102

AFRICA AND THE WEST

◆ ◆ ◆

VOLUME 1

AFRICA AND THE WEST

A Documentary History

SECOND EDITION

◆ ◆ ◆

VOLUME 1

From the Slave Trade to Conquest, 1441–1905

WILLIAM H. WORGER

NANCY L. CLARK

EDWARD A. ALPERS

OXFORD
UNIVERSITY PRESS

2010

OXFORD
UNIVERSITY PRESS

Copyright © 2001, 2010 by William H. Worger, Nancy L. Clark, and Edward A. Alpers

Published by Oxford University Press, Inc.
198 Madison Avenue, New York, New York 10016

www.oup.com

Africa and the West: A Documentary History from the Slave Trade to Independence,
by William H. Worger, Nancy L. Clark, and Edward A. Alpers, was originally published in hardcover by Oryx Press,
an imprint of Greenwood Publishing Group, Inc., Westport, CT. Copyright © 2001 by William H. Worger, Nancy L. Clark,
and Edward A. Alpers. This paperback edition by arrangement with Greenwood Publishing Group, Inc. All rights reserved.

Library of Congress Cataloging-in-Publication Data
Africa and the West : a documentary history / [edited by] William H. Worger, Nancy L. Clark, Edward A. Alpers.—2nd ed.
v.   cm.
Includes bibliographical references and index.
Contents: v. 1. From the slave trade to conquest, 1441–1905 — v. 2. From colonialism to independence, 1875 to the present.
ISBN 978-0-19-537348-6 (v. 1); 978-0-19-537313-4 (v. 2)
1. Africa, Sub-Saharan—Relations—Europe—History—Sources. 2. Europe—Relations—Africa, Sub-Saharan—History—
Sources. 3. Africa, Sub-Saharan—Relations—America—History—Sources. 4. America—Relations—Africa, Sub-Saharan—
History—Sources. 5. Slave-trade—History—Sources. I. Worger, William H. II. Clark, Nancy L. III. Alpers, Edward A.
DT353.5.E9A34 2010
303.48'26701821—dc22   2009034387

Printed in the United States of America
on acid-free paper

PREFACE

This two-volume work presents the story of Africa's relationship with the West through the perspective of those who lived its history. The words of African kings, slaves, and politicians, as well as European officials, missionaries, and slave traders, reproduced here in 133 select primary documents, tell the story of the colonial encounter between Africa and the West from the beginning of the fifteenth century to the beginning of the twenty-first. Although direct contact between Europe and North Africa has existed since ancient times, a fundamentally new relationship developed between Africa and Europe with the advent of the Atlantic slave trade. We have chosen to follow the developing contours of this relationship, particularly the ways in which Africans were incorporated into an Atlantic world that used their labor and their agricultural produce to build wealth in the West but caused poverty in Africa.

The story begins with Portuguese explorers who came looking for the source of West Africa's gold in reputed rivers of the precious metal and with the establishment of the first Portuguese settlements along the northwest coast of Africa (especially on the Atlantic islands of the Azores, Madeira, Cape Verde, and the Canaries). It continues, from the latter part of the fifteenth century well into the nineteenth, with the consequent forcible removal of Africans, who were taken across the Atlantic not as free settlers but as servile laborers to colonize the Americas. With the gradual ending of the slave trade, the story continues as European nations that had prospered from the slave trade identified new products for export and worked for nearly a century to gain control over those resources and African land and to maintain their control over African labor. The period of colonialism—the apex of European intervention and the means for the reshaping of the continent—was the culmination of the drive from the West to control Africa's resources. It also sowed the seeds for the emergence of new African leaders and a quest for independence that finally succeeded at the end of the twentieth century. The book ends at the beginning of a new millennium, with international energy companies drawn to the continent by reports of veritable lakes of oil beneath areas such as Darfur and with African nations facing a host of challenges—poverty and hunger among the most important, and most of them the legacy of the six-hundred-year relationship with the West.

The two volumes of this book are organized both chronologically and thematically. Attempting comprehensiveness across a continent with an area so large and with populations as diverse as those of Africa would be impossible (though we have focused on two countries in particular—Ghana and South Africa—because of the importance of each in the history of the encounter between Africa and the West and because of the richness of the sources that allow us to document that encounter). Volume 1 focuses on the initiation of contact with Africa through the slave trade, the so-called legitimate trade of the nineteenth century, and the eventual military conquest of most parts of Africa. Despite the eloquent pleas of Africans that they could initiate whatever changes they wanted free of outside intervention, this volume ends with the deaths of tens of thousands of Africans defending their autonomy against the inevitable military intervention of European powers. Volume 2 starts with discussions of the aims of colonialism, as expressed by some of its architects, and the concurrent criticisms made by colonial subjects (or victims, as increasingly they saw themselves). It examines the linkages between nineteenth- and twentieth-century political and economic practices, especially in the development of authoritarian forms of colonial rule, and the transformation of slavery into new forms of forced labor. Volume 2 ends with the struggle (ultimately successful) of people in the Portuguese and white-settler-ruled areas of Africa (Angola, Guinea-Bissau, Mozambique, Namibia, South Africa, and Zimbabwe) to achieve independence and the difficulties and contradictions of life after colonialism for people in the rest of Africa. While "freedom," in Nkrumah's stirring words, came to Africa with the end of formal colonialism, political independence has not translated into the types of freedom that most people expected.

In revising this work, originally published in one volume in 2001, we find continuing signs of hope and concern in Africa's most recent history. When we completed the first edition of this book, we ended the volume with a stirring speech given by Nelson Mandela at his inauguration as president of South Africa in May 1994, an oration that he concluded with the words "Let freedom reign!" But we also noted the continuing evidence of what we termed "reminders of the harsh legacy of colonialism," including genocide in Rwanda with a million dead in a hundred days; civil war in Sierra Leone, where all of the vying parties, "government" and "rebel" alike, used child soldiers and committed atrocities shockingly similar—dismemberment especially—to those carried out by Belgian colonialists in the Congo a century earlier; and riots in northern Nigeria, with Muslims being blamed for the killing of several hundred Nigerian Christians. As we complete the second edition of this book in 2009, the perpetrators of the Rwandan genocide have been sentenced to life in prison. Charles Taylor, considered responsible for the deaths of thousands in the wars that raged in Sierra Leone and Liberia throughout the 1990s, remains on trial. Riots have again taken place in Nigeria with evident tensions between Muslims and Christians.

At the same time, we find new challenges and reminders of the troubled past. Africans have the lowest life expectancy in the world, sometimes half that of people living in the West. They have the highest under-five child mortality rates in the world. There are more poor people (three hundred million) living in Africa than in any other part of the world, and they account for 76 percent of the world's "ultrapoor," as those living on less than fifty cents a day have been defined. They are hungry. In 2007 a survey of food intake in seven African countries (Burundi, Ethiopia, Kenya, Malawi, Rwanda, Senegal, and Zambia) found that the percentage of the population defined as the "ultrahungry" (consuming fewer than sixteen hundred calories a day) ranged from 27 percent of the people living in Kenya to 60 percent of Burundi's population.[1] In Africa, more people are dying of AIDS than in the rest of the world combined, with twelve million children orphaned by the disease by 2008. In the past five years, five million people have died in the Congo as a result of violence, and few people elsewhere seem to have noticed. Darfur captures the world's attention with concerns about geno-

---

1. Akhter U. Ahmed, Ruth Vargas Hill, Lisa C. Smith, Doris M. Wiesmann, and Tim Frankenberger, *The World's Most Deprived: Characteristics and Causes of Extreme Poverty and Hunger* (Washington, D.C.: International Food Policy Research Institute, 2007), xii; http://www.ifpri.org/sites/default/files/publications/vp43.pdf.

cide, but few perceive the growing importance of oil in the Sudan and Chad as world powers embark on a new quest for dominance, one based on the control of strategic minerals rather than the land mass so common during colonialism and still evident during the Cold War. Our hope is that the injustices and brutality that so characterized interactions between Africa and the West, as recounted in these two volumes, will not be repeated in the future.

We have endeavored in this collection to compile a text that will be of interest to a wide range of audiences from middle school, high school, and college students and beyond to anyone interested in the history of the African continent. For some of us—and we are of a generation that came of age in the 1960s and the 1970s—the decolonizing of Africa was a time of hope, and the names of people like Frantz Fanon, Kwame Nkrumah, and Julius Nyerere are very familiar. Later generations are likely to be more familiar with those who fought against continuing oppression in Africa, whether it be Nelson Mandela and his struggles to end apartheid in South Africa or Jack Mapanje, who denounced the shortcomings of Malawi's president for life, Hastings Banda, or perhaps they will be aware of Africa mainly as a place of poverty and political unrest. Believing as historians that the present cannot be explained without a grasp of the past, we hope that readers of every generation will find these documents of value in understanding the history of Africa and gaining some insight into the problems and the potential with which the continent is currently contending.

The documents collected here were written by people who participated in the events described. They capture, in first-person narratives, poetry, letters, formal political speeches, and many other forms of writing, the hopes, aspirations, doubts, and sometimes hypocrisy that mark all human endeavors. Editorially, we have aimed to present selections lengthy enough to enable the reader to capture a sense of what each author intended. We have avoided cutting texts to reflect certain lines of interpretation, and we have kept the explanatory text to a minimum (though clearly the selection of the documents itself reflects our collective and individual points of view). With the exception of minor changes in punctuation, the replacement of the letter *f* by *s* in some of the older English documents, and the reduction of some excessive capitalization (by today's standards), we have maintained the spelling, grammatical forms, and some capitalization from the original documents. In addition, we have dated the documents to reflect the period of time in which the events described took place, sometimes different from the actual publication date. Most important, we have retained without exception the documents' original language—always powerful, moving, and sometimes rough. The people whose words you read here were and still are exceptionally eloquent.

ACKNOWLEDGMENTS

In preparing the first edition of this work, we benefited at Cal Poly and UCLA from the research skills of Henry Trotter (who did much of the groundwork), Gibril Cole, Karen Flint, and Kristin Haynes and at Oryx Press from the editorial expertise of Jake Goldberg, Sean Tape, and Ann Thompson.

This second, revised, two-volume edition would not have happened without the energy and determination of the indefatigable Nancy Toff of Oxford University Press. Claire Cox of Greenwood Press went the extra step in sorting out the complex copyright issues. The three anonymous readers selected by Oxford provided numerous helpful suggestions for additions to and revisions of the first edition. We have benefited from answers to questions and a generous willingness to share material offered by Nwando Achebe, Gibril Cole, Jeremy Ball, Richard L. Betz, Elri Liebenberg, Bill Minter, Honoré Vinck, and David Rumsey. Ruby Bell-Gam of the Young Research Library (YRL) at UCLA answered every difficult bibliographic question with immense skill and alacrity. The YRL staff in circulation and interlibrary loan efficiently and graciously fielded an inordinate number of requests. Members of Special Collections at YRL provided high-quality reproductions of some of the illustrations. The Dean of Libraries at LSU, Jennifer Cargill, and the staffs of the Hill and Middleton libraries were always ready to help. The Dean of Social Sciences at UCLA provided a subvention for the costs of obtaining reprint permission for the copyrighted material included in this work. At OUP, we have also benefited from the sterling work of Jane Slusser, Leora Bersohn, Liz Smith, and Carol Hoke.

CONTENTS

ILLUSTRATIONS

PART I

Africa in the Era of the Slave Trade (1441–1899)

INTRODUCTION

The arrival of Europeans on African shores initiated a direct search for all of the continent's legendary wealth. Although Europe had obtained goods from Africa since before the advent of the Christian era, these items (gold especially) had been acquired through African middlemen. With the rise of Islam in the seventh century, access to African gold—the main source of that precious metal until the discovery of the Americas—became even more difficult and more expensive for the Christian West. With the development of new methods of navigation in the fifteenth century, however, Europeans for the first time were able to gain direct access to the coast of sub-Saharan Africa and to interior trade networks without having to deal with Muslim middlemen.

Though European voyaging aimed initially at getting direct access to West African gold producers and to locating in East Africa the legendary Christian monarch Prester John (viewed as a possible ally in the religious wars against Islam), an export trade in African slaves soon dominated practically all interaction between the West and Africa beginning in the 1440s and continuing for about four hundred years. During those four centuries, between 10 and 15 million Africans, two-thirds of them males, were forcibly taken from Africa and sent across the Atlantic to work in new colonies established primarily by the Spanish, the Portuguese, and the British in the Americas. The bulk of the slaves went to the Caribbean and to Portuguese South America (Brazil); the smallest number (approximately half a million) were sent to the American South. These people were purchased from African middlemen and transported for resale in the Americas by merchants from every European country in a trade that did not cease completely until the end of the nineteenth century.

The story of this devastating trade started fitfully with the first arrival of Europeans into Africa in the fifteenth century. Between the 1430s and the end of the century the Portuguese moved steadily southward along the northwestern coast of the continent, south of the Senegal and Gambia rivers to what became known as the Gold Coast (present-day Ghana) by the 1470s, to the mouth of the Congo River by the mid-1480s, and to the southern tip of the continent at the end of that decade. Finally, in 1497, Vasco da Gama traveled around the Cape of Good Hope into the Indian Ocean, where he came in contact with the Swahili trading towns of the East African coast and reached southern India and the spice trade networks of the East.

The Dutch eventually followed, establishing a trading post at Cape Town in 1652, with the French and British landing along the African coast in the eighteenth century.

Europeans landed initially in Africa looking for a variety of goods, particularly gold, but out of frustration with experienced African producers they soon turned to a trade in human beings that quickly became a business. Trading in people and bringing them to Portugal for sale as slave workers provided an additional means by which the early voyagers could turn a profit on a trading voyage. The rise of plantation agriculture, first in sugar on Mediterranean islands, then on islands off the coast of Africa (especially São Tomé and Principe), and most significant of all in the Americas with labor-intensive crops such as sugar, cotton, and tobacco, created a huge new demand for nearly endless supplies of cheap labor. The economic benefits of plantation agriculture were so great that the pope sanctioned the trade in an effort to maintain a Catholic monopoly in the face of attempts by competing traders to gain access to such a highly profitable commerce.

The demand for slaves quickly changed the nature of trade and initiated a nightmarish experience for those captured. Whereas the first slaves had been captured in raids or were war captives or criminals acquired through trade with local African leaders, over time the "production" of slaves became a major industry within Africa. Europeans remained based along the West African coastline in a series of trading forts, largely due to the massive mortality rates they experienced from malaria, sleeping sickness, and other diseases endemic to the interior. As a result, they were dependent for their continued presence on the favor of local kings. In these forts, European merchants traded manufactured goods such as cloth and firearms for people, and the terms of trade were continually renegotiated. The slaves were brought from the interior, acquired often by raids especially for the purpose of taking people into bondage or through wars increasingly fought for the same purpose, and transported to the coast along the river networks that served as the hub of internal trade. Frequently such slaves changed owners several times in a series of transactions, and the trip to the coast could be very lengthy. On the coast the slaves were sold to European merchants who, in constant attempts to maximize their profits, transported them across the Atlantic in the most appalling conditions. While the memoirs of those transported into slavery are riveting, so too are the business-as-usual accounts of those who managed the trade. The matter-of-fact business rationale of slavery is evident, too, in the justifications for the utilization of imported slave labor in the Cape of Good Hope, the only significant European colony in Africa prior to the nineteenth century and one whose agricultural economy was built on slave labor imported from East Africa, Madagascar, and southeast Asia.

Although millions of people were enslaved, they did not go peaceably. They fought against their captors, took flight when they had the chance, and rose up in revolt on occasion. Historians have recorded several hundred shipboard uprisings. Growing public revulsion at the practices of slave traders, especially as documented by writers like Olaudah Equiano, the frightening prospect of perhaps more successful slave revolts such as that of Toussaint l'Ouverture in Haiti, and the growing demand for free labor rather than servile as a result of the impact of the Industrial Revolution together reinforced demands for the end of the trade in slaves.

The eventual abolition of the slave trade enacted by Britain and the United States at the beginning of the nineteenth century had little immediate impact. Indeed, slave exports reached their highest peak ever in the 1820s and 1830s, when an average of almost 120,000 people a year were shipped across the Atlantic. Though the British and the Americans sent out ships to interdict the trade and freed some people who were then transported to Sierra Leone and Liberia (established by British and American antislavers respectively as havens for freed slaves), slavers moved their bases of operations, with a huge increase in slave raiding (much of it run by Muslim slavers) on the east coast of Africa and its hinterland in the nineteenth century that had not been present in the eighteenth.

The arrival of Europeans and the long experience of the slave trade had an enormous and lasting impact on Africa. It had the immediate result of initiating a massive increase in violence within the continent. Some of this violence was perpetrated by states (like Dahomey) that built their power and their wealth on raiding other societies for a product that could be sold for export. Other states, like Asante, did not engage in slave raiding for commercial purposes but did view the export trade as a useful way in which to get rid of captives acquired in wars of conquest who otherwise might practice sedition. Over the longer term, the removal from Africa of so many people during the most productive years of their lives (slave traders did not want the old, the ill, or the infirm) cannot but have had an immense impact on production within Africa. Moreover, instead of engaging in the production of local goods for trade within Africa, the slave trade led to a focus on the export of people in exchange for European manufactured goods (especially cloth, but also guns, which were used to expand the mercenary trade, metal manufactures, and other items). The demographic impact was also likely to have been considerable with so many people removed from the continent. Some estimates have suggested that Africa's population by the end of the nineteenth century was perhaps 50 percent less than it would have been without the slave trade. Indeed, when European travelers to Africa finally explored thoroughly the interior of the continent in the mid-nineteenth century, their remarks on the violence witnessed, the low levels of population in large areas, and the apparent (at least to them) lack of an active internal economy other than that built around slavery did not take into account the extent to which what they witnessed was a product of four hundred years of trade with Europe.

CHAPTER ONE

European Discovery and the Beginnings
of the Slave Trade (1441–1654)

1 • The beginnings of a regular European
trade in slaves from Africa (1441)

From the 1430s until his death in 1460, Prince Henry of Portugal sponsored a series of voyages to explore the West African coast. The Portuguese were seeking direct sea access to the gold of West Africa (otherwise obtainable only via Muslim traders who transported it across the Sahara) and hoped also to locate the legendary Christian monarch Prester John, reputed to live on the east coast of Africa and viewed as a potential ally for the Portuguese in their wars against the followers of Islam. Gomes Azurara, royal librarian, chronicler, and keeper of the Portuguese archives, compiled the earliest and most complete record of these early Portuguese voyages. Using as much as possible the testimony of participants in the events he described, Azurara, who completed his account in 1453, charted how the initial quest for gold and allies turned into a pattern of raiding for African slaves to work on farms and plantations in Portugal. The events described take place on the coast of present-day Mauritania.[1]

How Antam Gonçalvez brought back the first Captives

Now it was so that in this year 1441, when the affairs of this realm [Portugal] were somewhat more settled though not fully quieted, that the Infant [Prince Henry] armed a little ship, of the which he made captain one Antam Gonçalvez, his chamberlain, and a very young man; and the end of that voyage was none other, according to my Lord's commandment, but to ship a cargo of the skins and oil . . .

But when he had accomplished his voyage, as far as concerned the chief part of his orders, Antam Gonçalvez, called to him Affonso Goterres, another groom of the chamber . . . and all the others that were in the ship, being one and twenty in all, and spoke to them in this wise: "Friends and brethren! We have already got our cargo, as you perceive, by the which the chief part of our ordinance is accomplished, and we may well turn back, if we wish not to toil beyond that which was principally commanded of us; but I would know from all whether seemeth to you well that we should attempt something further, that he who sent us here may

---

1. Gomes Eannes De Azurara, *The Chronicle of the Discovery and Conquest of Guinea*, c.1453, translated by Charles Beazley and Edgar Prestage (London: Hakluyt Society, 1896–97), vol. 1, 39–50, 54–58, 60–68, 79–83.

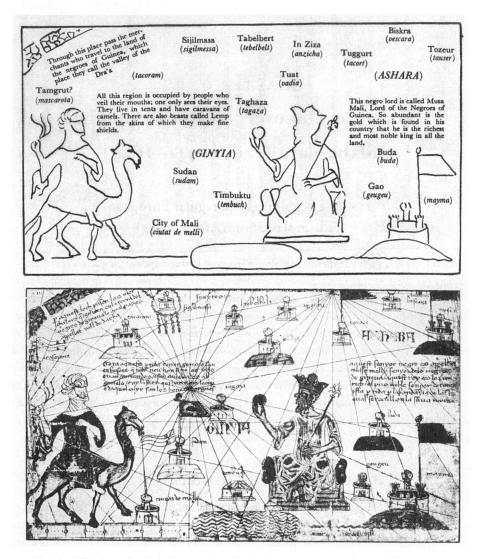

FIGURE 1 This Spanish map of 1375, on which the first Portuguese explorers relied in planning their expeditions, depicts an Africa as perceived by Europeans, who had never been there but who thought of it as a continent full of rivers of gold and powerful kingdoms. The map was drawn by Jewish mapmakers who had derived their information from Muslim travelers who had visited the capitals of Mansa Musa (center, with crown) and other African rulers. E. W. Bovill, *The Golden Trade of the Moors*, 1970.

have some example of our good wills; for I think it would be shameful if we went back into his presence just as we are . . . O how fair a thing it would be if we, who have come to this land for a cargo of such petty merchandise, were to meet with the good luck to bring the first captives before the face of our Prince . . . I would fain go myself this next night with nine men of you (those who are most ready for the business), and prove a part of this land along the river to see if I find any inhabitants; for I think we of right ought to meet with some, since 'tis certain there are people here, who traffic with camels and other animals that bear their freights. Now the traffic of these men must chiefly be to the seaboard; and since they have as yet no knowledge of us, their gathering cannot be too large for us to try their strength; and, if God grant us to encounter them, the very least part of our victory will be the capture of one of them, with the which the Infant will feel no small content, getting knowledge by that means of what kind are the other dwellers of this land. And as to our reward, you can estimate what it will be by the great expenses and toil he has undertaken in years past, only for this end" . . . they determined to do his bidding, and follow him as far as they could make their way. And as soon as it was night Antam Gonçalvez chose nine men who seemed to him most fitted for the undertaking, and made his voyage with them as he had before determined. And when they were about a league distant from the sea they came on a path which they kept, thinking some man or woman might come by there whom they could capture; but it happened otherwise; so Antam Gonçalvez asked the others to consent to go forward and follow out his purpose; for, as they had already come so far, it would not do to return to the ship in vain like that. And the others being content they departed thence, and, journeying through that inner land for the space of three leagues, they found the footmarks of men and youths, the number of whom, according to their estimate, would be from forty to fifty, and these led the opposite way from where our men were going. The heat was very intense, and so by reason of this and of the toil they had undergone in watching by night and travelling thus on foot, and also because of the want of water, of which there was none, Antam Gonçalvez perceived their weariness that it was already very great, as he could easily judge from his own sufferings: So he said, "My friends, there is nothing more to do here; our toil is great, while the profit to arise from following up this path meseemeth small, for these men are travelling to the place whence we have come, and our best course would be to turn back towards them, and perchance, on their return, some will separate themselves, or may be, we shall come up with them when they are laid down to rest, and then, if we attack them lustily, peradventure they will flee, and, if they flee, someone there will be less swift, whom we can lay hold of according to our intent; or may be our luck will be even better, and we shall find fourteen or fifteen of them, of whom we shall make a more profitable booty." Now this advice was not such as to give rise to any wavering in the will of those men, for each desired that very thing. And, returning towards the sea, when they had gone a short part of the way, they saw a naked man following a camel, with two assegais in his hand, and as our men pursued him there was not one who felt aught of his great fatigue. But though he was only one, and saw the others that they were many; yet he had a mind to prove those arms of his right worthily and began to defend himself as best he could, shewing a bolder front than his strength warranted. But Affonso Goterres wounded him with a javelin, and this put the Moor in such fear that he threw down his arms like a beaten thing. And after they had captured him, to their no small delight, and had gone on further, they espied, on the top of a hill, the company whose tracks they were following, and their captive pertained to the number of these. And they failed not to reach them through any lack of will, but the sun was now low, and they wearied, so they determined to return to their ship, considering that such enterprise might bring greater injury than profit. And, as they were going on their way, they saw a black Mooress come along (who was slave of those on the hill), and though some of our men were in favour of letting her pass to avoid a fresh skirmish . . . Antam Gonçalvez bade them go at her; for if (he said) they scorned that encounter, it might make their foes pluck up courage against them. And now you see how the word of a captain prevaileth among men used to obey; for, following his will, they seized the Mooress. And those on the hill had a mind to come to the rescue, but when they perceived our people ready to receive them, they not only retreated to their former position, but departed elsewhere, turning their backs to their enemies . . .

Now . . . Nuno Tristam, a youthful knight . . . brought with him an armed caravel, with the special command of his Lord, that he should pass beyond the Port of the Galley, as far as he could, and that he should bestir himself as well to capture some of the people of the country, as best he could. And he, pursuing his voyage, now arrived at the place where Antam Gonçalvez was. . . . "You . . . my friend Antam Gonçalvez, are not ignorant of the will of the Infant our Lord, and you know that to execute this purpose of his he hath incurred many and great expenses, and yet up till now, for a space of fifteen years, he hath toiled in vain in this part of the world, never being able to arrive at any certainty as to the people of this land, under what law or lordship they do live. And although you are carrying off these two captives, and by their means the Infant may come to know something about this folk, yet that doth not prevent what is still better, namely, for us to carry off many more; for, besides the knowledge which the Lord Infant will gain by their means, profit will also accrue to him by their service or ransom. Wherefore, it seemeth to me that we should do well to act after this manner. That is to say, in this night now following, you should choose ten of your men and I another ten of mine—from the best which each of us may have—and let us then go together and seek those whom you have found. And since you say that, judging from the fighting you had with them, they were not more than twenty men fit for battle, and the rest women and boys, we ought to capture them all very quickly. And even if we do not meet with the very same that you encountered, nevertheless we shall surely find others, by means of whom we can make as good a booty, or perhaps even better."

"I cannot well believe," replied Antam Gonçalvez, "that our expedition in search of those we found before, will have any sure result, for the place is all one great bare hill, in the which there is no house or hut where one could fancy they would lodge, and the more so since we saw them turn again like men that had come there from another part. And what seemeth to me worst of all is that those men will have forewarned all the others, and, peradventure, when we think to capture them we may ourselves become their booty . . ."

Yet, although this counsel of Antam Gonçalvez was good . . . there were there two squires, in whom these reasons did not suffice to oppose their desire of doing brave deeds . . . And these two persuaded the Council to depart from the advice which Antam Gonçalvez had given . . . as soon as it was night, they set out according to the order that Nuno Tristam gave at first. And so it chanced that in the night they came to where the natives lay scattered in two encampments, either the same that Antam Gonçalvez had found before or other like it. The distance between the encampments was but small, and our men divided themselves into three parties, in order that they might the better hit upon them. For they had not yet any certain knowledge of the place where they lay, but only a perception of them; as you see the like things are perceived much more readily by night than by day. And when our men had come nigh to them, they attacked them very lustily, shouting at the top of their voices, "Portugal" and "Santiago;" the fright of which so abashed the enemy, that it threw them all into disorder. And so, all in confusion, they began to fly without any order or carefulness. Except indeed that the men made some show of defending themselves with their assegais (for they knew not the use of any other weapon), especially one of them, who fought face to face with Nuno Tristam, defending himself till he received his death. And besides this one, whom Nuno Tristam slew by himself, the others killed three and took ten prisoners, what of men, women and boys. And it is not to be doubted that they would have slain and taken many more, if they had all fallen on together at the first onslaught. But among those who were taken there was one greater than the rest, who was called Adahu, and was said to be a noble; and he shewed in his countenance right well that he held the pre-eminence of nobility over the others . . . Then those captains returned to the ships and bade that Arab [translator] whom Nuno Tristam had brought with him, to sit with those Moors but they were not able to understand him, because the language of these people was not Moorish, but Azaneguy of Sahara, for so they name that land [between present-day Morocco and Senegal]. But the noble, in that he was of better breeding than the other captives, so had he seen more things and better than they; and had been to other lands where he had learned the Moorish tongue; forasmuch as he understood that Arab and answered to whatever matter was asked of him by the same. And the further to try the people of the land and to have of them more certain knowledge, they put that Arab on shore, and one of the Moorish women whom they had taken captive; who were to say to the others, that if they wished to come and speak to them about the ransom of some of those whom they had taken prisoners, or about traffick in merchandise, they might do so. And at the end of two days there came to that place about 150 Moors on foot and thirty-five on horses and camels, bringing the Moorish slave with them. And although outwardly they seemed to be a race both barbarous and bestial, yet was there not wanting in them something of astuteness, wherewith they sought to ensnare their enemies. For only three of them appeared on the shore, and the rest lay in ambush, to the end that our men, being unaware of their treachery, might land, when they who lay hid could seize them, which thing they might have done by sheer force of numbers, if our men had been a whit less cautious than they. But the Moors, perceiving that their wiles were discovered by us—because they saw that the men in the boat turned about on seeing that the slave did not appear—revealed their dissembling tricks and all came into sight on the shore, hurling stones and making gestures. And there they also displayed that Arab who had been sent to them, held as one whom they wished to keep in the subjection of a captive. And he called out to them that they should be on their guard against those people; for they would not have come there, except to take them at a disadvantage if they could. Thereupon our men turned back to the ships, where they made their partition of the captives, according to the lot of each, and the other Moors betook themselves to their encampments, taking the Arab with them. And Antam Gonçalvez, because he had now loaded his ship with cargo, as the Infant had commanded, returned to Portugal . . .

How Antam Gonçalvez went to make the first ransom

As you know that naturally every prisoner desireth to lie free, which desire is all the stronger in a man of higher reason or nobility whom fortune has condemned to live in subjection to another; so that noble [Adahu] of whom we have already spoken, seeing himself held in captivity, although he was very gently treated, greatly desired to be free, and often asked Antam Gonçalvez to take him back to his country, where he declared he would give for himself five or six Black Moors; and also he said that there were among the other captives two youths for whom a like ransom would be given.

And here you must note that these blacks were Moors like the others, though their slaves, in accordance with ancient custom, which I believe to have been because of the curse which, after the Deluge, Noah laid upon his son Cain, cursing him in this way—that his race should be subject to all the other races of the world.

And from his race these blacks are descended, as wrote the Archbishop Don Roderic of Toledo, and Josephus in his book on *The Antiquities of the Jews*... The will of Antam Gonçal-vez to return to that land, for desire of the ransom and profit he would get, was not so great as his desire to serve the Infant his lord—and therefore he asked leave to go on this journey, say-ing, that (forasmuch as he perceived the great desire his Grace had to know part of that land) if that were not sufficient which he had ascertained from that Moor, that he should give him license to go and ransom him and the other captive youths with him.

For as the Moor told him, the least they would give for them would be ten Moors, and it was better to save ten souls than three—for though they were black, yet had they souls like the others, and all the more as these blacks were not of the lineage of the Moors but were Gen-tiles, and so the better to bring into the path of salvation.

Also he said that the blacks could give him news of land much further distant, and he promised that when he spoke about the traffic with the natives, he would find means to learn as much news as possible.

The Infant answered all this and said that he was obliged by his offer, and that he not only desired to have knowledge of that land, but also of the Indies, and of the land of Prester John, if he could.

Antam Gonçalvez made ready to go with his captives ... and arriving at the boundaries of that land where the ransom had to be made ... resolved to put on shore that Moorish noble, that he might go and make ready his ransom at the place where he had agreed to meet Antam Gonçalvez again.

The Moor was very well clad in garments given him by the Infant, who considered that, for the excellence of his nobility that he had above the others, if he received benefits, he would be able to be of profit to his benefactors by encouraging his own people and bringing them to traffic. But as soon as he was free, he forgot very quickly all about his promises, on the secu-rity of which Antam Gonçalvez had trusted him, thinking that the nobility he displayed would be the chief hindrance of any breach of faith on his part; but his deceit thenceforth warned all our men not to trust one of that race except under the most certain security.

And now Antam Gonçalvez entering the Rio D'Ouro with his ship for a space of four leagues, dropped anchor, and waited for seven days without getting a message from any, or a glimpse of one single inhabitant of that land; but on the eighth day there arrived a Moor seated on a white camel, and another with him, who gave a message that they should await the others who would come and make the ransom, and that on the next day they would appear, as in fact they did.

And it was very clear that those youths [Gonçalvez's captives] were in great honour among them, for a good hundred Moors, male and female, were joined in their ransom, and Antam Gonçalvez received for his two captives, ten blacks, male and female, from various countries—one Martin Fernandez, the Infant's Alfaqueque [captive ransomer], managing the business between the parties.

And it was clear that the said Martin had great knowledge of the Moorish tongue, for he was understood among these people, where the other Arab, who was Moor by nation, could only find one person to understand him.

And besides the blacks that Antam Gonçalvez received in that ransom, he got also a little gold dust and a shield of ox-hide, and a number of ostrich eggs, so that one day there were served up at the Infant's table three dishes of the same, as fresh and as good as though they had been the eggs of any other domestic fowls. And we may well presume that there was no other Christian prince in this part of Christendom, who had dishes like these upon his table.

And according to the account of those Moors there were merchants in that part, who traded in that gold, which it seemed was found among them; but the Moorish noble never returned to fulfil his promise, neither did he remember the benefits he had received.

And by thus losing him, Antam Gonçalvez learnt to be cautious where before he was not. And returning to the Infant, his lord, he received his reward . . .

The growth of the trade in slaves

[A]t the beginning of the colonisation of the islands [Canary Islands and Cape Verde], people murmured as greatly as if he [Prince Henry] were spending some part of their property on it . . . But when they saw the first Moorish captives brought home, and the second cargo . . . they confessed their mistake . . . And so they were forced to turn their blame into public praise; for they said it was plain the Infant was another Alexander; and their covetousness now began to wax greater. And, as they saw the houses of others full to overflowing of male and female slaves, and their property increasing, they thought about the whole matter, and began to talk among themselves.

And because that after coming back from Tangier, the Infant usually remained always in the kingdom of Algarve, by reason of his town which he was then having built, and because the booty that his captains brought back was discharged at Lagos, therefore the people of that place were the first to move the Infant to give them license to go to that land whence came those Moorish captives . . . And the first who interposed to beg for this license, was a squire [Lançarote] . . . [who was] Almoxarife [collector of taxes] for the King in that town of Lagos . . . A man of great good sense, he understood well how the matter stood, and the profit that he would be able to gain by his expedition . . . So Lançarote prepared six armed caravels to carry out his purpose and spoke to the Infant about a license; saying that he begged he would grant it him that he might do him service, as well as obtain honour and profit for himself . . . And the Infant was very glad of this and at once commanded his banners to be made, with the Cross of the Order of Jesus Christ, one of which each caravel was to hoist . . . And pursuing their voyage, they arrived at the Isle of Herons [in the Bay of Arguin], on the eve of Corpus Christi Day . . . They took with them thirty men, to wit, six in each boat, and set out from the island where they were, about sunset. And rowing all that night, they arrived about daybreak at the island that they sought . . . They looked towards the settlement and saw that the Moors, with their women and children, were already coming as quickly as they could out of their dwellings, because they had caught sight of their enemies. But they, shouting out "St. James," "St. George," "Portugal," at once attacked them, killing and taking all they could.

Then might you see mothers forsaking their children, and husbands their wives, each striving to escape as best he could. Some drowned themselves in the water; others thought to escape by hiding under their huts; others stowed their children among the seaweed, where our men found them afterwards, hoping they would thus escape notice. And at last our Lord God, who giveth a reward for every good deed, willed that for the toil they had undergone in his service, they should that day obtain victory over their enemies, as well as a guerdon and a payment for all their labour and expense; for they took captive of those Moors, what with men, women, and children, 165, besides those that perished and were killed. And when the battle was over, all praised God for the great mercy that he had shewn them, in that he had willed to give them such a victory, and with so little damage to themselves. And as soon as they had their captives put safely in their boats, and others securely tied on land (because the boats were small and they were not able to store so many in them at once), they sent a man to go as far as possible along the shore, to see if he could get sight of the caravels. He set out at once; and one full league from the place where the others were staying, he had sight of the caravels coming; for Lançarote, as he had promised, had started as soon as it was dawn . . .

And when Lançarote, with those squires and brave men that were with him, had received the like news of the good success that God had granted to those few that went to the island; and saw that they had enterprised so great a deed; and that God had been pleased that they should bring it to such a pass; they were all very joyful, praising loudly the Lord God for that he had deigned to give such help to such a handful of his Christian people . . . Lançarote did not forget to learn from the Moorish prisoners what it was his duty to learn, about the place in which he was now staying and its opportunities; and he ascertained of them by his interpreter, that all about there were other inhabited islands, where they would be able to make large captures with little trouble . . .

The caravels arrived at Lagos, whence they had set out, having excellent weather for their voyage, for fortune was not less gracious to them in the serenity of the weather than it had been to them before in the capture of their booty.

And from Lagos the news reached the Infant . . . And next day Lançarote, as he who had taken the main charge of the expedition, said to the Infant: "My lord, your grace well knoweth that you have to receive the fifth of these Moors, and of all that we have gained in that land, whither you sent us for the service of God and of yourself . . ." The Infant said that he was well pleased, and on the next day very early, Lançarote bade the masters of the caravels that they should put out the captives, and take them to that field, where they were to make the divisions . . . But before they did anything else in that matter, they took as an offering the best of those Moors to the church of that place; and another little Moor, who afterwards became a friar of St. Francis, they sent to St. Vincent do Cabo, where he lived ever after as a Catholic Christian, without having understanding or perception of any law than that true and holy law in which all we Christians hope for our salvation. And the Moors of that capture were in number 235 . . .

O, Thou heavenly Father—who with Thy powerful hand, without alteration of Thy divine essence, governest all the infinite company of Thy Holy City, and controllest all the revolutions of higher worlds, divided into nine spheres, making the duration of ages long or short according as it pleaseth Thee—I [Azurara] pray Thee that my tears may not wrong my conscience; for it is not their religion but their humanity that maketh mine to weep in pity for their sufferings. And if the brute animals, with their bestial feelings, by a natural instinct understand the sufferings of their own kind, what wouldst Thou have my human nature to do on seeing before my eyes that miserable company, and remembering that they too are of the generation of the sons of Adam.

On the next day, which was the 8th of the month of August, very early in the morning, by reason of the heat, the seamen began to make ready their boats, and to take out those captives, and carry them on shore, as they were commanded. And these, placed all together in that field, were a marvellous sight; for amongst them were some white enough, fair to look upon, and well proportioned; others were less white like mulattoes; others again were as black as Ethiops, and so ugly, both in features and in body, as almost to appear (to those who saw them) the images of a lower hemisphere. But what heart could be so hard as not to be pierced with piteous feeling to see that company? For some kept their heads low and their faces bathed in tears, looking one upon another; others stood groaning very dolorously, looking up to the height of heaven, fixing their eyes upon it, crying out loudly, as if asking help of the Father of Nature; others struck their faces with the palms of their hands, throwing themselves at full length upon the ground; others made their lamentations in the manner of a dirge, after the custom of their country. And though we could not understand the words of their language, the sound of it right well accorded with the measure of their sadness. But to increase their sufferings still more, there now arrived those who had charge of the division of the captives, and who began to separate one from another, in order to make an equal partition of the fifths; and then was it needful to part fathers from sons, husbands from wives, brothers from brothers. No respect was shewn either to friends or relations, but each fell where his lot took him ... And who could finish that partition without very great toil? for as often as they had placed them in one part the sons, seeing their fathers in another, rose with great energy and rushed over to them; the mothers clasped their other children in their arms, and threw themselves flat on the ground with them; receiving blows with little pity for their own flesh, if only they might not be torn from them.

And so troublously they finished the partition; for besides the toil they had with the captives, the field was quite full of people, both from the town and from the surrounding villages and districts, who for that day gave rest to their hands (in which lay their power to get their living) for the sole purpose of beholding this novelty. And with what they saw, while some were weeping and others separating the captives, they caused such a tumult as greatly to confuse those who directed the partition.

The Infant was there, mounted upon a powerful steed, and accompanied by his retinue, making distribution of his favours, as a man who sought to gain but small treasure from his share; for of the forty-six souls who fell to him as his fifth, he made a very speedy partition of these, for his chief riches lay in his purpose; for he reflected with great pleasure upon the salvation of those souls that before were lost.

And certainly his expectation was not in vain; for ... as soon as they understood our language they turned Christians with very little ado; and I who put together this history into this volume, saw in the town of Lagos boys and girls (the children and grandchildren of those first captives, born in this land) as good and true Christians as if they had directly descended, from the beginning of the dispensation of Christ, from those who were first baptised.

2 • The pope grants to the Portuguese a monopoly of trade with Africa (1455)

Prince Henry argued that navigation of the African coast was part of a holy war and sought the support of the Catholic Church both for his missionary enterprise and to ward off other European powers. During the 1440s, Pope Eugenius IV had remained neutral with regard to the competing claims of Portugal and Spain, but in a papal bull issued in 1452 Pope Nicholas V gave King Alfonso of Portugal "power to conquer and enslave pagans." In another bull, Romanus Pontifex, *issued in 1455, Nicholas extended the king of Portugal's authority to include "exclusive control over the newly discovered territory." Note that "Guinea" in the papal bulls and in the correspondence of the Portuguese referred generally to all of West Africa south of the Saharan desert.*[2]

The Roman pontiff, successor of the key-bearer of the heavenly kingdom and vicar of Jesus Christ, contemplating with a father's mind all the several climes of the world and the characteristics of all the nations dwelling in them and seeking and desiring the salvation of all, wholesomely ordains and disposes upon careful deliberation those things which he sees will be agreeable to the Divine Majesty and by which he may bring the sheep entrusted to him by God into the single divine fold, and may acquire for them the reward of eternal felicity, and obtain pardon for their souls. This we believe will more certainly come to pass, through the aid of the Lord, if we bestow suitable favors and special graces on those Catholic kings and princes, who, like athletes and intrepid champions of the Christian faith, as we know by the evidence of facts, not only restrain the savage excesses of the Saracens and of other infidels, enemies of the Christian name, but also for the defense and increase of the faith vanquish them and their kingdoms and habitations, though situated in the remotest parts unknown to us, and subject them to their own temporal dominion, sparing no labor and expense, in order that those kings and princes, relieved of all obstacles, may be the more animated to the prosecution of so salutary and laudable a work.

We have lately heard, not without great joy and gratification, how our beloved son, the noble personage Henry, infante of Portugal, uncle of our most dear son in Christ, the illustrious Alfonso, king of the kingdoms of Portugal and Algarve, treading in the footsteps of John, of famous memory, king of the said kingdoms, his father, and greatly inflamed with zeal for the salvation of souls and with fervor of faith, as a Catholic and true soldier of Christ, the Creator of all things, and a most active and courageous defender and intrepid champion of the faith in Him, has aspired from his early youth with his utmost might to cause the most glorious name of the said Creator to be published, extolled, and revered throughout the whole

---

2. Papal bull *Romanus Pontifex* (Nicholas V), Jan. 8, 1455. In Frances Davenport, *European Treaties bearing on the History of the United States and Its Dependencies to 1648* (Washington, D.C.: Carnegie Institute, 1917), vol. 1, 20–24. Davenport has the original Latin text, as well as this translation into English.

FIGURE 2 Prince Henry of Portugal, known as the Navigator, sent out the first voyages of European exploration along the western, southern, and eastern coasts of Africa in the mid-1400s. The original quest was for gold, but a trade in slaves soon proved more profitable. Richard Henry Major, *The Life of Prince Henry of Portugal*, 1868.

world, even in the most remote and undiscovered places, and also to bring into the bosom of his faith the perfidious enemies of him and of the life-giving Cross by which we have been redeemed, namely the Saracens and all other infidels whatsoever, [and how] after the city of Ceuta, situated in Africa [on the northwestern tip nearest Spain], had been subdued by the said King John to his dominion, and after many wars had been waged, sometimes in person, by the said infante, although in the name of the said King John, against the enemies and infidels aforesaid, not without the greatest labors and expense, and with dangers and loss of life and property, and the slaughter of very many of their natural subjects, the said infante being neither enfeebled nor terrified by so many and great labors, dangers, and losses, but growing daily more and more zealous in prosecuting this his so laudable and pious purpose, has peopled with orthodox Christians certain solitary islands [Azores, Madeira, Canary Islands] in the ocean sea, and has caused churches and other pious places to be there founded and built, in which divine service is celebrated. Also by the laudable endeavor and industry of the said infante, very many inhabitants or dwellers in divers islands situated in the said sea, coming to the knowledge of the true God, have received holy baptism, to the praise and glory of God, the salvation of the souls of many, the propagation also of the orthodox faith, and the increase of divine worship.

Moreover, since, some time ago, it had come to the knowledge of the said infante that never, or at least not within the memory of men, had it been customary to sail on this ocean sea toward the southern and eastern shores, and that it was so unknown to us Westerners that we had no certain knowledge of the peoples of those parts, believing that he would best perform his duty to God in this matter, if by his effort and industry that sea might become navigable as far as to the Indians who are said to worship the name of Christ, and that thus he might be able to enter into relation with them, and to incite them to aid the Christians against the Saracens and other such enemies of the faith, and might also be able forthwith to subdue certain gentile or pagan peoples, living between, who are entirely free from infection by the sect of the most impious Mahomet [Muhammad], and to preach and cause to be preached to them the unknown but most sacred name of Christ, strengthened, however, always by the royal authority, he has not ceased for twenty-five years past to send almost yearly an army of the peoples of the said kingdoms, with the greatest labor, danger, and expense, in very swift ships called caravels, to explore the sea and coast lands toward the south and the Antarctic pole. And so it came to pass that when a number of ships of this kind had explored and taken possession of very many harbors, islands, and seas, they at length came to the province of Guinea, and having taken possession of some islands and harbors and the sea adjacent to that province, sailing farther they came to the mouth of a certain great river commonly supposed to be the Nile, and war was waged for some years against the peoples of those parts in the name of the said King Alfonso and of the infante, and in it very many islands in that neighborhood were subdued and peacefully possessed, as they are still possessed together with the adjacent sea. Thence also many Guineamen and other negroes, taken by force, and some by barter of unprohibited articles, or by other lawful contract of purchase, have been sent to the said kingdoms. A large number of these have been converted to the Catholic faith, and it is hoped, by the help of divine mercy, that if such progress be continued with them, either those peoples will be converted to the faith or at least the souls of many of them will be gained for Christ.

But since, as we are informed, although the king and infante aforesaid (who with so many and so great dangers, labors, and expenses, and also with loss of so many natives of their said kingdoms, very many of whom have perished in those expeditions, depending only upon the aid of those natives, have caused those provinces to be explored and have acquired and possessed such harbors, islands, and seas, as aforesaid, as the true lords of them), fearing lest strangers induced by covetousness should sail to those parts, and desiring to usurp to themselves the perfection, fruit, and praise of this work, or at least to hinder it, should therefore, either for the sake of gain or through malice, carry or transmit iron, arms, wood used for construction, and other things and goods prohibited to be carried to infidels, or should teach those infidels the art of navigation, whereby they would become more powerful and obstinate enemies to the king and infante, and the prosecution of this enterprise would either be hindered, or would perhaps entirely fail, not without great offense to God and great reproach to all Christianity, to prevent this and to conserve their right and possession, [the said king and infante] under certain most severe penalties then expressed, have prohibited and in general have ordained that none, unless with their sailors and ships and on payment of a certain tribute and with an express license previously obtained from the said king or infante, should presume to sail to the said provinces or to trade in their ports or to fish in the sea, [although the king and infante have taken this action, yet] in time it might happen that persons of other kingdoms or nations, led by envy, malice, or covetousness, might presume, contrary to the prohibition aforesaid, with-out license and payment of such tribute, to go to the said provinces, and in the provinces, harbors, islands, and sea, so acquired, to sail, trade, and fish; and thereupon between King Alfonso and the infante, who would by no means suffer themselves to be so trifled with in these things, and the presumptuous persons aforesaid, very many hatreds, rancors, dissensions, wars, and scandals, to the highest offense of God and danger of souls, probably might and would ensue. We weighing all and singular the premises with due meditation, and noting that since we had formerly by other letters of ours granted among other things free and ample faculty to the aforesaid King Alfonso—to invade, search out, capture, vanquish, and subdue all Saracens and pagans whatsoever, and other enemies of Christ wheresoever placed, and the kingdoms, dukedoms, principalities, dominions, possessions, and all movable and immovable goods whatsoever held and possessed by them and to reduce their persons to perpetual slavery, and to apply and appropriate to himself and his successors the kingdoms, dukedoms, counties, principalities, dominions, possessions, and goods, and to convert them to his and their use and profit—by having secured the said faculty, the said King Alfonso, or, by his authority, the aforesaid infante, justly and lawfully has acquired and possessed, and doth possess, these islands, lands, harbors, and seas, and they do of right belong and pertain to the said King Alfonso and his successors . . . We do by the tenor of these presents decree . . . to the aforesaid king and to his successors and to the infante . . . that the right of conquest which in the course of these letters we declare to be extended from the capes of Bojador and of Não [on the northwest African coast just south of the Canary Islands], as far as through all Guinea, and beyond toward that southern shore, has belonged and pertained, and forever of right belongs and pertains, to the said King Alfonso, his successors, and the infante, and not to any others.

3 • The first convert to Christianity (1488)

Religion, trade, and politics were inextricably linked from the very beginning of contact between Portuguese and Africans. The Portuguese proselytized in the name of Christianity as they sought allies against Muslim trading competitors and political enemies and a way to secure the support of the papacy. The new religion had distinct attractions for some Africans, especially those who saw it as a political ideology that would gain them new allies in their own contests for power within Africa. In 1488, Bemoym, king of Jalofo (at the mouth of the Senegal River), who was a Muslim, and the newly arrived Portuguese found that they had interests in common—Bemoym to regain his kingdom with Portuguese arms, the Portuguese to establish a base on the coast. Neither party expected the outcome that resulted.[3]

In this year one thousand four hundred and eighty-eight, while the king [John II] was in Setuvel [Setubal], he made a Christian of Bemoym, a negro prince of the kingdom of Gelof [Jalofo], which is at the entrance of the Rio de Çanaga [Senegal] in Guinee. His motives and reasons for this and the manner of doing it were briefly and truthfully as follows. During the previous year, while Gonçalo Coelho, a dependent of the king, was trafficking at the mouth of the said river, the said Bemoym, who at that time with prosperity and great power governed the said kingdom of Gelof, was informed through the interpreters of the royal perfection and

3. Ruy de Pina, *Chronica del Rey Joao II,* c.1500. In J. W. Blake, trans. and ed., *Europeans in West Africa, 1450–1560* (London: Hakluyt Society, 1942), vol. 1, 2d ser. no. 86, 80–86.

the many virtues of the king, and, desiring to serve him, through the said Gonçalo Coelho he sent him a rich present of gold and one hundred slaves, all young men, with some products of his land. This man, by virtue of a huge manilla of gold, which he gave the king as a letter of credence, according to his custom and being illiterate, sent to him to ask for arms and ships; to which the king refused consent with just reasons, based on the excommunications and the apostolic prohibitions, since he [Bemoym] was not a Christian. Then in this year, because the said Bemoym was treacherously driven out of his kingdom, he determined to embark on one of the caravels of the trade, which frequent the coast, and to come in person to seek aid, assistance and justice from the king, who was in Setuvel. Bemoym arrived in Lixboa, accompanied by some negroes of his own royal blood and sons of persons closely related to men of importance. When the king had been informed of their arrival, he commanded that they should come to be entertained at Palmella, where he forthwith commanded his men to make abundant provision for him and to serve him with silver and attendants and every other civility which was proper to his station. Also he commanded all to be given rich and fine clothes to wear, according as the quality and merit of their persons demanded. And when they were in a condition to come up to the court, the king sent horses and mules, very well appareled, to them all; and on the day when they were to make their entrance, the king commanded that Bemoym should be received by Dom Francisco Coutinho, Count of Marialva, and with him all lords and noblemen of the court, whom the king purposely ordered to be robed and adorned as well as possible. The king was lodged in the house of the exchequer of the said town, and the queen in other houses next to him, and both residences were all furnished and decorated with very expensive cloths of silk and serge and provided with a royal dais with a canopy of brocade. With the king was the duke Dom Manuel, accompanied by many titled lords and bishops and many other nobles, robed with much gentility and exact perfection. With the queen was the prince, her son, because it was ordained that one should forthwith visit the queen immediately after seeing and speaking with the king. The king and the duke adorned their persons with the very rich robes of their authority, all trimmed with gold and many precious stones. Bemoym appeared to be forty years old, and he was a man of great stature, very dark, with a very long beard, limbs all well proportioned and a very gracious presence; and being dressed, he entered the king's rooms, and the king came forward two or three paces from the dais to receive him, raising his cap a little. Then he led him to the dais, on which there was a throne; but the king did not sit thereon, and, leaning against it, thus on foot gave ear to him. Then the said Bemoym and all his men threw themselves at his feet to kiss them, and they made a show of taking the earth from under them and, in token of their subjection and his overlordship and of their great respect, threw it over their heads. But the king with much honour and courtesy made him rise, and through the negro interpreters, who were already present for this purpose, commanded him to speak. Thereupon, Bemoym with great ease, majesty and considerable gravity made a public speech, which lasted for a long time, and he used such notable words and sentences in support of his case that they did not seem to come from a savage negro but from Prince Grego, educated in Athenas. The substance of his speech was to recount to the king with swift sighs and many tears the tale of his miserable ill-fortune, caused by the treason which had been directed against him in his kingdom, and he declared this at large. Furthermore, he said that he was only reminding the king of this, because he was confidant in the hope of revenge, aid and assistance and above all justice; for he alone in the world could and ought to give it to him, since not only was he so noble, power-ful, just and pious a king, but also principally he was the lord of Guinee, to whom he, as his vassal, came, seeking assistance, justice and mercy; also he said that in the event of his royal escutcheon being richly decorated to his glory and praise with evidence of his victories over kings, it would also now be embellished with memorials of the kings whom he had made; the former would be primarily the accidental benefit of good fortune, whereas the latter would be the result of his own goodness and greatness of heart. Moreover, he said to him: "Most powerful lord, God knows how, when I heard of thy greatness and thy royal virtues, my spir-its were always eager and my eyes desirous to see thee; and I do not know why it was, because the more it pleased me, when I was free and in all my prosperity, the less do my overthrow and exile, by their sad condition, justify my faith and my words; but, if it were thus ordained from above that I should not come and do it so well in other circumstances more favourable to me, since it was ordained for me to see thee, I praise God fervently for my ruin; and this gladness already so satisfies me that I shall not return from this journey discontented." Proceeding fur-ther in a word, he said that, if perhaps in reply to his petition for justice and help men should deny that he was a Christian, even as upon other occasions word had been sent to him by way of an excuse for refusing another similar request, there should now be no doubt or contra-diction about it, because he and all his men who were present, among whom there were not wanting men of noble and royal birth, advised at other times by His holy warnings, had come in order that in his kingdoms and at his hands they might at once become Christians. He said that the only sorrow and truly grave anxiety, which they had thereby experienced, arose out of the fact that it seemed that the force of his necessity rather than of his faith had caused him to do it. With these he coupled many other sound reasons touching his purpose. Then the king replied to him in a few words, and devoted great care and much wisdom to everything, expressing great pleasure at their meeting and even more pleasure at his final intention to be a Christian. Therefore he gave him hope in this world of assistance in his cause and of restora-tion to his kingdom, and in the other that of glory and eternal salvation. Thereupon, he dis-missed him, and Bemoym went to speak to the queen and to the prince, before whom he made a short speech, in which with shrewd judgment and very natural dignity he asked them for favour and assistance with the king. The queen and the prince dismissed him, shewing him much honour and kindness. Then, on another day, Bemoym came to speak with the king, and, alone and apart, with an interpreter, they both conversed for a long time. Here Bemoym again recounted his affairs with great prudence; and he also replied very wisely and exactly to the questions which the king asked him, and the king remained very satisfied with this. In his ho-nour the king ordered bull-fights and tournaments, and he held fancy dress-balls and dances, and in order that he might see them he gave orders for a chair to be placed at the upper end of the state room opposite the king. Moreover, it was the king's wish that Bemoym, before becoming a Christian, should first be instructed in matters of the faith; for Bemoym was of the sect of Malamede [Muhammad] in whom he believed, because of his being a neighbour of, and dealer with, the Azanegues, and he had some knowledge of the contents of the Bible. For this reasons, theologians and learned men conversed with him and taught and advised him. Then it was decided that he should see and listen to a mass for the king, and this mass was said in pontifical and with great formality and ceremonial in the church of Santa Maria de Todolos Santos. Bemoym with his men and with learned Christians was in the choir, and, at the elevation of the body of Our Lord, when he saw all on their knees with their hands raised in the act of prayer, his hand went up to the cap which he had on his head; and thus, like everybody, with his knees on the ground and his head uncovered, he prayed. Then he said with many indications of truth that the remorse, which he experienced in his heart in that hour, he took as clear proof that this was the only true God of salvation. Then for two days the king proceeded to banquet publicly, for which purpose he put on his robes and he commanded that the house and the table were to be furnished with plate and tapestries, dishes and service, and there were to be minstrels and dances, and all in great perfection; for the king was deliberately very particular and exact about ceremonial above all in matters touching his estate. At the second hour of the night of the third day of the month of November, the said Bemoym, and six of the principal persons who had come with him, became Christians in the chamber of the queen, which was decorated for the occasion with elaborate formality. His godfathers were the king, the queen, the prince, the duke, a commissary of the pope who was at the court, and the bishop of Tanger who at the time was the licentiate Calçadilha. Dom Justo, bishop of Cepta, who in pontifical performed the office, baptized them, and Bemoym received the name Dom Joham for love of the king. Moreover, on the seventh day of November, the king dubbed him a knight; and twenty-four others of his men were made Christians in the counting-house of the said town. The king gave him a coat-of-arms consisting of a golden cross on a red field surrounded by the escutcheon of the arms of Portugal. On this same day, in a solemn act and speaking as a great lord he rendered obedience and paid homage to the king. Also he sent another submission, written in Latin, to the pope, wherein he gave an account of his case and of his conversion to the faith in words of deep devotion and high praise to the king. The king determined to give him help and assistance, and gave him twenty armed caravels. The captain of the caravels was Pero Vaaz da Cunha, who carried orders to build at the entrance of the Rio da Çanaga a fortress, which was not to be given to the said Bemoym, but was always to belong to the king. For this purpose a great quantity of stones and planed timber was then prepared, and also priests were assembled and a great number of articles for churches and for the business of conversion; and Master Alvaro, preacher to the king, of the order of Sam Domingos, was selected to be the principal person. One of the very chief reasons which inspired the king to prepare this fleet, and especially to undertake the building of a fortress at the entrance of this river, was his conviction that the said river, penetrating far into the interior, flowed to the city of Tambucutu [Timbuktu] and by Mombare, where are the richest trades and markets of gold in the world, from which all Berberia from east and west up to Jherusalem is supplied and provided. For he believed that the said fortress in order to free and safeguard the trade would provide great security in such a place for his men and the merchandise. This region up to the river and a little beyond was discovered in the time and by the command of the Infante Dom Anrique, the inventor and discoverer of this enterprise and the conquest of Guinee; and in his letters and records it appears that he called this river the Nillo, not that which enters the Mar do Levante at Alexandria, but another branch of it which the cosmographers say runs out to this ocean sea. But the real truth of this up to now—which is the time of our lord King Dom Manuel the First—has yet to be learned. Nevertheless, all these works, expenses and plans of Bemoym were changed to deeds of evil; because, after the said Pero Vaaz had put to land and entered into the said river, by readily believing suspicions of disloyalty and treason against Bemoym, or more truthfully because he wanted to return to the kingdom, he slew the said Bemoym with a sword, and then returned to this kingdom; whereat the king, being in Tavilla, grew very sad; and he overlooked this crime by Pero Vaaz, seeing that he did not visit heavy punishment upon him or many others who served it for the same reason; yet the king strongly disapproved of their killing him, since, being accomplices in such an error, they ought to have been treated as they treated him, because they had him freely in their power without offence or peril.

4 • The wealth of Africa (1508)

As the Portuguese moved farther and farther along the coast of Africa, they reported on the great amounts of trade in which the local people engaged, the wealth and power of many of the communities, and the skill evident in the production of items such as delicately carved ivory necklaces and finely woven mats. This was a continent teeming with people and commerce. And where the Portuguese could not go, such as inland areas where the followers of Islam ruled, they imagined the existence of dog-faced people and men with bristles like those of pigs. Duarte Pacheco Pereira wrote this account of Africa's wealth in 1505–8 after spending many years in the late 1400s as a ship's captain employed by King John II of Portugal. He was involved in the building of Elmina Castle, traveled to India in the early 1500s, and returned to serve as governor of the castle from 1520 to 1522.[4]

The Senegal River and its hinterland

The first black men are found at the Rio de Çanaguá [Senegal River]. This river is the beginning of the kingdom of Jalofo, which extends nearly a hundred leagues in length and forty in breadth; on the north the Rio de Çanaguá divides it from the Azanegues; on the south it borders Mandingua and on the east the kingdom of Turucol . . . The King of Jalofo can put 10,000 horsemen into the field and 100,000 footmen; they are all naked except the nobles and honourable men, who wear blue cotton shorts and drawers of the same stuff. These peoples, as those of the great kingdom of Mandingua and of Turucol and other negroes, are all circumcised and worship in the false sect of Mahomet. They are given to vice and are rarely at peace with one another, and are very great thieves and liars, great drunkards and very ungrateful and shameless in their perpetual begging.

All these people and others who dwell near them are ignorant of the source of the Rio de Çanaguá, which is so large and deep that they call it the Rio Negro. Many intelligent Ethiopians who know different provinces and countries for five hundred leagues up this river have told us that its source is unknown; but from its course and beginnings we know that it rises in a great lake of the river Nile thirty leagues long and ten broad, so that it seems that this is the branch which the Nile throws out through Ethiopia in a westerly direction, the other branch flowing north and disemboguing by four months in the sea of Egypt . . . At the head of this lake is a kingdom called Tambucutu, which has a large city of the same name on the edge of

4. Duarte Pacheco Pereira, *Esmeraldo de Situ Orbis,* c.1505–8, ed. and trans. George H. T. Kimble (London: Hakluyt Society, 1937), 2d ser., no. LXXIX, 78–82, 87–90, 90–94, 97–101.

the lake. There also is the city of Jany, inhabited by negroes and surrounded by a stone wall, where there is great wealth of gold; tin and copper are greatly prized there, likewise red and blue cloths and salt, all except the cloths being sold by weight; also greatly prized here are cloves, pepper and saffron, and fine thin silk and sugar. The commerce of this land is very great, and in the above-mentioned places and in Cooro as well, fairs are held; every year a million gold ducats go from this country to Tunis, Tripoli of Soria and Tripoli of Berbery and to the kingdom of Boje and Feez and other parts. This Rio de Çanaguá would be navigable for small vessels were it not for a great rock a little over 250 leagues from its mouth before one arrives at Tambucutu and the other towns. This rock is called Feleuu and it runs across the river so that no ship or boat can pass, as the water pours over it in a cataract. The ships of your Highness ascend this river only so far as the kingdom of Turocol, which the tide reaches sixty leagues from the mouth and bar of the river. There six or seven slaves are bartered for one horse of no great value, and some gold in return for kerchiefs and red cloths and stones called "alaquequas," which we are familiar with as stones that staunch blood. In this country there are very large snakes, twenty feet long and more and very thick . . . There are also in this river very large lizards, many of them twenty-two feet long, and their mouths are so large that they can easily swallow a man . . . This river is rife with fever . . .

The Gambia River and its hinterland

150 leagues from its mouth is a district called Cantor, where there are four towns, the principal of which is called Sutucoo and has some four thousand inhabitants; the names of the other three are Jalancoo, Dobancoo and Jamnamsura; they are all enclosed with wooden palisades and are distant from the river by half a league, a league and a league and a half. At Sutucoo is held a great fair, to which the Mandinguas bring many asses; these same Mandinguas, when the country is at peace and there are no wars, come to our ships (which at the bidding of our prince visit these parts) and buy common red, blue and green cloth, kerchiefs, thin coloured silk, brass bracelets, caps, hats, the stones called "alaquequas" and much more merchandise, so that in time of peace, as we have said, five and six thousand doubloons of good gold are brought thence to Portugal. Sutucoo and these other towns belong to the kingdom of Jalofo, but being on the frontier of Mandingua they speak the language of Mandingua. This Rio de Guambea divides the kingdom of Jalofo from the great kingdom of Mandingua . . . When ascending the Guabuu [Gambia River] the kingdom of Jalofo is on the N and that of Mandingua on the S, extending nearly 200 leagues in length and eighty in breadth. The king of Mandingua can put into the field twenty thousand horsemen, and infantry without number for they take as many wives as they choose; when their king is very old and cannot govern or when he is afflicted with a prolonged illness, they kill him and make one of his sons or relatives king. 200 leagues from this kingdom of Mandingua is a region where there is abundance of gold; it is called Toom. The inhabitants of this region have the faces and teeth of dogs and tails like dogs; they are black and shun conversation, not liking to see other men. The inhabitants of the towns called Beetu, Banbarranaa and Bahaa go to this country of Toom to obtain gold in exchange for merchandise and slaves which they take thither. Their mode of purchase is as follows: he who wishes to sell a slave or other article goes to a certain place appointed for the purpose and ties the slave to a tree and makes a hole in the ground as large as

he thinks fit, and then goes some way off; then the Dogface comes and if he is content with the size of the hole he fills it with gold, and if not he covers up the hole and makes another smaller one and goes away; the seller of the slave then returns and examines the hole made by the Dogface and if he is satisfied he goes away again, and the Dogface returns and fills the hole with gold. That is their mode of commerce, both in slaves and other merchandise, and I have spoken with men who have seen this. The merchants of Mandingua go to the fairs of Beetu and Banbarranaa and Bahaa to obtain gold from these monstrous folk . . . The people of this country all speak the language of Mandingua and follow the sect of Mahomet.

South to Serra Lyoa

There is a river called Casamansa, the people on whose banks belong to the Mandingua. Here are some shallows of mud, with five or six fathoms, running out two leagues into the sea, and at the end of this mud there are shallows of sand with twelve and fifteen fathoms, extending for four leagues. In this Rio de Casamansa iron is greatly prized, and slaves are bartered for horses and handkerchiefs and red cloths . . . I will not speak of the channel of this river, for it often changes; he who would enter it must take soundings at its bar to find the deepest part . . .

The Rio Grande has at its mouth five or six islands, very low and full of woods . . . the channels flowing between them are not very narrow, but in places they have bad shallows of rock through which the tide runs with great force . . . The tidal waters flow in so strongly that . . . leagues above its mouth there is a *macareo* [tidal bore] where the incoming tide raises the water twelve and fifteen fathoms and runs with such violence that a ship at anchor there could only escape being swamped by a miracle . . .

The coast from Rio Grande to Cabo da Verga lies NW by N and SE by S and occupies thirty-five leagues. This country is very low and difficult to recognise; the bottom is foul with great reefs of rock and on that account very dangerous, so that it should only be navigated by day; for greater security it should only be done in small vessels of from 25 to 30 tons, for a larger ship will run the risk of being wrecked. All the negroes of this country are idolators, and although they are ignorant of the law, they are circumcised; this is due to the fact that they are neighbours of the Mandinguas and other peoples who are Mohammedans . . . In all this country along the coast there is a certain amount of gold, for which we barter bloodstones, yellow and green beads, tin, linen, brass bracelets, red cloth and basins such as barbers use, and we obtain slaves there in exchange for such merchandise. The houses in this country are thatched huts and the inhabitants are usually at war with one another; they possess elephants . . . and various other animals and birds of strange kinds; they live on rice and maize and other vegetables, and also meat and fish, of which there is an abundance . . .

Concerning Serra Lyoa

The greater part of the inhabitants of this land are called Bouloos, a very warlike people and rarely at peace; they call gold "emloan" and water "men." Sometimes these negroes eat one another, but this is less usual here than in other parts of Ethiopia; they are all idolators and sorcerers and are ruled by witchcraft, placing implicit faith in oracles and omens. In this country there is gold in small quantity, which the Boulooes barter for salt. They take the salt to a place called Coya, whence the gold comes; it is very fine, of nearly twenty-three carats . . . In this land they make ivory necklaces more delicately carved than in any other country, also very fine and beautiful mats of palm-leaf which they call "bicas." In this country are many elephants . . . and many other animals such as are not to be found in Spain or in any other country of Europe. Here, as well, are wild men, whom the ancients called satyrs. They are covered with hairs almost as coarse as the bristles of a pig; they seem human and lie with their wives after our fashion, but instead of speaking they shout when they are hurt . . . Many believe that Serra Lyoa is so-called because there are lions here, but this is not so, for Pero de Sintra, a knight of Prince Henry's household, who discovered Serra Lyoa at the prince's bidding, seeing that it was a wild, rough country, called it the Lioness, and there was no other reason; and there can be no doubt of this, for he told me so himself . . .

In all this Serra Lyoa there is much fish, rice, maize, hens, capons, and a few cows and other cattle, but whoever comes here must guard against the negroes, for they are very bad people and shoot with poisoned arrows . . . In this country there are large canoes made from a single tree, many of which carry fifty men; they use them for war and other purposes. The country is full of woods which extend for nearly a thousand leagues along the coast . . . At this point the discoveries undertaken by the virtuous Prince Henry came to an end . . .

We must therefore pray God for his soul; he died on the 13th of November in the year 1460 and is buried in the monastery of Santa Maria da Vitoria da Batalha, in the chapel of King John his father. The benefits conferred on Portugal by the virtuous Prince Henry are such that its kings and people are greatly indebted to him, for in the country which he discovered a great part of the Portuguese people now earn their livelihood and the Kings of Portugal derive great profit from this commerce; for, from the Rio de Çanaguá on the frontier of the kingdom of Jalofo, where are the first negroes . . . to Serra Lyoa inclusive, when the trade of this country was well ordered, it yielded nearly 3,500 slaves and more, many tusks of ivory, gold, fine cotton cloths and much more merchandise. Therefore we must pray God for the soul of Prince Henry, for his discovery of this land led to the discovery of the other Guinea beyond Serra Lyoa and to the discovery of India, whose commerce brings us such an abundance of wealth.

5 • The king of Spain regulates the importation of African slaves into the Americas (1518)

The regular shipment of slaves from Africa to European possessions in the Americas began in the early 1500s (although the greatest growth would not take place until the spread of plantation agriculture, especially sugar, after the 1640s). The development of colonial labor needs arose from a combination of the exhaustion of indigenous stores of precious metals by European looting, together with the decimation of the local populations by diseases introduced from Europe. In order to make their colonies pay, the Spanish needed workers to produce goods and people able to resist the diseases that caused such high death rates among Native Americans and European settlers. The first slaves imported on a regular basis were Africans from Portugal, who had first been converted to Christianity. As the demand for slave labor increased, the requirement of conversion was allowed to lapse, as did the practice of importing only Africans who had first been brought to Europe. At the same time, the Spanish Crown anticipated earning considerable revenues from monopolizing and licensing slave imports into the Americas (which the pope had proclaimed a Spanish possession). The first significant license granted by the Crown was that given in 1518 by King Charles to Lorenzo de Gomenot, governor of Bresa, for the right to ship 4,000 Africans to Hispaniola, Cuba, Jamaica, and Puerto Rico.[5]

The king

Our officials who reside in the city of Seville in our House of Trade of the Indies; Know ye that I have given permission, and by the present [instrument] do give it, to Lorenzo de Gorrevod, governor of Bresa, member of my Council, whereby he, or the person or persons who may have his authority therefor, may proceed to take to the Indies, the islands and the mainland of the ocean sea already discovered or to be discovered, four thousand negro slaves both male and female, provided they be Christians, in whatever proportions he may choose. Until these are all taken and transported no other slaves, male or female, may be transported, except those whom I have given permission [to take] up to the present date. Therefore, I order you to allow and consent to the governor of Bresa aforesaid or the person or persons aforesaid who may have his said authority to transport and take the four thousand slaves male and female, without molesting him in any way; and, if the said governor of Bresa or the persons aforesaid who may have his authority, should make any arrangements with traders or other persons to ship the said slaves, male or female, direct from the isles of Guinea and other regions from which they are wont to bring the said negroes to these realms and to Portugal, or from any other region they please, even though they do not bring them to register in that house, they may do so provided that you take sufficient security that they bring you proof of how many they have taken to each island and that the said negroes male and female, have become Christians on reaching each island, and how they have paid the customs duties there, in order that those taken be known and be not in excess of the aforesaid number. Notwithstanding any prohibition and order that may exist to the contrary, I require you and order you in regard to this not to collect any duty in that house [of trade] on the said slaves but rather you are to allow them to be taken freely and this my cedula shall be written down in the books of that house [of trade].

Done in Saragossa, the eighteenth day of August of the year 1518.

I THE KING

6 • Trying to regulate the trade in slaves (1526)

In 1491, Nzinga a Nkuwu, king of the Kongo kingdom, which was inland and south of the Congo River, adopted Christianity and was baptized by the Portuguese as João I. His son, Afonso Mvemba a Nzinga, who took the throne as Afonso I in 1509, made Christianity the state religion. Both kings

---

5. Elizabeth Donnan, ed., *Documents Illustrative of the History of the Slave Trade to America* (Washington, D.C.: Carnegie Institute, 1930), vol. 1, 41–42.

engaged in an expanding trade with the Portuguese, first in copper, which the Kongolese forged into high-quality manillas (bracelets), which were used as a unit of currency, and then, increasingly, in slaves, which the Portuguese needed for their plantations on São Tomé. However, the demand was more than Afonso could manage, and in 1526 he wrote a series of letters to the king of Portugal asking for the latter's help in regulating the behavior of the European merchants, a request that went unanswered.[6]

Sir, Your Highness should know how our Kingdom is being lost in so many ways that it is convenient to provide for the necessary remedy since this is caused by the excessive freedom given by your factors and officials to the men and merchants who are allowed to come to this Kingdom to set up shops with goods and many things which have been prohibited by us, and which they spread throughout our Kingdoms and Domains in such an abundance that many of our vassals, whom we had in obedience, do not comply because they have the things in greater abundance than we ourselves; and it was with these things that we had them content and subjected under our vassalage and jurisdiction, so it is doing a great harm not only to the service of God, but to the security and peace of our Kingdoms and State as well.

And we cannot reckon how great the damage is since the mentioned merchants are taking every day our natives, sons of the land and sons of our noblemen and vassals and our relatives, because the thieves and men of bad conscience grab them wishing to have the things and wares of this Kingdom which they are ambitious of; they grab them and get them to be sold; and so great, Sir, is the corruption and licentiousness that our country is being completely depopulated, and Your Highness should not agree with this or accept it as in your service. And to avoid it we need from those [your] Kingdoms no more than some priests and a few people to teach in schools, and no other goods except wine and flour for the holy sacrament. That is why we beg of Your Highness to help and assist us in this matter, commanding your factors that they should not send here either merchants or wares, because it is *our will that in these Kingdoms there should not be any trade in slaves or outlets for them* ... [emphasis in original] (July 6, 1526)

◆

Sir ... many of our people, keenly desirous as they are of the wares and things of Your Kingdoms, which are brought here by your people, and in order to satisfy their voracious appetite, seize many of our people, freed and exempt men; and very often it happens that they kidnap even noblemen and sons of noblemen, and our relatives, and take them to be sold to the white men who are in our Kingdoms; and for this purpose they have concealed them; andothers are brought during the night so that they might not be recognized.

And as soon as they are taken by the white men they are immediately ironed and branded with fire, and when they are carried to be embarked, if they are caught by our guards' men the whites allege that they have bought them but they cannot say from whom, so that it is our duty to do justice and to restore to the freemen their freedom, but it cannot be done if your subjects feel offended, as they claim to be.

6. Basil Davidson, *The African Past: Chronicles from Antiquity to Modern Times* (Boston: Little, Brown, 1964), 194–97.

And to avoid such a great evil we passed a law so that any white man living in our King-doms and wanting to purchase goods in any way should first inform three of our noblemen and officials of our court whom we rely upon in this matter . . . who should investigate if the mentioned goods are captives or free men, and if cleared by them there will be no further doubt nor embargo for them to be taken and embarked. But if the white men do not comply with it they will lose their aforementioned goods. And if we do them this favour and conces-sion it is for the part Your Highness has in it, since we know that it is in your service too that these goods are taken from our Kingdom, otherwise we should not consent to this . . . (Oc-tober 18, 1526)

◆

Sir, Your Highness has been kind enough to write to us saying that we should ask in our letters for anything we need, and that we shall be provided with everything, and as the peace and health of our Kingdom depend on us, and as there are among us old folks and people who have lived for many days, it happens that we have continuously many and different diseases which put us very often in such a weakness that we reach almost the last extreme; and the same happens to our children, relatives and natives owing to the lack in this country of physi-cians and surgeons who might know how to cure properly such diseases. And as we have got neither dispensaries nor drugs which might help us in this forlornness, many of those who had been already confirmed and instructed in the holy faith of Our Lord Jesus Christ perish and die; and the rest of the people in their majority cure themselves with herbs and breads and other ancient methods, so that they put all their faith in the mentioned herbs and cere-monies if they live, and believe that they are saved if they die; and this is not much in the ser-vice of God.

And to avoid such great error and inconvenience, since it is from God in the first place and then from your Kingdoms and from Your Highness that all the good and drugs and med-icines have come to save us, we beg of you to be agreeable and kind enough to send us two physicians and two apothecaries and one surgeon, so that they may come with their drug-stores and all the necessary things to stay in our kingdoms, because we are in extreme need of them all and each of them. We shall do them all good and shall benefit them by all means, since they are sent by Your Highness, whom we thank for your work in their coming. We beg of Your Highness as a great favour to do this for us, because besides being good in itself it is in the service of God as we have said above. (October 18, 1526)

7 ◆ British attempts to break the Portuguese and Spanish monopolies of slave trading (1564–68)

The papal bulls excluded all Europeans other than those approved by the Portuguese and Spanish Crowns from the export trade in slaves from Africa and the import trade into the Americas. Such formal prohibition did not, however, prevent buccaneers attracted by the profits of the trade from attempting to participate, and in the 1560s Sir John Hawkins, an English sailor and trader, made three expeditions to West Africa in quest of slaves that he planned to sell to Spanish settlers in the Caribbean. As his accounts of his second (1564) and third (1567–68) voyages demonstrate, success in these endeavors was very difficult especially because of the actions taken by African rulers to use the European intruders for their own purposes.[7]

The 27th [December 1564] the captain was advertised by the Portugals of a town of the Negros called Bymba, being in the way as they returned [from the interior], where there was not only great quantity of gold, but also that there were not above forty men, and an hundred women and children in the town, so that if he would give the adventure upon the same, he might get a hundred slaves: with the which tidings he being glad . . . determined to stay before the town three or four hours to see what he could do: and thereupon prepared his men in armour and weapon together, to the number of forty men well appointed, having to their guides certain Portugals, in a boat, who brought some of them to their death: we landing boat after boat, and diverse of our men scattering themselves, contrary to the captain's will, by one or two in a company, for the hope that they had to find gold in their houses, ransacking the same, in the meantime the Negros came upon them, and hurt many being thus scattered, whereas if five or six had been together, they had been able, as their companions did, to give the overthrow to 40 of them, and being driven down to take their boats, were followed so hardly by a route of Negros, who by that took courage to pursue them to their boats, that not only some of them, but others standing on shore, not looking for any such matter by means that the Negros did flee at the first, and our company remained in the town, were suddenly so set upon that some with great hurt recovered their boats; othersome not able to recover the same, took the water, and perished by means of the ooze. While this was doing, the captain who with a dozen men, went through the town, returned finding 200 Negros at the waters side, [the English] shooting at them in the boats, and cutting them in pieces which were drowned in the water, at whose coming, they all ran away: so he entered his boats, and before he could put off from the shore, they returned again, and shot very fiercely and hurt diverse of them. Thus we returned back somewhat discomforted, although the captain in a singular wise manner carried himself, with countenance cheerful outwardly, as though he did little weigh the death of his men, not yet the great hurt of the rest, although his heart inwardly was broken in pieces for it; done to this end, that the Portugals being with him, should not presume to resist against him, nor take occasion to put him to further displeasure or hindrance for the death of our men: having gotten by our going ten Negros, and lost seven of our best men . . . and we had 27 of our men hurt . . .

The ships departed from Plymouth, the second day of October, Anno 1567 . . . and arrived at Cape Verde, the eighteenth of November; where we landed 150 men, hoping to obtain some Negros, where we got but few, and those with great hurt and damage to our men, which chiefly proceeded of their envenomed arrows; and although in the beginning they seemed to be but small hurts, yet there hardly escaped any that had blood drawn of them, but died in strange sort, with their mouths shut some ten days before they died, and after their wounds were whole; where I myself had one of the greatest wounds, yet thanks be to God, escaped. From thence we passed the time upon the coast of Guinea, searching with all diligence

7. Richard Hakluyt, *The Principal Navigations, Voyages, Traffiques & Discoveries of the English Nation Made by Sea or Over-land to the Remote and Farthest Distant Quarters of the Earth at Any Time within the Compass of these 1600 Yeeres* (London: G. Bishop, R. Newberie, and R. Barker, 1598–1600), vol. 10, 21–23, 65–67.

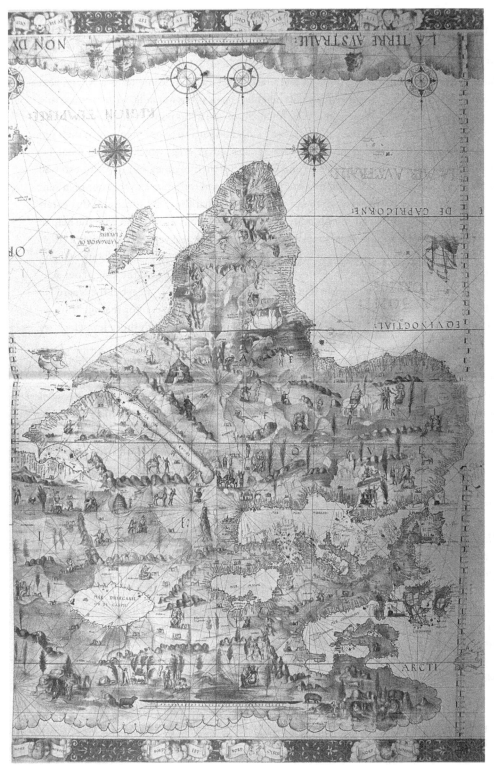

FIGURE 3 In this French map of 1546, the outline of the African coast is accurately depicted based on the travels of Portuguese voyagers, but the interior is filled with imagined peoples and beasts rather than the real kingdoms shown on the Catalan map of two centuries earlier. Special Collections, Young Research Library, UCLA.

the rivers from Rio Grande, unto Sierra Leone, till the twelfth of January, in which time we had gotten together a hundred and fifty Negros . . . thus having nothing wherewith to seek the coast of the West Indies, I was with the rest of our company in consultation to go to the coast of the Mina [Elmina], hoping there to have obtained some gold for our wares, and thereby to have defrayed our charge. But even in that present instant, there came to us a Negro, sent from a king, oppressed by other Kings his neighbours, desiring our aide, with promise that as many Negros as by these wars might be obtained as well of his part as of ours, should be at our pleasure; whereupon we concluded to give aid, and sent 120 of our men, which the 15 of January, assaulted a town of the Negros of our allies' adversaries, which had in it 8,000 inhabitants, being very strongly impaled and fenced after their manner, but it was not so well defended, that our men prevailed not, but lost six men and forty hurt: so that our men sent forthwith to me for more help: whereupon considering that the good success of this enterprise might highly further the commodity of our voyage, I went myself, and with the help of the king of our side, assaulted the town, both by land and sea, and very hardly with fire (their houses being covered with dry palm leaves) obtained the town, put the inhabitants to flight, where we took 250 persons, men, women, & children, and by our friend the king of our side, there were taken 600 prisoners, whereof we hoped to have had our choice; but the Negro (in which nation is seldom or never found the truth) meant nothing less: for that night he removed his camp and prisoners, so that we were fain to content us with those few which we had gotten ourselves.

Now we had obtained between four and five hundred Negros, wherewith we thought it somewhat reasonable to seek the coast of the West Indies, and there, for our Negros, and other [of] our merchandize, we hoped to obtain, whereof to countervail our charges with some gains, whereunto we proceeded with all diligence . . . and departed the coast of Guinea the third of February [1568].

8 • A Jesuit justifies the trade in African slaves to a skeptical colleague (1610)

Not all Europeans who engaged in the early slave trade accepted without question the legal and moral basis of the commerce in persons. In 1610, a Catholic priest in Brazil, Father Sandoval, inquired of a colleague in Angola, Luis Brandaon, rector of the College of the Society of Jesus at St. Paul de Loando [Luanda], Angola, as to the ways in which Africans were enslaved and how they were treated before being exported. Angola was the main source of slaves for Portuguese possessions in the Americas. It was also, for practically the entire period of the Atlantic slave trade, the largest supplier by far of slaves shipped to the Americas, accounting for almost half of all slave exports from Africa in the 1700s and the 1800s. This is Brother Luis Brandaon's response, dated March 12, 1610.[8]

8. Elizabeth Donnan, ed., *Documents Illustrative of the History of the Slave Trade to America* (Washington, D.C.: Carnegie Institute, 1930), vol. 1, 123–24.

Your Reverence writes me that you would like to know whether the negroes who are sent to your parts have been legally captured. To this I reply that I think your Reverence should have no scruples on this point, because this is a matter which has been questioned by the Board of Conscience in Lisbon, and all its members are learned and conscientious men. Nor did the bishops who were in São Thomé, Cape Verde, and here in Loando—all learned and virtuous men—find fault with it. We have been here ourselves for forty years and there have been [among us] very learned Fathers; in the Province of Brazil as well, where there have always been Fathers of our order eminent in letters, never did they consider this trade as illicit. Therefore we and the fathers of Brazil buy these slaves for our service without any scruple. Furthermore, I declare that if any one could be excused from having scruples it is the inhabitants of those regions, for since the traders who bring those negroes bring them in good faith, those inhabitants can very well buy from such traders without any scruple, and the latter on their part can sell them, for it is a generally accepted opinion that the owner who owns anything in good faith can sell it and that it can be bought. Padre Sánchez thus expresses this point in his Book of Marriage, thus solving this doubt of your Reverence. Therefore, we here are the ones who could have greater scruple, for we buy these negroes from other negroes and from people who perhaps have stolen them; but the traders who take them away from here do not know of this fact, and so buy those negroes with a clear conscience and sell them out there with a clear conscience. Besides I found it true indeed that no negro will ever say he has been captured legally. Therefore your Reverence should not ask them whether they have been legally captured or not, because they will always say that they were stolen and captured illegally, in the hope that they will be given their liberty. I declare, moreover, that in the fairs where these negroes are bought there are always a few who have been captured illegally because they were stolen or because the rulers of the land order them to be sold for offenses so slight that they do not deserve captivity, but these are few in number and to seek among ten or twelve thousand who leave this port every year for a few who have been illegally captured is an impossibility, however careful investigation may be made. And to lose so many souls as sail from here—out of whom many are saved—because some, impossible to recognize, have been captured illegally does not seem to be doing much service to God, for these are few and those who find salvation are many and legally captured.

9 • The importation of slaves into the Cape of Good Hope (1654)

In 1652, the Dutch East Indies Company, established to break the monopoly of the Portuguese and the Spanish on trade to Africa and Asia, founded a settlement on the southern coast of Africa from which to resupply ships sailing between Holland and trading ports along the West and East African coasts and in South and Southeast Asia. Initially, the directors of the company hoped to use local people to provide the labor needs of the settlement. However, the refusal of local Khoisan to work on the terms offered by the company led the first governor, Jan van Riebeeck, to send an expedition to the east coast of Africa in search of foodstuffs and slaves. From the 1650s until the first half of the next century, settlers at the Cape of Good Hope relied on slaves imported from Madagascar,

Mauritius, the east coast of Africa, and parts of South and Southeast Asia for their domestic and agricultural labor needs. While all European forts and settlements along the West and East African coasts used some slave labor, the Dutch settlement at the cape produced the largest and most continuous use of slave labor by Europeans within Africa. On May 8, 1654, van Riebeeck gave the following instructions to the officers of the Roode Vos *on their voyage to Mauritius and Madagascar.*[9]

As you are well aware from our resolution of the 27th April, why the galiot is to proceed to the above named islands [the settlement had been "reduced to great straits," had "nothing left of beans, cadjang, arrack, etc.," and had "resolved to send for supplies to Madagascar"], we merely now order you to proceed with the first fair wind straight to Mauritius and deliver our letter to the Commander there, and obtain the information required for trading at Madagascar, in order to secure rice, arrack, etc., hastening as much as possible to reach that island with the men which he may give you, that you may trade for the following provisions for the [cape] station: 25 or 30 tons rice, among them one or two padi. Arrack as much as you can stow away in casks or pots . . . Besides 30 or 40 slaves, more or less as you may be able to conveniently take on board—among them 10 or 12 slave girls from 12 to 15 or 16 years of age—the men slaves, however, to range in age between 16 to 20 and 23 years.

Should you meet with amber, musk, silver, ivory, skins or anything profitable for the Company you may bring us some as a trial. Also some sandal or other wood to see whether some profits may not likewise be secured for India. Above all, provide yourselves with rice, as we are much in want of it, and the men will long for it with their empty stomachs—for this especially the voyage is to be made with the hope that Providence will make it successful. Amen.

9. H. C. V. Leibbrandt, *Précis of the Archives of the Cape of Good Hope, Letters Despatched from the Cape, 1652–1662* (Cape Town: W. A. Richards and Sons, 1900), vol. 1, 300–302.

CHAPTER TWO

The Business of the Slave Trade (1672–1729)

10 ✦ An attempt to create an English
monopoly of trade in West Africa (1672)

When Britain's buccaneering attempts to break the Portuguese and Spanish monopolies met only limited success or failure, the English Crown sought to create trading monopolies of its own in a move to carve out a large share of trade on the West African coast. In 1618, James I chartered the Company of Adventurers of London Trading into Parts of Africa, but all of its trading voyages ended in disaster, with the ships lost at sea or the traders attacked on shore. Charles I in 1631 gave another group of English traders an exclusive right to regulate commerce in West Africa for thirty-one years, though again none of the expeditions was particularly successful. With the growth of English sugar plantations in the Caribbean from the mid-1600s onward, however, the demand for slave labor grew enormously. To meet this demand, the English sought to establish a new monopoly company for West Africa, matching the East India Company, which controlled English trade in South Asia and along the East African coast. The new enterprise, the Royal African Company, first chartered as the Company of Royal Adventurers Trading to Africa at the time of the restoration of the monarchy in 1660 and then reorganized in 1672, aimed to create an English monopoly that would challenge those of its European competitors (particularly the French and the Dutch, who by the mid-1600s had largely pushed the Portuguese out of much of West Africa). The company traded primarily in gold and slaves and based its African enterprises at Cape Coast Castle on the Gold Coast (present-day Ghana). According to the terms of its 1672 charter, the company had the right not only to establish an exclusive monopoly of West African trade but also to raise armies, declare wars, and enslave "Negroes."[1]

We [Charles the Second by the Grace of God King of England Scotland France and Ireland, Defender of the Faith, etc.] do hereby, for us, our heirs and Successors, grant unto the said Royal African Company of England and their Successors, that it shall and may be lawful to and for the said Company and their Successors, and none others, from time to time to set to Sea such and so many shipps, pinnaces, and barks as shall be thought fitting . . . And shall here-after have, use and enjoy all mines of Gold and Silver . . . which are or shall be found in any of the places above mentioned, And the whole, entire and only Trade, liberty, use and privilege of Trade and Traffic into and from the said parts of Africa above mentioned (that is to say) . . . all . . . places now or at any time heretofore called or known by the name or names of South

---

1. Elizabeth Donnan, ed., *Documents Illustrative of the History of the Slave Trade to America* (Washington, D.C.: Carnegie Institute, 1930), vol. 1, 177–92.

FIGURE 4 In the mid-1600s, Loango, north of the Congo River, was a major city with palaces, banquet halls, and royal gardens. This drawing, based on descriptions provided by European travelers to the city, provides an image very different from the stereotypical depictions of "tribal villages" found in nineteenth- and twentieth-century representations of "traditional" African communities. Olfert Dapper, *Umbständliche und eigentliche Beschreibung von Africa*, 1670–71.

Barbary, Guinny, Buiny or Angola . . . or any other Region or Countries or places within the bounds and limits aforesaid, and into and from all and singular Ports, Havens, Rivers, Creeks, Islands and places in the parts of Africa to them or any of them belonging, or being under the obedience of any King, State, or Potentate, of any Region, Dominion or Country in South Barbary, Guinny, Buiny or Angola, or limits aforesaid, for the buying, selling, bartering, and exchanging of, for, or with any Gold, Silver, Negroes, Slaves, goods, wares and merchandizes whatsoever to be rented or found at or within any of the Cities, Towns, places, Rivers situate or being in the Countries, islands, Places, Ports and Coasts aforementioned . . .

[W]e do hereby prohibit and forbid, all the subjects of us . . . to visit, frequent, trade or adventure to traffic into or from the said Regions . . . and places aforesaid or any of them to . . . import any Red Wood, Elephant's Teeth, Negro Slaves, Hydes, Wax, Gums, grains or any other the Commodities of the said Countries . . . unless it be with license and consent of the said Company . . .

We do hereby . . . grant and give full power and authority unto the said Royal African Company of England and their successors for the time being, that they, by themselves, their factors [agents], deputies and assigns, shall and may, from time to time, and at all times hereafter, enter into any Ship, Vessel, house, shop, Cellar or work-house and attack, arrest, take and seize all manner of ships, vessels, Negroes, Slaves, goods, Wares and Merchandizes whatsoever which shall be brought from or carried to the places before mentioned, or any of them, contrary to our Will and pleasure . . .

And we do . . . give and grant unto the said Royal African Company of England . . . full power to make and declare war with any of the heathen nations that are or shall be natives of any countries within the said territories within the said parts of Africa . . . [W]e do . . . give to them [the governors of the company] full power and authority to raise armies, train and muster such military forces as to them shall seem requisite and necessary and to execute and use within the said plantations the Laws called the Marshall Laws, for the defence of the said plantations against any foreign or domestic insurrection or Rebellion . . .

We have thought fit to erect and establish . . . a Court of Judicature to be held at such place or places, for our forts, plantations or factories upon the said coasts . . . which Court shall consist of one person learned in the Civil Laws, and two merchants . . . [who] shall have cognizance and power to hear and determine all cases of forfeiture and seizures of any ship or ships, goods and merchandizes trading and coming upon any of the said coasts . . . and also all cases of mercantile or maritime bargains buying selling and bartering of wares whatsoever . . . and all cases of trespasses, injuries and wrongs done or committed upon the high sea or in any of the regions, territories, countries or places aforesaid concerning any person or persons residing coming or being in the parts of Africa within the bounds and limits aforesaid . . .

In Witness etc., Witness the king at Westminster the seven and twentieth day of September [1672].

BY THE KING

11 • Sources of slaves for the Royal African Company (1678)

The Royal African Company held a legal monopoly on English trade on the West African coast until 1698. One of its main trading forts was on an island in the mouth of the Gambia River, and from this base, company traders annually acquired thousands of African slaves. The local agent of the company, Thomas Thurloe, wrote to his London superiors, March 15, 1678, a report on trading conditions on the West African coast.[2]

The next most considerable place for Trade is within this River of Gamboa for Slaves, Teeth, Wax and Hydes and may yield yearly between 5 and 6000 Slaves, 14 or 15 tuns of Teeth and wax and about 10,000 Hydes, the prices differ according to the persons the Goods are bought of, the dearest rates are those we give to the Portugueze which are 30 Bars for a Slave 18 Barrs per Cent for Teeth 16 for wax and 3 Hydes per b'l. To the natives wee give not so much but agree with them as wee can. But wee buy farr more of the Portugueze than of the Natives. If the Portugueze be kept poore then they will certainly bring their goods to the Islands but if they begin to grow rich then they will stand upon high terms and carry their goods to any Interloper's Strange Ship that comes in unless wee comply with them in every particular

2. Donnan, *Documents Illustrative of the History of the Slave Trade to America*, vol. 1, 234–35.

therefore this method ought to be used, to lend the best of them soe much and no more as with the proffitt of the goods wee lend them they may pay us againe and just maintaine their families soe that they wilbe allwayes in a necessity of borrowing and consequently only trade for us and not dare to sell what they gett to any strange Ship for fear wee should deny the lending of them. Once a Year (*vizt.*) about the ende of February a Vessell should be sent up the River to buy Slaves and Teeth of Merchants who come to such a particular place about 200 leagues up on purpose to meet with us and the Portugueze where those Comodityes are purchased at a cheaper rate than here below; and there is itt where wee buy the Country clothes which are very necessary to buy provisions here for wee spend 10 or 1200 every Year.

A third place to Trade in is betweene Cape Verde and this Rivers mouth which yeilds a good quantity of Negroes and Hydes but dearer than here for being an open place the French and Spaniards use it continually which hath raised the price of their Comodities, wee have not used that place because the Dutch had a Factor there; but since their Island hath been taken per the French, I sent thither to see what might be done and In a month or five weeks time bought 26 Negroes and 1400 Hydes, and if Goree were settled per the English, for the Dutch are taken and the French have left it, soe that tis free for the first commer, without wee might have a Considerable trade upon that Coast for it yeilds at best 500 Negroes and 50,000 hydes Yearly.

As for the sending out of Ships hither, it would be convenient to order it soe that none may be here In the raine time for that may prove the overthrow of a Voyage. 4 every Year would be enough (*Vizt.*) 2 for Negroes one to goe from hence at Christmas and the other at the latter end of May, and may both be dispatched from hence, for all the time betweene June and Christmas will be to buy ones Cargoe and from Christmas to June the other . . . this day I have sent another Ship to that Coast to buy Slaves and Hydes.

12 • The log of the *Arthur*, a ship carrying slaves for the Royal African Company from West Africa to Barbados (1677–78)

The Arthur *was part of the "triangular" trade, sailing from England to West Africa to purchase slaves, paying primarily with cloth manufactured in Europe and imported from India, beads, cowrie shells (the main form of currency used in Africa), and pieces of brass. The slaves were then shipped to the Caribbean and sold for sugar, which was then transported by the same vessels back to England. The log of the* Arthur *reprinted here details particularly the daily occurrence of death among the captives.*[3]

Dec. 5th 1677. A Journall of a voyage att New Callabarr in the shipp the *Arthur* Capt'n Rob't Doegood Commander: one the accompt of the Royall Affrican Company of England, of all actions and transactions from Gravesend to New Callabar and from thence to the Island of Barbados our portt of Discharge.

3. Donnan, *Documents Illustrative of the History of the Slave Trade to America,* vol. 1, 226–34.

Feb. 1678. Wed. 5 Wee Brake ground at Gravesend by five of the Clock in the mourninge and came to Anchor againe 7th day att twelve the wind att s.e . . .

Munday 11 February 1678. This day aboutt nine in the morninge Came one Board the Kinge of New Calabarr with some others of his gen'tes and after a Long discourse Came to Agreem'tt for Currentt for negro man 36 Copper Barrs: for one negro woman 30 and for one monello eight yames.

Tuesday 12th Feb'y 1678. This morninge Came one Board of us some Cannowse [canoes] Belonninge to Bandy with negroes but nott any wee did like: from which persons wee had Intelligence of Capt'n Wilkinse your Hon'rs Ship and that he had been gone from thence aboutt two moones and whilst he lay there was enforced to putt his negroes all on shore By reason of fire which appeared to be in his forecastell insoemuch that hee was very Likely to have Lost his ship By fire had nott the inhabitants [on] shore been kinde to him and helped him in the quenching of the fire and did honnorably deliver him againe all his negroes.

Wednesday 13 February 1678. The 12th day wee Bought 3 men 3 women as your hon'rs will finde one my Books of Acc'tt and this day we Bo[ought] 14 men and 18 women very good and young negroes with some provisions for them . . .

Sunday 17th Feby. 1678. Bo't 10 men 5 women 1 Boy and 3 girles all very likely negroes nott one of them exceedinge 30 years nor one under 14 yeares.

Monday 18th Feby 1678. This day wee Bo't 4 men and 4 women havinge noe encouridgrn't to By more by Reason of shore Remissniss in Bringing us provisions Doubtinge wee should have more Negroes then wee were Likely to have provisions and soe they to take advantage that did forbarre to Bye sendinge away again severall negroes and keepinge only such as we had minde to.

Wednesday 20th Feb. 1678. This day we had Cannows from Callabar and wee Bought 6 men 6 women and one Boye but had very Littell provisions for them.

Thursday 21st Feby 1678. This day we had severall Cannows on Board of us with Negroes Butt very few provisions wee Bo't 9 men and 11 women which were very stoute negroes indeed Butt nott many yames more then what before this day was promised to Bee Brought: the goods in our hands we kept till such Tyme as they had Brought enough for those negroes we had Bo't of them.

Friday Feby 22 1678. This day we sentt our Boat att Donus to see whatt might be done there, wee findinge negroes to be Brought one Board of us fast enough but were nott free to deale in many fearing lest wee should take in negroes and have noe provisions for them and the Boate returned againe with 1000 yames which they had purchased from severall of those on shore findinge yames very scarce this day, wee Bo't 7 men and 4 Women with some provisions as your hon'r may finde one the Booke of acc'tt . . .

Sattday 2 March 1678. This day wee Brought 2 men and 2 women havinge nott many Cannows one Board of us did Forbare to Buy too many expectinge to have as wee did Resolve our Choice of negroes: wee have made Choice of negroes to the Best of our skill and judgm'tt and as likely negroes as a man should see yett wee finde that some of them doe decay and grow Leane and some are sick they want for no thinge havinge dealy as much provision as they cann make use of neither doe the[y] want for any Comfortt not suffering any man one Board to strike them.

Acctt of what Negroes Dyd every day

Sunday 3 March 1678. This day wee Bought 5 men and 5 women and some provitions: aboutt 2 in the morning died one of our seamen after 5 days sickness and about 4 in the afternoon died one negro man: have 5 others sick.

Monday 4 March 1678. This day wee Bought 3 men and 4 women and 7 Girles very Likely Captives wee had some provitions and some oyle for them as will appere pr accontt.

Tuesday 5. This day wee Bought 5 men and 5 women wee forgett nott your hon'rs Interests mindeinge if possible to gett most men: if they are any way promisinge Butt as yett wee finde the women generally Better then the men.

Wednesday 6. This day wee Bought 3 men: 1 women with some provitions as pr accompt will appeare very good negroes nott forgetfinge your hon'rs orders that none exceed the age of fourteen neither under the age of twelve yeeres as heatherto had Been minded and accordingly Bo't.

Fryday 8. This day wee Bought 2 men and 1 woman haveinge nott many Cannows one Board to take greater Choice therfore did forbare to purchase expecting more for to Chuse for your hon'rs Better advantage Resolvinge as was befor minded to Buye not any Butt such as might If Life might bee permitted Answer your hon'rs expectation and advantage:

The 7 day aboutt four in the afternoon died one woman. This day as will appeare y're accompt wee did nott purchase any Negroes Butt some provitions for negroes: wee have many sick Captives Butt take the greatest Care wee can to preserve [them].

Sattday 9, March 1678 This day wee Bought 8 men and 6 women very Likely Negroes with some provitions—wee had died this day one man and severall others that are sick nottwithstandinge our Care with the Docktors phisick there is nothinge wantinge to them ...

Tuesday 12, March 1678 This day wee purchased 1 man 4 women and 1 Boy with some provitions as will appeare pr Accontt and att 10 in the forenoon died one man which to our knolidge had nott been sick 12 houres.

Wednsday 13, March 1678. This day haveing many Cannows on Board wee Bought 9 men and 8 women with some provitions many others wee might have Bott more but wee had noe Reason findinge many bad negroes, and the sickniss of ours one Board did soe much troble us takeing them in very Likely and stout negroes to fall sick in soe short Tyme that wee Littell in Curagm'tt. this day died 1 man and 1 Boy.

Thursday 14, March 1678. This day wee Bought 1 man and 1 woman with some provitions wee are nott free to Buy to many all one Tyme our Complem'tt Beinge all most up Butt are very Likely to Loose more here haveinge many very sick.

Fryday 15. This day wee haveinge many Cannewes, on bord and very Likely negroes wee Bought 11 men, 4 women, 2 Boyes and 1 Girle wee had not purchase soe many Butt findeinge them very Likely negroes and haveinge then many sick: ... died this day one man.

Sattday 16. This day wee Bought 3 men and 1 woman with some provitions wee hope to depart this place in few dayes our Complement beinge up: nether intend to purchase one negroe more except more dye to make our full number when wee shall come clare ofe: wee have many sick and doubt will not long live. the reason of ouer Byinge is bye the Loss of Negroes here ...

Monday 18. haveing soe many very sick expecting in few dayes the Loss of some negroes and haveinge very likely Negroes By the side wee Bought 4 men and some provitions:
this day died 1 woman . . .

Wedsday 20. died this day one man and one woman.

Thursday 21 . . . died one man haveing many more very sick . . .

Wednsday 27 . . . this day died one man. died of our negroes befor such tyme as wee
could gett over the Barr 12 men 6 woman and 1 Boy: have sevarall others sick.

Thursday 28 . . . in the afternoone I causd a muster of the negroes haveing all that were
well downe btween deck and soe told them up, on and on, giveinge all tobaco as they came
up: and found to bee one Board a life 175 men: 135 women: 9 Boyes: and 10 Girles and nott
one Negro more in the Shipp; myselfe sarchinge both betwen decks: and likewise the hold:
and am very Certaine there was not one Negroe more Bought for I paied the goods my selfe
for every Negroe was purchasd this voyage, this day died one man: and 2 women.

Fryday 29 . . . this day died one woman.

Sattday 30 . . . this day wee had died two men—haveinge att Least 30 more very sick.

Sunday 31 . . . in the morninge died one of our seamen and in the afternoon that day died
our docktor w'ch wee did accon'tt a great Lost haveinge 6 white men very sick and many
negroes sick: had not been sick passinge three dayes and wee had Been att sea of from the
Barr when he died, 5 dayes this day died one woman and one Girle.

Aprill, 1678.

Munday 1 . . . this day died one man and one woman.

Tuesday 2 . . . this day died two men—wee haveinge many more sick takeinge the greatest Care wee Could for there preservation.

Munday 8 . . . our negroes fallinge sick very many to our greate Troble Resolved to goe
at Cape Lopuse [Cape Lopez] to take some Refreshinge for them there aboutt 4 in the afternoon wee had a fresh gale: this day died one man.

Tuesday 9 . . . died this day and last night [two women].

Wedsday 10. there was att Cape Lopus when wee Came in a Dutchman, Belonginge to
the mine [Elmina], which had traded upon the Coast 5 months for Teeth, the next day after
wee Came in he went away from Cape Lopus this day wee sentt our Boat one shore for water:
this day died [one woman].

Thursday 11. This morninge our men went ashore woodinge and some for water, wee
had one Board Load of wood this day and 4 Tunn of Water: this day died one man.

Fryday 12. This day wee had 2 Boates Load of wood on Board and some water. wee finde
our Negroes to a mend and to be very well Refreshed wee Concludee itt to be By Reson of the
Change of the water: this day died one woman.

Sattday .13, Wee are now Cleeninge our ship: in the hold throwinge away the Rotton
yames wch are a great many more than wee thought. wee doubt wee shall not have good in the
ship 30,000 yames and shall be forced to take in provition here. this day died one woman . . .

Munday 15. This day aboutt 2 of the Clock in the morninge wee sett seale from Cape
Lopus . . . wee finde that the negroes are greatly refreshed By the stoping a Littell tyme. this
day died one man.

Tuesday 16 . . . this day died one man.

Fryday 19 . . . this day and Last night died 2 negro men.

Sunday 21 . . . this day died one Negroe man: some more wee have sick and though wee have noe Docktor yett wee doe the Best wee Cann for them giveinge them Brandy and Mallagetta: there is nothinge wantinge to them. this day died one man.

Munday 22. This day the winde nott Blowinge soe Fresh I did Muster the Negroes Causeing all to goe Downe Between decks that were weell and soe counted them up giveinge as they Came up one after one, Beinge all out of sheckells, Tobacco: and found to be alife 155 men 119 women 9 Boyes 9 Girles and noe more, this afternoone died one woman . . .

May.

Wedsday 1. our negroes are now for the most part in health.

Tuesday 14 . . . this day died one man—wee finde our negroes provitions to fall shortt By Reason of the many yames w'ch are Rotten.

Wedsday 15 . . . I tooke acco'tt of the Negroes Causeinge all that were well to goe downe Between decks: and soe Countinge the sick alought in the fore Castell and upon deck first: then Causeing the woman to Come up first one after one: and after the men: and I found to bee alife then 144 men: 110, women: 9 Boyes and 9 Girles and noe more, this eveninge about seaven of the Clock died one woman.

Thursday 16. this morninge and Last night died two men: one Boye: god Continue the gale otherwise wee doubt itt will be hard for us all intendinge to give our Negroes white mens provitions if theres should fall shortt w'ch wee doubt as yett wee have nott abated the negroes any thinge of there victialls but have as much as att first.

Sattday 18 . . . this afternoone died one man.

Tuesday 21 . . . aboutt 4 of the Clock in the afternoone wee had sight of the Island of Barbadoss, suppossinge too Late to gett in that night wee stood away.

Wednsday 22. The morninge Beinge hasie and darke wee Could not see the Island for two houres after wee stood towards itt wee made seale and seald N. W. and By 12 Of the Clock that day wee Anchord in Caleele Bay in Barbadoss: aboutt two houres after wee Came to Anchor; the Commander ordered his Boat to be mand who goes one shore and gives your hon'rs agentts accompt of the ships arrivall: my selfe Continge [continuing] one Board: expecting there Worshipps, one Board that night.

Thursday 23. This day wee expected your hon'rs Agentts on Board but did not Come. I went into the hold to see what was Left of the Negroes provition and found about 240 yames a few dryed plantaines w'ch was Left of that wee tooke in att Cape Lopus: 18 stock Fish: 3 parts of a hdd. of Beanes: a very small matter of Mallagetta [pepper] and about 10 l. of Tobaco: this is that w'ch was Left of there provitions: w'ch was not enough to give them Sattisfacktion three dayes: wherefor your honrs Agentts did order partatoes one Board whiles they Remaind there.

Fryday 24. This day I wentt one shore to your hon'rs Agentts and gave there W'rships the Charter p'tt and alsoe an accompt of what Negroes wee Bought what died one the Coast: what in the passage and how many wee Brought into Barbadoss alife: alsoe there worshipps had the sight of the Invoyces with the Declaration and proclamation: there worships intendinge the next day to Bee one Board and Lotte the negroes: w'ch after I had sattisfied there worshipps what they desired I went one Board againe. died one woman.

Sattday 25. This day your hon'r Agentts were one Board and Lotted the Negroes: which beinge done I showed there Worships my Booke of Accompt and whatt provitions was Left alsoe the Accompt of Teeth purchased and what goods Remayned of the Cargoe shipt one Board by your hon'rs Beinge now in the ship the *Arthur* eight hole Chest of Copper Barrs: and 34 Barrs in a Broken Chest, 26 Iron Barrs 16 Tapseels [type of cloth from India] 10 pentadoss [type of cloth from Southeast Asia] 16 dozen of Knives—this day died one negro man w'ch your hon'rs agentts had the sight of.

Sunday 26. Tuesday Followinge is intended the day for sale of Negroes: I am ordered to Tarry one Board w'ch accodingly doe. this day died one man.

Tuesday 28. This day were many of your hon'rs Negroes sold: the next day Beinge Keept: there were none sold untill Thursday. Wednsday Beinge the 29 May.

Thursday 30. this day the negroes were very thinn upon haveinge nott many Left.

31. The next day Rainy weather were not many Buyers one Board: if itt had Been Fare Weather suppose had sold all the Negroes—there were 23 Left unsold [the *Arthur* contained 265 living slaves when the sale began]: and the next day Beinge Satterday Mr. man Came on Board By your hon'rs Agentts order and Caused them to be Caryed away. I suppose the[y] were sold: after the negroes were all outt I Left the shipp and went one shore and the 7th of June Came outt of Barbadoss in the shipp the *Edward and Ann* Captn Nathaniell Green Commander: in Company with eleven seale more Bound for England.

Your Hon'rs Sav't

Geo. Kingston

13 • The Council of the Indies answers questions from the king of Spain concerning the introduction of slaves into Spanish America (1685)

In 1685, the king of Spain, Charles II, asked the Council of the Indies (the chief administrative body for the Spanish empire in the Americas and the Philippines) to explain the need for slavery in the Americas and to determine whether the religious aims of the Catholic church were being undermined by contracting with "Dutch heretics" to obtain large supplies of slaves. In their reply, the members of the council argued that the use of "heretics" did not undermine the religious aims of the Spanish colonists. Moreover, they stressed that without the use of slave labor Spain could not afford to retain its American colonies.[4]

Question:

By decree of July 5, 1685, his Majesty was pleased to order the Council of the Indies to inform him at once concerning the advantage of the negroes in America and what damage would follow in case they could not be had; whether there had been held any meetings by theologians and jurists to decide whether it was considered lawful to buy them as slaves and form asientos [concessions or contracts] for them; whether there were any authors who had written about this particular matter and who they were . . .

4. Donnan, *Documents Illustrative of the History of the Slave Trade to America*, vol. 1, 346–51.

The council answered as follows:

[The committee of the council] unanimously declared that they had no doubt with regard to this matter [the religious question] . . . the intercourse was lawful when there was no danger of perversion; and this could not be feared even remotely, for, although the administration of the contract was entrusted to Dutch persons, this present manager had to reside in these realms [Spanish], the business dealings were to be handled by Catholics, and if any Dutch trader had to assist tradesmen in their dealings, they were to obtain the advantages of such an one who had never had any business experiences in the Indies. Although many heretics of different sects have gone to the Indies, not one of them has ever tried to introduce his creed there. In case any such should go there, measures had been taken and orders had been given to the officials of the Inquisition, to punish them through their tribunal if they trespassed the permission granted them. The Faith was so firmly rooted in the Indies, and especially at ports where transports with negro slaves had to put in, that it could safely be said that it could not be more assured in the ports of Castile. There were no Indians at these ports nor even at a great distance from them, among whom they might, on account of their ready compliance, introduce their erroneous beliefs; and they cannot go into the interior of the country, because of the prohibitions in the laws of the Indies. As many cautions as possible were taken with regard to the two warships allowed to be manned by Flemish and Dutch crews in order to prevent these men from going ashore and from having any intercourse whatsoever with the Catholics . . . [Moreover, the intercourse was lawful] since it was certain that the Indies could not be maintained without negroes, because the lack of Indians has made it necessary that they be supplemented by making use of these people both for the labor of the estates, and for service in the families, as it is impossible to obtain Spaniards or creoles who are willing to do this kind of work; also the Dutch own the factories whence the negroes are brought. The public reason for maintaining those realms makes the trading lawful, because the Catholic could purchase from the infidel what was distinctly for necessary use, and not only the purchase is lawful, but also the delivery of the goods by the same hand, especially when, notwithstanding the many efforts made, no Spaniard could be found who was willing to take the asiento, inasmuch as the Consulado, which alone could handle the trade and which had done so before, refused it. Wherever the public weal is concerned, intercourse and trading are not only permitted but also the alliance with and use of armed auxiliaries, even of heretics, in defense of those domains proper, in case assistance cannot be obtained in any other way, as has been done in many instances in the past . . .

From the absolute need of these slaves, the fatal consequences which would result from not having them were easily deduced, for if they are the ones who cultivate the haciendas, and there is no one else who could do it, because of a lack of Indians, and where Indians were to be found they would not be forced to render personal services, it would follow that if a prohibition were issued to discontinue bringing them, the food needed for the support of the whole kingdom would cease to be produced; the landed properties, the main wealth of which consists chiefly of negro slaves, would be lost, and America would face absolute ruin. This was experienced when the kingdom of Portugal separated itself from the Spanish Crown [1640], for since [then] the asientos had lapsed and the bringing of negroes from Cape Verde and the factories owned by the Portuguese in Africa had ceased, and although certain permits were issued, they were not half enough to provide America where great poverty was suffered in consequence. It was then, in order to repair the loss, because the public weal demanded the support of those dominions, that the asiento was made with Domingo Grillo, slaves were provided, and immediately the benefit of their introduction was felt. Everything else connected with this question and deemed useful was considered.

14 • The voyage of the *Hannibal,* carrying slaves from West Africa to Barbados (1693–94)

This account of a slave voyage differs from that of the Arthur *in that the author, Thomas Phillips, provides information on the negotiations that took place between African and European traders. He also describes in some detail the conditions to which slaves were subjected on the Atlantic crossing and recounts the ways in which they struggled to escape their recent captivity. Phillips had purchased the* Hannibal, *a vessel of 450 tons and 36 guns, in 1693 with funds supplied by one of the London members of the Royal African Company, Sir Jeffrey Jeffreys, who was interested particularly in trade to Virginia. Other members of the company also invested as part owners with Phillips and Jeffreys. The* Hannibal, *together with five other ships, departed the English coast in October 1693 for a slaving voyage to West Africa. The vessels arrived at Cape Coast Castle near the end of February 1694 and then sailed along the coast until reaching Whydah (in present-day Benin) in late May.*[5]

Our factory [at Whydah] lies about three miles from the sea-side, where we were carry'd in hamocks, which the factor Mr. Joseph Peirson, sent to attend our landing, with several arm'd blacks that belong'd to him for our guard; we were soon truss'd in a bag, toss'd upon negroes heads, and convey'd to our factory . . .

Our factory built by Capt. Wiburne, Sir John Wiburne's brother, stands low near the marshes, which renders it a very unhealthy place to live in; the white men the African company send there, seldom returning to tell their tale: 'tis compass'd round with a mud-wall, about six foot high, and on the south-side is the gate; within is a large yard, a mud thatch'd house, where the factor lives, with the white men; also a store-house, a trunk for slaves, and a place where they bury their dead white men, call'd, very improperly, the hog-yard; there is also a good forge, and some other small houses . . . And here I must observe that the rainy season begins about the middle of May, and ends the beginning of August, in which space it was my misfortune to be there, which created sicknesses among my negroes aboard, it being noted for the most malignant season by the blacks themselves, who while the rain lasts will hardly be prevail'd upon to stir out of their huts . . . The factory prov'd beneficial to us in another kind; for after we had procured a parcel of slaves, and sent them down to the sea-side to be carry'd off, it sometimes proved bad weather, and so great a sea, that the canoes could not come ashore to fetch them, so that they returned to the factory, where they were secured and

5. Thomas Phillips, "A Journal of a Voyage made in the *Hannibal* of London . . . 1693, 1694," published originally in Awnsham Churchill and John Churchill, *Collection of Voyages and Travels* (London: H. Lintot, 1744–46), 6 vols., here excerpted from Donnan, *Documents Illustrative of the History of the Slave Trade to America,* vol. 1, 399–410.

provided for till good weather presented, and then were near to embrace the opportunity, we sometimes shipping off a hundred of both sexes at a time.

The factor, Mr. Peirson, was a brisk man, and had good interest with the king, and credit with the subjects, who knowing their tempers, which is very dastard, had good skill in treating them both civil and rough, as occasion requir'd; most of his slaves belonging to the factory, being gold coast negroes, who are very bold, brave, and sensible, ten of which would beat the best forty men the king of Whidaw had in his kingdom; besides their true love, respect and fidelity to their master, for whose interest or person they will most freely expose their own lives . . .

As soon as the king understood of our landing, he sent two of his cappasheirs, or noblemen, to compliment us at our factory, where we design'd to continue, that night, and pay our devoirs to his majesty next day, which we signify'd to them, and they, by a foot-express, to their monarch; whereupon he sent two more of his grandees to invite us there that night, saying he waited for us, and that all former captains used to attend him the first night: whereupon being unwilling to infringe the custom, or give his majesty any offence, we took our hamocks, and Mr. Peirson, myself, Capt. Clay, our surgeons, pursers, and about 12 men, arm'd for our guard, were carry'd to the king's town, which contains about 50 houses . . .

We returned him thanks by his interpreter, and assur'd him how great affection our masters, the royal African company of England, bore to him, for his civility and fair and just dealings with their captains; and that notwithstanding there were many other Places, more plenty of negro slaves that begg'd their custom, yet they had rejected all the advantageous offers made them out of their good will to him, and therefore had sent us to trade with him, to supply his country with necessaries, and that we hop'd he would endeavour to continue their favour by his kind usage and fair dealing with us in our trade, that we may have our slaves with all expedition, which was the making of our voyage; that he would oblige his cappasheirs to do us justice, and not impose upon us in their prices; all which we should faithfully relate to our masters, the royal African company, when we came to England. He answer'd that the African company was a very good brave man; that he lov'd him; that we should be fairly dealt with, and not impos'd upon; But he did not prove as good as his word; nor indeed (tho' his cappasheirs shew him so much respect) dare he do any thing but what they please . . . so after having examin'd us about our cargoe, what sort of goods we had, and what quantity of slaves we wanted, etc., we took our leaves and return'd to the factory, having promised to come in the morning to make our palavera, or agreement, with him about prices, how much of each of our goods for a slave.

According to promise we attended his majesty with samples of our goods, and made our agreement about the prices, tho' not without much difficulty; he and his cappasheirs exacted very high, but at length we concluded as per the latter end; then we had warehouses, a kitchen, and lodgings assign'd us, but none of our rooms had doors till we made them, and put on locks and keys; next day we paid our customs to the king and cappasheirs, as will appear hereafter; then the bell was order'd to go about to give notice to all people to bring their slaves to the trunk to sell us: this bell is a hollow piece of iron in shape of a sugar loaf, the cavity of which could contain about 50 lb. of cowries: This a man carry'd about and beat with a stick, which made a small dead sound . . .

Capt. Clay and I had agreed to go to the trunk to buy the slaves by turns, each his day, that we might have no distraction or disagreement in our trade, as often happens when there are here more ships than one, and the commanders can't set their horses together, and go hand in hand in their traffick, whereby they have a check upon the blacks, whereas their dis-agreements create animosities, underminings, and out-bidding each other, whereby they enhance the prices to their general loss and detriment, the blacks well knowing how to make the best use of such opportunities, and as we found make it their business, and endeavour to create and foment misunderstandings and jealousies between commanders, it turning to their great account in the disposal of their slaves.

When we were at the trunk, the king's slaves, if he had any, were the first offer'd to sale, which the cappasheirs would be very urgent with us to buy, and would in a manner force us to it ere they would shew us any other, saying they were the Reys Cosa [slaves of the king], and we must not refuse them, tho' as I observ'd they were generally the worst slaves in the trunk, and we paid more for them than any others, which we could not remedy, it being one of his majesty's prerogatives: then the cappasheirs each brought out his slaves according to his degree and quality, the greatest first, etc. and our surgeon examin'd them well in all kinds, to see that they were sound wind and limb, making them jump, stretch out their arms swiftly, looking in their mouths to judge of their age; for the cappasheirs are so cunning, that they shave them all close before we see them, so that let them be never so old we can see no grey hairs in their heads or beards; and then having liquor'd them well and sleek with palm oil, 'tis no easy matter to know an old one from a middle-age one, but by the teeths decay; but our greatest care of all is to buy none that are pox'd, lest they should infect the rest aboard . . .

When we had selected from the rest such as we liked, we agreed in what goods to pay for them, the prices being already stated before the king, how much of each sort of merchandize we were to give for a man, woman, and child, which gave us much ease, and saved abundance of disputes and wranglings, and gave the owner a note, signifying our agreement of the sorts of goods; upon delivery of which the next day he receiv'd them; then we mark'd the slaves we had bought in the breast, or shoulder, with a hot iron, having, the letter of the ship's name on it, the place being before anointed with a little palm oil, which caus'd but little pain, the mark being usually well in four or five days, appearing very plain and white after.

When we had purchas'd to the number of 50 or 60 we would send them aboard, there being a cappasheir, intitled the captain of the slaves, whose care it was to secure them to the water-side, and see them all off; and if in carrying to the marine any were lost, he was bound to make them good, to us, the captain of the trunk being oblig'd to do the like, if any ran away while under his care, for after we buy them we give him charge of them till the captain of the slaves comes to carry them away: These are two officers appointed by the king for this pur-pose, to each of which every ship pays the value of a slave in what goods they like best for their trouble, when they have done trading; and indeed they discharged their duty to us very faith-fully, we not having lost one slave thro' their neglect in 1300 we bought here.

There is likewise a captain of the sand, who is appointed to take care of the merchandize we have come ashore to trade with, that the negroes do not plunder them, we being often forced to leave goods a whole night on the sea shore, for want of porters to bring them up; but notwithstanding his care and authority, we often came by the loss, and could have no redress.

When our slaves were come to the seaside, our canoes were ready to carry them off to the longboat, if the sea permitted, and she convey'd them aboard ship, where the men were all put in irons, two and two shackled together, to prevent their mutiny, or swimming ashore.

The negroes are so wilful and loth to leave their own country, that they have often leap'd out of the canoes, boat and ship, into the sea, and kept under water till they were drowned, to

avoid being taken up and saved by our boats, which pursued them; they having a more dreadful apprehension of Barbadoes than we can have of hell, tho' in reality they live much better
there than in their own country; but home is home, etc: we have likewise seen divers of them
eaten by the sharks, of which a prodigious number kept about the ships in this place, and I
have been told will follow her hence to Barbadoes, for the dead negroes that are thrown overboard in the passage. I am certain in our voyage there we did not want the sight of some every
day, but that they were the same I can't affirm.

We had about 12 negroes did wilfully drown themselves, and others starv'd themselves
to death; for 'tis their belief that when they die they return home to their own country and
friends again.

I have been inform'd that some commanders have cut off the legs and arms of the most
wilful, to terrify the rest, for they believe if they lose a member, they cannot return home
again: I was advis'd by some of my officers to do the same, but I could not be perswaded to
entertain the least thought of it, much less put in practice such barbarity and cruelty to poor
creatures, who, excepting their want of Christianity and true religion (their misfortune more
than fault) are as much the works of God's hands, and no doubt as dear to him as ourselves;
nor can I imagine why they should be despis'd for their colour, being what they cannot help,
and the effect of the climate it has pleas'd God to appoint them. I can't think there is any in-
trinsick value in one colour more than another, nor that white is better than black, only we
think so because we are so, and are prone to judge favourably in our own case, as well as the
blacks, who in odium of the colour, say, the devil is white, and so paint him . . .

The present king often, when ships are in a great strait for slaves, and cannot be supply'd
otherwise, will sell 3 or 400 of his wives to compleat their number, but we always pay dearer
for his slaves than those bought of the cappasheirs, his measure for booges [type of cowry
shell] being much larger than theirs, and he was allow'd accordingly in all other goods we had.

For every slave the cappasheirs sold us publickly, they were oblig'd to pay part of the
goods they receiv'd for it to the king, as toll or custom, especially the booges, of which he
would take a small dishfull out of each measure; to avoid this they would privately send for us
to their houses in the night, and dispose of two or three slaves at a time, and we as privately
would send them the goods agreed upon for them; but this they did not much practise for fear
of offending the king, should he come to know it, who enjoyns them to carry all their slaves
to be sold publickly at the trunk with his own; sometimes after he had sold one of his wives or
subjects, he would relent, and desire us to exchange for another, which we freely did often,
and he took very kindly . . .

After we are come to an agreement for the prices of our slaves, ere the bell goes round to
order all people to bring their slaves to the trunk to be sold, we are oblig'd to pay our customs
to the king and cappasheirs for leave to trade, protection and justice; which for every ship are
as follow, *viz.*

To the king six slaves value in cowries, or what other goods we can perswade him to take,
but cowries are most esteem'd and desir'd; all which are measur'd in his presence, and he
would wrangle with us stoutly about heaping up the measure.

To the cappasheirs in all two slaves value, as above.

The usual charges here which we pay at our departure when we have finish'd our trade,
in any goods that remain, are One slave value to the captain of the trunk for his care of our
slaves while there; one slave value to the captain of the sand for his care of our goods; one

ditto to the captain of the slaves who conducts them safe to the sea-side; one ditto to captain Tom the interpreter, for his trouble; one ditto for filling water; half a slave, or as much cowries as the cavity of the bell can contain, to the bell-man.

Besides all which our factory charges, victualling the negroes after bought till they get aboard, and hire of porters to bring up the goods from the sea-side, which is seven miles at least, and the stoutest fellow would not bring above two bars of iron at a time, and make but one trip in a day, took up great quantities of our cowries, we paying these last charges in nothing else but these shells.

The best goods to purchase slaves here are cowries, the smaller the more esteem'd; for they pay them all by tale, the smallest being as valuable as the biggest, but take them from us by measure or weight, of which about 100 pounds for a good man-slave.

The next in demand are brass neptunes or basons, very large, thin, and flat; for after they have bought them they cut them in pieces to make anilias or bracelets, and collars for their arms legs and necks.

The other preferable goods are blue paper sletias, cambricks or lawns, caddy chints, broad ditto [all types of cloth], coral, large, smooth, and of a deep red, rangoes [beads] large and red, iron bars, powder, and brandy.

With the above goods a ship cannot want slaves here, and may purchase them for about three pounds fifteen shillings a head, but near half the cargo value must be cowries or booges, and brass basons, to set off the other goods that we buy cheaper, as coral, rangoes, iron, etc. else they will not take them; for if a cappasheir sells five slaves, he will have two of them paid for in cowries, and one in brass, which are dear slaves; for a slave in cowries costs us above four pounds in England; whereas a slave in coral, rangoes, or iron, does not cost fifty shillings; but without the cowries and brass they will take none of the last goods, and but small quantities at best, especially if they can discover that you have good store of cowries and brass aboard, then no other goods will serve their turn, till they have got as much as you have; and after, for the rest of the goods they will be indifferent, and make you come to their own terms, or else lie a long time for your slaves, so that those you have on board are dying while you are buying others ashore; therefore every man that comes here, ought to be very cautious in making his report to the king at first, of what sorts and quantities of goods he has, and be sure to say his cargo consists mostly in iron, coral, rangoes, chints, etc. so that he may dispose of those goods as soon as he can, and at last his cowries and brass will bring him slaves as fast as he can buy them; but this is to be understood of a single ship: or more, if the captains agree, which seldom happens; for where there are divers ships, and of separate interests, about buying the same commodity they commonly undermine, betray, and out-bid one the other; and the Guiney commanders words and promises are the least to be depended upon of any I know use the sea; for they would deceive their fathers in their trade if they could . . .

The only money they have here are these cowries or shells we carry them, being brought from the East-Indies, and were charg'd to us at four pounds per cent. of which we gave 100 lb. for a slave; as soon as the negroes have them, they bore holes in the backs of them, and string them on rushes, 40 shells on each, which they call a foggy; and five of such foggys being tied together, is call'd a galina, being 200 shells, which is their way of accounting their shell-money . . .

The canoes we buy on the gold coast, and strengthen them with knees and weatherboards fore and aft, to keep the sea out, they plunging very deep when they go against a sea. . . .

those that are most fit for the use at Whidaw, are five hand or seven hand canoes; of which each ship that buys many slaves ought to carry two, for they are very incident to be staved by the great sea when they overset, and here is none for supply, and without them there is no landing or coming off for goods or men: The canoe-men we bring from Cape Corce [Cape Coast Castle] being seven in number, of which one is boatswain, and is commonly one of the most skillful canoe-men in Guiney. . . . their pay is certain and stated, half of which we pay them in gold at Cape Corce, and the rest in goods when we have done with them at Whidaw; 'tis also customary to give them a canoe to carry them back, and cut up the other for fire-wood, unless an opportunity offers to sell it, which is very rare. They lost us six or seven barrels of cowries, above 100 bars of iron, and other goods, by the over-setting of the canoes in landing them, which we could never recover, or have the least satisfaction for, but were forced to give them good words, lest they should, in revenge, play us more such tricks; we kept two men ashore here constantly to fill water, which lay and eat at the factory, which fill'd our small hogsheads in the night, and roll'd them over the sand to the sea-side, ready to raft off in the morning, before the sea breeze came in, which is the only time, we having no other way to get it off but by rafting, and in halling off to the longboat the great sea would often break our raft, and stave our cask, whereby we lost a great many . . .

When our slaves are aboard we shackle the men two and two, while we lie in port, and in sight of their own country, for 'tis then they attempt to make their escape, and mutiny; to prevent which we always keep sentinels upon the hatchways, and have a chest full of small arms, ready loaden and prim'd, constantly lying at hand upon the quarter-deck, together with some granada shells; and two of our quarter-deck guns, pointing on the deck thence, and two more out of the steerage, the door of which is always kept shut, and well barr'd; they are fed twice a day, at 10 in the morning, and 4 in the evening, which is the time they are aptest to mutiny, being all upon deck; therefore all that time, what of our men are not employ'd in distributing their victuals to them, and settling them, stand to their arms; and some with lighted matches at the great guns that yaun upon them, loaden with partridge, till they have done and gone down to their kennels between decks: Their chief diet is call'd dabbadabb, being Indian corn ground as small as oat-meal, in iron mills, which we carry for that purpose; and after mix'd with water, and boil'd well in a large copper furnace, till 'tis as thick as a pudding, about a peck-ful of which in vessels, call'd crews, is allow'd to 10 men, with a little salt, malagetta [pepper], and palm oil, to relish; they are divided into messes of ten each, for the easier and better order in serving them: Three days a week they have horse-beans boil'd for their dinner and supper, great quantities of which the African company do send aboard us for that purpose; these beans the negroes extremely love and desire, beating their breast, eating them, and crying Pram! Pram! which is Very good! they are indeed the best diet for them, having a binding quality, and consequently good to prevent the flux, which is the inveterate distemper that most affects them, and ruins our voyages by their mortality: The men are all fed upon the main deck and forecastle, that we may have them all under command of our arms from the quarter-deck, in case of any disturbance; the women eat upon the quarter-deck with us, and the boys and girls upon the poop; after they are once divided into messes, and appointed their places, they will readily run there in good order of themselves afterwards; when they have eaten their victuals clean up, (which we force them to for to thrive the better) they are order'd down between decks, and every one as he passes has a pint of water to drink after his meat, which is serv'd them by the cooper out of a large tub, fill'd before-hand ready for them . . .

When we come to sea we let them all out of irons, they never attempting then to rebel, considering that should they kill or master us, they could not tell how to manage the ship, or must trust us, who would carry them where we pleas'd; therefore the only danger is while we are in sight of their own country, which they are loth to part with; but once out of sight out of mind: I never heard that they mutiny'd in any ships of consequence, that had a good number of men, and the least care; but in small tools where they had but few men, and those negligent or drunk, then they surpriz'd and butcher'd them, cut the cables, and let the vessel drive ashore, and every one shift for himself. However, we have some 30 or 40 gold coast negroes, which we buy, and are procur'd us there by our factors, to make guardians and overseers of the Whidaw negroes, and sleep among them to keep them from quarrelling; and in order, as well as to give us notice, if they can discover any caballing or plotting among them, which trust they will discharge with great diligence: they also take care to make the negroes scrape the decks where they lodge every morning very clean, to eschew any distempers that may engender from filth and nastiness; when we constitute a guardian, we give him a cat of nine tails as a badge of his office, which he is not a little proud of, and will exercise with great authority. We often at sea in the evenings would let the slaves come up into the sun to air themselves, and make them jump and dance for an hour or two to our bag-pipes, harp, and fiddle, by which exercise to preserve them in health; but notwithstanding all our endeavour, 'twas my hard fortune to have great sickness and mortality among them.

Having bought my complement of 700 slaves, *viz.* 480 men and 220 women, and finish'd all my business at Whidaw, I took my leave of the old king, and his cappasheirs, and parted, with many affectionate expressions on both sides, being forced to promise him that I would return again the next year, with several things he desired me to bring him from England; and having sign'd bills of lading to Mr. Peirson, for the negroes aboard, I set sail the 27th of July in the morning, accompany'd with the *East-India Merchant,* who had bought 650 slaves, for the island of St. Thomas, with the wind at W.S.W . . .

We supply'd ourselves with some Indian corn, figolas, or kidneybeans, plantins, yams, potatoes, cocoa-nuts, limes, oranges, etc., for the use and refreshment of our negroes . . .

Having completed all my business ashore in fourteen days that I lay here, yesterday in the afternoon I came off with a resolution to go to sea. Accordingly about six in the evening we got up our anchors, and set sail for Barbadoes, being forc'd to leave the *East-India Merchant* behind, who could not get ready to sail in nine or ten days; which time I could not afford to stay, in respect to the mortality of my negroes, of which two or three died every day, also the small quantity of provisions I had to serve for my passage to Barbadoes . . . I deliver'd alive at Barbadoes to the company's factors 372, which being sold, came out at about nineteen pounds per head. . . .

15 • Willem Bosman describes the Dutch trade for slaves on the West African coast (1704)

During the seventeenth century, Dutch traders expanded aggressively into the international seaborne trade, driving the Portuguese from many of their bases in West and East Africa, the Indian subcontinent, and Southeast Asia. They wrested much of Brazil from Portuguese control in 1630 (though they were driven out in 1654) and established their own sugar plantations in the Caribbean.

In search of slaves for their plantations and making considerable profits as suppliers of slaves to
other European settlers, the Dutch had their main base at Elmina (in present-day Ghana), which
they had seized from the Portuguese in 1637. Willem Bosman, the author of this account, had first
traveled to West Africa as a sixteen-year-old in the late 1680s. Later he returned as head of the
Dutch trading fort at Elmina and published one of the earliest and most thorough books on slave
trading on the African coast.⁶

The first business of one of our factors [agents] when he comes to Fida [Whydah], is to satisfy the customs of the king and the great men, which amount to about 100 pounds in guinea
value, as the goods must yield there. After which we have free licence to trade, which is published throughout the whole land by the crier.

But yet before we can deal with any person, we are obliged to buy the king's whole stock
of slaves at a set price; which is commonly one third or one fourth higher than ordinary: After
which we obtain free leave to deal with all his subjects of what rank soever. But if there happen to be no stock of slaves, the factor must then resolve to run the risk of trusting the inhabitants with goods to the value of one or two hundred slaves; which commodities they send
into the inland country, in order to buy with them slaves at all markets, and that sometimes
two hundred miles deep in the country: For you ought to be informed that markets of men
are kept here in the same manner as those of beasts with us.

Not a few in our country fondly imagine that parents here sell their children, men their
wives, and one brother the other: But those who think so deceive themselves; for this never
happens on any other account but that of necessity, or some great crime: But most of the
slaves that are offered to us are prisoners of war, which are sold by the victors as their booty.

When these slaves come to Fida, they are put in prison all together, and when we treat
concerning buying them, they are all brought out together in a large plain; where, by our surgeons, whose province it is, they are thoroughly examined, even to the smallest member,
and that naked too both men and women, without the least distinction or modesty. Those
which are approved as good are set on one side; and the lame or faulty are set by as invalids,
which are here called *mackrons*. These are such as are above five and thirty years old, or are
maimed in the arms, legs, hands or feet, have lost a tooth, are grey-haired, or have films over
their eyes; as well as all those which are affected with any venereal distemper, or with several
other diseases.

The invalids and the maimed being thrown out, as I have told you, the remainder are
numbered, and it is entered who delivered them. In the mean while a burning iron, with the
arms or name of the companies, lies in the fire; with which ours are marked on the breast.

This is done that we may distinguish them from the slaves of the English, French or others; (which are also marked with their mark) and to prevent the Negroes exchanging them for
worse; at which they have a good hand.

I doubt not but that this trade seems very barbarous to you, but since it is followed by
mere necessity it must go on; but we yet take all possible care that they are not burned too
hard, especially the women, who are more tender than the men.

6. Willem Bosman, *A New and Accurate Description of the Coast of Guinea, divided into the Gold, the Slave, and
the Ivory Coasts* (London: J. Knapton, 1705, first published in a Dutch edition in 1704), 363–65.

We are seldom long detained in the buying of these slaves, because their price is established, the women being one fourth or fifth part cheaper than the men. The disputes which we generally have with the owners of these slaves are, that we will not give them such goods as they ask for them, especially the *boesies* [cowry shells] (as I have told you, the money of this country;) of which they are very fond, though we generally make a division on this head in order to make one sort of goods help off another, because those slaves which are paid for in *boesies* cost the company one half more than those bought with other goods . . .

When we have agreed with the owners of the slaves, they are returned to their prison; where from that time forwards they are kept at our charge, cost us two pence a day a slave; which serves to subsist them, like our criminals, on bread and water: So that to save charges we send them on board our ships with the very first opportunity; before which their masters strip them of all they have on their backs; so that they come aboard stark naked as well women as men. In which condition they are obliged to continue, if the master of the ship is not so charitable (which he commonly is) as to bestow something on them to cover their nakedness.

You would really wonder to see how these slaves live on board; for though their number sometimes amounts to six or seven hundred, yet by the careful management of our masters of ships, they are so regulated that it seems incredible: And in this particular our nation exceeds all other Europeans; for as the French, Portuguese and English slave-ships, are always foul and stinking; on the contrary ours are for the most part clean and neat.

The slaves are fed three times a day with indifferent good victuals, and much better than they eat in their own country. Their lodging-place is divided into two parts; one of which is appointed for the men the other for the women; each sex being kept apart. Here they lie as close together as is possible for them to be crowded.

We are sometimes sufficiently plagued with a parcel of slaves, which come from a far inland country, who very innocently persuade one another, that we buy them only to fatten and afterwards eat them as a delicacy.

When we are so unhappy as to be pestered with many of this sort, they resolve and agree together (and bring over the rest to their party) to run away from the ship, kill the Europeans, and set the vessel ashore; by which means they design to free themselves from being our food.

I have twice met with this misfortune; and the first time proved very unlucky to me, I not in the least suspecting it; but the uproar was timely squashed by the master of the ship and myself, by causing the abettor to be shot through the head, after which all was quiet.

But the second time it fell heavier on another ship, and that chiefly by the carelessness of the master, who having fished up the anchor of a departed English ship, had it laid in the hold where the male slaves were lodged; who, unknown to any of the ship crew, possessed themselves of a hammer; with which, in a short time, they broke all their fetters in pieces upon the anchor: after this they came above deck and fell upon our men; some of whom they grievously wounded, and would certainly have mastered the ship, if a French and English ship had not very fortunately happened to lie by us; who perceiving by our firing a distressed gun, that something was in disorder of board, immediately came to our assistance with shallops [a type of sloop] and men, and drove the slaves under deck: Notwithstanding which before all was appeased about twenty of them were killed.

The Portuguese have been more unlucky in this particular than we; for in four years time they have lost four ships in this manner.

16 ◆ In support of slavery and against monopoly (1729)

Not all merchants believed that profits could be won only through the establishment of national monopolies like that of the Royal African Company. Joshua Gee, a London merchant, argued that only the final demise of the company would encourage competition and result in much greater numbers of slaves being exported from Africa to British plantations in the Caribbean. At the time of Gee's writing the company was already well into decline. Within two decades it disappeared altogether and was replaced in 1752 by the Company of Merchants Trading to Africa, membership in which was open to all English traders.[7]

Our trade with Africa is very profitable to the Nation in general; it has this Advantage that it carries no Money out, and not only supplies our Plantations with Servants, but brings in a great Deal of Bullion for those that are sold to the Spanish West Indies, besides Gold Dust, and other Commodities, as Red-wood, Teeth, Guinea Grain, &c. some of which are re-exported. The supplying our Plantations with Negroes is of that extraordinary Advantage to us, that the Planting Sugar and Tobacco, and carrying on Trade there could not be supported without them; which Plantations, as I have elsewhere observed, are the great Causes of the Increase of the Riches of the Kingdom. There has been great Struggles by the African Company to engross that Trade to themselves; by which Means they would not only prevent the large Profits that are brought into the Nation by the Trade private Adventurers drive thither, but would also be one great Means of ruining our Plantations; for, as I have already observed, our Plantations are supported by the Labour of Slaves, and our Profit either more or less, according to the Numbers there employed; and as the Trade is now drove on by private Adventurers, they push it with all imaginable Vigour, and the Planters have not only very great Numbers of Slaves brought in, but they are also afforded them at moderate Prices. But if this Trade should fall into the Hands of the Company, the Management, I am afraid, would be as it has been in some other Companies, carried on to the enriching [of] particular Persons, who too often trade away the Company's Estates; whereas private Traders put themselves into all Methods of Frugality, Industry and good Management; which indeed evidently appears by the Trade the Company drove and what private Adventurers have done. For the Company at best, by what I apprehend, never traded for above Five or Six Thousand Negroes yearly, whereas private Adventurers have traded for Thirty Thousand or upwards; And if ever our Trade should come to be put under a Company, I shall take it for granted, that our Improvements in the Plantations, which is carried on by the Labour of Negroes, would soon decline.

7. Joshua Gee, *The Trade and Navigation of Great-Britain Considered* (London: S. Buckley, 1729), 25–26.

CHAPTER THREE

The Slave Experience (1785–98)

17 • Venture Smith describes his capture into slavery (1798)

Broteer, or Venture Smith, as he was later named, was born the son of a West African prince. In the 1730s, Broteer, who was only six years old at the time, was captured by enemies of his father, transported to the coast, and sold into slavery. He was sent to North America, where eventually, at age thirty-six, he was able to purchase his freedom. Later he also bought the freedom of his wife, two sons, and a daughter and became a man of some property, even purchasing three slaves for his own use. When he died in Connecticut in 1805, he left a hundred-acre farm and three houses to his heirs. He published his autobiography in 1798, and like that of his near contemporary, Olaudah Equiano, Broteer's text became an important weapon in the hands of those calling at the end of the eighteenth century for the abolition of the slave trade.[1]

I was born at Dukandarra, in Guinea, about the year 1729. My father's name was Saungm Furro, Prince of the Tribe of Dukandarra. My father had three wives. Polygamy was not uncommon in that country, especially among the rich, as every man was allowed to keep as many wives as he could maintain. By his first wife he had three children. The eldest of them was myself, named by my father, Broteer. The other two were named Cundazo and Soozaduka. My father had two children by his second wife, and one by his third. I descended from a very large, tall and stout race of beings, much larger than the generality of people in other parts of the globe, being commonly considerable above six feet in height, and every way well proportioned.

The first thing worthy of notice which I remember was, a contention between my father and mother, on account of my father marrying his third wife without the consent of his first and eldest, which was contrary to the custom generally observed among my countrymen. In consequence of this rupture, my mother left her husband and country, and travelled away with her three children to the eastward. I was then five years old. She took not the least sustenance along with her, to support either herself or children. I was able to travel along by her side; the other two of her offspring she carried one on her back, and the other being a sucking child, in her arms. When we became hungry, our mother used to set us down on the ground, and gather some of the fruits which grew spontaneously in that climate. These served us for food on the way. At night we all lay down together in the most secure place we could find, and reposed ourselves until morning. Though there were many noxious animals there; yet so kind

1. Venture Smith, *A Narrative of the Life and Adventures of Venture, a Native of Africa, but Resident above Sixty Years in the United States of America* (New London, Conn.: C. Holt, 1798), 5–13.

was our Almighty protector, that none of them were ever permitted to hurt or molest us. Thus we went on our journey until the second day after our departure from Dukandarra, when we came to the entrance of a great desert. During our travel in that we were often affrighted with the doleful howlings and yellings of wolves, lions, and other animals. After five days travel we came to the end of this desert, and immediately entered into a beautiful and extensive interval country. Here my mother was pleased to stop and seek a refuge for me. She left me at the house of a very rich farmer. I was then, as I should judge, not less than one hundred and forty miles from my native place, separated from all my relations and acquaintance. At this place my mother took her farewell of me, and set out for my own country. My new guardian, as I shall call the man with whom I was left, put me into the business of tending sheep, immediately after I was left with him. The flock which I kept with the assistance of a boy, consisted of about forty. We drove them every morning between two and three miles to pasture, into the wide and delightful plains. When night drew on, we drove them home and secured them in the cote. In this round I continued during my stay here. One incident which befell me when I was driving my flock from pasture, was so dreadful to me in that age, and is to this time so fresh in my memory, that I cannot help noticing it in this place. Two large dogs sallied out of a certain house and set upon me. One of them took me by the arm, and the other by the thigh, and before their master could come and relieve me, they lacerated my flesh to such a degree, that the scars are very visible to the present day. My master was immediately sent for. He came and carried me home, as I was unable to go myself on account of my wounds. Nothing remarkable happened afterwards until my father sent for me to return home. . . . My father sent a man and horse after me. After settling with my guardian for keeping me, he took me away and went for home. It was then about one year since my mother brought me here. Nothing remarkable occurred to us on our journey until we arrived safe home.

I found then that the difference between my parents had been made up previous to their sending for me. On my return, I was received both by my father and mother with great joy and affection, and was once more restored to my paternal dwelling in peace and happiness. I was then about six years old.

Not more than six weeks had passed after my return, before a message was brought by an inhabitant of the place where I lived the preceding year to my father, that that place had been invaded by a numerous army, from a nation not far distant, furnished with musical instruments, and all kinds of arms then in use; that they were instigated by some white nation who equipped and sent them to subdue and possess the country; that his nation had made no preparation for war, having been for a long time in profound peace; that they could not defend themselves against such a formidable train of invaders, and must therefore necessarily evacuate their lands to the fierce enemy, and fly to the protection of some chief; and that if he would permit them they would come under his rule and protection when they had to retreat from their own possessions. He was a kind and merciful prince, and therefore consented to these proposals.

He had scarcely returned to his nation with the message, before the whole of his people were obliged to retreat from their country, and come to my father's dominions.

He gave them every privilege and all the protection his government could afford. But they had not been there longer than four days before news came to them that the invaders had laid waste their country, and were coming speedily to destroy them in my father's territories.

This affrighted them, and therefore they immediately pushed off to the southward, into the unknown countries there, and were never more heard of.

Two days after their retreat, the report turned out to be but too true. A detachment from the enemy came to my father and informed him, that the whole army was encamped not far out of his dominions, and would invade the territory and deprive his people of their liberties and rights, if he did not comply with the following terms. These were to pay them a large sum of money, three hundred fat cattle, and a great number of goats, sheep, asses, etc.

My father told the messenger he would comply rather than that his subjects should be deprived of their rights and privileges, which he was not then in circumstances to defend from so sudden an invasion. Upon turning out those articles, the enemy pledged their faith and honor that they would not attack him. On these he relied and therefore thought it unnecessary to be on his guard against the enemy. But their pledges of faith and honor proved no better than those of other unprincipled hostile nations; for a few days after a certain relation of the king came and informed him, that the enemy who sent terms of accommodation to him and received tribute to their satisfaction, yet meditated an attack upon his subjects by surprise and that probably they would commence their attack in less than one day, and concluded with advising him, as he was not prepared for war, to order a speedy retreat of his family and subjects. He complied with this advice.

The same night which was fixed upon to retreat, my father and his family set off about the break of day. The king and his two younger wives went in one company, and my mother and her children in another. We left our dwellings in succession, and my father's company went on first. We directed our course for a large shrub plain, some distance off, where we intended to conceal ourselves from the approaching enemy, until we could refresh ourselves a little. But we presently found that our retreat was not secure. For having struck up a little fire for the purpose of cooking victuals, the enemy who happened to be encamped a little distance off, had sent out a scouting party who discovered us by the smoke of the fire, just as we were extinguishing it, and about to eat. As soon as we had finished eating, my father discovered the party, and immediately began to discharge arrows at them. This was what I first saw, and it alarmed both me and the women, who being unable to make any resistance, immediately betook ourselves to the tall thick reeds not far off, and left the old king to fight alone. For some time I beheld him from the reeds defending himself with great courage and firmness, till at last he was obliged to surrender himself into their hands.

They then came to us in the reeds, and the very first salute I had from them was a violent blow on the back part of the head with the fore part of a gun, and at the same time a grasp round the neck. I then had a rope put about my neck, as had all the women in the thicket with me, and were immediately led to my father, who was likewise pinioned and haltered for leading. In this condition we were all led to the camp. The women and myself being pretty submissive, had tolerable treatment from the enemy, while my father was closely interrogated respecting his money which they knew he must have. But as he gave them no account of it, he was instantly cut and pounded on his body with great inhumanity, that he might be induced by the torture he suffered to make the discovery. All this availed not in the least to make him give up his money, but he despised all the tortures which they inflicted, until the continued exercise and increase of torment, obliged him to sink and expire. He thus died without informing his enemies where his money lay. I saw him while he was thus tortured to death. The shocking scene is to this day fresh in my mind, and I have often been overcome while thinking on it. He was a man of remarkable stature. I should judge as much as six feet and six or seven inches high, two feet across his shoulders, and every way well proportioned. He was a man of remarkable strength and resolution, affable, kind and gentle, ruling with equity and moderation.

The army of the enemy was large, I should suppose consisting of about six thousand men. Their leader was called Baukurre. After destroying the old prince, they decamped and immediately marched towards the sea, lying to the west, taking with them myself and the women prisoners. In the march a scouting party was detached from the main army. To the leader of this party I was made waiter, having to carry his gun, etc. As we were a scouting we came across a herd of fat cattle, consisting of about thirty in number. These we set upon, and immediately wrested from their keepers, and afterwards converted them into food for the army. The enemy had remarkable success in destroying the country wherever they went. For as far as they had penetrated, they laid the habitations waste and captured the people. The distance they had now brought me was about four hundred miles. All the march I had very hard tasks imposed on me, which I must perform on pain of punishment. I was obliged to carry on my head a large flat stone used for grinding our corn, weighing as I should suppose, as much as twenty-five pounds; besides victuals, mat and cooking utensils. Though I was pretty large and stout at my age, yet these burdens were very grievous to me, being only six years and a half old.

We were then come to a place called Malagasco. When we entered the place we could not see the least appearance of either houses or inhabitants, but upon stricter search found, that instead of houses above ground they had dens in the sides of hillocks, contiguous to ponds and streams of water. In these we perceived they had all hid themselves, as I suppose they usually did on such occasions. In order to compel them to surrender, the enemy contrived to smoke them out with faggots. These they put to the entrance of the eaves and set them on fire. While they were engaged in this business, to their great surprise some of them were desperately wounded with arrows which fell from above on them. This mystery they soon found out. They perceived that the enemy discharged these arrows through holes on the top of the dens directly into the air. Their weight brought them back, point downwards on their enemies heads, whilst they were smoking the inhabitants out. The points of their arrows were poisoned, but their enemy had an antidote for it, which they instantly applied to the wounded part. The smoke at last obliged the people to give themselves up. They came out of their caves, first spatting the palms of their hands together, and immediately after extended their arms, crossed at their wrists, ready to be bound and pinioned. I should judge that the dens above mentioned were extended about eight feet horizontally into the earth, six feet in height and as many wide. They were arched over head and lined with earth, which was of the clay kind, and made the surface of their walls firm and smooth.

The invaders then pinioned the prisoners of all ages and sexes indiscriminately, took their flocks and all their effects, and moved on their way towards the sea. On the march the prisoners were treated with clemency, on account of their being submissive and humble. Having come to the next tribe, the enemy laid siege and immediately took men, women, children, flocks, and all their valuable effects. They then went on to the next district which was contiguous to the sea, called in Africa, Anamaboo. The enemies provisions were then almost spent, as well as their strength. The inhabitants knowing what conduct they had pursued, and what were their present intentions, improved the favorable opportunity, attacked them, and took enemy, prisoners, flocks and all their effects. I was then taken a second time. All of us were then put into the castle, and kept for market. On a certain time I and other prisoners were put on board a canoe, under our master, and rowed away to a vessel belonging to Rhode Island, commanded by Captain Collingwood, and the mate Thomas Mumford. While we were going to the vessel, our master told us all to appear to the best possible advantage for sale. I was bought on board by one Robertson Mumford, steward of said vessel, for four gallons of rum, and a piece of calico, and called VENTURE, on account of his having purchased me with his own private venture. Thus I came by my name. All the slaves that were bought for that vessel's cargo, were two hundred and sixty.

18 • Olaudah Equiano becomes a slave (1789)

Olaudah Equiano, also known by his slave name, Gustavus Vassa, was born in the mid-1740s. An Igbo speaker from the eastern part of present-day Nigeria, Equiano, along with his sister, was captured by local slave raiders in the mid-1750s and eventually sold to slavers bound for the British Caribbean. Near the end of his life (he died in 1797), he became a well-known opponent of the slave trade and a strong supporter of the repatriation of freed slaves to the British colony of Sierra Leone. His autobiography, published in 1789, won considerable support for the abolitionist cause with its graphic depiction of the horrors of slavery. It was an enormous publishing success, going into eight editions in England alone within five years of its first publication, circulating in multiple editions in the United States, and being translated into Dutch, German, and Russian in the 1790s. So powerful was the impact of Equiano's two-volume account of his life on public opinion that contemporary advocates of the slave trade sought to question (without apparent factual basis or success) its veracity by claiming that the author had been born in the Caribbean and had never set foot in Africa until he returned later in life as an advocate of slave repatriation.[2]

My father, besides many slaves, had a numerous family, of which seven lived to grow up, including myself and a sister, who was the only daughter. As I was the youngest of the sons, I became, of course, the greatest favorite with my mother, and was always with her; and she used to take particular pains to form my mind. I was trained up from my earliest years in the art of war: my daily exercise was shooting and throwing javelins; and my mother adorned me with emblems, after the manner of our greatest warriors. In this way I grew up till I was turned the age of eleven, when an end was put to my happiness in the following manner. Generally when the grown people in the neighborhood were gone far in the fields to labor, the children assembled together in some of the neighboring premises to play; and commonly some of us used to get up a tree to look out for any assailant, or kidnapper, that might come upon us, for they sometimes took those opportunities of our parents' absence, to attack and carry off as many as they could seize. One day as I was watching at the top of a tree in our yard, I saw one of those people come into the yard of our next neighbor but one to kidnap, there being many

---

2. Olaudah Equiano, *The Interesting Narrative of the Life of Olaudah Equiano, or Gustavus Vassa, the African, Written by Himself* (London: Printed and sold by the author, 1789), vol. 1, 30–52.

stout young people in it. Immediately on this I gave the alarm of the rogue, and he was surrounded by the stoutest of them, who entangled him with cords, so that he could not escape till some of the grown people came and secured him. But, alas! ere long it was my fate to be thus attacked, and to be carried off, when none of the grown people were nigh. One day, when all our people were gone out to their works as usual, and only I and my dear sister were left to mind the house, two men and a woman got over our walls, and in a moment seized us both, and, without giving us time to cry out, or make resistance, they stopped our mouths, and ran off with us into the nearest wood. Here they tied our hands, and continued to carry us as far as they could, till night came on, when we reached a small house, where the robbers halted for refreshment, and spent the night. We were then unbound, but were unable to take any food; and, being quite overpowered by fatigue and grief, our only relief was some sleep, which allayed our misfortune for a short time. The next morning we left the house, and continued travelling all the day. For a long time we had kept the woods, but at last we came into a road which I believed I knew. I had now some hopes of being delivered; for we had advanced but a little way before I discovered some people at a distance, on which I began to cry out for their assistance; but my cries had no other effect than to make them tie me faster and stop my mouth, and then they put me into a large sack. They also stopped my sister's mouth, and tied her hands; and in this manner we proceeded till we were out of sight of these people. When we went to rest the following night, they offered us some victuals, but we refused it; and the only comfort we had was in being in one another's arms all that night, and bathing each other with our tears. But alas! we were soon deprived of even the small comfort of weeping together. The next day proved a day of greater sorrow than I had yet experienced; for my sister and I were then separated, while we lay clasped in each other's arms. It was in vain that we besought them not to part us; she was torn from me, and immediately carried away, while I was left in a state of distraction not to be described. I cried and grieved continually; and for several days did not eat any thing but what they forced into my mouth. At length, after many days travelling, during which I had often changed masters, I got into the hands of a chieftain, in a very pleasant country. This man had two wives and some children, and they all used me extremely well, and did all they could to comfort me; particularly the first wife, who was something like my mother. Although I was a great many days' journey from my father's house, yet these people spoke exactly the same language with us. This first master of mine, as I may call him, was a smith, and my principal employment was working his bellows, which were the same kind as I had seen in my vicinity. They were in some respects not unlike the stoves here in gentlemen's kitchens, and were covered over with leather; and in the middle of that leather a stick was fixed, and a person stood up, and worked it in the same manner as is done to pump water out of a cask with a hand pump. I believe it was gold he worked, for it was of a lovely bright yellow color, and was worn by the women on their wrists and ankles. I was there I suppose about a month, and they at last used to trust me some little distance from the house. This liberty I used in embracing every opportunity to inquire the way to my own home; and I also sometimes, for the same purpose, went with the maidens, in the cool of the evenings, to bring pitchers of water from the springs for the use of the house. I had also remarked where the sun rose in the morning, and set in the evening, as I had travelled along; and I had observed that my father's house was towards the rising of the sun. I therefore determined to seize the first opportunity of making my escape, and to shape my course for that quarter; for I was quite oppressed and weighed down by grief after my mother and friends; and my love of liberty, ever great, was strengthened by the mortifying circumstance of not daring to eat with the free-born children, although I was mostly their companion. While I was projecting my escape one day, an unlucky event happened, which quite disconcerted my plan, and put an end to my hopes. I used to be sometimes employed in assisting an elderly slave to cook and take care of the poultry; and one morning, while I was feeding some chickens, I happened to toss a small pebble at one of them, which hit it on the middle, and directly killed it. The old slave, having soon after missed the chicken, inquired after it; and on my relating the accident, (for I told her the truth, for my mother would never suffer me to tell a lie), she flew into a violent passion, and threatened that I should suffer for it; and, my master being out, she immediately went and told her mistress what I had done. This alarmed me very much, and I expected an instant flogging, which to me was uncommonly dreadful, for I had seldom been beaten at home. I therefore resolved to fly; and accordingly I ran into a thicket that was hard by, and hid myself in the bushes. Soon afterwards my mistress and the slave returned, and, not seeing me, they searched all the house, but not finding me, and I not making answer when they called to me, they thought I had run away, and the whole neighborhood was raised in the pursuit of me. In that part of the country, as in ours, the houses and villages were skirted with woods, or shrub-beries, and the bushes were so thick that a man could readily conceal himself in them, so as to elude the strictest search. The neighbors continued the whole day looking for me, and several times many of them came within a few yards of the place where I lay hid. I expected every moment, when I heard a rustling among the trees, to be found out, and punished by my master; but they never discovered me, though they were often so near that I even heard their conjectures as they were looking about for me, and I now learned from them that any attempts to return home would be hopeless. Most of them supposed I had fled towards home; but the distance was so great, and the way so intricate, that they thought I could never reach it, and that I should be lost in the woods. When I heard this I was seized with a violent panic, and abandoned myself to despair. Night, too, began to approach, and aggravated all my fears. I had before entertained hopes of getting home, and had determined when it should be dark to make the attempt; but I was now convinced it was fruitless, and began to consider that, if possibly I could escape all other animals, I could not those of the human kind; and that, not knowing the way, I must perish in the woods. Thus was I like the hunted deer—

> "Every leaf and every whisp'ring breath,
> Convey'd a foe, and every foe a death."

I heard frequent rustlings among the leaves, and being pretty sure they were snakes, I expected every instant to be stung by them. This increased my anguish and the horror of my situation became now quite insupportable. I at length quitted the thicket, very faint and hungry, for I had not eaten or drank any thing all the day, and crept to my master's kitchen, from whence I set out at first, which was an open shed, and laid myself down in the ashes with an anxious wish for death, to relieve me from all my pains. I was scarcely awake in the morning, when the old woman slave, who was the first up, came to light the fire, and saw me in the fire place. She was very much surprised to see me, and could scarcely believe her own eyes. She now promised to intercede for me, and went for her master, who soon after came, and, having slightly reprimanded me, ordered me to be taken care of, and not ill treated.

Soon after this, my master's only daughter, and child by his first wife, sickened and died, which affected him so much that for some time he was almost frantic, and really would have killed himself, had he not been watched and prevented. However, in short time afterwards he recovered, and I was again sold. I was now carried to the left of the sun's rising, through many dreary wastes and dismal woods, amidst the hideous roarings of wild beasts. The people I was sold to used to carry me very often, when I was tired, either on their shoulders or on their backs. I saw many convenient well built sheds along the road, at proper distances, to accommodate the merchants and travellers, who lay in those buildings along with their wives, who often accompany them; and they always go well armed.

From the time I left my own nation, I always found somebody that understood me till I came to the sea coast. The languages of different nations did not totally differ, nor were they so copious as those of the Europeans, particularly the English. They were therefore, easily learned; and, while I was journeying thus through Africa, I acquired two or three different tongues. In this manner I had been travelling for a considerable time, when, one evening, to my great surprise, whom should I see brought to the house where I was but my dear sister! As soon as she saw me, she gave a loud shriek, and ran into my arms. I was quite overpowered: neither of us could speak; but, for a considerable time, clung to each other in mutual embraces, unable to do any thing but weep. Our meeting affected all who saw us; and, indeed, I must acknowledge, in honor of those sable destroyers of human rights, that I never met with any ill treatment, or saw any offered to their slaves, except tying them, when necessary, to keep them from running away. When these people knew we were brother and sister, they indulged us to be together; and the man, to whom I supposed we belonged, lay with us, he in the middle, while she and I held one another by the hands across his breast all night; and thus for a while we forgot our misfortunes, in the joy of being together; but even this small comfort was soon to have an end; for scarcely had the fatal morning appeared when she was again torn from me forever! I was now more miserable, if possible, than before. The small relief which her presence gave me from pain, was gone, and the wretchedness of my situation was redoubled by my anxiety after her fate, and my apprehensions lest her sufferings should be greater than mine, when I could not be with her to alleviate them. Yes, thou dear partner of all my childish sports! thou sharer of my joys and sorrows! happy should I have ever esteemed myself to encounter every misery for you and to procure your freedom by the sacrifice of my own. Though you were early forced from my arms, your image has been always rivetted in my heart, from which neither time nor fortune have been able to remove it; so that, while the thoughts of your sufferings have damped my prosperity, they have mingled with adversity and increased its bitterness. To that Heaven which protects the weak from the strong, I commit the care of your innocence and virtues, if they have not already received their full reward, and if your youth and delicacy have not long since fallen victims to the violence of the African trader, the pestilential stench of a Guinea ship, the seasoning in the European colonies, or the lash and lust of a brutal and unrelenting overseer.

I did not long remain after my sister. I was again sold, and carried through a number of places, till after travelling a considerable time, I came to a town called Tinmah, in the most beautiful country I had yet seen in Africa. It was extremely rich, and there were many rivulets which flowed through it, and supplied a large pond in the centre of the town, where the people washed. Here I first saw and tasted cocoa nuts, which I thought superior to any nuts I had ever tasted before; and the trees which were loaded, were also interspersed among the houses, which had commodious shades adjoining, and were in the same manner as ours, the insides being neatly plastered and whitewashed. Here I also saw and tasted for the first time, sugar-cane. Their money consisted of little white shells, the size of the finger nail. I was sold here for one hundred and seventy-two of them, by a merchant who lived and brought me there. I had been about two or three days at his house, when a wealthy widow, a neighbor of his, came there one evening, and brought with her an only son, a young gentleman about my own age and size. Here they saw me; and, having taken a fancy to me, I was bought of the merchant, and went home with them. Her house and premises were situated close to one of those rivulets I have mentioned, and were the finest I ever saw in Africa: they were very extensive, and she had a number of slaves to attend her. The next day I was washed and perfumed, and when meal time came, I was led into the presence of my mistress, and ate and drank before her with her son. This filled me with astonishment; I could scarce help expressing my surprise that the young gentleman should suffer me, who was bound, to eat with him who was free; and not only so, but that he would not at any time either eat or drink till I had taken first, because I was the eldest, which was agreeable to our custom. Indeed, every thing here, and all their treatment of me, made me forget that I was a slave. The language of these people resembled ours so nearly, that we understood each other perfectly. They had also the very same customs as we. There were likewise slaves daily to attend us, while my young master and I, with other boys, sported with our darts and bows and arrows, as I had been used to do at home. In this resemblance to my former happy state, I passed about two months; and I now began to think I was to be adopted into the family, and was beginning to be reconciled to my situation, and to forget by degrees my misfortunes, when all at once the delusion vanished; for, without the least previous knowledge, one morning early, while my dear master and companion was still asleep, I was awakened out of my reverie to fresh sorrow, and hurried away even amongst the uncircumcised.

Thus, at the very moment I dreamed of the greatest happiness, I found myself most miserable; and it seemed as if fortune wished to give me this taste of joy only to tender the reverse more poignant. The change I now experienced, was as painful as it was sudden and unexpected. It was a change indeed, from a state of bliss to a scene which is inexpressible by me, it discovered to me an element I had never before beheld, and till then had no idea of, and wherein such instances of hardship and cruelty continually occurred, as I can never reflect on but with horror.

All the nations and people I had hitherto passed through, resembled our own in their manners, customs, and language: but I came at length to a country, the inhabitants of which differed from us in all those particulars. I was very much struck with this difference, especially when I came among a people who did not circumcise, and ate without washing their hands. They cooked also in iron pots, and had European cutlasses and cross bows, which were unknown to us, and fought with their fists among themselves. Their women were not so modest as ours, for they ate, and drank, and slept with their men. But above all, I was amazed to see no sacrifices or offerings among them. In some of those places the people ornamented themselves with scars, and likewise filed their teeth very sharp. They wanted sometimes to ornament me in the same manner, but I would not suffer them; hoping that I might some time be among a people who did not thus disfigure themselves, as I thought they did. At last I came to the banks of a large river which was covered with canoes, in which the people appeared to live with their household utensils, and provisions of all kinds. I was beyond measure astonished at this, as I had never before seen any water larger than a pond or a rivulet: and my surprise was mingled with no small fear when I was put into one of these canoes, and we began to paddle and move along the river. We continued going on thus till night, and when we came to land, and made fires on the banks, each family by themselves; some dragged their canoes on shore, others stayed and cooked in theirs, and laid in them all night. Those on the land had mats, of which they made tents, some in the shape of little houses; in these we slept; and after the morning meal, we embarked again and proceeded as before. I was often very much astonished to see some of the women, as well as the men, jump into the water, dive to the bottom, come up again, and swim about. Thus I continued to travel, sometimes by land, sometimes by water, through different countries and various nations, till, at the end of six or seven months after I had been kidnapped, I arrived at the sea coast . . .

The first object which saluted my eyes when I arrived on the coast, was the sea, and a slave ship, which was then riding at anchor, and waiting for its cargo. These filled me with astonishment, which was soon converted into terror, when I was carried on board. I was immediately handled, and tossed up to see if I were sound, by some of the crew; and I was now persuaded that I had gotten into a world of bad spirits, and that they were going to kill me. Their complexions, too, differing so much from ours, their long hair, and the language they spoke, (which was very different from any I had ever heard) united to confirm me in this belief. Indeed, such were the horrors of my views and fears at the moment, that, if ten thousand worlds had been my own, I would have freely parted with them all to have exchanged my condition with that of the meanest slave in my own country. When I looked round the ship too, and saw a large furnace of copper boiling, and a multitude of black people of every description chained together, every one of their countenances expressing dejection and sorrow, I no longer doubted of my fate; and, quite overpowered with horror and anguish, I fell motionless on the deck and fainted. When I recovered a little, I found some black people about me, who I believed were some of those who had brought me on board, and had been receiving their pay they talked to me in order to cheer me, but all in vain. I asked them if we were not to be eaten by those white men with horrible looks, red faces, and long hair. They told me I was not: and one of the crew brought me a small portion of spirituous liquor in a wine glass, but, being afraid of him, I would not take it out of his hand. One of the blacks, therefore, took it from him and gave it to me, and I took a little down my palate, which, instead of reviving me, as they thought it would, threw me into the greatest consternation at the strange feeling it produced, having never tasted any such liquor before. Soon after this, the blacks who brought me on board went off, and left me abandoned to despair.

I now saw myself deprived of all chance of returning to my native country, or even the least glimpse of hope of gaining the shore, which I now considered as friendly; and I even wished for my former slavery in preference to my present situation, which was filled with horrors of every kind, still heightened by my ignorance of what I was to undergo. I was not long suffered to indulge my grief; I was soon put down under the decks, and there I received such a salutation in my nostrils as I had never experienced in my life: so that, with the loathsomeness of the stench, and crying together, I became so sick and low that I was not able to eat, nor had I the least desire to taste any thing. I now wished for the last friend, death, to relieve me;

but soon, to my grief, two of the white men offered me eatables; and, on my refusing to eat, one of them held me fast by the hands, and laid me across, I think the windlass, and tied my feet, while the other flogged me severely. I had never experienced any thing of this kind before, and although not being used to the water, I naturally feared that element the first time I saw it, yet, nevertheless, could I have got over the nettings, I would have jumped over the side, but I could not; and besides, the crew used to watch us very closely who were not chained down to the decks, lest we should leap into the water; and I have seen some of these poor African prisoners most severely cut, for attempting to do so, and hourly whipped for not eating. This indeed was often the case with myself. In a little time after, amongst the poor chained men, I found some of my own nation, which in a small degree gave ease to my mind. I inquired of these what was to be done with us? They gave me to understand, we were to be carried to these white people's country to work for them. I then was a little revived, and thought, if it were no worse than working, my situation was not so desperate; but still I feared I should be put to death, the white people looked and acted, as I thought, in so savage a manner; for I had never seen among any people such instances of brutal cruelty; and this not only shown towards us blacks, but also to some of the whites themselves. One white man in particular I saw, when we were permitted to be on deck, flogged so unmercifully with a large rope near the foremast, that he died in consequence of it; and they tossed him over the side as they would have done a brute. This made me fear these people the more; and I expected nothing less than to be treated in the same manner. I could not help expressing my fears and apprehensions to some of my countrymen; I asked them if these people had no country, but lived in this hollow place? (the ship) they told me they did not, but came from a distant one. "Then," said I, "how comes it in all our country we never heard of them?" They told me because they lived so very far off. I then asked where were their women? had they any like themselves? I was told they had. "And why," said I, "do we not see them?" They answered, because they were left behind. I asked how the vessel could go? They told me they could not tell but that there was cloth put upon the masts by the help of the ropes I saw, and then the vessel went on and the white men had some spell or magic they put in the water when they liked, in order to stop the vessel. I was exceedingly amazed at this account, and really thought they were spirits. I therefore wished much to be from amongst them, for I expected they would sacrifice me; but my wishes were vain—for we were so quartered that it was impossible for any of us to make our escape.

While we stayed on the coast I was mostly on deck; and one day, to my great astonishment, I saw one of these vessels coming in with the sails up. As soon as the whites saw it, they gave a great shout, at which we were amazed; and the more so, as the vessel appeared larger by approaching nearer. At last, she came to an anchor in my sight, and when the anchor was let go, I and my countrymen who saw it, were lost in astonishment to observe the vessel stop and were now convinced it was done by magic. Soon after this the other ship got her boats out, and they came on board of us, and the people of both ships seemed very glad to see each other. Several of the strangers also shook hands with us black people, and made motions with their hands, signifying I suppose, we were to go to their country, but we did not understand them.

At last, when the ship we were in, had got in all her cargo, they made ready with many fearful noises, and we were all put under deck, so that we could not see how they managed the vessel. But this disappointment was the least of my sorrow. The stench of the hold while we were on the coast was so intolerably loathsome, that it was dangerous to remain there for any time, and some of us had been permitted to stay on the deck for the fresh air; but now that the whole ship's cargo were confined together, it became absolutely pestilential. The closeness of the place, and the heat of the climate, added to the number in the ship, which was so crowded that each had scarcely room to turn himself, almost suffocated us. This produced copious perspirations, so that the air soon became unfit for respiration, from a variety of loathsome smells, and brought on a sickness among the slaves, of which many died—thus falling victims to the improvident avarice, as I may call it, of their purchasers. This wretched situation was again aggravated by the galling of the chains, now became insupportable; and the filth of the necessary tubs, into which the children often fell, and were almost suffocated. The shrieks of the women, and the groans of the dying, rendered the whole a scene of horror almost inconceivable. Happily perhaps, for myself, I was soon reduced so low here that it was thought necessary to keep me almost always on deck; and from my extreme youth I was not put in fetters. In this situation I expected every hour to share the fate of my companions, some of whom were almost daily brought upon deck at the point of death, which I began to hope would soon put an end to my miseries. Often did I think many of the inhabitants of the deep much more happy than myself. I envied them the freedom they enjoyed, and as often wished I could change my condition for theirs. Every circumstance I met with, served only to render my state more painful, and heightened my apprehensions, and my opinion of the cruelty of the whites.

One day they had taken a number of fishes; and when they had killed and satisfied themselves with as many as they thought fit, to our astonishment who were on deck, rather than give any of them to us to eat, as we expected, they tossed the remaining fish into the sea again, although we begged and prayed for some as well as we could, but in vain; and some of my countrymen, being pressed by hunger, took an opportunity, when they thought no one saw them, of trying to get a little privately; but they were discovered, and the attempt procured them some very severe floggings. One day, when we had a smooth sea and moderate wind, two of my wearied countrymen who were chained together, (I was near them at the time) preferring death to such a life of misery, somehow made through the nettings and jumped into the sea: immediately, another quite dejected fellow, who, on account of his illness, was suffered to be out of irons, also followed their example; and I believe many more would very soon have done the same, if they had not been prevented by the ship's crew, who were instantly alarmed. Those of us that were the most active, were in a moment put down under the deck, and there was such a noise and confusion amongst the people of the ship as I never heard before, to stop her, and get the boat out to go after the slaves. However, two of the wretches were drowned, but they got the other, and afterwards flogged him unmercifully, for thus attempting to prefer death to slavery. In this manner we continued to undergo more hardships than I can now relate, hardships which are inseparable from this accursed trade. Many a time we were near suffocation from the want of fresh air, which we were often without for whole days together. This, and the stench of the necessary tubs, carried off many.

During our passage, I first saw flying fishes, which surprised me very much; they used frequently to fly across the ship, and many of them fell on the deck. I also now first saw the use of the quadrant; I had often with astonishment seen the mariners make observations with it, and I could not think what it meant. They at last took notice of my surprise; and one of them, willing to increase it, as well as to gratify my curiosity, made me one day look through it. The clouds appeared to me to be land, which disappeared as they passed along. This heightened my wonder; and I was now more persuaded than ever, that I was in another world, and that every thing about me was magic. At last, we came in sight of the island of Barbadoes, at which the whites on board gave a great shout, and made many signs of joy to us. We did not know what to think of this; but as the vessel drew nearer, we plainly saw the harbor, and other ships of different kinds and sizes, and we soon anchored amongst them, off Bridgetown. Many merchants and planters now came on board, though it was in the evening. They put us in separate parcels, and examined us attentively. They also made us jump, and pointed to the land, signifying we were to go there. We thought by this, we should be eaten by these ugly men, as they appeared to us; and, when soon after we were all put down under the deck again, there was much dread and trembling among us, and nothing but bitter cries to be heard all the night from these apprehensions, insomuch, that at last the white people got some old slaves from the land to pacify us. They told us we were not to be eaten, but to work, and were soon to go on land, where we should see many of our country people. This report eased us much. And sure enough, soon after we were landed, there came to us Africans of all languages.

We were conducted immediately to the merchant's yard, where we were all pent up together, like so many sheep in a fold, without regard to sex or age. As every object was new to me, every thing I saw filled me with surprise. What struck me first, was, that the houses were built with bricks and stories, and in every other respect different from those I had seen in Africa; but I was still more astonished on seeing people on horseback. I did not know what this could mean; and, indeed, I thought these people were full of nothing but magical arts. While I was in this astonishment, one of my fellow-prisoners spoke to a countryman of his, about the horses, who said they were the same kind they had in their country. I understood them, though they were from a distant part of Africa; and I thought it odd I had not seen any horses there; but afterwards, when I came to converse with different Africans, I found they had many horses amongst them, and much larger than those I then saw.

We were not many days in the merchant's custody, before we were sold after their usual manner, which is this. On a signal given, (as the beat of a drum), the buyers rush at once into the yard where the slaves are confined, and make choice of that parcel they like best. The noise and clamor with which this is attended, and the eagerness visible in the countenances of the buyers, serve not a little to increase the apprehension of terrified Africans, who may well be supposed to consider them as the ministers of that destruction to which they think themselves devoted. In this manner, without scruple, are relations and friends separated, most of them never to see each other again. I remember, in the vessel in which I was brought over, in the men's apartment, there were several brothers, who, in the sale, were sold in different lots; and it was very moving on this occasion, to see and hear their cries at parting. O, ye nominal Christians! might not an African ask you—Learned you this from your God, who says unto you, Do unto all men as you would men should do unto you? Is it not enough that we are torn from our country and friends, to toil for your luxury and lust of gain? Must every tender feeling be likewise sacrificed to your avarice? Are the dearest friends and relations, now rendered more dear by their separation from their kindred, still to be parted from each other, and thus prevented from cheering the gloom of slavery, with the small comfort of being together, and mingling their sufferings and sorrows? Why are parents to lose their children, brothers their sisters, or husbands their wives? Surely, this is a new refinement in cruelty, which, while it has no advantage to atone for it, thus aggravates distress, and adds fresh horrors even to the wretchedness of slavery.

19 • Anders Sparrman describes the treatment of slaves in South Africa (1785)

Anders Sparrman (1748–1820) was a Swedish physician and naturalist who had trained as a student of Carl Linnaeus. He first traveled overseas as a ship's surgeon on a voyage to China in 1765. In 1772 he visited the Cape of Good Hope at the direction of the Swedish East India Company with instructions to investigate the natural life of the country. Later that same year, he joined Captain James Cook's expedition to the South Pacific and Antarctica, returning to the Cape in 1775 after twenty-eight months of voyaging. Before returning to Sweden in 1776, Sparrman made a lengthy expedition into the interior of the cape. His three-volume Swedish (two-volume English) account of these travels focuses on the flora and fauna of the cape, but it also provides detailed commentary on all of the people that he encountered. Sparrman, who later gave testimony in England about the cruelties of the slave trade, was highly critical of the Dutch. In this section he relates a story told to him in April 1776 about the sufferings of a Dutch woman whose husband had been killed by a slave to illustrate the harsh ways in which slaves were treated at the cape.[3]

In the evening we came to *Nana-rivier.* At this time there lived here a widow, whose husband had several years before met with the dreadful catastrophe of being beheaded by his own slaves. His son, then about 13 or 14 years of age, was obliged to be eye-witness to his father's fate, and was even threatened with being made to partake of it, but luckily found an opportunity of giving them the slip; and after eluding their most vigilant search, hid himself up close from the forenoon till it was dark at night; when at last he ventured forth, with a view to seek a safer asylum at a neighbouring farm, and to accuse his father's murderers. These villains had resolved likewise to murder the mother, who was expected that day home from the Cape; but fortunately for her, though very much to her dissatisfaction, she was delayed by some accident on the road till the next day. By means of her son, who had made his escape, she received advice of what had happened. As the whole premises on the farm consisted merely of two houses, situated on a plain quite open on all sides, excepting that it was covered with a few straggling bushes, which grew along the little river or brook that ran close by the spot, the lad's contrivance to hide himself, though in fact extremely painful as well as singular, was the only one that could at this time possibly save him. It consisted in this, viz. that he sat, or rather sank himself up to his nose in the river; taking care at the same time to hide his face behind the boughs that hung over the water. The murderers not being able to find him any where, he having as it were entirely vanished out of their sight, immediately began to conclude, that, in order to avoid the stroke of the bloody axe, he had rather chose to put an end to his life himself, by jumping into the river: notwithstanding this, however, they attempted to make themselves

3. Anders Sparrman, *A Voyage to the Cape of Good Hope, towards the Antarctic Polar Circle and round the World: But Chiefly into the Country of the Hottentots and Caffres, from the Year 1772, to 1776* (London: G. G. J. and J. Robinson, 1785, first published in Swedish in 1783), vol. 2, 337–44.

certain whether he was drowned or not. The means they took in order to effect this, was to sound the brook all over with the branches of a tree; but they luckily forgot just the particular place where the boy was sitting, probably as the river was in that part shallower, and had a brisker current.

I should doubtless have brought the tears into the eyes of our hosts, and at the same time made them a bad return for their civilities, had I, by questioning them closely concerning the particulars of this story, endeavoured so unseasonably to satisfy my curiosity. For this reason, I have contented myself with taking it down, just as I have related it above, from the accounts given me by Mr. Immelman and others; and consequently was not able to learn with any certainty, whether the deceased had by any unusual act of severity provoked his slaves to commit this crime, by way of revenging themselves; or else whether these latter had acted thus, from a persuasion that the same crimes and predatory practices by which violence had been offered to their persons, and they had been deprived of their liberties, might likewise lawfully be had recourse to, for the recovery of this precious right bestowed on them by nature, and might consequently be very pardonable when exercised on their tyrants.

Yet, whatever might be the real reason of the committing this dreadful crime, I am convinced, that it has its origin in the very essence and nature of the commerce in slaves, in whatever manner and in whatever country it may be practised; a motive which I found had as much influence among the Christians in many places, as among the Turks on the coast of Barbary, to induce the unhappy slaves, and still more their tyrannical masters, to behave very strangely; nay, sometimes to be guilty of the most horrid cruelties. I have known some colonists, not only in the heat of their passion, but even deliberately and in cool blood, undertake themselves the low office (fit only for the executioner) of not only flaying, for a trifling neglect, both the backs and limbs of their slaves by a peculiar slow lingering method, but likewise, exceeding the very tigers in point of cruelty, throw pepper and salt over the wounds. But what appeared to me more strange and horrible, was to hear a colonist, not only describe with great seeming satisfaction the whole process of this diabolical invention, but even pride himself on the practice of it; and rack his brains, in order to find sophisms in defence of it, as well as of the slave trade; in which occupation the important post he enjoyed in the colony, and his own interest, had engaged him. He was, however, an European by birth; of a free and civilized nation; and, indeed, gave evident proofs of possessing a kind and tender heart; so that, perhaps, it would be difficult to shew any where a greater contradiction in the disposition of man, though in a world composed almost entirely of contradictions.

Many a time, especially in the mornings and evenings, have I seen in various places unhappy slaves, who with the most dismal cries and lamentations, were suffering the immoderately severe punishments inflicted on them by their masters; during which, they are used, as I was informed, to beg not so much for mercy, as for a draught of water; but as long as their blood was still inflamed with the pain and torture, it was said that great care must be taken to avoid allowing them the refreshment of any kind of drink; as experience had shewn, that in that case, they would die in the space of a few hours, and sometimes the very instant after they had drank it. The same thing is said to happen to those who are impaled alive, after having been broken upon the wheel, or even without having previously suffered this punishment. The spike in this case is thrust up along the backbone and the vertebrae of the neck, between the skin and the cuticle, in such a manner, that the delinquent is brought into a sitting posture. In this horrid situation, however, they are said to be capable of supporting life for several days, as long as there comes no rain; as in that case, the humidity will occasion their sores to mortify, and consequently put an end to their sufferings in a few hours.

I am glad that, during my residence in the town, no opportunity presented itself to me of seeing any one undergo this punishment; which, though it is only destined for incendiaries, or for such as are guilty of sedition, or murder, aggravated with peculiar circumstances of cruelty and barbarity, yet it appears not less shocking and revolting to human nature, than the very crimes themselves, and actually irritates more than it is generally thought to do, the other slaves in the town; whom I have seen compelled to be present even at such public punishments as do not affect the life of the culprit, in order that they might take warning from it. But the slave who is punished for sedition, is always, in the eyes of his fellow-slaves a martyr, that suffers for the common cause, and for having maintained the dearest rights bestowed upon them by nature, which is their liberty. Spikes, wheels, red-hot pincers, and all the rest of the horrid apparatus employed by their executioners, will never have with the sufferers the effect of convincing them of the contrary doctrine; on the contrary, they become still more obstinate in supposing themselves tyrannized over, and in thinking that such of their fellow-slaves as have had the courage to take away the lives of their own tyrants, and prefer death and tortures to the basely groveling and crawling any longer upon the earth in an opprobrious state of bondage, are examples worthy of imitation, and that at least they deserve to be venerated, pitied, and even revenged . . .

I have before observed, that the Bugunese slaves [brought to the cape from Dutch possessions on Celebes Island of Southeast Asia] are particularly strict and scrupulous with respect to the administration of justice. Those slaves are a sort of Mohamedans, and nearly of the same complexion as the people of Java, though they are taken upon other islands in the East-Indies. They are not moreover of a humour to put up with harsh expressions or abusive language, still less when they are not deserving of it, and not at all from a woman; looking upon it as the greatest shame, to suffer themselves to be disciplined by the weaker sex. Many a master and mistress of a family, who have happened to forget themselves with respect to this point, have, when a proper opportunity has offered, been made to pay for this mistake of theirs with their lives. These same slaves, on the other hand, when they know that they are in the wrong, are said to thank their master for each stroke he bestows upon them; at the same time commending his rigour and justice, nay even kissing his feet; a circumstance of which I myself have been an eye-witness. In fine, they are reported to be capable of bearing the most cruel torments with wonderful fortitude, as though they were entirely devoid of feeling. There have been instances of their not having uttered the least cry or complaint when impaled alive, or broken upon the wheel. But should a Bugunese slave at any time happen to betray the least want of resolution in this point, his countrymen are said to feel themselves hurt by it, considering it as a reproach to the whole nation. The female slaves belonging to these people, are reported to be extremely constant in love, as likewise to exact the strictest fidelity from their lovers. In short, the bold and intrepid character of this nation, is the cause that people at the Cape are not fond of buying them; and that the importation of them is prohibited, though in fact it is sometimes practised. The slaves from other parts, such as from Mosambique, Madagascar, Malabar, etc. are in general not so dangerous to their unreasonable and tyrannical masters. On account of this great tameness shewn by them, they are more generally made to bow beneath the yoke; and the mistress of a family may venture to give as free a scope to all her whims and fancies as her husband himself, with respect to these slaves. There is a law, indeed, existing in the colonies, which prohibits masters from killing their slaves, or from flogging or otherwise chastising them with too great severity; but how is a slave to go to law with his master, who is, as it were, his sovereign, and who, by the same laws, has a right (or at least may by dint of bribes purchase that right) to have him flogged at the public whipping-post, not absolutely to death, indeed, yet not far from it; and this merely on the strength of the master's own testimony, and without any farther inquisition into the merits of the case? The master has, besides, so far his slave's life in his hands, that by rating and abusing him day after day, as likewise by proper family discipline, as it is called, such as heavy iron chains, hard work, and little meat, he may, without controul, by little and little, though soon enough for his purpose, worry the poor fellow out of his life. In consequence of this, the unhappy slaves, who are frequently embued with finer feelings and nobler sentiments of humanity, though for the most part actuated by stronger passions than their white masters, often give themselves up totally to despondency, and commit various acts of desperation and violence. Divers circumstances and considerations may, perhaps, concur to induce a wretch in this situation to exempt his tyrant from the dagger, which he plunges in his own bosom; content with being thus able to put an end to his misery, and at the same time to disappoint his greedy master of the profits arising from the sweat of his brow. A female slave, who had been just bought at a high price, and rather prematurely treated with severity by her mistress, who lived in the Roode-zand district, hanged herself the same night out of revenge and despair, just at the entrance of her new mistress's bedchamber. A young man and woman, who were slaves at the Cape, and were passionately fond of each other, solicited their master, in conformity to the established custom, for his consent to their being united in wedlock, though all in vain, as from some whim or caprice he was induced absolutely to forbid it. The consequence was, that the lover was seized with a singular fit of despair, and having first stabbed the heart of the object of his dearest wishes, immediately afterwards put an end to his own life. But how many hundred instances, not less dreadful than these, might be produced for this purpose! These, however, may suffice to create all that abhorrence for the slave trade, which so unnatural a species of commerce deserves; we will, therefore, at present dismiss this disagreeable subject.

20 • Alexander Falconbridge describes his experiences as a physician on slave ships (1788)

Criticism of the treatment of slaves and of the Atlantic slave trade grew throughout the latter half of the eighteenth century and reached a peak in the late 1780s. In response to the criticism, the English parliament held a series of official inquiries into slavery and the export of slaves from Africa. One of the most riveting accounts of the slave trade was written by Alexander Falconbridge, a physician who had served as ship's surgeon on four slaving voyages. On the basis of his shipboard experiences he became a strong supporter of abolition, testifying against the trade before official British commissions, working closely with leading abolitionists such as Thomas Clarkson, and volunteering to travel to Sierra Leone, established in 1787 as a colony for freed slaves, to rebuild settlements burnt down by slavers.[4]

The Manner in Which the Slaves are Procured

After permission has been obtained for *breaking trade,* as it is termed, the captains go ashore, from time to time, to examine the negroes that are exposed to sale, and to make their purchases. The unhappy wretches thus disposed of, are bought by the black traders at fairs, which are held for that purpose, at a distance of upwards of two hundred miles from the sea coast; and these fairs are said to be supplied from an interior part of the country. Many negroes, upon being questioned relative to the places of their nativity have asserted, that they have travelled during the revolution of several moons (their usual method of calculating time) before they have reached the places where they are purchased by the black traders. At these fairs, which are held at uncertain periods, but generally every six weeks, several thousands are frequently exposed to sale, who had been collected from all parts of the country for a very considerable distance round. While I was upon the coast, during one of the voyages I made, the black traders brought down, in different canoes, from twelve to fifteen hundred negroes, which had been purchased at one fair. They consisted chiefly of men and boys, the women seldom exceeding a third of the whole number. From forty to two hundred negroes are generally purchased at a time by the black traders, according to the opulence of the buyer; and consist of those of all ages, from a month, to sixty years and upwards. Scarce any age or situation is deemed an exception, the price being proportionable. Women sometimes form a part of them, who happen to be so far advanced in their pregnancy, as to be delivered during their journey from the fairs to the coast; and I have frequently seen instances of deliveries on board ship. The slaves purchased at these fairs are only for the supply of the markets at Bonny, and Old and New Calabar.

There is great reason to believe, that most of the negroes shipped off the coast of Africa, are *kidnapped.* But the extreme care taken by the black traders to prevent the Europeans from gaining any intelligence of their modes of proceeding; the great distance inland from whence the negroes are brought; and our ignorance of their language, (with which, very frequently, the black traders themselves are equally unacquainted) prevent our obtaining such information on this head as we could wish. I have, however, by means of occasional inquiries, made through interpreters, procured some intelligence relative to the point, and such, as I think, puts the matter beyond a doubt.

From these I shall select the following striking instances. While I was in employ on board one of the slave ships, a negroe informed me, that being one evening invited to drink with some of the black traders, upon his going away, they attempted to seize him. As he was very active, he evaded their design, and got out of their hands. He was however prevented from effecting his escape by a large dog, which laid hold of him, and compelled him to submit. These creatures are kept by many of the traders for that purpose; and being trained to the inhuman sport, they appear to be much pleased with it.

4. Alexander Falconbridge, *An Account of the Slave Trade on the Coast of Africa* (London: J. Phillips, 1788), 12–36.

I was likewise told by a negroe woman, that as she was on her return home, one evening, from some neighbours, to whom she had been making a visit by invitation, she was kidnapped; and, notwithstanding she was big with child, sold for a slave. This transaction happened a considerable way up the country, and she had passed through the hands of several purchasers before she reached the ship. A man and his son, according to their own information, were seized by professed kidnappers, while they were planting yams, and sold for slaves. This likewise happened in the interior parts of the country, and after passing through several hands, they were purchased for the ship to which I belonged.

It frequently happens, that those who kidnap others, are themselves, in their turns, seized and sold. A negroe in the West-Indies informed me, that after having been employed in kidnapping others, he had experienced this reverse. And he assured me, that it was a common incident among his countrymen.

Continual enmity is thus fostered among the negroes of Africa, and all social intercourse between them destroyed; and which most assuredly would not be the case, had they not these opportunities for finding a ready sale for each other.

During my stay on the coast of Africa, I was an eye-witness of the following transaction. A black trader invited a negroe, who resided a little way up the country, to come and see him. After the entertainment was over, the trader proposed to his guest, to treat him with a sight of one of the ships lying in the river. The unsuspicious countryman readily consented, and accompanied the trader in the canoe to the side of the ship, which he viewed with pleasure and astonishment. While he was thus employed, some black traders on board, who appeared to be in the secret, leaped into the canoe, seized the unfortunate man, and dragging him into the ship, immediately sold him.

Previous to my being in this employ, I entertained a belief, as many others have done, that the kings and principal men *breed* negroes for sale, as we do cattle. During the different times I was in the country, I took no little pains to satisfy myself in this particular; but notwithstanding I made many inquiries, I was not able to obtain the least intelligence of this being the case, which it is more than probable I should have done, had such a practice prevailed. All the information I could procure, confirms me in the belief, that to *kidnapping*, and to crimes, (and many of these fabricated as a pretext) the slave trade owes its chief support.

The following instance tends to prove, that the last mentioned artifice is often made use of. Several black traders, one of whom was a person of consequence, and exercised an authority somewhat similar to that of our magistrates, being in want of some particular kind of merchandize, and not having a slave to barter for it, they accused a fisherman, at the river Ambris, with extortion in the sale of his fish; and as they were interested in the decision, they immediately adjudged the poor fellow guilty, and condemned him to be sold. He was accordingly purchased by the ship to which I belonged, and brought on board.

As an additional proof that kidnapping is not only the general, but almost the sole mode, by which slaves are procured, the black traders, in purchasing them, choose those which are the roughest and most hardy; alleging, that the smooth negroes have been *gentlemen.* By this observation we may conclude they mean that nothing but fraud or force could have reduced these smooth-skinned gentlemen to a state of slavery.

It may not be here unworthy of remark, in order to prove that the wars among the Africans do not furnish the numbers they are supposed to do, that I never saw any negroes with recent wounds; which must have been the consequence, at least with some of them, had they been taken in battle. And it being the particular province of the surgeon to examine the slaves when they are purchased, such a circumstance could not have escaped my observation. As a further corroboration, it may be remarked, that on the Gold and Windward Coasts, where fairs are not held, the number of slaves procured at a time are usually very small.

The preparations made at Bonny by the black traders, upon setting out for the fairs which are held up the country, are very considerable. From twenty to thirty canoes, capable of containing thirty or forty negroes each, are assembled for this purpose; and such goods put on them as they expect will be wanted for the purchase of the number of slaves they intend to buy. When their loading is completed, they commence their voyage, with colours flying and musick playing; and in about ten or eleven days, they generally return to Bonny with full cargoes. As soon as the canoes arrive at the trader's landing-place, the purchased negroes are cleaned, and oiled with palm oil; and on the following day they are exposed for sale to the captains.

The black traders do not always purchase their slaves at the same rate. The speed with which the information of the arrival of the ships upon the coast is conveyed to the fairs, considering it is in the interest of the traders to keep them ignorant, is really surprising. In a very short time after the ships arrive upon the coast, especially if several make their appearance together, those who dispose of the negroes at the fairs are frequently known to increase the price of them.

These fairs are not the only means, though they are the chief, by which the black traders on the coast are supplied with negroes. Small parties of them, from five to ten, are frequently brought to the houses of the traders, by those who make a practice of kidnapping; and who are constantly employed in procuring a supply, while purchasers are to be found.

When the negroes, whom the black traders have to dispose of, are shewn to the European purchasers, they first examine them relative to their age. They then minutely inspect their persons, and inquire into the state of their health; if they are afflicted with any infirmity, or are deformed, or have bad eyes or teeth; if they are lame, or weak in the joints, or distorted in the back, or of a slender make, or are narrow in the chest; in short, if they have been, or are afflicted in any manner, so as to render them incapable of much labour; if any of the foregoing defects are discovered in them, they are rejected. But if approved of, they are generally taken on board the ship the same evening. The purchaser has liberty to return on the following morning, but not afterwards, such as upon re-examination are found exceptionable.

The traders frequently beat those negroes which are objected to by the captains, and use them with great severity. It matters not whether they are refused on account of age, illness, deformity, or for any other reason. At New Calabar, in particular, the traders have frequently been known to put them to death. Instances have happened at that place, that the traders, when any of their negroes have been objected to, have dropped their canoes under the stern of the vessel, and instantly beheaded them, in sight of the captain.

Upon the Windward Coast, another mode of procuring slaves is pursued; that is, by what they term *boating*; a mode that is very pernicious and destructive to the crews of the ships. The sailors, who are employed upon this trade, go in boats up the rivers, seeking for negroes, among the villages situated on the banks of them. But this method is very slow, and not always effectual. For, after being absent from the ship during a fortnight or three weeks, they sometimes return with only from eight to twelve negroes. Numbers of these are procured in consequence of alleged crimes, which, as before observed, whenever any ships are upon the coast, are more productive than at any other period. Kidnapping, however, prevails here.

I have good reason to believe, that of one hundred and twenty negroes, which were purchased for the ship to which I then belonged, then lying at the river Ambris, by far the greater part, if not the whole, were kidnapped. This, with various other instances, confirms me in the belief that kidnapping is the fund which supplies the thousands of negroes annually sold off these extensive Windward, and other Coasts, where boating prevails.

The Treatment of the Slaves

As soon as the wretched Africans, purchased at the fairs, fall into the hands of the black traders, they experience an earnest of those dreadful sufferings which they are doomed in future to undergo. And there is not the least room to doubt, but that even before they can reach the fairs, great numbers perish from cruel usage, want of food, travelling through inhospitable deserts, etc. They are brought from the places where they are purchased to Bonny, etc., in canoes; at the bottom of which they lie, having their hands tied with a kind of willow twigs, and a strict watch is kept over them. Their usage in other respects, during the time of the passage, which generally lasts several days, is equally cruel. Their allowance of food is so scanty, that it is barely sufficient to support nature. They are, besides, much exposed to the violent rains which frequently fall here, being covered only with mats that afford but a slight defence; and as there is usually water at the bottom of the canoes, from their leaking, they are scarcely ever dry.

Nor do these unhappy beings, after they become the property of the Europeans (from whom, as a more civilized people, more humanity might naturally be expected) find their situation in the least amended. Their treatment is no less rigorous. The men negroes, on being brought aboard the ship, are immediately fastened together, two and two, by hand-cuffs on their wrists, and by irons rivetted on their legs. They are then sent down between the decks, and placed in an apartment partitioned off for that purpose. The women likewise are placed in a separate apartment between decks, but without being ironed. And an adjoining room, on the same deck, is besides appointed for the boys. Thus are they all placed in different apartments.

But at the same time, they are frequently stowed so close, as to admit of no other posture than lying on their sides. Neither will the height between decks, unless directly under the grating, permit them the indulgence of an erect posture; especially where there are platforms, which is generally the case. These platforms are a kind of shelf, about eight or nine feet in breadth, extending from the side of the ship towards the centre. They are placed nearly midway between the decks, at the distance of two or three feet from each deck. Under these the negroes are stowed in the same manner as they are on the deck underneath.

In each of the apartments are placed three or four large buckets, of a conical form, being near two feet in diameter at the bottom, and only one foot at the top, and in depth about twenty-eight inches; to which, when necessary, the negroes have recourse. It often happens, that those who are placed at a distance from the buckets, in endeavouring to get to them, tumble over their companions, in consequence of their being shackled. These accidents, although unavoidable, are productive of continual quarrels, in which some of them are always bruised. In this distressed situation, unable to proceed, and prevented from getting to the tubs, they desist from the attempt; and, as the necessities of nature are not to be repelled, ease themselves as they lie. This becomes a fresh source of broils and disturbances, and tends to render the conditions of the poor captive wretches still more uncomfortable. The nuisance arising from these circumstances, is not infrequently increased by the tubs being much too small for the purpose intended, and their being usually emptied but once every day. The rule for doing this, however, varies in different ships, according to the attention paid to the health and convenience of the slaves by the captain.

About eight o'clock in the morning the negroes are generally brought upon deck. Their irons being examined, a long chain, which is locked to a ring-bolt, fixed in the deck, is run through the rings of the shackles of the men, and then locked to another ring-bolt, fixed also in the deck. By this means fifty or sixty, or sometimes more, are fastened to one chain, in order to prevent them from rising, or endeavouring to escape. If the weather proves favourable, they are permitted to remain in that situation till four or five in the afternoon, when they are disengaged from the chain, and sent down.

The diet of the negroes, while on board, consists chiefly of horse-beans, boiled to the consistence of a pulp; of boiled yams and rice, and sometimes of a small quantity of beef or pork. The latter are frequently taken from the provisions laid in for the sailors, They sometimes make use of a sauce, composed of palm-oil, mixed with flour, water, and pepper, which the sailors call *slabber-sauce*. Yams are the favourite food of the Eboe, or Bight negroes, and rice or corn, of those from the Gold and Windward Coasts; each preferring the produce of their native soil.

In their own country, the negroes in general live on animal life and fish, with roots, yams, and Indian corn. The horse-beans and rice, with which they are fed aboard ship, are chiefly taken from Europe, The latter, indeed, is sometimes purchased on the coast, being far superior to any other.

The Gold Coast negroes scarcely ever refuse any food that is offered them, and they generally eat larger quantities of whatever is placed before them, than any other species of negroes, whom they likewise excel in strength of body and mind. Most of the slaves have such an aversion to the horse-beans, that unless they are narrowly watched, when fed upon deck, they will throw them overboard, or in each other's faces when they quarrel.

They are commonly fed twice a day, about eight o'clock in the morning and four in the afternoon. In most ships they are only fed with their *own food* once a day. Their food is served up to them in tubs, about the size of a small water bucket. They are placed around these tubs in companies of ten to each tub, out of which they feed themselves with wooden spoons. These they soon lose, and when they are not allowed others, they feed themselves with their hands. In favourable weather they are fed upon the deck, but in bad weather their food is given them below. Numberless quarrels take place among them during their meals; more especially when they are put upon short allowance, which frequently happens, if the passage from the coast of Guinea to the West-India islands proves of unusual length. In that case, the weak are obliged to be content with a very scanty portion. Their allowance of water is about half a pint at every meal. It is handed round in a bucket, and given to each negroe in a pannekin; a small utensil with a strait handle, somewhat similar to a sauce-boat. However, when the ships approach the islands with a favourable breeze, they are no longer restricted.

Upon the negroes refusing to take sustenance, I have seen coals of fire, glowing hot, put on a shovel, and placed so near their lips, as to scorch and burn them. And this has been accompanied with threats, of forcing them to swallow the coals, if they any longer persisted in refusing to eat. These means have generally had the desired effect. I have also been credibly informed, that a certain captain in the slave trade, poured melted lead on such of the negroes as obstinately refused their food.

Exercise being deemed necessary for the preservation of their health, they are sometimes obliged to dance, when the weather will permit their coming on deck. If they go about it reluctantly, or do not move with agility, they are flogged; a person standing by them all the time with a cat-o'-nine-tails in his hand for that purpose. Their musick, which upon these occasions, consists of a drum, sometimes with only one head; and when that is worn out, they do not scruple to make use of the bottom of one of the tubs before described. The poor wretches are frequently compelled to sing also; but when they do, their songs are generally melancholy lamentations of their exile from their native country.

The women are furnished with beads for the purpose of affording them some diversion. But this end is generally defeated by the squabbles which are occasioned, in consequence of their stealing them from each other.

On board some ships, the common sailors are allowed to have intercourse with such of the black women whose consent they can procure. And some of them have been known to take the inconstancy of their paramours so much to heart, as to leap overboard and drown themselves. The officers are permitted to indulge their passions among them at pleasure, and sometimes are guilty of such brutal excesses, as disgrace human nature.

The hardships and inconveniences suffered by the negroes during the passage, are scarcely to be enumerated or conceived. They are far more violently affected by the sea-sickness, than the Europeans. It frequently terminates in death, especially among the women. But the exclusion of the fresh air is among the most intolerable. For the purpose of admitting this needful refreshment, most of the ships in the slave-trade are provided, between the decks, with five or six air-ports on each side of the ship, of about five inches in length, and four in breadth; in addition to which, some few ships, but not one in twenty, have what they denominate windsails. But whenever the sea is rough, and the rain heavy, it becomes necessary to shut these, and every conveyance by which the air is admitted. The fresh air being thus excluded, the negroes rooms very soon grow intolerably hot. The confined air, rendered noxious by the effluvia exhaled from their bodies, and by being repeatedly breathed, soon produces fevers and fluxes, which generally carries off great numbers of them.

During the voyages I made, I was frequently witness to the fatal effects of this exclusion of the fresh air. I will give one instance, as it serves to convey some idea, though a very faint one, of the sufferings of those unhappy beings whom we wantonly drag from their native country, and doom to perpetual labour and captivity. Some wet and blowing weather having occasioned some port-holes to be shut, and the grating to be covered, fluxes and fevers among the negroes ensued. While they were in this situation, my profession requiring it, I frequently went down among them, till at length their apartments became so extremely hot, as to be only sufferable for a very short time. But the excessive heat was not the only thing that rendered their situation intolerable. The deck, that is, the floor of their rooms, was so covered with the blood and mucus which had proceeded from them in consequence of the flux, that it resembled a slaughter-house. It is not in the power of the human imagination to picture to itself a situation more dreadful or disgusting. Numbers of the slaves having fainted, they were carried upon deck, where several of them died, and the rest were, with great difficulty, restored. It had nearly proved fatal to me also. The climate was too warm to admit the wearing of any clothing but a shirt, and that I had pulled off before I went down; notwithstanding which, by only continuing among them for about a quarter of an hour, I was so overcome with the heat, stench and foul air, that I had nearly fainted; and it was not without assistance, that I could get upon deck. The consequence was, that I soon fell sick of the same disorder, from which I did not recover for several months.

A circumstance of this kind, sometimes repeatedly happens in the course of a voyage; and often to a greater degree than what has just been described; particularly when the slaves are much crowded, which was not the case at that time, the ship having more than a hundred short of the number she was to have taken in.

This devastation, great as it was, some few years ago was greatly exceeded on board a Liverpool ship. I shall particularize the circumstances of it, as a more glaring instance of an insatiable thirst for gain, or of less attention to the lives and happiness of even of that despised and oppressed race of mortals, the sable inhabitants of Africa, perhaps was never exceeded; though indeed several similar instances have been known.

This ship, though a much smaller ship than that in which the event I have just mentioned happened, took on board at Bonny, at least six hundred negroes; but according to the information of the black traders, from whom I received the intelligence immediately after the ship sailed, they amounted to near *seven hundred*. By purchasing so great a number, the slaves were so crowded, that they were even obliged to lie one upon another. This occasioned such a mortality among them, that, without meeting with unusual bad weather, or having a longer voyage than common, nearly one half of them died before the ship arrived in the West-Indies.

That the publick may be able to form some idea of the almost incredible small space into which so large a number of negroes were crammed, the following particulars of this ship are given. According to Liverpool custom she measured 235 tons. Her width across the beam, 25 feet. Length between the decks, 92 feet, which was divided into four rooms, thus:

Store room, in which there were not any negroes placed		15 feet
Negroes rooms	mens room	about 45 feet
	womens ditto	about 10 feet
	boys ditto	about 22 feet
	Total room for negroes	77 feet

Exclusive of the platform before described, from 8 to 9 feet in breadth, and equal in length to that of the room.

It may be worthy of remark, that the ships in this trade, are usually fitted out to receive only one third women negroes, or perhaps a smaller number, which the dimensions of the room allotted for them, above given, plainly shew, but in a greater disproportion.

One would naturally suppose, that an attention to their own interest, would prompt the owners of the Guinea ships not to suffer the captains to take on board a greater number of negroes than the ship would allow room sufficient for them to lie with ease to themselves, or, at least, without rubbing against each other. However that may be, a more striking instance than the above, of avarice, completely and deservedly disappointed, was surely never displayed;

for there is little room to doubt, but that in consequence of the expected premium usually allowed to the captains, of 6 per cent sterling on the produce of the negroes, this vessel was so thronged as to occasion such a heavy loss.

The place allotted for the sick negroes is under the half deck, where they lie on the bare planks. By this means, those who are emaciated, frequently have their skin, and even their flesh, entirely rubbed off, by the motion of the ship, from the prominent parts of the shoulders, elbows, and hips, so as to render the bones in those parts quite bare. And some of them, by constantly lying in the blood and mucus, that had flowed from those afflicted with the flux, and which, as before observed, is generally so violent as to prevent their being kept clean, have their flesh much sooner rubbed off, than those who have only to contend with the mere friction of the ship. The excruciating pain which the poor sufferers feel from being obliged to continue in such a dreadful situation, frequently for several weeks, in case they happen to live so long, is not to be conceived or described. Few, indeed, are ever able to withstand the fatal effects of it. The utmost skill of the surgeon is here ineffectual. If plaisters be applied, they are very soon displaced by the friction of the ship; and when bandages are used, the negroes very soon take them off, and appropriate them to other purposes.

The surgeon, upon going between decks, in the morning, to examine the situation of the slaves, frequently finds several dead; and among the men, sometimes a dead and living negroe fastened by their irons together. When this is the case, they are brought upon the deck, and being laid on the grating, the living negroe is disengaged, and the dead one thrown overboard.

It may not be improper here to remark, that the surgeons employed in the Guinea trade, are generally driven to engage in so disagreeable an employ by the confined state of their finances. An exertion of the greatest skill and attention could afford the diseased negroes little relief, so long as the causes of their diseases, namely the breathing of a putrid atmosphere, and wallowing in their own excrements, remain. When once the fever and dysentery get to any height at sea, a cure is scarcely ever effected.

Almost the only means by which the surgeon can render himself useful to the slaves, is, by seeing that their food is properly cooked, and distributed among them. It is true, when they arrive near the markets for which they are destined, care is taken to polish them for sale, by an application of the lunar caustic to such as are afflicted with the yaws. This, however, affords but a temporary relief, as the disease most assuredly breaks out, whenever the patient is put upon a vegetable diet.

It has been asserted, in favour of the captains in this trade, that the sick slaves are usually fed from their tables. The great number generally ill at a time, proves the falsity of such an assertion. Were even a captain *disposed* to do this, how could he feed half the slaves in the ship from his own table? for it is well known, *that more than half* are often sick at a time. Two or three perhaps may be fed.

The loss of slaves, through mortality, arising from the causes just mentioned, are frequently very considerable. In the voyage lately referred to (not the Liverpool ship beforementioned) one hundred and five, out of three hundred and eighty, died in the passage. A proportion seemingly very great, but by no means uncommon. One half, sometimes two thirds, and even beyond that, have been known to perish. Before we left Bonny River, no less than fifteen died of fevers and dysenteries, occasioned by their confinement. On the Windward

Coast, where slaves are procured more slowly, very few die, in proportion to the numbers which die at Bonny, and at Old and New Calabar, where they are obtained much faster; the latter being of a more delicate make and habit.

The havock made among the seamen engaged in this destructive commerce, will be noticed in another part; and will be found to make no inconsiderable addition to the unnecessary waste of life just represented.

As very few of the negroes can so far brook the loss of their liberty, and the hardships they endure, so as to bear them with any degree of patience, they are ever upon the watch to take advantage of the least negligence in their oppressors. Insurrections are frequently the consequence; which are seldom suppressed without much bloodshed. Sometimes these are successful, and the whole ship's company is cut off. They are likewise always ready to seize every opportunity for committing some act of desperation to free themselves from their miserable state; and notwithstanding the restraints under which they are laid, they often succeed.

While a ship, to which I belonged, lay in Bonny River, one evening, a short time before our departure, a lot of negroes, consisting of about ten, was brought on board; when one of them, in a favourable moment, forced his way through the net-work on the larboard side of the vessel, jumped overboard, and was supposed to have been devoured by the sharks.

During the time we were there, fifteen negroes belonging to the vessel from Liverpool, found means to throw themselves into the river; very few were saved; and the residue fell a sacrifice to the sharks. A similar instance took place in a French ship while we lay there.

Circumstances of this kind are very frequent. On the coast of Angola, at the River Ambris, the following incident happened. During the time of our residing on shore, we erected a tent to shelter ourselves from the weather. After having been there several weeks, and being unable to purchase the number of slaves we wanted, through the opposition of another English slave vessel, we determined to leave the place. The night before our departure, the tent was struck; which was no sooner perceived by some of the negroe women on board, than it was considered a prelude to our sailing; and about eighteen of them, when they were sent between decks, threw themselves into the sea through one of the gun ports; the ship carrying guns between decks. They were all of them, however, excepting one, soon picked up; and that which was missing, was, not long after, taken about a mile from the shore.

I once knew a negroe woman, too sensible of her woes, who pined for a considerable time, and was taken ill of a fever and dysentery; when declaring it to be her determination to die, she refused all food and medical aid, and, in about a fortnight after, expired. On being thrown overboard, her body was instantly torn to pieces by the sharks.

The following circumstance also came within my knowledge. A young female negroe, falling into a desponding way, it was judged necessary, in order to attempt her recovery, to send her on shore, to the hut of one of the black traders. Elevated with the prospect of regaining her liberty by this unexpected step, she soon recovered her usual cheerfulness; but hearing, by accident, that it was intended to take her on the ship again, the poor young creature hung herself.

It frequently happens that the negroes, on being purchased by the Europeans, become raving mad; and many of them die in that state; particularly the women. While I was one day ashore at Bonny, I saw a middle aged stout woman, who had been brought down from a fair the preceding day, chained to the post of a black trader's door, in a sate of furious insanity. On board a ship in Bonny River, I saw a young negroe woman chained to the deck, who had lost her senses, soon after she was purchased and taken on board. In a former voyage, on board a ship to which I belonged, we were obliged to confine a female negroe, of about twenty-three years of age, on her becoming a lunatic. She was afterwards sold during one of her lucid intervals.

One morning, upon examining the place allotted for the sick negroes, I perceived that one of them, who was so emaciated as scarcely to be able to walk, was missing, and was convinced that he must have gone overboard in the night, probably to put a more expeditious period to his sufferings. And, to conclude on this subject, I could not help being sensibly affected, on a former voyage, at observing with what apparent eagerness a black woman seized some dirt from off an African yam, and put it into her mouth; seeming to rejoice at the opportunity of possessing some of her native earth.

From these instances I think it may be clearly deduced, that the unhappy Africans are not bereft of finer feelings, but have a strong attachment to their native country, together with a just sense of the value of liberty. And the situation of the miserable beings above described, more forcibly urge the necessity of abolishing a trade which is the source of such evils, than the most eloquent harangue, or persuasive arguments could do.

Sale of the slaves

When the ships arrive in the West-Indies, (the chief mart for this inhuman merchandize), the slaves are disposed of, as I have before observed, by different methods. Sometimes the mode of disposal, is that of selling them by what is termed a *scramble;* and a day is soon fixed for that purpose. But previous thereto, the sick, or refuse slaves, of which there are frequently many, are usually conveyed on shore, and sold at a tavern by vendue, or public auction. These, in general, are purchased by the Jews and surgeons, but chiefly the former, upon speculation, at so low a price as five or six dollars a head. I was informed by a mulatto woman, that she purchased a sick slave at Grenada, upon speculation, for the small sum of one dollar, as the poor wretch was apparently dying of the flux. It seldom happens that any, who are carried ashore in the emaciated state to which they are generally reduced by that disorder, long survive their landing. I once saw fifteen conveyed on shore, and sold in the foregoing manner, the whole of them died before I left the island, which was within a short time after. Sometimes the captains march their slaves through the town at which they intend to dispose of them; and then place them in rows where they are examined and purchased.

The mode of selling them by scramble having fallen under my observation the oftenest, I shall be more particular in describing it. Being some years ago, at one of the islands in the West-Indies, I was witness to a sale by scramble, where about 250 negroes were sold. Upon this occasion all the negroes scrambled for bear an equal price; which is agreed upon between the captains and the purchasers before the sale begins.

On a day appointed, the negroes were landed, and placed together in a large yard, belonging to the merchants to whom the ship was consigned. As soon as the hour agreed on arrived, the doors of the yard were suddenly thrown open, and in rushed a considerable number of purchasers, with all the ferocity of brutes. Some instantly seized such of the negroes as they could conveniently lay hold of with their hands. Others, being prepared with several handkerchiefs tied together, encircled with these as many as they were able. While others, by means of a rope, effected the same purpose. It is scarcely possible to describe the confusion of which this mode of selling is productive. It likewise causes much animosity among the purchasers, who, not infrequently upon these occasions, fall out and quarrel with each other. The poor astonished negroes were so much terrified by these proceedings, that several of them, through fear, climbed over the walls of the court yard, and ran wild about the town; but were soon hunted down and retaken.

While on a former voyage from Africa to Kingston in Jamaica, I saw a sale there by scramble, on board a snow [a type of sailing vessel]. The negroes were collected together upon the main and quarter decks, and the ship was darkened by sails suspended over them, in order to prevent the purchasers from being able to see, so as to pick or chuse. The signal being given, the buyers rushed in, as usual, to seize their prey; when the negroes appeared to be extremely terrified, and near thirty of them jumped into the sea. But they were all soon retaken, chiefly by boats from other ships.

On board a ship, lying at Port Maria, in Jamaica, I saw another scramble; in which, as usual, the poor negroes were greatly terrified. The women, in particular, cling to each other in agonies scarcely to be conceived, shrieking through excess of terror, at the savage manner in which their brutal purchasers rushed upon them, and seized them. Though humanity, one would imagine, would dictate the captains to apprize the poor negroes of that mode by which they were to be sold, and by that means to guard them, in some degree, against the surprize and terror which must attend it, I never knew that any notice of the scramble was given to them. Nor have I any reason to think that it is done; or that this mode of sale is less frequent at this time, than formerly.

Various are the deceptions made use of in the disposal of the sick slaves; and many of these, such as must excite in every humane mind, the liveliest sensations of horror. I have been well informed, that a Liverpool captain boasted of his having cheated some Jews by the following stratagem. A lot of slaves, afflicted with the flux, being about to be landed for sale, he directed the surgeon to stop the anus of each of them with oakum. Thus prepared, they were landed, and taken to the accustomed place of sale; where, being unable to stand but for a very short time, they are usually permitted to sit. The Jews, when they examine them, oblige them to stand up, in order to see if there be any discharge, and when they do not perceive this appearance, they consider it as a symptom of recovery. In the present instance, such an appearance being prevented, the bargain was struck, and they were accordingly sold. But it was not long before a discovery ensued. The excruciating pain which the prevention of a discharge of such an acrimonious nature occasioned, not being able to be borne by the poor wretches, the temporary obstruction was removed, and the deluded purchasers were speedily convinced of the imposition.

So grievously are the negroes sometimes afflicted with this troublesome and painful disorder, that I have seen large numbers of them, after being landed, obliged by the virulence of the complaint, to stop almost every minute, as they passed on.

21 • The plan of the slave ship *Brookes* (1788)

The Brookes *was one of eighteen Liverpool slave ships officially examined and measured in 1788 during parliamentary discussions about the possible regulation of slave vessels. Using these mea-*

surements, Thomas Clarkson, a prominent proponent of the abolition of the slave trade, had a sketch of the Brookes *drawn to show what the ship would look like when fully loaded with slaves. The sketch, though slightly incorrect in failing to show the spaces by which slaves could be fed and dead bodies removed, proved a highly effective piece of political propaganda. When Clarkson visited France in 1789 to gain support for the abolitionist cause, Louis XVI's chief minister refused to show the sketch to the king on the grounds that it would distress him too much, while future revolutionaries such as Condorcet, Mirabeau, and Lafayette were all much affected. Mirabeau had a model of the* Brookes *made in wood, the better to depict the barbarity of the slaves' conditions, and Lafayette became a supporter of the antislavery cause. Nearly four thousand copies of the diagram were distributed in Philadelphia. Captain Perry, the official who had measured the eighteen Liverpool slave ships in 1788, described the dimensions of the* Brookes *as follows.*[5]

Length of the lower deck, gratings and bulkheads included, at A A, 100 feet, breadth of beam on lower deck inside, B B, 25 feet 4 inches, depth of Hold, O O O, from ceiling to ceiling, 10 feet, height between decks, from deck to deck, 5 feet 8 inches, length of the men's room, C C, on the lower deck, 46 feet, breadth of the men's room, C C, on the lower deck, 25 feet 4 inches, length of the platforms, D D, in the men's room, 46 feet, breadth of the platforms in the men's room on each side, 6 feet, length of the boy's room, E E, 13 feet 9 inches, breadth of the boy's room, 25 feet, breadth of platforms, F F, in boy's room, 6 feet, length of women's room, G G, 28 feet 6 inches, breadth of women's room, 23 feet 6 inches, length of platforms, H H, in women's room, 28 feet 6 inches, breadth of platforms in women's room, 6 feet, length of gun-room, I I, on the lower deck, 10 feet 6 inches, breadth of the gun-room on the lower deck, 12 feet, length of the quarter-deck, K K, 33 feet 6 inches, breadth of the quarter-deck, 19 feet, 6 inches, length of the cabin, L L, 14 feet, height of the cabin, 6 feet 2 inches, length of the half-deck, M M, 16 feet 6 inches, height of the half-deck, 6 feet 2 inches, length of the platforms, N N, on the half-deck, 16 feet 6 inches, breadth of the platforms on the half-deck, 6 feet, upper deck, P P . . .

Let it now be supposed that the above are the real dimensions of the ship *Brookes,* and further, that every man slave is to be allowed six feet by one foot four inches for room, every woman five feet ten by one foot four, it will follow that the annexed plan of a slave vessel will be precisely the representation of the ship *Brookes,* and of the exact number of persons neither more nor less, that could be stowed in the different rooms of it upon these data. These, if counted [deducting the women stowed at Z in subfigures VI and VII in Figure 5 since by an act of Parliament that space was reallocated to seamen] will be found to amount to *four hundred and fifty-one.* Now, if it be considered that the ship *Brookes* is of three hundred and twenty tons, and that she is allowed to carry by act of Parliament *four hundred and fifty-four persons,* it is evident that if three more could be wedged among the number represented in the plan, this plan would contain precisely the number which the act directs.

5. Elizabeth Donnan, ed., *Documents Illustrative of the History of the Slave Trade to America* (Washington, D.C.: Carnegie Institute, 1930), vol. 2, 592 and facing 592.

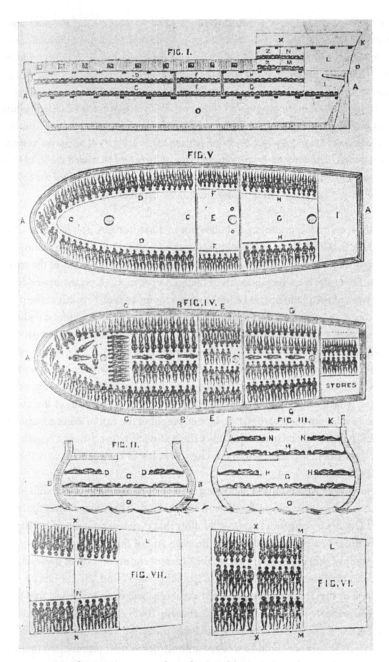

FIGURE 5 The *Brookes* was a slave ship used by British traders to transport African slaves to the Caribbean and North America. According to measurements made in 1788, the total amount of space allotted to each African during the transatlantic passage was 6 feet by 18 inches for a man, 5 feet 10 inches by 12 inches for a woman, 5 feet by 14 inches for a boy, and 4 feet 6 inches by 12 inches for a girl. Four hundred fifty-one individuals were crammed into the *Brookes*. Library of Congress.

22 ◆ In support of the continued importation
of slaves into South Africa (1797)

Despite the growing calls for abolition in the late eighteenth century, proslavers continued for the moment to speak with a dominant voice, especially by pointing out the economic basis of slavery. After the British, concerned in 1795 that the French might gain control of the sea route to India, conquered the Dutch East Indies Company's settlement at the Cape of Good Hope, they instructed the first governor, Lord Macartney, to examine the feasibility of ending the importation of slaves. For advice on this question, Macartney turned to W. S. van Ryneveld, who, despite being a member of the company's governing body at the time of the conquest, was considered an expert on matters of local administration. In responding to Macartney's questionnaire, van Ryneveld argued that putting an end to the importation of slaves would result in the economic collapse of the cape. The British took van Ryneveld's advice. Between 1797 and 1808, they imported another 3,500 slaves into South Africa and, even after the passage of legislation prohibiting the trade, brought another 2,100 "prize negroes" into the colony between 1808 and 1816. The latter were captives "released" from slaving vessels interdicted by British frigates and forced to enter fourteen-year "apprenticeships" with European employers at the cape. Macartney's questions and van Ryneveld's answers follow.[6]

Question: What material injury or inconvenience would result to the Colony, if the importation of slaves were to be prohibited?

Answer: An immediate interdiction to the importation of slaves, would, of course, effectuate that the culture, especially the two principal branches thereof . . . corn and wine, first would begin to languish, and afterwards entirely to decay.

We know very well, that here, both within and without the Colony, no sufficient number of white people can be obtained to perform in culture the labour of the slaves; and, on the other hand, experience shows us every day that the procreation of slaves, in proportion to number, is very trifling, and even not worth mentioning; and that, moreover, a very considerable number of slaves is lost by continual disorders, especially by bile and putrid fevers, to which they are very subject.

The political state of this Colony, I think, is actually of that nature that, however injurious slavery of itself may be to the morals and industry of the inhabitants, still the keeping of slaves has now become, as it is styled, a necessary evil; and, at least, a sudden interdiction to the importation of slaves would occasion a general injury, as long as such a number of hands as is requisite for the culture cannot be obtained from another part, at a rate that may be thought proportionate to the produce arising from the lands . . . It is very true that at present there may be found some white or free persons apt for that purpose; yet apart from the number of these persons not being sufficient in any degree to supply the number of slaves wanted, the high hire and expensive maintenance of such free labourers would still render the employing of them impracticable . . .

6. Replies of W. S. Ryneveld to Governor Macartney's questionnaire, Nov. 29, 1797, reprinted in André du Toit and Hermann Giliomee, eds., *Afrikaner Political Thought* (Berkeley: University of California Press, 1983), vol. 1, 46–49.

Question: If there were no slaves at the Cape, would not the white peasants become more industrious and useful to the State? Does not the facility of procuring slaves, and the general custom of making use of them, render the white inhabitants more haughty, more lazy and more brutal? . . .

Answer: There are (to return properly to my subject) two principle causes that prevent the white people here from doing rural labour, viz.:

1st. The great extent of the country, without sufficient population, so that the country is really in want of hands for carrying on the tillage;

2nd. The introduction of slavery.

I perfectly acknowledge . . . that if there were no slaves at the Cape the peasants would then be more industrious and useful to the State, and that the facility of procuring slaves renders the inhabitants of this country lazy, haughty and brutal.

Every kind of vice and a perfect corruption of morals is owing to that. But how to help it? If slavery had been interdicted at the first settling of this Colony, then the inhabitants would doubtless have become more industrious and useful to each other; they would be obliged to associate in a narrower compass of land, and the Colony would never have so exceedingly extended beyond its ability and beyond the exigence of its population.

Yet, the business is done. Slavery exists and is now even indispensable. It is absolutely necessary because there are no other hands to till this extensive country, and therefore it will be the work, not of years, but as it were of centuries to remove by attentive and proper regulation this evil established with the first settling of the Colony.

Should the slaves be now declared free, that would immediately render both the country and these poor creatures themselves miserable; not only all tillage would then be at an end, but also the number of freemen, instead of their being (as now) useful members of, would then really become a charge to, society. And should the importation of slaves be interdicted, on a sudden, without any means being provided towards supplying other hands for the tillage, then the Colony would thereby be caused to languish (the procreation of slaves being so inconsiderable in comparison with their mortality) and especially the culture of grain would thereby be reduced to decay.

In order to improve gradually the industry of this Colony, it will be absolutely necessary, on the one hand, to obviate the further enlarging of this settlement. As long as one may infringe upon the countries of the Kaffirs, Bushmen, etc., to take their lands and to live upon the breeding of cattle, then so long no person will be anxious about the state of his children, so long no sufficient number of hands will be to be obtained in the country itself to carry on the tillage, so long the inhabitants will never enter into the service of each other, and, finally, so long the importation of slaves also will be necessary for the sake of the culture of grain. While on the other hand a person will never scruple to settle himself throughout the whole country of Africa among all the nations, and, by so doing, at length to become like those wild nations.

The Government, intending to frame from this Colony a regular Society, where diligence and industry are to compose the foundation of the prosperity of the people, ought therefore, and in the first place, to take care that no person do in future settle beyond the boundaries of this Colony, and that by that regulation the young people be, of course, obliged to endeavour to earn their subsistence in the bosom of the Colony itself; from doing which, sufficient motives will then always and in proportion to the increase of population arise, to be industrious and so to promote both their own welfare and the prosperity of the community in general . . .

23 • Mungo Park describes taking slaves from the interior of Africa to the coast (1796–97)

Like his South African contemporary van Ryneveld, Mungo Park (1771–1806), the first European to explore the hinterland of the Gambia River, considered slavery a necessary evil. Park, who had trained as a surgeon at Edinburgh University and was a protégé of Sir Joseph Banks (famed naturalist and president of the Royal Society), embarked on his travels at the direction of the African Association, an organization founded in 1788 by, as Park put it, "noblemen and gentlemen, associated for the purpose of prosecuting discoveries in the interior of Africa." One of their main aims was to gain information about the legendary trading cities of the interior, especially Timbuktu, still renowned as it had been three hundred years earlier in the publications of Ibn Battuta and Leo Africanus as the chief entrepôt for the transfer of African gold across the Sahara. Park began his expedition into the interior with "a passionate desire to examine into the productions of a country so little known, and [aiming] to become experimentally acquainted with the modes of life and character of the natives." Though exhaustion and illness prevented him from reaching Timbuktu on his first trip, he explored more of the interior of West Africa than any other European up to that point. He returned in 1806 but was killed when, firing on Africans that he believed to be unfriendly, he and a companion were attacked in turn. In his published journal Park provides an eyewitness description of the collection of slaves in the interior, their transfer to the coast, and the Atlantic crossing. Park arrived at Kamalia, northeast of the headwaters of the Gambia River, on September 16, 1796.[7]

On my arrival at Kamalia, I was conducted to the house of a Bushreen [Muslim] named Karfa Taura . . . He was collecting a coffle [caravan] of slaves, with a view to sell them to the Europeans on the Gambia, as soon as the rains should be over. I found him sitting in his baloon [visitor's room], surrounded by several Slatees [African merchants], who proposed to join the coffle. He was reading to them from an Arabic book; and inquired, with a smile, if I understood it. Being answered in the negative, he desired one of the Slatees to fetch the curious little book, which had been brought from the west country. On opening this small volume, I was surprised and delighted, to find it our *Book of Common Prayer;* and Karfa expressed great joy to hear that I could read it: for some of the Slatees, who had seen the Europeans upon the coast, observing the colour of my skin (which was now become very yellow from sickness), my long beard, ragged clothes, and extreme poverty; were unwilling to admit that I was a white man, and told Karfa that they suggested I was some Arab in disguise . . . [I]n the beginning of December, a Sera-Woolli Slatee, with five slaves, arrived from Sego: this man too, spread a number of malicious reports concerning me; but Karfa paid no attention to them, and continued to show me the same kindness as formerly. As I was one day conversing, with

7. Mungo Park, *Travels in the Interior Districts of Africa, Performed under the Direction of the African Association, in the Years 1795, 1796, and 1797* (London: G. and W. Nicol, 1799), 253, 256–57, 287–90, 318–21, 323–25, 327–28, 330, 331–34, 338–40, 346–50, 353–54, 356–57, 360–62.

FIGURE 6 Mungo Park made three lengthy expeditions into the interior of West Africa in the late 1700s and early 1800s on behalf of British investors interested in finding out about the economic resources of the continent. He drowned on his third expedition up the Niger River. Mungo Park, *Travels in the Interior Districts of Africa,* 1816.

the slaves which this Slatee had brought, one of them begged me to give him some victuals. I told him I was a stranger, and had none to give. He replied, "I gave *you* victuals when you was hungry. Have you forgot the man who brought you milk at Karrankalla? But (added he with a sigh) *the irons were not then upon my legs!*" I immediately recollected him, and begged some ground nuts from Karfa to give him, as a return for his former kindness. He told me that he had been taken away by the Bambarrans the day after the battle of Joka, and sent to Sego, where he had been purchased by his present master, who was carrying him down to Kajaaga. Three more of these slaves were from Kaarta, and one from Wassela, all of them prisoners of war. They stopped four days at Kamalia, and were then taken to Bala, where they remained until the river Kokoro was fordable, and the grass burnt.

In the beginning of December, Karfa proposed to complete his purchase of slaves; and for this purpose collected all the debts which were owing to him in his own country, and on the 19th, being accompanied by three Slatees, he departed for Kancaba, a large town on the banks of the Niger; and a great slave market. Most of the slaves who are sold at Kancaba come from Bambarra; for Mansong, to avoid the expence and danger of keeping all his prisoners at Sego, commonly sends them in small parties, to be sold at the different trading towns; and as Kancaba is much resorted to by merchants, it is always supplied with slaves, which are sent thither up the Niger in canoes . . .

The slaves in Africa, I suppose, are nearly in the proportion of three to one to the freemen. They claim no reward for their services except food and clothing, and are treated with

kindness or severity, according to the good or bad disposition of their masters. Custom, however, has established certain rules with regard to the treatment of slaves, which it is thought
dishonourable to violate. Thus, the domestic slaves, or such as are born in a man's own house,
are treated with more lenity than those which are purchased with money. The authority of the
master over the domestic slave . . . extends only to reasonable correction; for the master cannot sell his domestic, without having first brought him to a public trial, before the chief men
of the place. But these restrictions on the power of the master extend not to the case of prisoners taken in war, nor to that of slaves purchased with money. All these unfortunate beings
are considered as strangers and foreigners, who have no right to the protection of the law, and
may be treated with severity, or sold to a stranger, according to the pleasure of their owners.
There are, indeed, regular markets, where slaves of this description are bought and sold, and
the value of a slave, in the eye of an African purchaser, increases in proportion to his distance
from his native kingdom: for when slaves are only a few days' journey from the place of their
nativity, they frequently effect their escape, but when one or more kingdoms intervene, escape being more difficult, they are more readily reconciled to their situation. On this account,
the unhappy slave is frequently transferred from one dealer to another, until he has lost all
hopes of returning to his native kingdom. The slaves which are purchased by the Europeans
on the Coast, are chiefly of this description; a few of them are collected in the petty wars,
hereafter to be described, which take place near the Coast; but by far the greater number are
brought down in large caravans from the inland countries, of which many are unknown, even
by name, to the Europeans. The slaves which are thus brought from the interior may be divided into two distinct classes; *first,* such as were slaves from their birth, having been born of
enslaved mothers; *secondly,* such as were born free, but who afterwards, by whatever means,
became slaves. Those of the first description are by far the most numerous; for prisoners taken
in war (at least such as are taken in open and declared war, when one kingdom avows hostilities against another), are generally of this description . . . it must be observed that men of free
condition have many advantages over the slaves, even in war time. They are in general better
armed, and well mounted, and can either fight or escape with some hope of success; but the
slaves who have only their spears and bows, and of whom great numbers are loaded with baggage, become an easy prey. Thus, when Mansong, King of Bambarra, made war upon Kaarta
. . . he took in one day nine hundred prisoners, of which number not more than seventy were
free men. This account I received from Daman Jumma, who had thirty slaves at Kemmoo, all
of whom were made slaves by Mansong. Again, when a free man is taken prisoner, his friends
will sometimes ransom him, by giving two slaves in exchange; but when a slave is taken, he
has no hopes of such redemption. To these disadvantages, it is to be added, that the Slatees,
who purchase slaves in the interior countries, and carry them down to the Coast for sale, constantly prefer such as have been in that condition of life from their infancy, well knowing that
these have been accustomed to hunger and fatigue, and are better able to sustain the hardships of a long and painful journey, than free men; and on their reaching the Coast, if no opportunity offers of selling them to advantage, they can easily be made to maintain themselves
by their labour; neither are they so apt to attempt making their escape, as those who have
once tasted the blessings of freedom.

Slaves of the second description [those born free], generally become such by one of
the following causes, 1. *Captivity.* 2. *Famine.* 3. *Insolvency.* 4. *Crimes.* A free man may, by the

established customs of Africa, become a slave by being taken in war. War is, of all others, the most productive source, and was probably the origin of slavery . . .

On the 24th of January [1797] Karfa returned to Kamalia with a number of people, and thirteen prime slaves which he had purchased . . .

The slaves which Karfa had brought with him were all of them prisoners of war; they had been taken by the Bambarran army in the kingdoms of Wassela and Kaarta, and carried to Sego, where some of them had remained three years in irons. From Sego they were sent, in company with a number of other captives, up the Niger, in two large canoes, and offered for sale at Yamina, Bammakoo, and Kancaba; at which places the greater number of the captives were bartered for gold dust, and the remainder sent forward to Kankaree.

Eleven of them confessed to me that they had been slaves from their infancy; but the other two refused to give any account of their former condition. They were all very inquisitive; but they viewed me at first with looks of horror, and repeatedly asked if my countrymen were cannibals. They were very desirous to know what became of the slaves after they had crossed the salt water. I told them, that they were employed in cultivating the land; but they would not believe me; and one of them putting his hand upon the ground, said with great simplicity, "have you really got such ground as this, to set your feet upon?" A deeply rooted idea, that the whites purchase Negroes for the purpose of devouring them, or of selling them to others that they may be devoured hereafter, naturally makes the slaves contemplate a journey towards the Coast with great terror; insomuch, that the Slatees are forced to keep them constantly in irons, and watch them very closely, to prevent their escape. They are commonly secured by putting the right leg of one, and the left of another, into the same pair of fetters. By supporting the fetters with a string, they can walk, though very slowly. Every four slaves are likewise fastened together by the necks, with a strong rope of twisted thongs; and in the night, an additional pair of fetters is put on their hands, and sometimes a light iron chain passed round their necks.

Such of them as evince marks of discontent, are secured in a different manner. A thick billet of wood is cut, about three feet long, and a smooth notch being made upon one side of it, the ankle of the slave is bolted to the smooth part by means of a strong iron staple, one prong of which passes on each side of the ankle. All these fetters and bolts are made from native iron; in the present case they were put on by the blacksmith, as soon as the slaves arrived from Kancaba, and were not taken off until the morning on which the coffle departed for Gambia.

In other respects, the treatment of the slaves during their stay at Kamalia, was far from being harsh or cruel. They were led out in their fetters, every morning, to the shade of the tamarind tree, where they were encouraged to play at games of hazard, and sing diverting songs, to keep up their spirits; for though some of them sustained the hardships of their situation with amazing fortitude, the greater part were very much dejected, and would sit all day in a sort of sullen melancholy, with their eyes fixed upon the ground. In the evening their irons were examined, and their hand fetters put on; after which they were conducted into two large huts, where they were guarded during the night by Karfa's domestic slaves. But notwithstanding all this, about a week after their arrival, one of the slaves had the address to procure a small knife, with which he opened the rings of his fetters, cut the rope, and made his escape; more of them would probably have got off had they assisted each other: but the slave no sooner found himself at liberty, than he refused to stop, and assist in breaking the chain which was fastened round the necks of his companions.

As all the Slatees and slaves belonging to the coffle were now assembled, either at Kamalia, or at some of the neighbouring villages, it might have been expected that we should have set out immediately for Gambia; but though the day of our departure was frequently fixed, it was always found expedient to change it. Some of the people had not prepared their dry provisions; others had gone to visit their relations, or collect some trifling debts, and last of all, it was necessary to consult whether the day would be a lucky one. On account of one of these, or other such causes, our departure was put off, day after day, until the month of February was far advanced, after which, all the Slatees agreed to remain in their present quarters, until the *fast moon was over* . . .

April 19th. The long wished-for day of our departure was at length arrived, and the Slatees having taken the irons from their slaves, assembled with them at the door of Karfa's house, where the bundles were all tied up, and every one had his load assigned him. The coffle, on its departure from Kamalia, consisted of twenty-seven slaves for sale, the property of Karfa and four other Slatees; but we were afterwards joined by five at Maraboo and three at Bala; making in all thirty-five slaves. The free men were fourteen in number, but most of them had one or two wives, and some domestic slaves, and the schoolmaster, who was now upon his return for Woradoo, the place of his nativity, took with him eight of his scholars; so that the number of free people and domestic slaves amounted to thirty-eight, and the whole amount of the coffle was seventy-three. Among the free men were six Jillakeas (singing men), whose musical talents were frequently exerted, either to divert our fatigue, or obtain us a welcome from strangers. When we departed from Kamalia, we were followed for about half a mile, by most of the inhabitants of the town, some of them crying, and others shaking hands with their relations, who were now about to leave them; and when we had gained a piece of rising ground from which we had a view of Kamalia, all the people belonging to the coffle were ordered to sit down in one place, with their faces towards the west, and the townspeople were desired to sit down in another place, with their faces towards Kamalia. In this situation, the schoolmaster with two of the principal Slatees, having taken their places between the two parties, pronounced a long and solemn prayer; after which they walked three times round the coffle, making an impression in the ground with the ends of their spears, and muttering something by way of charm. When this ceremony was ended, all the people belonging to the coffle sprang up, and without taking a formal farewell of their friends, set forwards. As many of the slaves had remained for years in irons, the sudden exertion of walking quick, with heavy loads upon their heads, occasioned spasmodic contractions of their legs; and we had not proceeded above a mile, before it was found necessary to take two of them from the rope, and allow them to walk more slowly until we reached Maraboo, a walled village where some people were waiting to join the coffle. Here we stopt about two hours, to allow the strangers time to pack up their provisions, and then continued our route . . .

As this was the first town [Kinytakooro] beyond the limits of Manding, greater etiquette than usual was observed. Every person was ordered to keep in his proper station, and we marched towards the town, in a sort of procession, nearly as follows. In front, five or six singing men, all of them belonging to the coffle; these were followed by the other free people; then came the slaves fastened in the usual way by a rope round their necks, four of them to a rope, and a man with a spear between each four; after them came the domestic slaves, and in the rear the women of free condition, wives of the Slatees, etc. In this manner we proceeded, until we came within a hundred yards of the gate; when the singing men began a loud song, well calculated to flatter the vanity of the inhabitants, by extolling their known hospitality to strangers, and their particular friendship for the Mandingoes. When we entered the town we proceeded to the Bentang, where the people gathered round us to hear our *dentegi* (history). This was related publicly by two of the singing men: they enumerated every little circumstance which had happened to the coffle, beginning with the events of the present day, and relating everything in a backward series, until they reached Kamalia. When this history was ended, the master of the town gave them a small present, and all the people of the coffle, both free and enslaved, were invited by some person or other, and accommodated with lodging and provisions for the night . . .

As soon as we had crossed the river [Wonda] Karfa gave orders, that all the people of the coffle should in future keep close together, and travel in their proper station; the guides and young men were accordingly placed in the van, the women and slaves in the centre, and the free men in the rear. In this order we travelled with uncommon expedition . . .

April 24th. Before daybreak the Bushreens said their morning prayers, and most of the free people drank a little *moening* (a sort of gruel), part of which was likewise given to such of the slaves as appeared least able to sustain the fatigues of the day. One of Karfa's female slaves was very sulky, and when some gruel was offered to her, she refused to drink it. As soon as day dawned we set out, and travelled the whole morning over a wild and rocky country, by which my feet were much bruised; and I was sadly apprehensive that I should not be able to keep up with the coffle during the day; but I was, in a great measure, relieved from this anxiety, when I observed that others were more exhausted than myself. In particular, the woman slave, who had refused victuals in the morning, began now to lag behind, and complain dreadfully of pains in her legs. Her load was taken from her, and given to another slave, and she was ordered to keep in the front of the coffle. About eleven o'clock, as we were resting by a small rivulet, some of the people discovered a hive of bees in a hollow tree, and they were proceeding to obtain the honey, when the largest swarm I ever beheld, flew out, and attacking the people of the coffle, made us fly in all directions. I took the alarm first, and I believe was the only person who escaped with impunity. When our enemies thought fit to desist from pursuing us, and every person was employed in picking out the stings he had received, it was discovered that the poor woman abovementioned, whose name was Nealee, was not come up; and as many of the slaves in their retreat had left their bundles behind them, it became necessary for some persons to return, and bring them. In order to do this with safety, fire was set to the grass, a considerable way to the eastward of the hive, and the wind driving the fire furiously along, the party pushed through the smoke, and recovered the bundles. They likewise brought with them poor Nealee, whom they found lying by the rivulet. She was very much exhausted, and had crept to the stream, in hopes to defend herself from the bees by throwing water over her body; but this proved ineffectual; for she was stung in the most dreadful manner.

When the Slatees had picked out the stings as far as they could, she was washed with water, and then rubbed with bruised leaves; but the wretched woman obstinately refused to proceed any farther; declaring, that she would rather die than walk another step. As entreaties and threats were used in vain, the whip was at length applied; and after bearing patiently a few strokes, she started up, and walked with tolerable expedition for four or five hours longer, when she made an attempt to run away from the coffle, but was so very weak, that she fell down in the grass. Though she was unable to rise, the whip was a second time applied, but without effect; upon which Karfa desired two of the Slatees to place her upon the ass which carried our dry provisions; but she could not sit erect; and the ass being very refractory, it was found impossible to carry her forward in that manner. The Slatees however were unwilling to abandon her, the day's journey being nearly ended: they therefore made a sort of litter of bamboo canes, upon which she was placed, and tied on it with slips of bark: this litter was carried upon the heads of two slaves, one walking before the other, and they were followed by two others, who relieved them occasionally. In this manner the woman was carried forward until it was dark, when we reached a stream of water, at the foot of a high hill called Gankaran-Kooro; and here we stopt for the night, and set about preparing our supper. As we had only eat one handful of meal since the preceding night, and travelled all day in a hot sun, many of the slaves, who had loads upon their heads, were very much fatigued; and some of them *snapt their fingers,* which among the Negroes is a sure sign of desperation. The Slatees immediately put them all in irons; and such of them as had evinced signs of great despondency, were kept apart from the rest, and had their hands tied. In the morning they were found greatly recovered.

April 25th. At daybreak poor Nealee was awakened; but her limbs were now become so stiff and painful, that she could neither walk nor stand; she was therefore lifted, like a corpse, upon the back of the ass; and the Slatees endeavoured to secure her in that situation, by fastening her hands together under the ass's neck, and her feet under the belly, with long slips of bark; but the ass was so very unruly, that no sort of treatment could induce him to proceed with his load; and as Nealee made no exertion to prevent herself from falling, she was quickly thrown off, and had one of her legs much bruised. Every attempt to carry her forward being thus found ineffectual, the general cry of the coffle was, *kang-tegi, kang-tegi,* "cut her throat, cut her throat;" an operation I did not wish to see performed, and therefore marched onwards with the foremost of the coffle. I had not walked above a mile, when one of Karfa's domestic slaves came up to me, with poor Nealee's garment upon the end of his bow, and exclaimed *Nealee affilita* (Nealee is lost). I asked him whether the Slatees had given him the garment, as a reward for cutting her throat; he replied, that Karfa and the schoolmaster would not consent to that measure, but had left her on the road; where undoubtedly she soon perished, and was probably devoured by wild beasts.

The sad fate of this wretched woman, notwithstanding the outcry beforementioned, made a strong impression on the minds of the whole coffle, and the schoolmaster fasted the whole of the ensuing day, in consequence of it. We proceeded in deep silence, and soon afterward crossed the river Furkoomah, which was about as large as the river Wonda. We now travelled with great expedition, every one being apprehensive he might otherwise meet with the fate of poor Nealee. It was however with great difficulty that I could keep up, although I threw away my spear, and every thing that could in the least obstruct me. About noon we saw a large herd of elephants, but they suffered us to pass unmolested, and in the evening we halted near a thicket of bamboo, but found no water; so that we were forced to proceed four miles farther, to a small stream, where we stopt for the night. We had marched this day, as I judged, about twenty-six miles ...

In the afternoon [April 28] we passed several villages, at none of which could we procure a lodging; and in the twilight we received information, that two hundred Jallonkas had assembled near a town called Melo, with a view to plunder the coffle. This induced us to alter our course, and we travelled with great secrecy until midnight, when we approached a town called Koba. Before we entered the town, the names of all the people belonging to the coffle were called over, and a freeman and three slaves were found to be missing. Every person immediately concluded that the slaves had murdered the freeman, and made their escape. It was therefore agreed, that six people should go back as far as the last village, and endeavour to find his body, or collect some information concerning the slaves. In the meantime the coffle was ordered to lie concealed in a cotton field near a large nitta tree, and nobody to speak, except in a whisper. It was towards morning before the six men returned, having heard nothing of the man or the slaves. As none of us had tasted victuals for the last twenty-four hours, it was agreed that we should go into Koba, and endeavour to procure some provisions. We accordingly entered the town before it was quite day, and Karfa purchased from the chief man, for three strings of beads, a considerable quantity of ground nuts, which we roasted and eat for breakfast; we were afterwards provided with huts, and rested here for the day.

About eleven o'clock, to our great joy and surprise, the freeman and slaves, who had departed from the coffle the preceding night, entered the town. One of the slaves, it seems, had hurt his foot, and the night being very dark, they soon lost sight of the coffle. The free man, as soon as he found himself alone with the slaves, was aware of his own danger, and insisted on putting them in irons. The slaves were at first rather unwilling to submit, but when he threatened to stab them one by one with his spear, they made no further resistance, and he remained with them among the bushes until morning, when he let them out of irons, and came to the town in hopes of hearing which route the coffle had taken. The information that we received concerning the Jallonkas, who intended to rob the coffle, was this day confirmed, and we were forced to remain here until the afternoon of the 30th; when Karfa hired a number of people to protect us, and we proceeded to a village called Tinkingtang. Departing from this village on the day following, we crossed a high ridge of mountains to the west of the Black river, and travelled over a rough stony country until sunset, when we arrived at Lingicotta, a small village in the district of Woradoo. Here we shook out the last handful of meal from our dry provision bags, this being the second day (since we crossed the Black river), that we had travelled from morning until night, without tasting one morsel of food . . .

May 13th. In the morning, as we were preparing to depart, a coffle of slaves belonging to some Serawoolli traders, crossed the river, and agreed to proceed with us to Baniserile, the capital of Dentila; a very long day's journey from this place. We accordingly set out together, and travelled with great expedition, through the woods, until noon, when one of the Serawoolli slaves dropt a load from his head, for which he was smartly whipped. The load was replaced; but he had not proceeded above a mile before he let it fall a second time, for which he received the same punishment. After this he travelled in great pain until about two o'clock, when we stopt to breathe a little, by a pool of water, the day being remarkably hot. The poor slave was now so completely exhausted, that his master was obliged to release him from the rope, for he lay motionless on the ground. A Serawoolli therefore undertook to remain with him, and endeavour to bring him to the town during the cool of the night: in the meanwhile we continued our route, and after a very hard day's travel, arrived at Baniserile late in the evening . . .

About eight o'clock the same evening, the Serawoolli, who had been left in the woods to take care of the fatigued slave, returned and told us that he was dead: the general opinion, however, was, that he himself had killed him, or left him to perish on the road; for the Serawoollis are said to be infinitely more cruel in their treatment of slaves than the Mandingoes. We remained at Baniserile two days, in order to purchase native iron, Shea-butter, and some other articles for sale on the Gambia; and here, the Slatee who had invited me to his house, and who possessed three slaves, part of the coffle, having obtained information that the price on the coast was very low, determined to separate from us, and remain, with his slaves, where he was, until an opportunity should offer of disposing of them to advantage ... [May 16 traveled from Baniserile to Kirwani]

Departing from Kirwani, on the morning of the 20th, we entered the Tenda Wilderness of two days' journey. The woods were very thick, and the country shelved towards the southwest. About ten o'clock we met a coffle of twenty-six people, and seven loaded asses, returning from Gambia. Most of the men were armed with muskets, and had broad belts of scarlet cloth over their shoulders, and European hats upon their heads. They informed us that there was very little demand for slaves on the Coast, as no vessel had arrived for some months past. On hearing this, the Serawoollies who had travelled with us from Falemé river, separated themselves and their slaves from the coffle. They had not, they said, the means of maintaining their slaves in Gambia until a vessel should arrive; and were unwilling to sell them to disadvantage: they therefore departed to the northward for Kajaaga. We continued our route through the Wilderness, and travelled all day through a rugged country, covered with extensive thickets of bamboo ...

[May 30th] ... Here [the town of Jallacotta] one of the slaves belonging to the coffle, who had travelled with great difficulty for the last three days, was found unable to proceed any farther; his master (a singing man) proposed therefore to exchange him for a young slave girl, belonging to one of the townspeople. The poor girl was ignorant of her fate, until the bundles were all tied up in the morning, and the coffle ready to depart; when, coming with some other young women to see the coffle set out, her master took her by the hand and delivered her to the singing man. Never was a face of serenity more suddenly changed into one of the deepest distress; the terror she manifested on having the load put upon her head, and the rope fastened around her neck, and the sorrow with which she bade adieu to her companions, were truly affecting ...

Being now [June 2, 1797] arrived within a short distance of Pisania, from whence my journey originally commenced, and learning that my friend Karfa was not likely to meet with an immediate opportunity of selling his slaves on the Gambia, it occurred to me to suggest to him, that he would find it for his interest to leave them at Jindey, until a market should offer. Karfa agreed with me in this opinion, and hired, from the chief man of the town, huts for their accommodation, and a piece of land on which to employ them, in raising corn, and other provisions for their maintenance. With regard to himself, he declared that he would not quit me until my departure from Africa. We set out accordingly, Karfa, myself, and one of the Foulahs belonging to the coffle, early on the morning of the 9th; but although I was now approaching the end of my tedious and toilsome journey, and expected, in another day, to meet with countrymen and friends, I could not part, for the last time, with my unfortunate fellow-travellers, doomed, as I knew most of them to be, to a life of captivity and slavery in a foreign land, without great emotion. During a wearisome peregrination of more than five hundred British miles, exposed to the burning rays of a tropical sun, these poor slaves, amidst their own infinitely greater sufferings, would commiserate mine; and frequently, of their own accord, bring water to quench my thirst, and at night collect branches and leaves to prepare me a bed in the Wilderness. We parted with reciprocal expressions of regret and benediction. My good wishes and prayers were all I could bestow upon them, and it afforded me some consolation to be told, that they were sensible I had no more to give . . .

[O]n the 15th [June], the ship Charles-Town, an American vessel, commanded by Mr. Charles Harris, entered the river. She came for slaves, intending to touch at Goree to fill up, and to proceed from thence to South Carolina. As the European merchants on the Gambia, had at this time a great many slaves on hand, they agreed with the captain to purchase the whole of his cargo, consisting chiefly of rum and tobacco, and deliver him slaves to the amount, in the course of two days. This afforded me such an opportunity of returning (through a circuitous route) to my native country, as I thought was not to be neglected. I therefore immediately engaged my passage in this vessel for America . . . I embarked at Kaye on the 17th day of June.

Our passage down the river was tedious and fatiguing, and the weather was so hot, moist, and unhealthy, that before our arrival at Goree, four of the seamen, the surgeon, and three of the slaves, had died of fevers. At Goree we were detained, for want of provisions, until the beginning of October.

The number of slaves received on board this vessel, both on the Gambia, and at Goree, was one hundred and thirty, of whom about twenty-five had been, I suppose, of free condition in Africa, as most of those, being Bushreens, could write a little Arabic. Nine of them had become captives in the religious war between Abdulkader and Damel, mentioned in the latter part of the preceding chapter. Two of the others had seen me as I passed through Bondou, and many of them had heard of me in the interior countries. My conversation with them, in their native language, gave them great comfort; and as the surgeon was dead, I consented to act in a medical capacity in his room for the remainder of the voyage. They had in truth need of every consolation in my power to bestow; not that I observed any wanton acts of cruelty practised either by the master, or the seamen, towards them; but the mode of confining and securing Negroes in the American slave ships, owing chiefly to the weakness of their crews, being abundantly more rigid and severe than in British vessels employed in the same traffic, made these poor creatures to suffer greatly, and a general sickness prevailed amongst them. Besides the three who died on the Gambia, and six or eight while we remained at Goree, eleven perished at sea, and many of the survivors were reduced to a very weak and emaciated condition.

In the midst of these distresses, the vessel, after having been three weeks at sea, became so extremely leaky, as to require constant exertion at the pumps. It was found necessary, therefore, to take some of the ablest of the Negro men out of irons, and employ them at this labour, in which they were often worked beyond their strength. This produced a complication of miseries not easily to be described. We were, however, relieved much sooner than I expected, for the leak continuing to gain upon us, notwithstanding our utmost exertions to clear the vessel, the seamen insisted on bearing away for the West Indies, as affording the only chance of saving our lives. Accordingly, after some objections on the part of the master, we directed our course for Antigua, and fortunately made that island in about thirty-five days after our departure from Goree. Yet even at this juncture we narrowly escaped destruction, for on approaching the north-west side of the island, we struck on Diamond Rock, and got into St John's harbour with great difficulty. The vessel was afterwards condemned as unfit for sea, and the slaves, as I have heard, were ordered to be sold for the benefit of the owners . . .

CHAPTER FOUR

The Impact of Abolition (1807–99)

24 ◆ Britain and the United States enact legislation to abolish the trade in slaves (1807)

In 1807, the governments of Britain and the United States enacted legislation to restrict the trade in slaves from Africa. By the terms of its legislative act, Great Britain aimed to end the export trade from Africa by making it illegal for anyone, no matter what the nationality of the offender, to engage in the "Purchase, Sale, Barter, or Transfer of Slaves, or of Persons intended to be sold, transferred, used, or dealt with as Slaves, practised and carried on, in, at, to or from any Part of the Coast or Countries of Africa." The United States focused on the import trade to North America rather than on the export trade from Africa, prohibiting the importation of any "negro, mulatto, or person of colour, with intent to hold, sell, or dispose of such . . . as a slave, or to be held to service or labour."[1]

Great Britain, An Act for the abolition of the slave trade, June 10 and 24, 1806, May 1, 1807

Whereas the Two Houses of Parliament did, by their Resolutions of the Tenth and Twenty-fourth Days of June One thousand eight hundred and six, severally resolve, upon certain Grounds therein mentioned, that they would, with all practicable Expedition, take effectual Measures for the Abolition of the African Slave Trade, in such Manner, and at such Period as might be deemed adviseable: And Whereas it is fit upon all and each of the Grounds mentioned in the said Resolutions, that the same should be forthwith abolished and prohibited, and declared to be unlawful; be it therefore enacted by the King's most Excellent Majesty, by and with the Advice and Consent of the Lords Spiritual and Temporal, and Commons, in this present Parliament assembled, and by the Authority of the same, That from and after the First Day of May One thousand eight hundred and seven, the African Slave Trade, and all manner of dealing and trading in the Purchase, Sale, Barter, or Transfer of Slaves, or of Persons intended to be sold, transferred, used, or dealt with as Slaves, practised and carried on, in, at, to or from any Part of the Coast or Countries of Africa, shall be, and the same is hereby utterly abolished, prohibited, and declared to be unlawful; and also that all and all manner of dealing, either by way of Purchase, Sale, Barter, or Transfer, or by means of any other Contract or Agreement whatever, relating to any Slaves, or to any Persons intended to be used or dealt with as Slaves, for the Purpose of such Slaves or Persons being removed

---

1. Elizabeth Donnan, ed., *Documents Illustrative of the History of the Slave Trade to America* (Washington, D.C.: Carnegie Institute, 1930), vol. 2, 659–69; vol. 4, 666–71.

and transported either immediately or by Transhipment at Sea or otherwise, directly or in-directly from Africa, or from any Island, Country, Territory, or Place whatever, in the West Indies, or in any other Part of America, not being in the Dominion, Possession, or Occupa-tion of His Majesty, to any other Island, Country, Territory or Place whatever, is hereby in like Manner utterly abolished, prohibited, and declared to be unlawful; and if any of His Majesty's Subjects, or any Person or Persons resident within this United Kingdom, or any of the Islands, Colonies, Dominions, or Territories thereto belonging, or in His Majesty's Occupation or Possession, shall from and after the Day aforesaid, by him or themselves, or by his or their Factors or Agents or otherwise howsoever, deal or trade in, purchase, sell, barter, or transfer, or contract or agree for the dealing or trading in, purchasing, selling, bartering, or transferring of any Slave or Slaves, or any Person or Persons intended to be sold, transferred, used, or dealt with as a Slave or Slaves contrary to the Prohibitions of this Act, he or they so offending shall forfeit and pay for every such Offence the Sum of One hundred Pounds of law-ful Money of Great Britain for each and every Slave so purchased, sold, bartered, or trans-ferred, or contracted or agreed for as aforesaid, the One Moiety thereof to the Use of His Majesty, His Heirs and Successors, and the other Moiety to the Use of any Person who shall inform, sue, and prosecute for the same . . .

And be it further enacted, That from and after the said First Day of May One thousand eight hundred and seven, it shall be unlawful for any of His Majesty's Subjects, or any Person or Persons resident in this United Kingdom, or in any of the Colonies, Territories or Do-minions thereunto belonging, or in His Majesty's Possession or Occupation, to carry away or remove, or knowingly and wilfully to procure, aid, or assist in the carrying away or removing, as Slaves, or for the Purpose of being sold, transferred, used, or dealt with as Slaves, any of the Subjects or Inhabitants of Africa, or of any Island, Country, Territory, or Place in the West Indies, or any other Part of America, whatsoever, not being in the Dominion, Possession, or Occupation of His Majesty, either immediately or by Transhipment at Sea or otherwise, di-rectly or indirectly from Africa, or from any such Island, Country, Territory, or Place as afore-said, to any other Island, Country, Territory, or Place whatever . . .

And Whereas it may happen, That during the present or future Wars, Ships or Vessels may be seized or detained as Prize, on board whereof Slaves or Natives of Africa, carried and detained as Slaves, being the Property of His Majesty's Enemies, or otherwise liable to Con-demnation as Prize of War, may be taken or found, and it is necessary to direct in what Man-ner such Slaves or Natives of Africa shall be hereafter treated and disposed of: And Whereas it is also necessary to direct and provide for the Treatment and Disposal of any Slaves or Na-tives of Africa carried, removed, treated or dealt with as Slaves, who shall be unlawfully car-ried away or removed contrary to the Prohibitions aforesaid, or any of them, and shall be afterwards found on board any Ship or Vessel liable to Seizure under this Act, or any other Act of Parliament made for restraining or prohibiting the African Slave Trade, or shall be else-where lawfully seized as forfeited under this or any other such Act of Parliament as aforesaid; and it is expedient to encourage the Captors, Seizors [sic] and Prosecutors thereof; Be it there-fore further enacted, That all Slaves and all Natives of Africa, treated, dealt with, carried, kept or detained as Slaves, which shall at any Time from and after the said First Day of May next be seized or taken as Prize of War, or liable to Forfeiture, under this or any other Act of Parlia-ment made for restraining or prohibiting the African Slave Trade, shall and may, for the Purposes only of Seizure, Prosecution, and Condemnation as Prize or as Forfeitures, be considered, treated, taken, and adjudged as Slaves and Property, in the same Manner as Negro Slaves have been heretofore considered, treated, taken, and adjudged, when seized as Prize of War, or as forfeited for any Offence against the Laws of Trade and Navigation respectively; but the same shall be condemned as Prize of War, or as forfeited to the sole Use of His Majesty, His Heirs and Successors, for the Purpose only of divesting and barring all other Property, Right, Title, or Interest whatever, which before existed, or might afterwards be set up or claimed in or to such Slaves or Natives of Africa so seized, prosecuted and condemned; and the same nevertheless shall in no case be liable to be sold, disposed of, treated or dealt with as Slaves, by or on the Part of His Majesty, His Heirs or Successors, or by or on the Part of any Person or Persons claiming or to claim from, by or under His Majesty, His Heirs and Successors, or under or by force of any such Sentence of Condemnation: Provided always, that it shall be lawful for His Majesty, His Heirs and Successors, and such Officers, Civil or Military, as shall, by any general or special Order of the King in Council, be from Time to Time appointed and empowered to receive, protect, and provide for such Natives of Africa as shall be so condemned, either to enter and enlist the same, or any of them, into His Majesty's Land or Sea Service as Soldiers, Seamen or Marines, or to bind the same, or any of them, whether of full Age or not, as Apprentices, for any Term not exceeding Fourteen Years, to such Person or Persons, in such Place or Places, and upon such Terms and Conditions, and subject to such Regulations, as to His Majesty shall seem meet, and as shall by any general or special Order of His Majesty in Council be in that Behalf directed and appointed; and any Indenture of Apprenticeship duly made and executed, by any Person or Persons to be for that Purpose appointed by any such Order in Council, for any Term not exceeding Fourteen Years, shall be of the same Force and Effect as if the Party thereby bound as an Apprentice had himself or herself, when of full Age upon good Consideration, duly executed the same; and every such Native of Africa who shall be so enlisted or entered as aforesaid into any of His Majesty's Land or Sea Forces as a Soldier, Seaman, or Marine, shall be considered, treated, and dealt with in all Respects as if he had voluntarily so enlisted or entered himself.

United States of America, Act to prohibit the importation of slaves into the United States, March 2, 1807

An Act to prohibit the importation of Slaves into any place within the jurisdiction of the United States, from and after the first day of January, in the year of our Lord one thousand eight hundred and eight.

Be it enacted by the Senate and House of Representatives of the United States of America in Congress assembled, That from and after the first day of January, one thousand eight hundred and eight, it shall not be lawful to import or bring into the United States or the territories thereof from any foreign kingdom, place, or country, any negro, mulatto, or person of colour, with intent to hold, sell, or dispose of such negro, mulatto, or person of colour, as a slave, or to be held to service or labour.

Sec. 2. *And be it further enacted,* That no citizen or citizens of the United States, or any other person, shall, from and after the first day of January, in the year of our Lord one thousand eight hundred and eight, for himself, or themselves, or any other person whatsoever, either as master, factor, or owner, build, fit, equip, load or otherwise prepare any ship or vessel, in any port or place within the jurisdiction of the United States, nor shall cause any ship or vessel to sail from any port or place within the same, for the purpose of procuring any negro, mulatto, or person of colour, from any foreign kingdom, place, or country, to be transported to any port or place whatsoever, within the jurisdiction of the United States, to be held, sold, or disposed of as slaves, or to be held to service or labour; and if any ship or vessel shall be so fitted out for the purpose aforesaid, or shall be caused to sail so as aforesaid, every such ship or vessel, her tackle, apparel, and furniture, shall be forfeited to the United States, and shall be liable to be seized, prosecuted, and condemned in any of the circuit courts or district courts, for the district where the said ship or vessel may be found or seized.

Sec. 3. *And be it further enacted,* That all and every person so building, fitting out, equipping, loading, or otherwise preparing or sending away, any ship or vessel, knowing or intending that the same shall be employed in such trade or business, from and after the first day of January, one thousand eight hundred and eight, contrary to the true intent and meaning of this act, or any ways aiding or abetting therein, shall severally forfeit and pay twenty thousand dollars, one moiety thereof to the use of the United States, and the other moiety to the use of any person or persons who shall sue for and prosecute the same to effect.

Sec. 4. *And be it further enacted,* If any citizen or citizens of the United States or any person resident within the jurisdiction of the same, shall, from and after the first day of January, one thousand eight hundred and eight, take on board, receive or transport from any of the coasts or kingdoms of Africa, or from any other foreign kingdom, place, or country, any negro, mulatto, or person of colour, in any ship or vessel, for the purpose of selling them in any port or place within the jurisdiction of the United States as slaves, or to be held to service or labour or shall be in any ways aiding or abetting therein, such citizen or citizens, or person, shall severally forfeit and pay five thousand dollars, one moiety thereof to the use of any person or persons who shall sue for and prosecute the same to effect; and every such ship or vessel in which such negro, mulatto, or person of colour, shall have been taken on board, received, or transported as aforesaid, her tackle, apparel, and furniture, and the goods and effects which shall be found on board the same, shall be forfeited to the United States, and shall be liable to be seized, prosecuted, and condemned in any of the circuit courts or district courts in the district where the said ship or vessel may be found or seized. And neither the importer, nor any person or persons claiming from or under him, shall hold any right or title whatsoever to any negro, mulatto, or person of colour, nor to the service or labour thereof, who may be imported or brought within the United States, or territories thereof, in violation of this law, but the same shall remain subject to any regulations not contravening the provisions of this act, which the legislatures of the several state or territories at any time hereafter may make, for disposing of any such negro, mulatto, or person of colour.

Sec. 5. *And be it further enacted,* That if any person or persons whatsoever, shall, from and after the first day of January, one thousand eight hundred and eight, purchase or sell any negro, mulatto, or person of colour, for a slave, or to be held to service or labour, who shall have been imported, or brought from any foreign kingdom, place, or country, or from the dominions of any foreign state, immediately adjoining to the United States, into any port or place within the jurisdiction of the United States, after the last day of December, one thousand eight hundred and seven, knowingly at the time of such purchase or sale, such negro, mulatto, or person of colour, was brought within the jurisdiction of the United States as aforesaid, such purchaser and seller shall severally forfeit and pay for every negro, mulatto, or person of colour, so purchased or sold as aforesaid, eight hundred dollars; one moiety thereof to the United States, and the other moiety to the use of any person or persons who shall sue for and prosecute to the same effect: *Provided,* that the aforesaid forfeiture shall not extend to the seller or purchaser of any negro, mulatto, or person of colour, who may be sold or disposed of in virtue of any regulation which may hereafter be made by any of the legislatures of the several states in that respect, in pursuance of this act, and the constitution of the United States . . .

25 • Ali Eisami recounts how he was taken into slavery and then freed (1818)

Though Britain outlawed the trade in slaves and then sent armed vessels to patrol the West African coast and intercept slaving ships, the export trade across the Atlantic continued, especially so long as slavery as an institution remained legal throughout the Americas. Between 1801 and 1867 more than three million West Africans were transported as slaves across the Atlantic. Some of these slaves were victims of a series of religious wars that erupted in West Africa during the first decades of the nineteenth century, when Islamic reformers engaged in jihads (holy wars) against societies that they believed had become corrupt.

Ali Eisami was born in the late 1780s in the Gazir province of Bornu, an Islamic state in the northeast of present-day Nigeria. The relatively privileged son of a Muslim scholar-teacher, Ali Eisami found his life transformed after 1808, when Fulbe reformers attacked Bornu. Ali was taken into slavery in 1818 and, after a series of transactions, ended up being sold to European slave merchants. By chance—the British had only two ships patrolling the entire West African coast in 1818—the vessel on which Ali Eisami was being transported to the Americas was interdicted, and Ali was released in Sierra Leone, at that time the only significant British territorial holding in West Africa. Ali Eisami dictated the story of his life to S. W. Koelle, a German linguist employed by the Church Missionary Society.[2]

In the town of Magriari Tapsoua, there was a man, named Mamade Atshi, son of Kodo, and he was my father. He was already a priest when he went and sought to marry my mother: so when their great people had consulted together, and come to a mutual understanding, my father prepared himself, sought a house, and the time for the wedding was fixed, which having arrived, my mother was married, and brought into my father's house. After they had been living in their house one year, my elder sister, Sarah, was born, next my elder brother Mamade, and after him myself; next to me, my younger sister Pesam, and then my younger sister Kadei were born; on their being born, our mother did not bear any more. As to myself, I was put to school when I was seven years of age. Then my younger sister Kadei and mine elder brother Mamade died, so that only three of us remained, of whom two were females and I alone a male. When I had been reading at school till I was nine years of age, they took me from school,

2. Sigismund William Koelle, *African Native Literature, or Proverbs, Tales, Fables, & Historical Fragments in the Kanuri or Bornu Language* (London: Church Missionary House, 1854), 248–56.

and put me into the house of circumcision; and after passing through the rite of circumcision, I returned to school, and having remained there two years longer, I left off reading the Koran. When I left off reading the Koran, I was eleven years old.

Two years later, there was an eclipse of the sun, on a Saturday, in the cold season. One year after this, when, in the weeding time, in the rainy season, about two o'clock in the afternoon, we looked to the West, the Kaman-locusts were coming from the West, forming a straight line (across the sky), as if one of God's thunder-storms were coming, so that day was turned into night. When the time of the locusts was past, the famine Ngeseneski took place, but did not last long, only three months. After it, the pestilence came, and made much havock in Bornu, completely destroying all the great people. Next, the wars of the Phula [Fulbe] came up. In the rainy season the Phula put to flight the Deia King with his family, and, as they were coming to our town, my Father said to me, "My son, times will be hard for you: this year thou hast been nineteen years of age, and though I said that, when thou art twenty, I will seek a girl for thee, and let thee marry, yet now the Phula have unsettled the land, and we do not know what to do: but what God has ordained for us, that shall we experience." When the guinea-corn which we were weeding had become ripe, and the harvest was past, the Phula roused both us and the Deiaese, so we went, and remained near the Capital, till the Phula arose and came to the Capital, on a Sunday, about two o'clock in the afternoon. When they were coming, the Commander went out to encounter them; but, after they had met and been engaged in a battle till four o'clock, the Commander's power was at an end. The King arose, passed out through the Eastgate, and started for Kurnoa. Then the Commander left the Phula, and followed the King; on seeing which, all the Phula came and entered the Capital. After they had entered, the tidings reached us about seven o'clock in the evening. When the tidings came, none knew where to lay their head. On the following morning, a great priest of the Phula said to us, "Let every one go and remain in his house, the war is over: let all the poor go, and each cultivate land!" Then my father called his younger brother, and we arose and went to our town; but when we came, there was nothing at all to eat. So my father called my mother at night, when all the people were gone, and said to her, "This our town is ruined; if we remain, the Phula will make an end of us: arise, and load our things upon our children!" Now there was a town, Magerari by name, which is subject to the Shoas; and the Phula never meddle with any place that is subject to the Shoas. So we arose, and went to that town; but when we had lived there one year, the King went, turned the Phula out of the Capital, and went in himself and abode there.

About one year after this event, when my father had died, as it were to-day, at two o'clock in the afternoon, and we had not yet buried him, intending to do so next day, then we slept, and on the following morning, my mother called me, and my elder and my younger sister, and said to us, "Live well together, ye three; behold, your father lies here a corpse, and I am following your father." Now there was just a priest with us who said to my mother, "Why dost thou say such things to thy children?" but my mother replied to the priest, "I say these things to my children in truth." Then she called me, and I rose up, went, and sat down before her. When I had sat down, she said to me, "Stretch out thy legs, that I may lay my head upon thy thighs." So I stretched out my legs, and she took her head, and laid it upon my thighs; but when the priest who was staying with us saw that my mother was laying her head upon my thighs, he arose, came, sat down by me, stretched out his legs, and took my mother's head from my thighs, and laid it upon his own. Then that moment our Lord sought my mother.

After this there came tears from mine eyes, and when the priest saw it, he said to me, "Let me not see tears in thine eyes! will thy father and thy mother arise again, and sit down, that thou mayest see them, if thou weepest?" I attended to what the priest said, and did not weep any more. With the corpse of our father before us, and with the corpse of our mother before us, we did not know what to do, till the people of the town went and dug graves for both of them, side by side, in one place, and came back again, when we took the corpses, carried and buried them, and then returned.

After waiting two months at home, I took my younger sister, and gave her to a friend of my father's in marriage, my elder sister being already provided with a husband. On one occasion I got up after night had set in, without saying any thing to my little mother, took my father's spear, his charms, and one book which he had, set out on a journey, and walked in the night, so that it was not yet day when I reached the town of Shagou, where there was a friend of my father's, a Shoa; and, when I came to the dwelling place of this friend of my father's, they were just in the place for prayer. When I came to him, and he saw me, he knew me, and I knew him. I having saluted him, he asked me, "Where is thy father?" I replied to him, saying, "My father is no more, and my mother is no more, so I left both my elder and my younger sister, and came to thee:" whereupon he said to me, "Come, my son, we will stay together; thy father did do good to me, and now since he is no more, and thou didst like me and come to me, I also like thee: I will do to thee what I do to my own son."

After I had been there about three years, I called a companion, saying, "Come and accompany me!" for I had a friend in a town of the name of Gubr. The youth arose, and we started together, but as we were going towards the town of Gubr, seven Phula waylaid us, seized us, tied our hands upon our backs, fettered us, put us in the way, and then we went till it became day. When it was day, both they and we became hungry in a hostile place, the land being the land of Ngesm. In this place we sat down, and ate the fruit of a certain tree called Ganga, till it became dark, when they took us again, and carried us to the town of Ngololo to market. On that day Hausas bought us, took us into a house, and put iron fetters on our feet; then, after five days, we arose, and were twenty-two days, ere we arrived in the Hausa land. When we arrived, we went to a town called Sangaya, where there are a great many dates. In this town we remained during the months of Asham, Soual, and Kide; but when only three days of the (month of) Atsbi were passed, they roused me up, and in a week we came to the Katsina Capital, where they slew the Easter-lamb, and after five days they rose again, and we started for Yauri. After marching a fortnight, we arrived at the Yauri Capital. Here the Hausas sold us, and took their goods, whilst Bargas bought us. The Bargas roused us up, and when we came to their town, the man who had bought me, did not leave me alone at all: I had iron fetters round my feet, both by night and by day. After I had stayed with him seven days, he took me, and brought me to the town of Sai, where a Yoruban bought me.

The Yoruban who bought me was a son of the Katunga King; he liked me, and called me to sit down before him, and, on seeing my tattoo-marks, he said to me, "Wast thou the son of a King in your country?" To this I replied, "My father, as for me, I will not tell lies, because times are evil, and our Lord has given me into slavery: my father was a scholar." Then he said,

"As for this youth and his father, his father must have been a fine man; I will not treat him ill;" and so he kept me in his house. In this place I remained a long time, so that I understood their language. After I had been there four years, a war arose: now, all the slaves who went to the war, became free [these were likely among the soldiers who captured Samuel Crowther—see the next extract]; so when the slaves heard these good news, they all ran there, and the Yorubans saw it. The friend of the man who had bought me, said to him, "If thou dost not sell this slave of thine, he will run away, and go [to] the war, so that thy cowries will be lost, for this fellow has sound eyes." Then the man took hold of me, and bound me, and his three sons took me to the town of Atshashe, where white men had landed; then they took off the fetters from my feet, and carried me before them to the white people, who bought me, and put an iron round my neck. After having bought all the people, they took us, brought us to the seashore, brought a very small canoe, and transferred us one by one to the large vessel.

The people of the great vessel were wicked: when we had been shipped, they took away all the small pieces of cloth which were on our bodies, and threw them into the water, then they took chains, and fettered two together. We in the vessel, great and small, were seven hundred, whom the white men had bought. We were all fettered round our feet, and all the stoutest died of thirst, for there was no water. Every morning they had to take many, and throw them into the water: so we entreated God by day and by night, and, after three months, when it pleased God to send breezes, we arose in the morning, and the doors were opened. When we had all come on deck, one slave was standing by us, and we beheld the sky in the midst of the water.

When I looked at the horizon, mine eye saw something far away, like trees. On seeing this, I called the slave, and said to him, "I see a forest yonder, far away;" whereupon he said to me, "Show it to me with thy finger!" When I had shown it to him, and he had seen the place at which my finger pointed, he ran to one of the white men who liked me, and would give me his shirts to mend, and then gave me food, he being a benefactor; now, when the slave told it him, the white man who was holding a roasted fowl in his hand, came to me, together with the slave. This slave who understood their language, and also the Hausa, came and asked me, saying, "Show me with thy finger what thou seest, that the white man also may see it!" I showed it, and when the white man brought his eye, and laid it upon my finger, he also saw what I pointed at. He left the roasted fowl which he held in his hand and wanted to eat, before me, and ran to their Captain. Then I took the fowl, and put it into my bag. All of them ran, and loaded the big big guns with powder and their very large iron. We, not knowing what it was, called the Hausa who understood it, and said to him, "Why do the white men prepare their guns?" and he said to us, "What thou sawest were not trees, but a vessel of war is coming towards us." We did not believe it, and said, "We have never seen any one make war in the midst of water;" but, after waiting a little, it came, and when it was near us, our own white men fired a gun at them; but it still went on. When the white men with us had fired a gun nine times, the white man of war was vexed and fired one gun at our vessel, the ball of which hit the middle mast with those very large sails, cut it off, and threw it into the water. Then the white men with us ran to the bottom of the vessel, and hid themselves. The war-chief, a short man, of the name of Captain Hick, brought his vessel side by side with ours, whereupon all the war-men came into our vessel, sword in hand, took all our own white men, and carried them to their vessel. Then they called all of us, and when we formed a line, and stood up in one place, they counted us, and said, "Sit down!" So we sat down, and they took off all the fetters from our feet, and threw them into the water, and they gave us clothes that we might cover our nakedness, they opened the water-casks, that we might drink water to the full, and we also ate food, till we had enough. In the evening they brought drums, and gave them to us, so that we played till it was morning. We said, "Now our Lord has taken us out of our slavery," and thanked him. Then came a white man, stood before me, and, after looking at me, slapped both my cheeks, took me to the place where they cooked food, and said to me, "Thou hast to cook, that thy people may eat." So I cooked food, and distributed the water with mine own hand, till they brought us and landed us in this town [Freetown, Sierra Leone], where we were a week in the King's house, and then they came and distributed us among the different towns.

We went and settled in the forests, at Bathurst. We met a white man in this town whose name was Mr. Decker, and who had a wife, and was a reverend priest. On the following morning we all went, and stood up in his house, and having seen all of us, he came, took hold of my hand, and drew me into his house, and I did not fear him; but I heard inside the house that my people without were talking, and saying, "The white man has taken Ali, and put him into the house, in order to slaughter him." So I looked at the white people, and they looked at me. When the white man arose and went to the top of the house, I prepared myself, and thought, "If this white man takes a knife, and I see it in his hand, I will hold it;" but the white man was gone up to fetch shirts, and trowsers, and caps down. On coming down, he said to me, "Stand up!" So when I stood up, he put me into a shirt, put trowsers over my legs, gave me a jacket, and put a cap upon my head. Then he opened the door, and when we came out, all our people were glad. He called a man who understood the white man's language, and said to him, "Say that this one is the chief of all his people;" then the man told me so. When they carried us to the forest the day before, my wife followed after me; and on the day after our arrival the white man married us, and gave me my wife, so we went and remained in the house of our people.

The white man was a benefactor, and he liked me. But, after a few days, his wife became ill, so we took her, and carried her to the town of Hog-brook; and then the illness exceeded her strength, and our Lord sought her. After this he arose in our town, and we took his things, and carried them to Freetown, where he said to us, "Go, and remain quiet; I go to our own country, not knowing whether I shall come back again, or not." Then he shook hands with us, bid us farewell, and went to their own country.

Until now our Lord has preserved me, but "God knows what is to come," say the Bornuese. I also heard the great men say, "What is to come even a bird with a long neck cannot see, but our Lord only." This is an account of what I experienced from my childhood till to-day, and what I have been telling thee is now finished.

26 • Samuel Crowther escapes slavery (1821–22)

Samuel Crowther was born around 1806 in the southwestern part of present-day Nigeria. His father was a weaver, and his mother a descendant of one of the Yoruba kings of Old Oyo and a renowned priestess in her own right. Crowther's life intersected with that of Ali Eisami in a number of ways. It was Yoruba people who at one point acquired Ali Eisami as a slave before selling him to European merchants. On the other hand, Crowther's hometown was destroyed by a Muslim army made up of freed slaves from Old Oyo, the same town where Eisami had spent time as a slave. Crowther was captured by these Islamic reformers in 1821 and sold to merchants in Lagos, who placed him on a slave ship bound for Brazil. The slave ship was intercepted by a British man-of-war, and Crowther and his fellow captives were put ashore at Freetown, Sierra Leone. Crowther converted to Christianity, became an active member of the Church Missionary Society, and was consecrated in 1864 as the first Anglican bishop of West Africa. He described his capture and escape in a letter written to the secretary of the Church Missionary Society, the Rev. William Jowett, on February 22, 1837.[3]

Rev. and Dear Sir,

As I think it will be interesting to you to know something of the conduct of Providence in my being brought to this Colony, where I have the happiness to enjoy the privilege of the Gospel, I give you a short account of it; hoping I may be excused if I should prove rather tedious in some particulars.

I suppose some time about the commencement of the year 1821, I was in my native country, enjoying the comforts of father and mother, and the affectionate love of brothers and sisters. From this period I must date the unhappy—but which I am now taught, in other respects, to call blessed day, which I shall never forget in my life. I call it *unhappy* day, because it was the day in which I was violently turned out of my father's house, and separated from relations; and in which I was made to experience what is called to be in slavery:—with regard to its being called *blessed,* it being the day which Providence had marked out for me to set out on my journey from the land of heathenism, superstition, and vice, to a place where His Gospel is preached.

For some years, war had been carried on in my Eyó [Oyo] country, which was always attended with much devastation and bloodshed; the women, such men as had surrendered or were caught, with the children, were taken captives. The enemies who carried on these wars were principally the Eyó Mahomedans, with whom my country abounds—with the Foulahs [Fulbe], and such foreign slaves as had escaped from their owners, joined together, making a formidable force of about 20,000, who annoyed the whole country. They had no other employment but selling slaves to the Spaniards and Portuguese on the coast.

The morning in which my town, Ochó-gu [Osugun], shared the same fate which many others had experienced, was fair and delightful; and most of the inhabitants were engaged in their respective occupations. We were preparing breakfast without any apprehension; when, about 9 o'clock A.M., a rumour was spread in the town, that the enemies had approached with intentions of hostility. It was not long after when they had almost surrounded the town, to prevent any escape of the inhabitants; the town being rudely fortified with a wooden fence, about four miles in circumference, containing about 12,000 inhabitants, which would produce 3,000 fighting men. The inhabitants not being duly prepared, some not being at home—those who were, having about six gates to defend, as well as many weak places about the fence to guard against, and, to say in a few words, the men being surprised, and therefore confounded—

---

3. *Journals of the Rev. James Frederick Schön and Mr. Samuel Crowther, who with the Sanction of Her Majesty's Government Accompanied the Expedition up the Niger, in 1841, in Behalf of the Church Missionary Society. With Appendices, and Map* (London: Hatchard and Son, 1842), 371–85.

the enemies entered the town after about three or four hours' resistance. Here a most sorrowful scene imaginable was to be witnessed!—women, some with three, four, or six children clinging to their arms, with the infants on their backs, and such baggage as they could carry on their heads, running as fast as they could through prickly shrubs, which, hooking their . . . loads, drew them down from the heads of the bearers. While they found it impossible to go along with their loads, they endeavoured only to save themselves and their children: even this was impracticable with those who had many children to care for. While they were endeavouring to disentangle themselves from the ropy shrubs, they were overtaken and caught by the enemies with a noose of rope thrown over the neck of every individual, to be led in the manner of goats tied together, under the drove of one man. In many cases a family was violently divided between three or four enemies, who each led his away, to see one another no more. Your humble servant was thus caught—with his mother, two sisters (one an infant about ten months old), and a cousin—while endeavouring to escape in the manner above described. My load consisted in nothing else than my bow, and five arrows in the quiver; the bow I had lost in the shrub, while I was extricating myself, before I could think of making any use of it against my enemies. The last view I had of my father was when he came from the fight, to give us the signal to flee: he entered into our house, which was burnt some time back for some offence given by my father's adopted son. Hence I never saw him more—Here I must take thy leave, unhappy, comfortless father!—I learned, some time afterward, that he was killed in another battle.

Our conquerors were Eyó Mahomedans, who led us away through the town. On our way, we met a man sadly wounded on the head, struggling between life and death. Before we got half way through the town, some Foulahs, among the enemies themselves, hostilely separated my cousin from our number . . . The town on fire . . . We were led by my grandfather's house, already desolate; and in a few minutes after we left the town to the mercy of the flame, never to enter or see it any more . . . We were now out of Ochó-gu, going into a town called Iseh'i [Iseyin], the rendezvous of the enemies, about twenty miles from our town. On the way, we saw our grandmother at a distance, with about three or four of my other cousins taken with her, for a few minutes . . . Several other captives were held in the same manner as we were: grandmothers, mothers, children, and cousins were all led captives. O sorrowful prospect!—The aged women were to be greatly pitied, not being able to walk so fast as their children and grandchildren: they were often threatened with being put to death upon the spot, to get rid of them, if they would not go as fast as others; and they were often as wicked in their practice as in their words. O pitiful sight! Whose heart would not bleed to have seen this? Yes, such is the state of barbarity in the heathen land. Evening came on; and coming to a spring of water, we drank a great quantity; which served us for breakfast, with a little parched corn and dried meat previously prepared by our victors for themselves.

During our march to Iseh'i, we passed several towns and villages which had been reduced to ashes. It was almost midnight before we reached the town, where we passed our doleful first night in bondage . . .

On the next morning our cords being taken off our necks, we were brought to the Chief of our captors—for there were many other Chiefs—as trophies at his feet. In a little while, a separation took place, when my sister and I fell to the share of the Chief, and my mother and the infant to the victors. We dared not vent our grief by loud cries, but by very heavy sobs. My mother, with the infant, was led away, comforted with the promise that she should see us again, when we should leave Iseh'i for Dah'dah [Dada], the town of the Chief. In a few hours after, it was soon agreed upon that I should be bartered for a horse in Iseh'i, that very day. Thus was I separated from my mother and sister for the first time in my life; and the latter not to be seen more in this world. Thus, in the space of twenty-four hours, being deprived of liberty and all other comforts, I was made the property of three different persons. About the space of two months, when the Chief was to leave Iseh'i for his own town, the horse, which was then only taken on trial, not being approved of, I was restored to the Chief, who took me to Dah'dah, where I had the happiness to meet my mother and infant sister again with joy, which could be described by nothing else but tears of love and affection; and on the part of my infant sister, with leaps of joy in every manner possible. Here I lived for about three months, going for grass for horses with my fellow captives. I now and then visited my mother and sister in our captor's house, without any fears or thoughts of being separated any more. My mother told me that she had heard of my sister; but I never saw her more.

At last, an unhappy evening arrived, when I was sent with a man to get some money at a neighbouring house. I went; but with some fears, for which I could not account; and, to my great astonishment, in a few minutes I was added to the number of many other captives, enfettered, to be led to the market-town early the next morning. My sleep went from me; I spent almost the whole night in thinking of my doleful situation, with tears and sobs, especially as my mother was in the same town, whom I had not visited for a day or two. There was another boy in the same situation with me: his mother was in Dah'dah. Being sleepless, I heard the first cock-crow. Scarcely the signal was given, when the traders arose, and loaded the men slaves with baggage. With one hand chained to the neck, we left the town. My little companion in affliction cried and begged much to be permitted to see his mother, but was soon silenced by punishment. Seeing this, I dared not speak, although I thought we passed by the very house my mother was in. Thus was I separated from my mother and sister, my then only comforts, to meet no more in this world of misery. After a few days' travel, we came to the market-town, I-jah'i [Ijaye]. Here I saw many who had escaped in our town to this place; or those who were in search of their relations, to set at liberty as many as they had the means of redeeming. Here we were under very close inspection, as there were many persons in search of their relations; and through that, many had escaped from their owners. In a few days I was sold to a Mahomedan woman, with whom I travelled to many towns in our way to the Popo country, on the coast, much resorted to by the Portuguese, to buy slaves. When we left I-jahi, after many halts, we came to a town called Tó-ko [Itoko]. From I-jahi to Tó-ko all spoke the Ebwah [Egba] dialect, but my mistress Eyó, my own dialect. Here I was a perfect stranger, having left my own Eyó country far behind. I lived in Tó-ko about three months; walked about with my owner's son with some degree of freedom, it being a place where my feet had never trod: and could I possibly have made my way out through many a ruinous town and village we had passed, I should have soon become a prey to some others, who would have gladly taken the advantage of me ...

Now and then my mistress would speak with me and her son, that we should by-and-by go to the Popo country, where we should buy tobacco, and other fine things, to sell at our return. Now, thought I, this was the signal of my being sold to the Portuguese; who, they often told me during our journey, were to be seen in that country. Being very thoughtful of this, my appetite forsook me, and in a few weeks I got the dysentery, which greatly preyed on me. I determined with myself that I would not go to the Popo country; but would make an end of myself, one way or another. In several nights I attempted strangling myself with my band; but had not courage enough to close the noose tight, so as to effect my purpose. May the Lord forgive me this sin! I determined, next, that I would leap out of the canoe into the river, when we should cross it in our way to that country. Thus was I thinking, when my owner, perceiving the great alteration that took place in me, sold me to some persons. Thus the Lord, while I knew Him not, led me not into temptation and delivered me from evil. After my price had been counted before my own eyes, I was delivered up to my new owners, with great grief and dejection of spirit, not knowing where I was now to be led. After the first cock-crowing, which was the usual time to set out with slaves, to prevent their being much acquainted with the way, for fear an escape should be made, we set out for Jabbo [Ijebu], the third dialect from mine.

After having arrived at Ik-ke-ku Yé-re [Ikereku-iwre], another town, we halted. In this place I renewed my attempt of strangling, several times at night; but could not effect my purpose. It was very singular, that no thought of making use of a knife ever entered my mind. However, it was not long before I was bartered, for tobacco, rum, and other articles. I remained here, in fetters, alone, for some time, before my owner could get as many slaves as he wanted. He feigned to treat us more civilly, by allowing us to sip a few drops of White Man's liquor, rum; which was so estimable an article, that none but chiefs could pay for a jar or glass vessel of four or five gallons: so much dreaded it was, that no one should take breath before he swallowed every sip, for fear of having the string of his throat cut by the spirit of the liquor. This made it so much more valuable.

I had to remain alone, again, in another town in Jabbo, the name of which I do not now remember, for about two months. From hence I was brought, after a few days' walk, to a slave-market, called I'-ko-sy [Ikosi], on the coast, on the bank of a large river, which very probably was the Lagos on which we were afterwards captured. The sight of the river terrified me exceedingly, for I had never seen any thing like it in my life. The people on the opposite bank are called E'-ko. Before sun-set, being bartered again for tobacco, I became another owner's. Nothing now terrified me more than the river, and the thought of going into another world. Crying was nothing now, to vent out my sorrow: my whole body became stiff. I was now bade to enter the river, to ford it to the canoe. Being fearful at my entering this extensive water, and being so cautious in every step I took, as if the next would bring me to the bottom, my motion was very awkward indeed. Night coming on, and the men having very little time to spare, soon carried me into the canoe, and placed me among the corn-bags, and supplied me with an Ab'-alah [steamed pudding] for my dinner. Almost in the same position I was placed I remained, with my Ab'-alah in my hand quite confused in my thoughts, waiting only every moment our arrival at the new world; which we did not reach till about 4 o'clock in the morning. Here I got once more into another dialect, the fourth from mine; if I may not call it altogether another language, on account of now and then, in some words, there being a faint shadow of my own. Here I must remark that during the whole night's voyage in the canoe, not a single thought of leaping into the river had entered my mind; but, on the contrary, the fear of the river occupied my thoughts.

Having now entered E'-ko [Lagos], I was permitted to go any way I pleased; there being no way of escape, on account of the river. In this place I met my two nephews, belonging to different masters. One part of the town was occupied by the Portuguese and Spaniards, who had come to buy slaves. Although I was in E'-ko more than three months, I never once saw a White Man; until one evening, when they took a walk, in company of about six, and came to the street of the house in which I was living. Even then I had not the boldness to appear distinctly to look at them, being always suspicious that they had come for me: and my suspicion was not a fanciful one; for, in a few days after, I was made the eighth in number of the slaves of the Portuguese. Being a veteran in slavery, if I may be allowed the expression, and having no more hope of ever going to my country again, I patiently took whatever came; although it was not without a great fear and trembling that I received, for the first time, the touch of a White Man, who examined me whether I was sound or not. Men and boys were at first chained together, with a chain of about six fathoms in length, thrust through an iron fetter on the neck of every individual, and fastened at both ends with padlocks. In this situation the boys suffered the most: the men sometimes, getting angry, would draw the chain so violently, as seldom went without bruises on their poor little necks; especially the time to steep, when they drew the chain so close to ease themselves of its weight, in order to be able to lie more conveniently, that we were almost suffocated, or bruised to death, in a room with one door, which was fastened as soon as we entered in, with no other passage for communicating the air than the openings under the eaves-drop. Very often at night, when two or three individuals quarrelled or fought, the whole drove suffered punishment, without any distinction. At last, we boys had the happiness to be separated from the men, when their number was increased, and no more chain to spare: we were corded together, by ourselves. Thus we were going in and out, bathing together, and so on.—The female sex fared not much better.—Thus we were for nearly the space of four months.

About this time, intelligence was given that the English were cruising the coast. This was another subject of sorrow with us—that there must be war also on the sea as well as on land— a thing never heard of before, or imagined practicable. This delayed our embarkation. In the meanwhile, the other slaves which were collected in Popo, and were intended to be conveyed into the vessel the nearest way from that place, were brought into E'-ko, among us. Among this number was Joseph Bartholomew, my Brother in the service of the Church Missionary Society.

After a few weeks' delay, we were embarked, at night in canoes, from E'-ko to the beach; and on the following morning were put on board the vessel, which immediately sailed away. The crew being busy embarking us, 187 in number, had no time to give us either breakfast or supper; and we, being unaccustomed to the motion of the vessel, employed the whole of this day in sea-sickness, which rendered the greater part of us less fit to take any food whatever. On the very same evening, we were surprised by two English men-of-war; and on the next morning found ourselves in the hands of new conquerors, whom we at first very much dreaded, they being armed with long swords. In the morning, being called up from the hold, we were astonished to find ourselves among two very large men-of-war and several other brigs. The men-of-war were, His Majesty's ships *Myrmidon,* Captain H. J. Leeke, and *lphigenia,* Captain Sir Robert Mends, who captured us on the 7th of April 1822, on the river Lagos.

Our owner was bound with his sailors, except the cook, who was preparing our breakfast. Hunger rendered us bold; and not being threatened at first attempts to get some fruits from the stern, we in a short time took the liberty of ranging about the vessel, in search of plunder of every kind. Now we began to entertain a good opinion of our conquerors. Very soon after breakfast, we were divided into several of the vessels around us. This was now cause of new fears, not knowing where our misery would end. Being now, as it were, one family, we began to take leave of those who were first transshipped, not knowing what would become of them and ourselves. About this time, six of us, friends in affliction, among whom was my Brother Joseph Bartholomew, kept very close together, that we might be carried away at the same time. It was not long before we six were conveyed into the *Myrmidon,* in which we discovered not any trace of those who were transshipped before us. We soon came to a conclusion of what had become of them, when we saw parts of a hog hanging, the skin of which was white— a thing we never saw before; for a hog was always roasted on fire, to clear it of the hair, in my country—and a number of cannonshots were arranged along the deck. The former we supposed to be the flesh, and the latter the heads of the individuals who had been killed for meat. But we were soon undeceived, by a close examination of the flesh with cloven foot, which resembled that of a hog; and, by a cautious approach to the shot, that they were iron.

In a few days we were quite at home in the man-of-war: being only six in number, we were selected by the sailors, for their boys; and were soon furnished with clothes. Our Portuguese owner and his son were brought over into the same vessel, bound in fetters; and, thinking that I should no more get into his hand, I had the boldness to strike him on the head, while he was shaving by his son—an act, however, very wicked and unkind in its nature. His vessel was towed along by the man-of-war, with the remainder of the slaves therein. But after a few weeks, the slaves being transshipped from her, and being stripped of her rigging, the schooner was left alone on the ocean . . .

One of the brigs, which contained a part of the slaves, was wrecked on a sand-bank: happily, another vessel was near, and all the lives were saved. It was not long before another brig sunk, during a tempest, with all the slaves and sailors, with the exception of about five of the latter, who were found in a boat after four or five days, reduced almost to mere skeletons, and were so feeble, that they could not stand on their feet. One hundred and two of our number were lost on this occasion.

After nearly two months and a half cruising on the coast, we were landed at Sierra Leone, on the 17th of June, 1822. The same day we were sent to Bathurst, formerly Leopold, under the care of Mr. Davey. Here we had the pleasure of meeting many of our country people, but none were known before. They assured us of our liberty and freedom; and we very soon believed them. But a few days after our arrival at Bathurst, we had the mortification of being sent for at Freetown, to testify against our Portuguese owner. It being hinted to us that we should be delivered up to him again, notwithstanding all the persuasion of Mr. Davey that we should return, we entirely refused to go ourselves, unless we were carried. I could not but think of my ill-conduct to our owner in the man-of-war. But as time was passing away, and our consent could not be got, we were compelled to go by being whipped; and it was not a small joy to us to return to Bathurst again, in the evening, to our friends.

From this period I have been under the care of the Church Missionary Society; and in about six months after my arrival in Sierra Leone, I was able to read the New Testament with some degree of freedom . . . The Lord was pleased to open my heart to hearken to those things which are spoken by His servants; and being convinced that I was a sinner, and desired to obtain pardon through Jesus Christ, I was baptized on the 11th of December, 1825 [and took the name Samuel Crowther after a benefactor of the Church Missionary Society] . . . May I ever have a fresh desire to be engaged in the service of Christ, for it is *perfect freedom* . . .

Thus the day of my captivity was to me a blessed day, when considered in this respect; though certainly it must be unhappy also, in my being deprived on it of my father, mother, sisters, and all other relations. I must also remark, that I could not as yet find a dozen Ochó-gu people among the inhabitants of Sierra Leone. I was married to a Christian woman on the 21st of September 1829. She was captured by His Majesty's Ship *Bann*, Capt. Charles Phillips, on the 31st of October 1822. Since, the Lord has blessed us with three children—a son, and two daughters.

That the time may come when the Heathen shall be fully given to Christ for His inheritance, and the uttermost part of the earth for His possession, is the earnest prayer of

> Your humble, thankful, and obedient Servant
> Samuel Crowther

27 ◆ The Asante king questions British motives in ending the slave trade (1820)

Not all Africans welcomed British attempts to end the trade in slaves. The Asante king Osei Bonsu, for one, expressed doubt that those who were opposed to the trade were influenced by humanitarian reasons. For his part, he argued that he had never enslaved people except through war (and then not wars fought for the purpose of getting slaves but for other reasons entirely) and that it was necessary for him to sell war captives lest they rise up against him. Osei Bonsu expressed these points in a discussion in 1820 with Joseph Dupuis, sent by the British to be their consul in the Asante capital city of Kumasi. Dupuis had been instructed by his superiors "to nurture the seeds of an accidental friendship as an essential preliminary step to the advancement of certain hopeful expectations connected with the manufacturing and commercial interests of Great Britain." Osei Bonsu wondered what he would trade with if he could not trade slaves for European manufactured goods.[4]

"Now," said the king, after a pause, "I have another palaver, and you must help me to talk it. A long time ago the great king liked plenty of trade, more than now; then many ships came, and they bought ivory, gold, and slaves; but now he will not let the ships come as before, and the people buy gold and ivory only. This is what I have in my head, so now tell me truly, like a friend, why does the king do so?" "His majesty's question," I replied, "was connected with a great palaver, which my instructions did not authorise me to discuss. I had nothing to say regarding the slave trade." "I know that too," retorted the king; "because, if my master liked that trade, you would have told me so before. I only want to hear what you think as a friend: this is not like the other palavers." I was confessedly at a loss for an argument that might pass as a satisfactory reason, and the sequel proved that my doubts were not groundless. The king

4. Joseph Dupuis, *Journal of a Residence in Ashantee, Comprising Notes and Researches relative to the Gold Coast, and the Interior of Western Africa; Chiefly Collected from Arabic MSS. And Information Communicated by the Moslems of Guinea: to which is Prefixed an Account of the Origin of the Causes of the Present War* (London: Henry Colburn, 1824), 162–64.

did not deem it plausible, that this obnoxious traffic should have been abolished from motives of humanity alone; neither would he admit that it lessened the number either of domestic or foreign wars.

Taking up one of my observations, he remarked, "the white men who go to council with your master, and pray to the great God for him, do not understand my country, or they would not say the slave trade was bad. But if they think it bad now, why did they think it good before? Is not your law an old law, the same as the Crammo [Muslim] law? Do you not both serve the same God, only you have different fashions and customs? Crammos are strong people in fetische, and they say the law is good, because the great God made the book; so they buy slaves, and teach them good things, which they knew not before. This makes every body love the Crammos, and they go every where up and down, and the people give them food when they want it. Then these men come all the way from the great water [Niger], and from Manding, and Dagomba, and Killinga; they stop and trade for slaves, and then go home. If the great king would like to restore this trade, it would be good for the white men and for me too, because Ashantee is a country for war, and the people are strong; so if you talk that palaver for me properly, in the white country, if you go there, I will give you plenty of gold, and I will make you richer than all the white men."

I urged the impossibility of the king's request, promising, however, to record his sentiments faithfully. "Well then," said the king, "you must put down in my master's book all I shall say, and then he will look to it, now he is my friend. And when he sees what is true, he will surely restore that trade. I cannot make war to catch slaves in the bush, like a thief. My ancestors never did so. But if I fight a king, and kill him when he is insolent, then certainly I must have his gold, and his slaves, and the people are mine too. Do not the white kings act like this? Because I hear the old men say, that before I conquered Fantee and killed the Braffoes and the kings, that white men came in great ships, and fought and killed many people; and then they took the gold and slaves to the white country: and sometimes they fought together. That is all the same as these black countries. The great God and the fetische made war for strong men every where, because then they can pay plenty of gold and proper sacrifice. When I fought Gaman, I did not make war for slaves, but because Dinkera (the king) sent me an arrogant message and killed my people, and refused to pay me gold as his father did. Then my fetische made me strong like my ancestors, and I killed Dinkera, and took his gold, and brought more than 20,000 slaves to Coomassy. Some of these people being bad men, I washed my stool in their blood for the fetische. But then some were good people, and these I sold or gave to my captains: many, moreover, died, because this country does not grow too much corn like Sarem, and what can I do? Unless I kill or sell them, they will grow strong and kill my people. Now you must tell my master that these slaves can work for him, and if he wants 10,000 he can have them. And if he wants fine handsome girls and women to give his captains, I can send him great numbers."

28 • A slave revolt in South Africa (1825)

In 1825, a twenty-six-year-old slave named Galant, angered by the constant floggings he received from his "master," Willem van der Merwe, and inspired by reports he had heard of the development of abolitionist sentiment in Britain, gathered together fellow slaves equally unhappy with their situation. Galant killed van der Merwe and two other farmers and took control of his former master's farm, but within days was captured along with those slaves who had joined him in revolt and was put on trial for treason. Though this was only the second insurrection to occur in two hundred years of slavery at the cape and was limited to one farm, slaveholders perceived Galant's revolt as a powerful threat to their way of life. The uprising took place during a period when the institution of slavery was coming under strong attack in Britain and in the cape, with missionaries in particular denouncing the ways in which Dutch slaveholders treated their servants. Moreover, less than two decades earlier, in October 1808, more than three hundred slaves, determined to overthrow slavery, had marched on Cape Town, and memories of that insurrection (which ended with the capture of the slaves and the execution of five of their leaders) remained strong in the minds of slaves and slaveholders alike. These connections were made clear in Galant's testimony and in the demand of the prosecutor, Daniel Denyssen, for the death penalty for the prisoners.

The trial of Galant and twelve other defendants concluded with two found not guilty and the remainder guilty. Galant, along with two coconspirators, was ordered to be hanged until dead, and his head, along with that of his chief ally, to be displayed publicly on iron spikes "until consumed by time and the birds of the air." The others convicted were sentenced to various forms of torture (scourging, branding, and flogging) and to lengthy terms of imprisonment. At the trial, Denyssen interrogated Galant.[5]

Question. With what intention did you assemble?

Answer. We meant to murder all the masters that did not treat their people well, to lay waste the country if we were strong enough, and then to escape to Caffreland; and if the Commando should be too strong, to remain at the places of the murdered people.

Question. As you say in the beginning of your statement that you had spoken with Abel [one of the accused] and the other people, had you any other conversation with them than about the ill usage?

Answer. Abel said he had heard his Master reading the newspaper about making the slaves free, and that he had heard his master say he would rather shoot all his slaves than make them free . . .

Question. Do you persist in this statement, and have you anything to add to or take from it?

Answer. I have something more to state, namely my master told me himself that he would shoot me. My master once when I came from the work also said to me that there was a newspaper come from another country in which stood that a black cat had been hatched under a white hen. The next day my master asked me what I understood by that expression? to which I answered that I did not know. My master repeated the question, and I said again, that I did not understand it; my Master then asked Achilles and Antony [both accused] if they also had an intention of going to their own Country, to which they answered yes, but said that they could not find the way there, but that they would go if the Governor would send them, al-

5. A full transcript of the court case is printed in G. M. Theal, ed., *Records of the Cape Colony* (London: Printed for the Government of the Cape Colony, 1905), vol. 20, 188–341. The excerpts here are from pp. 208–11, 312–16, 318–20, 322–23, and 328–30.

though they were afraid their parents were dead and that they should not be known by their nation. My master was thereupon silent, but my mistress said to my wife, a Hottentot named Betje, that a Newspaper was come from the Cape which she dare not break open, but that a time would be prescribed when it might be opened. When the Newspaper was opened my mistress said that it stood therein that there was another great nation that was unknown; that there were orders come to make the Slaves free, and that if it was not done the other nation would then come to fight against the Farmers. My mistress afterwards further told me that it was also said in the Newspapers that the Slaves must be free, but if the Farmers would not allow it then it would not take place, to which I did not say anything. Another Newspaper came afterwards, when my wife Betje told me that her mistress had said if we would go to the King for the money and bring it to her on the table, that then we might be free. I desired her to keep it quiet, which she did. Some time after, another Newspaper came, when my wife told me that her Mistress had said that the first Englishman who came to make the slaves free should be shot, as well as the slaves; upon which I again advised her to be silent, for that if our master should hear of it he would punish us, and that she must not tell it to anybody else; but I desired her to ask the Mistress why the slaves were to be free, as she spoke so often about it. She told me afterwards that she had asked her, and that her Mistress had said it was because there came too many white children among the black Negroes, and therefore that they must be free. I then desired her again not to tell it to anyone, and not to talk so much about it. Another Newspaper then came, when she informed me that her Mistress had said that the Farmers were too hardly off, and that they were obliged to put up with too much from the Blacks. My wife came to me one day to the land weeping, and on my asking her the reason she said that while she was in the kitchen she had asked for a piece of bread, and that her Master was so angry that he said he would shoot her and all the people in a lump, and leave us to be devoured by the crows and vultures. I again told her to be quiet, for that I could not well believe her although she was my wife, as she could not read or write no more than myself. Once that Barend van der Merwe [a neighbor of Willem van der Merwe] was at my Master's place on his return from Worcester where he had been to fetch the slave Goliath who had made a complaint, I was in the stable preparing forage for the horses. It was dark, so that nobody could see me in the stable. My master called Barend van der Merwe out and came with him into the stable without seeing me, when I heard my master ask him whether he had had his slave flogged, to which he answered no, for that the black people had more to say with the Magistrate of late than the Christians; further saying but he shall nevertheless not remain without a flogging, for when I come home he shall have one. I also heard Barend van der Merwe say to my Master on that occasion I wish that the Secretaries or Commissioners had died rather than that they should have come here, for that since that time they had been obliged to pay so much for the *Opgaaf* [tax receipt] and also for the Slaves. My master gave for answer I wish that the first Commissioner who put his foot on the wharf from on board had broken his neck, for that it was from that time one was obliged to pay so much for the Slaves, which they were not worth. My Master likewise said to Barend van der Merwe that he must keep himself armed in order to shoot the first Commissioner or Englishman who should come to the Country to make the Slaves free, together with the Slaves all in one heap. B. van der Merwe thereupon rode home, some time after which I again heard my master speaking to Barend Lubbe who was at my Master's place, when he asked Lubbe how it was in the upper Country, to which Lubbe answered he did not know, that he not having any slaves had not once inquired about it, and that what the gentlemen did was well done; my master replied that although he had not any Slaves he must nevertheless stand up for his Country, further saying that he would shoot the first Commissioner, Englishman, or magistrate who should come to his place to make the Slaves free, but first the Slaves. Lubbe then asked van der Merwe whether he was not afraid if he fought against the Magistrates that the Slaves would attack him from behind, to which my master answered for that reason the Slaves must be first shot. Subsequently I heard my master speaking for the third time with Hans Lubbe and Jan Bothma, whom having asked how it was in their part of the Country, they answered bad, for the black heathens have more privileges than us, and if the Christians go to the Landdrost to complain of their slaves, the Landdrost will not even look at us, but turns his backside to us, on which my master said the best advice I can give you is that you remain armed and keep your powder and ball together. Lubbe replied the first Gentleman that comes to me I will shoot with all the Slaves in a heap. Again for the fourth time I heard my Master talking with Schalk Lubbe, likewise at my master's place, whom he asked how it was here in the upper Country and if he had heard anything of the Newspaper and about the Slaves, he answered no, on which my master said lately we heard every day of new laws. I have asked for nothing, but I keep myself armed to shoot the first magistrate who comes to my place and the Blacks likewise.

For the fifth time I heard my Master conversing at his place with Johannes Jansen and Jan Verlee [both of whom were killed along with van der Merwe]; the former had made an ox sambok [rawhide whip] which he brought into the house, on which my master desired me to drive in a pig that had got out, which I accordingly did. Standing before the door of the pigsty in order to fasten it, I heard my master say to Jansen, you must promise me something the same as Verlee has done, namely to shoot the magistrate when he comes. Jansen answered that he would do so, for that he would stand up for his mother Country; on that my Master said that he should give orders to all the Slaves, and that if they did not obey them he would supple the sambok on them the next day, for, said my Master, if you punish a slave you must do it that he cannot be known before a magistrate. My Master ordered us to smear the treading floor and that the floor must be well laid the next morning when he got up, on that we made the plan to murder all the farmers; we did not smear the floor because it was evening and was dark; we also told my master this, but he notwithstanding would have that the floor should be smeared against the next morning. My master did not say anything more about it that evening, and we then immediately formed the plan, as I have already stated.

Speech of Fiscal D. Denyssen as public prosecutor at the trial of the Bokkeveld insurgents, March 18, 1825

. . . I shall begin with the head of the gang, namely the slave Galant. When we hear his statement, one will be easily led to suppose that he had been obliged to sigh under a continued chain of successive ill usage, that his child who could scarcely walk, had died in consequence of the repeated floggings he had received from his master, and this for no other reason than because he was displeased with his own wife; that he himself had been hoisted up by the arms and in this manner flogged by his master, that he had been incessantly, maltreated by his Master in the same way, and that he scarcely received sufficient clothes or victuals.

How unfortunate it is for the impartial investigation of the truth that the man, whom all these accusations regard, now lies low and cannot refute them, and that his widow, who is likewise implicated in the charges, although she still lives, cannot possibly appear here without suffering too much under the consequences of the wound so cruelly inflicted on her.

In the meantime if it be considered worth the trouble to stop the mouth of the prisoner Galant of his foul charges, I believe there exist proofs enough which can be adduced with success.

We have already seen in the investigation of these charges, for as far as we could ascertain the truth, that the foulest slander constitutes their principal feature . . . [I]t was not the ill treatment which Galant alleges to have suffered that brought him to the step, as he calls it, of fighting himself free; no, it was his disappointed hopes of freedom that induced him to it. I take his own words. When in his confrontation with the Witness Betje she says that Galant told her before the commencement of the present year he should wait till new year, and that if he were not made free then he would begin to murder, what else did Galant do than to acknowledge the truth of what Betje said, and to name the persons from whom he had heard last year that at the commencement of the new one a general freedom of the slaves should take place.

See there your Worships the ringleader's own confession, see there the pivot upon which the whole machine guided by his hand turned.

Such like false reports appear to have prevailed for some time, it is impossible to say how long they have been in circulation, but they have been communicated not only to the slaves but to the owners of slaves. No wonder then if some credulous and misled masters, imagining that their right of property to their slaves, which next to their lives they considered as most sacred, would be disputed, now and then expressed themselves in language characteristic of the bitterness of their internal feelings; and that the slaves, in whose presence such subjects were imprudently talked of, or who listened at such discourses or found an opportunity of getting a knowledge of them from the children of their masters, should on their part become exasperated against their owners from the opposition to their freedom which they supposed they met with at their hands.

No wonder if in this manner an enmity hitherto unknown arose and was cherished in the minds of slaves against their masters, and that the ruinous distrust of their masters, which so evidently appears in the statements of Galant, gained ground and produced those extremities to which they naturally must lead. It is in this point of view that I consider the statement of Galant with regard to the backwardness of the Masters to communicate to their slaves the news contained in the papers which they received from time to time, or the written orders which they received from the Landdrost respecting their slaves, and also with respect to his fishing out and listening to the discourses which he says were held between his master and others, and again those discourses themselves, which he states to have consisted in threats against his slaves and all others who should undertake to proclaim their freedom.

For why should we doubt of the truth of what Galant says, in this regard, that such discourses have been actually held by weak and credulous slave owners, who supposing that they were at once to be deprived of all their slaves, were driven by such an idea to the very borders of rage and despair.

It is not my task in the present prosecution to endeavour to trace out the authors of such evil and pernicious reports, this belongs to an investigation hereafter to be made by me. It is sufficient in the present instance if such reports did prevail, and if they were the leading cause, as Galant states them to have been, of his undertaking . . .

If we compare the examples of murders committed on slaves by their masters with the number of those committed on and by others, we shall soon see that the slave here is almost as safe under the protection of his Master as the child under that of the father; and especially those slaves who are born in the house, of which description both Abel and Galant are, with respect to whom the natural feeling of affection combines with self interest to make them find true friends and protectors in their masters . . .

Proceeding now to the grounds of my claim relative to the criminality and punishableness of the several points of accusation, I remark that the most heinous species of high treason consists in taking up arms against the state, and that all those are justly considered as guilty of this crime who combine to oppose the existing order of public affairs with violence and arms . . .

In a country where slavery exists, a rising of the slaves to fight themselves free is nothing else than a state of war, and therefore to such a rising the name of war has been given more than once in the Roman history, and justly, for hence states can be, and we know have been, totally overthrown . . .

One of the prisoners themselves, I believe Galant, called his act here in Court making *war.* According to the laws it is sufficient that the plan of such a rising and the junction of the partakers therein, is prepared, to consider the crime of sedition, properly called *Perduellis* (High treason) as consummated . . .

And now, your Worships, as it has fallen to my lot to claim the punishment of death against so many culprits who now stand before you, it only remains for me to see whether I am at liberty to recommend any mitigation to the Court. There exists a right of mitigation that the law gives to the Judge, namely when legal reasons can be adduced why the Judge is allowed to mitigate the ordinary punishment. But among these reasons I certainly do not find that of having been led away by Galant; for all of them have attained that age, and possess that portion of understanding and judgment, which could prevent them having been so seduced.

The eagerness to shake off the yoke of slavery, which had never before led to such excesses here, cannot be considered in any other light than as a desire to withdraw themselves from the laws of the land and from obedience to Government; a desire for blood, war and confusion leading to the most disastrous anarchy, the desire of freedom thus directed is a reason for the aggravation of the punishment. But perhaps it will be said, when so many are to suffer, humanity requires that the example to deter should extend to all, but the punishment to only few. Of this we find instances in history where great crimes have been committed by many persons. But this belongs to the rights reserved to the Sovereign. As Judges I am humbly of opinion that this court cannot go farther than the right with which judicial authority is vested with regard to crimes and punishments. The reasons which might induce His Excellency the Governor to spare any of those who may appear to have been led away are not within the pale of that authority, and they cannot constitute a subject of discussion at the present moment.

I therefore claim and conclude that the first ten prisoners, Galant, Abel, Isaac Rooy, Isaac Thys, Hendrik, Klaas, Achilles, Antony, Valentyn, and Vlak, and the 12th prisoner Pamela shall be declared by your Worships guilty of the crimes with which they are charged in the act of accusation; and the last mentioned prisoner Pamela in particular of not rendering any the least assistance to her Master and Mistress, but on the contrary deserting them, when she slept under the same roof and could have afforded help by warning them of the approaching evil and assisting them in their danger . . . and [recommend] therefore that they shall be condemned by sentence of your Worships to be brought to the usual place of execution here, and being there all with the exception of the 10th prisoner Vlak, delivered over to the executioner, the first eight prisoners, Galant, Abel, Isaac Rooy, Isaac Thys, Hendrik, Klaas, Achilles, and Antony, to be hanged by the necks till they are dead; the 12th prisoner Pamela to be strangled, and the 9th prisoner Valentyn to be tied to a stake and severely scourged with rods on the bare back, then branded, and thereupon confined to labour on the public works here for such term as this Worshipful Court shall deem requisite, that the bodies of the first six prisoners shall be afterwards taken down from the gallows and their heads separated therefrom with an axe at the public place of execution, and then thrown into sacks in order to be conveyed to Bokkeveld and there exposed to public view on separate poles to be erected on the most conspicuous places near the road, with a board over each, on which shall be painted in legible letters *The punishment of Rebels;* thus to remain till consumed by time and the birds of the air; and the 10th prisoner Vlak, after having witnessed the execution, to be severely flogged in the town prison by the black constables. . . .

29 • A Muslim explains the morality and practices of slavery (1890s)

Even as the Atlantic slave trade continued in the nineteenth century, though at a lower level than during the previous century, the use of slaves within Africa expanded. Many of those used as slaves were war captives and criminals who once would have been exported to the Americas but now were used for labor within Africa. There was a growing need for such labor, especially with the expansion of agricultural production to meet new European demands. As the export of slaves from the West Coast of Africa to the Americas declined in the face of increasing British pressure and larger naval squadrons, that from Central Africa to the East Coast and beyond grew. Arab spice plantations on the islands of Zanzibar and Pemba needed huge numbers of workers to meet the market demands of Europe. The French established plantations in the Indian Ocean to replace those that they had lost to slave revolts and British raids in the Caribbean. In addition, Muslim communities in Egypt, the Sudan, and the Arabian peninsula continued to import slaves. Between 1801 and 1896 more than a million and a half Africans were exported to communities ringing the Indian Ocean (Arabia, Iran, India, Zanzibar, and Pemba), as well as around the coast of southern Africa to Brazil. Many of these slaves lived in Muslim societies, and the rulers of these communities found it necessary to explain to European colonial officials why they considered slavery necessary and not the evil depicted by abolitionists.

This particular interview was recorded during the 1890s. A German linguist, Carl Velten, asked Swahili-speaking Africans living near the town of Bagamoyo in German East Africa (present-day Tanzania) to write down accounts of their traditions and customs. This they did in Arabic script, which Velten translated into German. Velten's main informant was Bwana Mtoro Mwinyi Bakari, a Muslim who traveled to Germany with Velten and taught Arabic in Berlin. While in

FIGURE 7 Although Europeans had traded in slaves from Africa since the mid-1400s, it was the Arab trade in African slaves in the mid-nineteenth century, here illustrated by an 1861 drawing from David Livingstone's accounts, that fueled popular demands for European conquest of Africa. Conquest, it was argued, would enable Europeans to end the trade in slaves that was represented in the drawings of Livingstone and others as an indigenous African and Arab practice and not as one in which Europeans still engaged despite much written evidence to the contrary. David Livingstone and Charles Livingstone, *Narrative of an Expedition to the Zambesi and Its Tributaries*, 1866.

Europe Bwana Mtoro married a German woman, but because of opposition from German settlers, was unable to live with her when he returned to Tanzania with his bride. Bwana Mtoro and his wife both returned to Germany, where they were able to spend the rest of their lives living openly as man and wife.[6]

Of Slavery: The Origin of Slaves

The origin is that a man is struck by some disaster such as war between one country and another. Those who are taken prisoner in war are not killed, but roped and taken to the town and told to remain as slaves. They do so, and they marry among themselves, and their offspring are slaves too. Or slavery may arise from a debt of blood money. If somebody has killed another and his family is poor and he has no money, he's liable for blood money; but if he cannot pay, he is taken and sold, or he goes as a slave to the creditor. If he has killed a freeman, the blood money is a large sum, and if he has a brother or an uncle, he also may accompany him into slavery. Or if a sorcerer has killed somebody, and known to be a sorcerer, he is killed, or he may go as a slave to the place where the killing took place. Or if an adulterer has lain with another's wife, he has to pay compensation. If he cannot, he becomes a slave. Compensa-

6. J. W. T. Allen, ed., *The Customs of the Swahili People: The Desturi za Waswahili of Mtoro bin Mwinyi Bakari and Other Swahili Persons* (Berkeley: University of California Press, 1981), 169–77.

tion for adultery used to be paid inland and on the coast, even among the Swahili. Or in time of famine people would sell themselves to each other. Or a person may pledge a child or a brother-in-law, and when he has not the money to redeem him, he becomes a slave. A man cannot pledge or sell his wife, even in a severe famine. If he cannot support her he will divorce her.

To return to consideration of the inland country: prisoners of war, pawns, and persons taken in adultery whose families cannot redeem them become slaves. Arab and other slave traders go inland and buy them and bring them to the coast and sell them to others. This is the origin of slavery. The purchaser of those brought to the coast must lose watch on them or they will run away, and some on arrival at the coast claim to be freemen.

In the time of Sayyid Barghash there was a famine, and the Zaramo sold and pawned each other. When the Zanzibar Arabs heard that slaves were easily obtained on the coast, they came to buy Zaramo slaves; but when they went to sleep at night, the Zaramo ran away and by morning was back at home. Once he was there it was hard to recover him. Those who were shipped to Zanzibar stayed for a month and then claimed not to be slaves but freemen and the courts were full complaints. When Sayyid Barghash found out that the Arabs were going to the coast to buy Zaramo, he rebuked them, saying, "Anybody who goes to the coast to buy Zaramo is throwing his money into the sea, and in addition I shall give him six months in fetters." The reason for this was that they were not being bought; when people were going out of the town into the country, and they saw Zaramo and children, they would seize them, gagging them so that they could not cry out, and bring them into the town to sell to the traders.

Many of the Arabs who traveled inland to make war on the pagan tribes enslaved those whom they made prisoner. Or a pagan would go to an Arab and offer his services. The Arab would agree, and if he had any family, they would come too. Then he made them slaves. That is why some of the inland or Manierna slaves give a lot of trouble on the coast, saying, "This Arab did not buy me. I took service with him, and now he wants to make a slave of me."

Types of Slaves

Mzalia is one whose mother came from inland. On arrival she was married to another slave and had a child. He is called mzalia. There are two sorts of mzalia, first-generation mzalia, second-generation mzalia, et cetera, until the seventh generation. The meaning of the seventh generation is that his mother was born in the town and his father likewise. Such a person's status is that of a freeman, he is simply said to be of slave origin.

Then there are raw slaves. Raw means that he has just arrived on the coast and does not know the language or customs, nor how to wash nor how to cook. He is called a raw slave, and if he is sold his price is smaller than that of a trained slave. The mzalia was not often sold in the past, unless he had bad manners and was rude to freemen. A freeman would marry a mzalia, for they became part of the family. Children born to a mzalia by a freeman are not slaves.

The Work of Raw Slaves

On purchase they were given new clothes and bought a hoe and sent to the fields. There there were an overseer and a headman. When the master came to the field, he called the overseer and the headman and said to them, "I have brought you a recruit." They said, "Good, we see him."

In the morning the overseer and the headman showed him where to dig, and his plot was marked out for him. He was given a task, that is, a section in which he must dig cassava and plant vegetables and beans. The master did not have to give him the yield of this plot unless he wished to do so. If he grew rice or sorghum, he gave him a little rice as pepeta or sorghum as msima out of kindness.

Some slaves have three days and some two. They, work in the fields from early morning until eleven o'clock, when they return to the houses. They go out again in the afternoon until five, when they knock off.

If a slave is unwell, he does not go to work. He tells the master that such a slave is unwell. If the illness is serious, the master treats him until he recovers. If he dies, he provides the winding sheet and tells the others to bury him.

Songs of Slaves after Work:

They sing:

> Overseer, your work is done,
> Give us something to straighten our backs.

or:

> If you go to Malindi, kanzu and vest,
> If you get any money, let it roll,
> Or Msengesi will ruin you.

or:

> Sir, I am not well, send me to the field to dig wild
>   jasmine and pomegranate.
> This is not smallpox but chicken pox.

or:

> The silver dollar never tells a lie.
> Though you put it in the mud
> Your heart rejoices and you have no bitterness.

The Work of Mzalia

The work of the mzalia is to serve in the house, to wash vessels and plates or clothes or to be taught to cook, to plait mats, to sweep the house, to go to the well to draw water, to go to the shop to buy rice or meat; when food is ready, to dish it up for the master, to hold the basin for him to wash his hands, sometimes to wash his feet, and to oil him; but only if his wife approves. If the wife wants to go into the country or to a mourning or a wedding, she accompanies her, and if she has an umbrella, she carries it for her.

A male mzalia travels with his master to tend him if he is unwell, to wash his clothes when they are dirty, to shop for him, and to do any other service that he wants. He may be sent into the yard to learn to sew a kanzu or to embroider clothes or caps, or to be taught carpentry, to make carved doors, or to build stone or timber houses. When he knows these things he retains his own profits, and if he is a good mzalia he remembers his master and gives part to him.

How Slave and Master Should Behave

A slave should obey his master; if he is told to do something, he should do it. If he is called, he should come at once to hear his orders. He should not answer his master back. If he sees his master carrying something, he should take it from him. If he goes into his master's room, he should take off his cap. When he is with his master, he should not go in front, and if they go where there are stools, he should not take one. Every morning and evening he should wait on his master to do anything required. When a slave greets his master, he does not offer his hand, even when they are traveling, nor does he ever enter his master's room without speaking. A slave must eat any food that the gentry are eating; but he does not eat with them. A mzalia eats with his master.

Of Slaves in the Past

In the past slaves were given no consideration by freemen on the coast. A slave was known by his dress, for never in his life did he wear a cap, whether a jumbe lived or died. He never wore sandals nor a kanzu long enough to cover his legs. Nor did a gentleman address him by name; he said, "You." He did not protect himself from the rain with an umbrella; although they did cover themselves in the rain with umbrellas made of doum palm. Nor did he ever in the house wear clogs. At parties they sat separately, not with the gentry, as the town crier said:

> The news horn,
> Its sound means that all is well.
> The horn of the jumbe and of the forty,
> Of the officers and the locally born slaves,
> Of gentlemen and their sons,
> Of the mzalia and of slaves.

After this introduction the required announcement was made. Female slaves accompanying free women do not wear a veil or a headcloth.

Nor does a slave sit on a cane chair nor have one in his house. If he does so, people say, "This slave thinks himself as good as us. He has cane chairs in his house."

Slaves began to give themselves airs some fifteen years ago. There was a jumbe who had many slaves. One day he went to the shop and bought kangas and kayas for his slave girls to wear. They were astonished, and the other jumbes heard that jumbe Kisoka had given kayas to his slaves. They went to ask him about it, and he said, "I want to please myself and my slaves, as anyone may do if he likes." All the jumbes were angry, and they wanted to oppose him; but others said, "That will not do; he has a lot of supporters, he is well born, and he has many relations in the town, but the jumbes hated him.

A year later there was in the quarter of Gongoni a jumbe called Gungurugwa, who said, "I am going to give my slaves kayas and umbrellas." The young citizens made no objection, and he put his domestic slaves into kayas, and they went around the town carrying umbrellas. The other jumbes were angry and said, "These jumbes are breaking the traditions and doing things that our ancestors never did. There will be trouble in the town. There will be a revolution if slaves are treated differently every month. Next time a jumbe dies, half the place will uncover in respect, and half will keep their caps on." There was a lot of disagreement, and to this day they do not uncover on the death of a Jumbe. Very few do so because they do not think it necessary. And the slaves no longer do the work that they used to do. They do as they like, and if they do not like it they do not do it. If one is disobedient, his master cannot correct him. He takes him to court and says, "This slave is disobedient and will not work in the house." The government punishes him. That is the difference between slaves now and in the past.

Marriage of Slaves

In the past, if a slave wanted a wife, he asked his master's permission to marry her. The master asked if they were agreed, and he said that they were. Then he told the slave to give him a dollar for his turban. A raw slave paid a dollar for the turban, which he gave to his master, and the bride-price was five dollars. After paying for the turban in accordance with old custom, they did not go to the teacher for the marriage, but the master said, "I marry you to your fellow slave so-and-so," and he went at once into his wife's house.

Now they go to the teacher to be married in accordance with custom. There are no wedding feast, no celebration, no invitations, and no sewing mattresses and pillows. These customs are not followed.

A freed slave does not inform his master of his proposal to a fellow slave. He finds the woman that he wants, and when they have agreed, he goes to his master to tell him that he wishes to get married, because to do so is respectful. The master says, "Very well, it is for you to decide."

On the day of the wedding the master comes to preside over the feast, for he is the father. If the freed slave can afford it, he has a celebration like a freeman with dancing and many invitations. The bride-price is ten to twenty dollars, and a turban of five dollars is given to the bride's father or brother or, if she has neither, to her owner. A freed slave, or, as the Swahili say, a slave of God, marries another slave of God. A freed domestic slave can marry a free woman, but a raw slave cannot.

Children both of whose parents are slaves are slaves. If a freeman marries a slave woman, their child is a slave; but if a free woman marries a slave man, their child is not a slave, because free birth is matrilineal.

Of Suria

A suria is when a man buys a slave girl and introduces her into his house, and she learns cooking and all domestic customs. When she is of age, her master says to her, "You are my suria, and you may not go outside. If you want anything, tell others to buy it for you." When her fellows realize that the master has spoken so, they give her respect. She is bought a bed and a mat and pillows and is given her own room like a wife. If the master is married, he spends three nights with his wife and one with his suria. If he is not married, the suria is his

Of Manumission

If a man has many slaves, he may see one under his authority and call him, saying, "Mabruk" or "Majuma, you shall have a deed of manumission and be no longer a slave." Or if he has but one slave who has been with him for many years, he may manumit him. If he has a little field, he gives it to him and makes him his brother or his son. Such deeds are usually written when a man is growing old and wants to do a good action, whether he has children or not. He says, "I wish to make slave so-and-so a slave of God, and when I die, let her be as your sister. Do not cast her off." Then a deed is written and given to her, and she is free. One with such a deed cannot be sold or used as security.

The Deed of Manumission

If a man wants to give his slave a deed of manumission, he writes, "I, A, son of B, hereby declare that I set so-and-so free before God, a free person. None may dispute this while I am alive or after my death. Any person altering what I have written in this deed is answerable to God for altering it. I have made him free. Any person making him a slave contrary to this deed must answer to God."

Such was the bond; but nowadays they go to the court, and the deed is drawn there and stamped with the seal of the central government.

30 • Tippu Tip, the "leopard" (1890s)

The most renowned slave trader in mid-nineteenth-century Africa was Sheikh Hamed bin Muhammed el Murjebi, known by Europeans as Tippu Tip, who with a base in Zanzibar roamed far into central Africa in search of ivory and slaves. Sheikh Hamed established his own state in the interior of Africa, where he built roads, laid out plantations, collected taxes, and attempted to impose a monopoly on the sale of ivory. After reaching the height of his power in the 1870s, he lost out to European competitors in the 1880s and retired to the East African coast still a rich man in the 1890s. In his autobiography, written while living in retirement in Zanzibar, Sheikh Hamed describes how he became a trader in ivory and slaves.[7]

1. When I was twelve, I started to go on local trips. I traded in gum-copal, together with my brother Muhammad bin Masud el Wardi and my uncle Bushir bin Habib, and Abdallah bin Habib el Wardijan. I only took small loads, as I was merely a youth. My brother and my uncles carried rather more. This trade we carried on for a year.

2. When I was eighteen, my father, Muhammed bin Juma went on a journey; he and his kinsmen decided to go to Ugangi. He brought me the news, saying, "I have decided to go on a trip to Ugangi, come, let us go!" I went with him and we arrived at Ugangi. After the Ugangi trip I came to Zanzibar. Then my father decided to go to Unyamwezi country, to Tabora. In

7. W. H. Whitely, *Maisha ya Hamed bin Muhammad el Murjebi: Yanni Tippu Tip, kwa Maneno yake Mwenyewe* (Kampala: East African Literature Bureau, 1966), 9, 11, 13, 15.

wife. Some people prefer a suria to a wife, because they say that a suria is a piece of luggag meaning that if you travel you take your suria with you; but a wife, first you have to persuad her, and then you have to consult her parents before you take her on a Journey. That is wh they prefer a suria. Others prefer a wife, because when they have a child, he can say, "My fa ther is so-and-so and my grandfather so-and-so, and my mother is so-and-so and her fathe so-and-so," because he has good blood on both sides. That is the reason for preferring a wif But the son of a suria is a freeman and may not be sold nor called a slave, although he has n rank through his mother.

Of Runaway Slaves

If a slave runs away, if you bought him in the town, you go to the vendor and say, "M slave has run away, please bring him to me if you see him." Or you go to the river or th seashore and say to the ferrymen, "My slave has run away; his description is like this—he i wearing such clothes, his tribe is Ganda or Sukuma, he is a raw slave, short and dark. If yo find him trying to cross, stop him, catch him, and bring him to me. I live at Bagamoyo near so and-so, and my name is." Then he goes back to the town.

If the slave comes to the river and the ferrymen see him, they ask him what he wants, an he does not know what to say, so they catch him and take him to the man's house in the town and he must pay a recovery fee of one dollar. In the old days the slave would be locked up i the house in a room by himself for two or three days. Then he was promised on oath that if h ran away again he should die.

Of Charms to Recover Slaves

If a man ran away, a coil rope was bought and Ya sini was recited over seven knots in i by the teacher. It was given to the owner of the runaway to take home. There he stood in th doorway and called his slave by name seven times. Then the rope was hung over the door, and if he was lucky the slave came back or was caught and brought back by others.

Of Giving a Slave as Security

Any debtor can send his slave as security, whether the slave likes it or not, if security is required of the master. Such a slave is allowed one day to go and visit his master and to return on the next day. A married slave can be used as security and his wife too, and they have to do the same work as they did for their master. If they are idle, he can send them back and demand his money.

Of Borrowing by Slaves

A slave cannot incur a debt without his master's authority. If a merchant advances money to a slave, he knows that if the slave takes the money and goes inland or dies or runs away and does not return to the coast, his money has fallen into the sea. He cannot go to the master to claim it. If it is a written agreement and he wants to borrow, he may do so by himself if he is in need of money; because if he loses it, he alone, and not his master, is liable.

FIGURE 8 Tippu Tip, an Arab slave trader, established his own state in East Africa in the 1860s and 1870s before being pushed out by European competitors in the 1880s and retiring to Zanzibar. He wrote an autobiography that was later translated into English. Henry M. Stanley, *In Darkest Africa, Or, the Quest, Rescue, and Retreat of Emin, Governor of Equatoria,* 1890.

Tabora he was comparable to a Chief. He had married from childhood the daughter of Chief Fundi Kira, one Karunde, and Karunde's mother was Fundi Kira's first and chief wife. And the chief wife at that time in Unyamwezi held power comparable with the Chief, so that my father was greatly respected. Whatever he wanted in and around Tabora he got, and when he went down to the coast he took his wife Karunde. He was given much ivory from the wealth of Chief Fundi Kira. He was also given other goods, was my father, and at this time he was as though Chief in the Nyamwezi manner, having much property and many followers, perhaps even as much as the Chiefs of Uganda and Karagwe.

3. At the time when I went to Tabora, I was stricken with smallpox en route, and when I reached Unyanyambe, Tabora, we stayed two months. My father decided to go on to Ujiji but when we arrived the price of ivory was rather high. Our fellow Arabs with whom we were travelling decided to go on to Urua, while my father preferred to return to Tabora, giving his property to a fellow from the Mrima coast at Mbwamaji, by name Mwinyi Bakari bin Mustafa. He said, "You go with him, travel together." At this time wealth at Urua was simply reckoned in beads and bangles, they didn't want cloth. And I replied, "I can't go on to Urua, with our property in the possession of a man from the Mrima coast and I following along with him. Better that I return with you." My father answered, "I wouldn't have given the stuff to the man had you not been a youth who was unversed in the practice of the area. That's why I gave it to him. But if you are able yourself to take the goods, so much the better." I replied, "Yes, try; if I fail then give it to someone else next trip." He left the goods with me and left to return to Tabora.

4. As for us, we crossed Lake Tanganyika, and at that time there were no proper boats, only dug-outs. There were about twenty of us who made the trip. We arrived at Urua at Mrongo Tambwe's place. We found that trade was moderate, neither good nor bad. We bought ivory; large tusks were expensive while the small were extremely cheap. Everyone was buying the large tusks, so I decided to go for the small, and collected a large number. At that time the price of the large tusks was high; people wanted the large ones because on the coast they fetched a higher price, the Babu "Ulaya" than did the Babu "Kutch." When we had finished trading we returned . . .

11. When I arrived in Zanzibar I was lucky. It was the small tusks which were fetching a good price and at the time a frasila (35 lbs.) fetched between 50–55 dollars (if this were the Maria Theresa dollar, value 3–4/-) and the tax was 9 dollars per frasila. So I sold the ivory and took back to my father the goods he had ordered. I did not go back again to Tabora but carried on my own business with my brother, Mohammed bin Masud el Wardi.

When my father and I had made our trip, he had gone to Ngao and Nyasa. Returning thence he went to Benadir. As for me, I had been to Mahenge to the Mafiti. I borrowed goods in Zanzibar about 1000 dollar's worth and went to Uhehe to Mtengera's.

There I had had to take a major decision, borrowed between 4000–7000 dollars and went on to Urori. There I found trade bad and so went on to Fipa, Nyamwanga, Ruemba and Urungu where I got a great quantity of ivory. Returning from this trip to Ruemba I saw my brother in Zanzibar for the first time in twelve years. Formerly, when I had arrived in Zanzibar, he had been in Ngao or Benadir; when he had been in Zanzibar I had been up-country; now when I returned from Ruemba he had just come from Benadir and that was when we met).

For my part, I had made tremendous profits, but he had resolved to have a change from sea-trips and so we decided to go up-country together . . .

13. I took 700 porters and left Zanzibar with the goods and went to Mbwamaji. We loaded (made into loads) the goods and when everything was ready the crowd of porters appeared and took off their loads. We started the journey and reached Mbezi, where we stayed seven days. Then we went off again and reached Mkamba. By this time the porters had eaten the maize and were carrying their loads on an empty stomach, so when we arrived at Mkamba we bought plenty of rice to give them adequate rations. For between there and Lufiyi (Rufiji) there was no likelihood of getting food and the porters were many. Each man was given food for six days because there was plenty available.

14. On the day we decided to leave, the porters were scattered throughout the many villages where they had set down their loads; a hundred men in one, sixty in another; they had dispersed.

In the morning we sounded the departure drum. There was no response. We sent out men to go and hurry them up but they encountered no one. All had deserted. When they brought me this news, I went myself to look in the villages where they had set down their loads. I saw no one. I lost my temper and brought the news to my brother and told him to bring me my guns, travelling clothes and a bed-roll and servants. Then I went back through the districts of Mbezi and Ndengereko. Within a few hours I had a force of eighty guns. I slept on the road and on the second day arrived in the porters' villages, but they had not yet arrived. I seized their elders and kinsmen, about 200 of them, and bound them up. Thereupon they beat their drums and met together, the whole lot of them. When they saw that we were ready they came back. I went on ahead to Ndengereko and then to Mbezi, seizing a large number of people. I went into every part of Zaramu country and in the space of five days had seized 800 men. They called me Kingugwa—the "leopard"—because the leopard attacks indiscriminately, here and there. I yoked the whole lot of them together and went back with them to Mkamba.

31 • Chisi Ndjurisiye Sichyajunga, slave (1890s)

Whatever the justifications given by slaveholders and supporters of the trade in slaves, the lives of those subjected to this coercive institution remained hard throughout the century. Indeed, for much of Africa, slavery was not denied a legal status until late in the nineteenth century or early in the twentieth. It remained legal in Nigeria until 1901; in French West Africa until 1903; in Kenya until 1907; in Angola until 1910; in Tanganyika until 1922; in Sierra Leone, supposed home of freed slaves, until 1928; and in Ethiopia (always proud of not having been conquered by Europeans in the nineteenth century) until 1937. Chisi Ndjurisiye Sichyajunga, born around 1870 in Central Africa, was one such person who experienced slavery well into the colonial era in Africa. Her story was recorded in the second decade of the twentieth century and likely was already retold frequently and well rehearsed by that time.[8]

Childhood

My home was in the Biza country, for we are Chawa. I do not know my family, for enemies carried me off when I was still a child. The name of my father was Sichyajunga, and the name of my mother was Ntundu.

I can just remember the death of my mother. I was a very little child and sat beside her before the door of our hut. My mother fed the baby with gruel while I held its hands. Suddenly a lion sprang upon us, seized my mother and tore her with its teeth, and scratched my leg with its claws. People drove off the lion and rescued my mother, but she died of her wounds. Near our home there were many lions. The lion which killed my mother had also killed two of my mother's sisters, my aunts.

After my mother's death we were alone with my father, who looked after us. My grandmother cared for the baby.

My older sister, Nsigwa, lived with her husband in another village. She sent a messenger to my father who said, "Your daughter wishes you to know that she is with child." When my father heard this he called my brother and told him to go and see how my sister was. Then I began to cry and said, "Father, let me go, too." But my father replied, "No, you cannot walk so far. You must stay here. Your brother shall go alone." I screamed, "I will go with him." At last my father said, "Go, if you must."

8. Marcia Wright, *Strategies of Slaves and Women: Life-stories from East/Central Africa* (New York: Lilian Barber, 1993), 81–85.

My brother and I set out. Part of the way he carried me, part of the way I walked. When we came to the village where my sister lived we found it was as the messenger had said. My brother did not spend the night there, but set out for home the same day, and I stayed with my sister.

Stolen from Home

Our land lies near the borders of the Bemba country, and the Bemba are our enemies. They are always making war on our land. That very night, as dawn was breaking while I lay asleep with my sister in her hut, the Bemba attacked the village.

There had been a beer drink the day before, so that everyone was drunk. The enemy killed all the men; not one escaped. Then they cut off their heads, put them in baskets, and carried them off to their own land to show to their chief.

Two of the enemy burst into our hut, seized my sister and me, and set out with us for luBemba. We spent the night on the way, and during the night my sister gave birth to twins, both girls.

The next morning my sister could not walk. The man who had taken her said to his companion, "What shall I do now?" His companion replied, "You dare not kill her, for the chief has forbidden the killing of women. If you are going to leave her behind, leave her alive." But the man said, "No, I will not leave her behind, for I have no other wife at home. I will look after her, and when she is better she will be my wife. Let the girl stay behind with me, too, so that she can look after her sister, and later I will give her back to you." The other agreed to this and went on alone, leaving me with my sister. We camped in that place for one more night.

The next day at dawn the man said to my sister, "Come along. We shall travel slowly and I will care for you." My sister set out, carrying one of the children, while the man carried the other. We traveled very slowly and spent ten nights on the way. At last we reached luBemba with both children safe and well.

In luBemba the chief said to my captor, "This is the first person you have taken in a raid, so she belongs to me, for it is the custom that the first person taken belongs to the chief." So it came to pass that my sister stayed in the hut of the man who had stolen her and became his wife, but that I was given to the chief.

Slavery

I stayed in luBemba for three years until I was ten or eleven years old. I must have been seven or eight years of age when I was stolen by the enemy. Then four coast people, an Arab and three black men, came to luBemba. After the chief had spoken with them in secret he brought them to the hut where I was and said, "Chisi, these men are my relations. You are to go home with them and stay with them. You shall return with me after a time when I go to visit them." Then he gave me meat and fish saying, "Eat this while you are with my relations."

I wept bitterly, but it was of no avail. The coast people took me to their hut, and there I met four boys and two girls. The coast people put food before me. I would not eat, but screamed and cried. At sunset we started our journey and traveled by night, for the moon was shining. We went toward wiNamwanga and were a long time on the way.

In wiNamwanga the Arab became so ill that he could not travel, and we stayed there for two and a half years.

When the Arab was somewhat better we set out once more and reached the village of Chief Zambi in uSafwa. We stayed there for three days. There the coast people said to one of the girls who was about my age, "You are to stay here with our relations until we come back and fetch you." But we found ivory in the hut and exclaimed, "Where did that come from? That was not here before! You have sold your sister for ivory!"

We left Zambi and traveled toward Intente. When we got there it was raining heavily and we were numb with cold. The coast people sat down and ate some honey. They said to my companion and me, "Go on, we shall catch up with you." The boys stayed with the men.

Escape

As we walked on, the other girl, who was bigger than I, said, "Child, let us run away and hide in the tall grass, for these coast people will kill us. One of us has already been left behind in Zambi. She has been sold for the ivory they are carrying. They will sell us, too. Come along, let us hide in the grass and later we will make our way home." I answered, "It is all very well for you, my friend, for you are big and can run faster than I. You will go ahead and leave me behind, for I am small and very cold." But she said, "No, I promise not to leave you. Come on, let us be off."

She put down the Arab's cooking pot which she carried and we plunged into the high grass and fled. My companion ran quickly and I soon fell behind, so I turned aside and went down to the stream and hid in a cave in the bank. I heard my companion call, "Hurry up, child, come to me." But I did not want to follow her, and stayed in the cave.

The coast people came along the road and found the cooking pot. They followed our tracks through the grass, but they lost mine where I had turned aside to the stream. They followed the other girl, and I have never heard whether they caught her or not.

The water began to rise in the cave where I was hidden, for much rain had fallen that day. I crawled out and looked around. Nearby were fields of the Safwa of Itende. I went toward the fields and came on some boys who had been weeding and taken shelter, from the rain. I stood still and thought, The Safwa will find me in their fields and will call out, "Thief, you are stealing our maize!" So I went on toward a hut with smoke rising from it. I was shivering with cold and thought, "I will go to that hut and there I shall die."

Marriage

I went up to the hut, which belonged to Ndeye. He was not there but his sister was in the hut. She looked up and said in Safwa, "Where do you come from?" But I did not understand Safwa[, and] the woman could not speak Biza. I tried to explain with signs [that] another girl and I had run away from the coast people, but I did not know where she was. Then the woman signaled come to the fire, and I drew near and warmed myself.

Ndeye's wife came in and found me there and asked, "Where does this girl come from?" Ndeye's sister answered, "Just think, she was traveling with the coast people and she had run away from them with another girl. Where the other is I know not. This one came into the hut suddenly."

The wife of Ndeye went to the chief and said, "A girl has come to my hut. She says she was traveling with the coast people and ran away from them." When the chief heard this he said, "Do not let her leave the hut. Keep her hidden there until Ndeye comes back."

When Ndeye came back and heard the whole story, he said, "It is well; my ancestors have sent this girl to my hut." So I stayed in the hut of Ndeye.

After a year the chief sent for Ndeye and said to him, "Bring the girl to me. I want to see her." Ndeye led me before the chief, who said, "Look after the girl as though she were your own child. Let men woo her, and he who wants her must work for her." But Ndeye replied, "Not so, O Chief, if I keep this girl she shall be my wife." So I stayed in the hut of Ndeye and grew up there. After four years, when I was fully grown, I became the wife of Ndeye and bore him a son, Mbindijeriye.

PART II

The Conquest of Africa (1809–1905)

INTRODUCTION

During the course of the nineteenth century, Europeans gradually developed a new relationship with the African continent, replacing the buying and selling of people with the appropriation of their labor and their lands. The movement from an export trade in slaves to European conquest was not a quick and straightforward process, nor was it one foreordained by the nature of the relationship that existed between the West and Africa at the beginning of the nineteenth century. But it was a process that in fundamental ways grew out of four hundred years of the Atlantic slave trade.

At the end of the eighteenth century and the beginning of the nineteenth, the slave trade was on the decline, and it was becoming evident to some European businessmen that new export products needed to be identified if they were to retain their commercial bases in Africa. People such as Mungo Park, funded by businessmen who wanted to find out about and tap into the trading networks of the interior, were sent to explore that region and to seek certain types of knowledge (commercial above all). The prospects did not look particularly good. Park favored continuing with the trade in slaves since he thought not enough money could be made from other products he found in West Africa to support an expanded European commercial presence. In South Africa, there was similar support for the continuance of slavery as absolutely necessary for the economic survival of the Cape Colony—and if not slavery, then certainly other forms of servile labor. Because of such testimony, in the early 1800s European powers such as Britain and France questioned the continued presence of their nationals in Africa.

Nevertheless, European interest in Africa continued to grow because of the emerging demand for African products that were useful in Europe's burgeoning factories. Palm, ground nut, and peanut oils found a use as lubricants, indigo was useful in dyes, and ivory became the primary component of billiard balls and piano keys for the new middle classes on the European and the American sides of the Atlantic. Europeans sought to acquire direct access to these goods by entering into treaty arrangements with African kings, though the terms of these treaties were often disputed when the resulting written form was explained to those Africans who had signed them and who claimed that their oral transactions had been misrepresented. But then, Europeans often believed that, since Africans were "barbarians," they did not have to be treated with as one would treat with a "civilized" person. The result was a considerable expansion not only in these export items but also in the use of slave labor by African producers on newly established plantations in collecting and transporting items such as ivory, and a further shift (already evident during the slave trade) away from food production.

Still, until the latter half of the nineteenth century Europeans did not have the ability to extend their physical presence into the interior of Africa. Often they relied on missionaries, the only group who really supported the continuance of a European presence in Africa. Most missionaries were members of the newly emergent middle class that developed as a result of the Industrial Revolution, who argued to their peers at home and to potential converts in Africa about the importance of a missionary presence for Christianizing and "civilizing" the otherwise "barbarous" and "warlike" people of the continent. They clearly had a considerable impact on labor legislation in South Africa, but in part because of their complaints about the settlers' treatment of the indigenous people, the area of white settlement expanded significantly, eventually reaching well beyond the boundaries envisaged by a British government concerned about the costs of foreign rule.

New medical and technological developments at midcentury, however, made the reliance on missionary initiative less important. Quinine proved a very effective prophylactic against malaria, and European death rates in the West African interior and on the coast in the 1850s and after dropped to levels that were only two to three times those experienced in Europe rather than a hundred times higher—or more, as in the 1840s and earlier. Steam-powered iron ships could be sailed against the current, thereby providing European merchants with direct access to the river networks of the interior, as well as the ability to use gunboats to extend the reach of their cannon. Perhaps most significant of all was the immense development of European firepower from the mid-nineteenth century onward, especially of rifled barrels and repeating mechanisms, which for the first time gave Europeans a huge military advantage over their opponents. This advantage was cemented by the development of early machine guns, especially the Maxim gun.

Still, at midcentury the European presence was a scattered, local phenomenon, and the likelihood of European colonization on a continental scale seemed remote. In South Africa, the Dutch-speaking settlers had established their own independent republics situated between African states, but theirs were essentially semisubsistence economies that utilized disguised forms of slave labor and were not likely to expand much. In West Africa the British and the French were interested in increasing their economic spheres of influence, especially up the rivers— such as the Senegal, Gambia, and Niger—through which large numbers of now illegal slaves were still exported. However, missionary-educated Africans, some who had never left Africa, and others who had returned from the Americas, like Samuel Crowther, Africanus Horton, and Edward Blyden, could still reasonably envisage a future Africa learning from Europe and other parts of the world but remaining politically autonomous.

That all changed in the 1870s. The discovery of a vast new store of diamonds in South Africa excited Europeans' expectations of finding new wealth deep within the interior of the continent. Images of Africa as backward and difficult were overcome by visions of vast fortune. Yet, as the South African diamond industry demonstrated, fortune could be ephemeral, and only the securing of large supplies of cheap labor within Africa would make it possible for Europeans to exploit fully the potential wealth of their anticipated empires. Using an imperial rhetoric that denounced Africans for being savage and announced a European commitment to ridding Africa of slavery, empire boosters—most of them business speculators—scrambled in the 1870s and 1880s to seize as large a share of Africa as they could. They organized themselves into companies chartered by their respective national states to have a supposed monopoly of trade in the territories that they sought to acquire. The resulting competition was often self-defeating. As a consequence, in 1884–85 the European powers (with participation by the United States), organized under the aegis of Otto von Bismarck, chancellor of the German Empire, a conference to allocate shares of territory in Africa. Significantly, the prime areas of concern were the river hinterlands that had been so important during the slave trade, especially those of the Niger and the Congo. The "scramble," already a decade in motion, was now much more carefully organized by a set of rules established in Berlin and with no African presence whatsoever at the negotiating table (despite endless rhetoric in the treaty resulting from the conference about Europe's commitment to ending slavery in Africa). Significantly, the treaty banned any trade in arms to Africa (meaning in practice to Africans since it was accepted that weapons were necessary for Europeans to "pacify" the continent).

The process of conquest was frequently duplicitous and often bloody. In their private writings and often in their public, the imperialists were not loath to admit that prospects of fortune drove them on and that trickery was often necessary to achieve their goals. Moreover, when trickery did not work, outright slaughter by means of the Maxim gun was always a sure means of success. It was not just a racial conquest, either, for when the control of South African gold was at issue, the British were quite ready to embark on their largest and most costly colonial campaign ever as they fought to destroy the Boer republics at the end of the nineteenth century and the beginning of the twentieth.

Conquest was a lengthy process. Africans did not give in easily in any part of the continent. Nor did initial defeats mean the end of resistance. Indeed, the process of conquest often extended over several decades and produced events and leaders who would long be celebrated for their resistance to European rule.

CHAPTER FIVE

Assessing the Costs and Benefits of European Engagement on the African Continent (1809–38)

32 • The subordination of labor in South Africa (1809)

One of the results of the 1807 British legislation prohibiting the export trade in slaves was a grow-ing shortage of labor within the one European settlement that depended extensively on the use of im-ported workers: the Cape of Good Hope. From the 1650s through to the beginning of the nineteenth century, European farmers at the cape depended entirely on slaves imported from the east coast of Africa, Madagascar, and Southeast Asia to meet their labor needs. In order to meet continued de-mands for workers while also adhering to the metropolitan British government's policy of amelio-rating the conditions of forced labor, in 1809 the cape colonial administration of the Earl of Cale-don introduced legislation requiring that local Khoisan peoples (known pejoratively as "Hottentots") be regulated "in regard to their places of abode and occupations." All male Khoisan were required to carry on their persons a "pass" stating whether they were entitled to live in a cer-tain area of the colony and whether they were employed by a European "master" and had fulfilled the conditions of their employment. Nonfulfillment of the conditions or lack of evidence of employ-ment was regarded as the equivalent of vagrancy and thus punishable by the state. The terms of the 1809 legislation, published in the Cape Governor's Proclamation no. 14, November 1, 1809, by His Excellency Du Pre, Earl of Caledon, were extended in 1812 to apply as well to children and young adults (euphemistically deemed "apprentices").[1]

WHEREAS it appears that the provisions made from time to time, for securing the fulfilling of Contracts of Hire between the Inhabitants of this Colony and Hottentots, are not sufficient for the intended purpose; and, whereas for the benefit of this Colony at large, it is necessary, that not only the Individuals of the Hottentot Nation, in the same manner as the other In-habitants, should be subject to proper regularity in regard to their places of abode and occu-pations, but also that they should find an encouragement for preferring entering the service of the Inhabitants to leading an indolent life, by which they are rendered useless both for themselves and the community at large.

I therefore have thought proper to establish and ordain, and by these Presents do estab-lish and ordain:

1. That all and every Hottentot in the different Districts of this Colony, in the same man-ner as all Inhabitants, shall have a fixed Place of Abode in some one of the Districts, and that

---

1. W. Wilberforce Bird, *State of the Cape of Good Hope in 1822* (London: John Murray, 1828), 244–48.

an entry of the same shall be made in the Office of the Fiscal, or the respective Landdrosts, and that they shall not be allowed to change their place of abode from one District to another, without a Certificate from the Fiscal, or Landdrost of the District from which they remove; which Certificate they shall be bound to exhibit to the Fiscal, or Landdrost of the District where they intend to settle, for the purpose of being entered in their Office; while every Hottentot neglecting this order, shall be considered as a Vagabond, and be treated accordingly.

2. That every Inhabitant who engages a Hottentot in his service for the space of a month, or any longer period, shall be bound with the same to make his appearance before the Fiscal, or Landdrost, or the Field-Cornet of his District, and there enter into, and sign in triplo, a proper written Contract, containing:

(a) The name of the Person who takes into service;
(b) The name of the Person who enters into service;
(c) The terms of the Contract;
(d) The amount of the Wages;
(e) The time of payment; and
(f) Such further Conditions as the Persons contracting shall agree upon....

13. That the Hottentots engaged in the manner prescribed in the 2nd article, shall be bound diligently and honestly to serve their masters during the period of their contract, and to behave with proper submission; on penalty, that in case any founded complaints against their non-complying with their contract be lodged against them, to the fiscal or respective Landdrosts, they shall, by order of the same, be subjected to domestic correction; or, if their misconduct deserves a severer punishment, they shall, upon a summary investigation of the case, by a committee of the court of justice or heemraden, be punished with confiscation of the wages due to them, or part of the same, or a temporary confinement, or a more severe domestic punishment...

15. That no Hottentot shall be taken into service without being provided with a certificate, either of his master, or the fiscal, landdrost, or field-cornet, under whose district he did serve, containing a declaration, that he has duly served out his time, or in case he has not served out his time, that he left the service of his former master with proper consent, or upon due authority ... any one taking into his service a Hottentot not provided with such certificate or discharge, shall forfeit one hundred rds [rix dollars]; one-third for the informer, one-third for the public treasury, and one-third for the magistrate who carries on the prosecution.

16. Lastly, the Hottentots going about the country, either on the service of their masters, or on other lawful business, must be provided with a pass, either of their commanding officer, if in the military service, or the master under whom they serve, or the magistrate in the district, on penalty of being considered and treated as vagabonds....

33 • The trade question in West Africa (1807–12)

The British legislation that abolished the export of slaves made illegal 90 percent of the trade engaged in by the Company of Merchants Trading to Africa, the loose association of merchants that had succeeded the Royal African Company. This issue raised the question of whether Britain should con-

tinue to maintain the series of eleven forts spread along 350 miles of the West African coast that were used as bases by British slavers. On the surface, abandonment seemed to make economic sense. Furthermore, the number of people based in the forts was minuscule, no more than about thirty-five Europeans "with a handful of men, half soldiers, half slaves." However, proponents of abolition argued that by maintaining bases on the West African coast and fostering new forms of trade, Britain could promote "civilization." In this approach, the abolitionists were joined by members of the Company of Merchants, who, rapidly casting off their proslavery views of the past, took up the cause of antislavery in arguing for an expansion of the British presence in West Africa. The first selection below is from a letter by Zachary Macaulay, governor of Sierra Leone from 1793 to 1799 (administered by the St. George's Bay or Sierra Leone Company), to the British secretary of state for war and the colonies. The second is from a letter sent by the Company of Merchants to the British treasury lords.[2]

Zachary Macaulay to Lord Castlereagh, May 8, 1807

The British Settlements in Africa form at present a very loose and disjointed whole, subjected to great diversity of management and pursuing ends which differ widely from each other. Goree is a Military Government immediately under the directions of His Majesty, Sierra Leone is at present governed by the Sierra Leone Company by the authority of a Charter of Justice obtained from the King. Bance Island, a fortified settlement in the same river, is the property of Messrs. John and Alexander Anderson of London, who hold it by virtue of an Act of Parliament, and who have hitherto used it as a slave factory. The forts on the Gold Coast, seven or eight in number, are in the hands of the African Company, who receive annually from Parliament the sums required for their maintenance; and who continue a Company for the sole purpose of managing these forts, which were originally constructed and hitherto been supported for the protection and encouragement of the slave trade.

With a view both to the British interests in Africa, and to the improvement of Africa itself it appears to deserve consideration whether these Establishments, as well as any other which may hereafter be formed in Africa, should not be taken under the immediate government of His Majesty, otherwise it is not likely that any uniform plan of policy can be pursued with respect to that country, nor any liberal and concurrent efforts made to amend the condition of its inhabitants. It was also in that case naturally become a question, whether the different settlements on the coast of Africa should be independent of each other, and subject only to the direct controul of which, the others might be placed. Supposing the latter, which seems the better plan, should be adopted, I should entertain no doubt, for reasons not now necessary to be specified, that Sierra Leone is the best situation for such a Presidency.

But whether the plan of uniting all our African Establishments under the Government of His Majesty is adopted or not, it appears to me that some steps might be taken, at the present moment, which would be attended with advantage both to Africa and Great Britain . . .

It appears to be in the first place desirable that for the course of the next year or two vessels of war should be stationed at different parts of the African coast . . . with a view both of

---

2. G. E. Metcalfe, ed., *Great Britain and Ghana: Documents of Ghana History, 1807–1957* (Legon: Institute of African Studies, University of Ghana, 1964), 4–6, 22–25.

giving effect to the provisions of the Act for Abolishing the Slave Trade, and for other purposes of considerable moment. The Commanders of His Majesty's ships are almost universally regarded with respect and deference by the native chiefs on the coast of Africa. Being recognised as the representatives and accredited agents of His Majesty they naturally possess a very considerable influence among those chiefs.

If such Naval Commanders therefore as may visit the Coast of Africa, were directed to convey to the chiefs to whom they may have an opportunity of communicating favourable views of the principles which have guided the British Government in abolishing the slave trade, and to point out to them the various means within their reach of improving the condition of their country, their representations, I have little doubt, would produce a considerable and very beneficial effect . . .

In particular it seems important to point out to them the advantage which they would derive from cultivating generally the *white* instead of the *red* rice, because in that case a vent might be easily obtained for their surplus produce of that article, either in Great Britain or the West Indies, the former species being a marketable article, while the other, though equally useful as food, would not find a sale out of Africa.

The other articles of exportable produce, the cultivation of which seems to me the best adapted to the present state of Africa are indigo, cotton and coffee, and these might be recommended to the attention of the chiefs . . .

I have already expressed an opinion that the Settlement of Sierra Leone is better calculated than any other for the presidency of the African Coast. Its local advantages are great when compared either with Goree, or Cape Coast Castle, and without taking into account that Goree may be given up to France at a peace. The existence also of a colonial establishment at this place, together with a considerable extent of territory will afford facilities for promoting the great object of African civilization which are enjoyed in no other place on the Coast, particularly as the circumstances, which hitherto have chiefly impeded this object will be removed by the abolition of the Slave Trade, and the transfer of the Colony from the Company to the Government. The example afforded by the Colony of a mild but firm and well-ordered Government, of rational liberty, and of secure and productive industry, would be of almost incalculable importance while the influence which its growing strength and respectability and its growing commercial importance must give it over the neighbouring chiefs, might be exerted in composing their differences, and inducing them to pursue plans of peaceful industry . . .

The forts of the Gold Coast, if properly employed might be made very important engines of promoting the mutual benefit of Great Britain and Africa. In addition to those which we already possess, it might be advisable to obtain possession of two or three Dutch forts situated on the same coast, which I apprehend would be a work of little difficulty. If this were effected, we should possess almost the entire controul of that line of Coast which extends from Cape Three Points to the Rio Volta. It is important here to remark, that at this moment the laws of this district of Africa are administered in a great degree by the Governors of these forts, who ordinarily proceed in administering them on the principles not of British but of African legislation. That is to say, the guilt of African criminals is tried, not by the received rules of evidence, but by the application of some ordeal which is regarded according to [the] effect which it produces, as decisive of guilt or innocence. Persons thus found guilty being liable to be sold as slaves, and the Governors of the forts being generally slave traders, it might be presumed that some degree of oppression has arisen from this source. It is obvious, however, that the power which has been thus employed, and that without being resisted, may be converted into an instrument of great good to Africa; and that the Governors who may now be appointed, being instructed to substitute equitable principles of law and benevolent maxims of policy, in place of those which have grown up under the former system, may by that change alone operate a very considerable amelioration in the civil condition of the inhabitants of a part of the coast which extends from three to four hundred miles in length . . .

The African Committee of the Company of Merchants, letter to the Lords of the Treasury, April 9, 1812

Settlements on the coast of Africa have hitherto been deemed valuable on two grounds; first, as conferring an exclusive right of trade upon the Power possessing them; and, secondly, as the only medium through which it can be safely and advantageously carried on. The trade with the Gold Coast principally consists in a traffic of native merchants who travel from the interior, and frequently from very great distances, to exchange their goods for articles of foreign production. As these merchants cannot wait for the ships to arrive, nor the ships for them, it results that resident traders are necessary for their mutual accommodation; and that country will trade to the most advantage which has the greatest number of them established at convenient stations on the coast. For the sake of security, both to their persons and property, these traders must necessarily reside in forts, or under the immediate protection of them . . .

By the abolition of the slave trade, the commerce of Africa was rendered so insignificant that it may have appeared scarcely worth the maintenance of the settlements on the coast. But it must be recollected that those settlements which are supported at so trifling an expense, were originally formed with no view to the slave trade, which was then neither in existence nor in contemplation and that one of the chief arguments urged for the abolition of that trade was that on the adoption of that measure, a new, more desirable, and more extensive commerce would, in process of time, be established in Africa. We will not pretend to determine the precise extent to which these bright anticipations are likely to be realized; but that considerable progress has already been made will appear from the [fact] . . . that in the three years which have elapsed since the abolition, the average export to that country has been £830,325, and that the imports have rapidly increased until they amounted in the year 1810 to above half a million sterling, exclusive of gold, which has been imported in far greater quantities than during the slave trade . . .

Before any material improvement can be expected to take place in any district of Africa, the slave trade must be completely annihilated, or at least driven from that part of the coast; for so long as any people carrying on that trade are in possession of a single fort in the same neighbourhood, their influence will be superior to ours, and we shall be considered as opposed to the interests of the natives and be regarded with feelings of enmity. It is, besides, unquestionable that the British trade will not be able to exist where the slave trade is carried on. Those engaged in the latter will monopolize the whole. Ships can always carry more goods than are required to purchase their complement of negroes, and with little additional expense and without loss of time, the surplus goods may be converted into gold, ivory, &c; whereas the British merchant must fit out his vessel expressly for the purpose of purchasing those articles . . .

So long as the vessels of other countries are allowed to frequent the coast, the forts will be unable to prevent the trade in slaves. Until, therefore, we can interdict such intercourse by foreign vessels, good policy would forbid our imposing the impracticable duty of attempting it by force, upon those whose prospects of success in the great work of introducing cultivation and civilization so essentially depend on their preserving the friendship, confidence and respect of the natives.

We are aware of but one mode by which the slave trade can be entirely abolished in this part of Africa, and that, we feel it our duty to recommend. It is the occupation by this nation of the whole of the Gold Coast . . . stationing good and respectable garrisons in the most commanding situation, [and,] at the rest, establishments sufficient to mark our possession. The sole right of external trade or internal being thereby vested in this country, two or three small ships of war, with some troops or an extra number of marines on board, should be kept constantly cruizing on the coast, to prevent the approach of all vessels not British . . .

34 • The king of Asante disputes the text of a treaty (1817–24)

The British government accepted the views of the proexpansionists and in 1821 took formal possession of the West African forts of the Company of Merchants. However, staying meant finding new trade items to replace slaves. It also necessitated the establishment of treaty relationships with African rulers in order to ensure that British traders got a monopoly of the new trades. Treaty making was a complex process, especially because of each party's limited understanding of the other's language and because of the eagerness of merchant representatives to claim to have received more than African rulers believed that they had given. The complexities are evident in the accounts left by participants to the first treaty that the British made with an African ruler, that with the king (or Asantehene) of Asante, Osei Bonsu, in 1817. The first three accounts come from Thomas Bowdich's description of his mission on behalf of the Company of Merchants to the Asante capital, Kumasi, in 1817. In the second account, the Asante king complains of Britain's failure to force coastal Africans living near Cape Castle, his subjects by conquest since 1807, to make adequate tribute payments. The third account is Bowdich's version (which implied that the king of Dwaben was coequal with rather than a vassal of the Asantehene) of the 1817 treaty. In the fourth and fifth extracts, from Joseph Dupuis' account of his mission to Kumasi in 1821 and William Hutton's account of the same expedition, the objections of the Asantehene are detailed. Continuing disagreement between the British and the king of Asante over control of the West African coast, especially the right of the Asante king to receive tribute from the coastal people, led to the British sending a punitive expedition under the command of British governor Sir Charles McCarthy into the interior in 1824. Macarthy's forces were defeated, and the governor was decapitated. Victorious Asante took his head to their capital of Kumasi, where it remained in the royal palace for more than half a century.[3]

3. A, B, C, T. Edward Bowdich, *Mission from Cape Coast Castle to Ashantee, with a Descriptive Account of that Kingdom* (London: Griffith and Farran, new ed., 1873; first ed., 1819), 3–7, 76–81, 143–45; D, Joseph Dupuis, *Journal of a Residence in Ashantee, Comprising Notes and Researches relative to the Gold Coast, and the*

A. Letter of instruction from the African Committee of the Company of Merchants to Thomas Bowdich

[W]e wish you to obtain permission from the King [of Asante] to send an Embassy to his capital; if granted, you will select three gentlemen (one of them from the medical department) for that service . . . In particular, it will be necessary for them to observe, and report upon, the nature of the country; its soil and products; the names, and distances, and the latitude and longitude of the principal places; and its most remarkable natural objects: the appearance, distinguishing characters, and manners of the natives; their religion, laws, customs, and forms of government, as far as they can be ascertained; and by whom each place is governed. When at Ashantee, they should endeavour to obtain the fullest information of the countries beyond, in each direction; particularly whether any high mountains, lakes, or large rivers are known; and the width, depth, course, and direction of the latter; and whether the water, as well of the lakes as the rivers, is salt or fresh. and how far, and under what circumstances, white men may travel with safety, especially in a northerly direction. They should collect the most accurate information possible of the extent, population, and resources of the Ashantee dominions, and should report fully their opinion of the inhabitants, and of the progress they may have made in the arts of civilized life. They should be directed also, to procure and bring away (with the consent of the chiefs) any specimens of vegetable and mineral productions they may be able: and to ascertain where and how the natives collect the gold, and the extent to which the trade in that article, and in ivory, might be carried on. It would, we conceive, be a most important advantage if the King of Ashantee, and some of his chiefs, could be prevailed upon to send one or more of their children to the Cape, to be educated at the expense of the Committee (to be attended by their own servants, if required), under the guarantee of the Governor and Council for their personal safety, and that they should be sent back when required.

Another great object would be, to prevail upon the King to form, and keep open, a path not less than six feet wide, from his capital, as far as his territories extend towards Cape Coast, you engaging on the part of the Committee to continue it from that point to Cape Coast, which we presume may be done at a very small expense, by means of monthly allowances to the chiefs of such villages as be in that line; upon condition that they shall not allow the path to be overgrown with underwood, or otherwise obstructed . . .

Besides the escort of which we have spoken, we think it necessary, or at least extremely important, that the Embassy should be accompanied by natives of character and consequence, conversant with the Ashantee language, in whom you have perfect confidence, selected, one from each of the towns of Cape Coast, Accra, and Appollonia, to whom you may make reasonable allowances for their time and trouble.

We have said that you should obtain the permission of the King of Ashantee to send the Embassy: we have doubts of the expediency of requiring hostages; but, we presume you will

---

Interior of Western Africa; Chiefly Collected from Arabic MSS. And Information Communicated by the Moslems of Guinea: to which is Prefixed an Account of the Origin of the Causes of the Present War (London: Henry Colburn, 1824), 135; E, William Hutton, *A Voyage to Africa: Including a Narrative of an Embassy to One of the Interior Kingdoms, in the Year 1820; with Remarks on the Course and Termination of the Niger, and Other Principal Rivers in that Country* (London: Longman, Hurst, Rees, Orme, and Brown, 1821), 447–51.

concur with us in thinking, it will be necessary, before it leaves Cape Coast, that a man of con-sequence should be specially sent down by the King, to serve as a guide and protector; and who, on his journey to Cape Coast, may arrange with the messenger whom you may send to the King, respecting the places at which the Embassy may stop to refresh, and give directions to open the paths that may be overgrown.

The gentlemen whom you may select, will of course be well advised by you not to inter-fere with any customs of the natives, however absurd; or in any way to give them offence. And they cannot too strongly impress upon the minds of the King and people of Ashantee, that the only objects his Britannic Majesty has in view, are, to extend the trade with that country; to prevent all interruption to their free communication with the waterside; and to instruct their children in reading, writing, &c., from which, as may be easily pointed out, the greatest advantages must arise to the Ashantees . . . [Y]ou, gentlemen will perceive, that in selecting the Embassy, it is important, that one of the persons composing it should be able to deter-mine the latitude and longitude of places, and that both shall be seasoned to the climate of ability, physical and mental; of cool tempers and moderate habits; and possessed of fortitude and perseverance; and that in the selection of their escort also, regard be had to the qualifica-tions of the parties in those respects. Among them there should be a bricklayer, carpenter, blacksmith, gunsmith, and cooper, with proper tools; if these persons can be spared for the purpose.

B. Sai Tootoo Quamina, King of Ashantee and its Dependencies, letter to John Hope Smith, Esquire, Governor-in-Chief of the British Settlements on the Gold Coast of Africa

The King sends his compliments to the Governor; he thanks the King of England and him very much for the presents sent to him, he thinks them very handsome. The King's sisters and all his friends have seen them, and think them very handsome, and thank him. The King thanks his God and his fetish that he made the Governor send the white men's faces for him to see, like he does now; he likes the English very much, and the Governor all the same as his brother.

The King of England has made war against all the other white people a long time, and killed all the people all about, and taken all the towns, French, Dutch, and Danish, all the towns all about. The King of Ashantee has made war against all the people of the water side, and all the black men all about, and taken all their towns.

When the King of England takes a French town, he says, "Come, all this is mine, bring all your books, and give me all your pay;" and if they don't do it, does the Governor think the King of England likes it? So the King [of Asante] has beat the Fantees now two times, and taken all their towns, and they send and say to him, "You are a great King, we want to serve you;" but he says, "Hah if you want to serve me, then bring all your books, what you get from the forts;" and then they send him four ackies [of tribute]; this vexes him too much . . . his captains swear that the Fantees are rogues and want to cheat him. When the white men see the Fantees do this, and the English officers bring him his four ackies, it makes him get up very angry, but he has no palaver with white men.

All Fantee is his, all the black man's country is his; he hears that white men bring all the things that come here; he wonders they do not fight with the Fantees, for he knows they cheat them. Now he sees white men, and he thanks God and his fetish for it . . .

This King, Sai, is young on the stool, but he keeps always in his head what old men say, for it is good, and his great men and linguists tell it him every morning. The King of England makes three great men, and sends one to Cape Coast, one to Annamaboe, and one to Accra; Cape Coast is the same as England. The King gets two ounces from Accra every moon, and the English wish to give him only four ackies for the big fort at Cape Coast, and the same for Annamaboe; do white men think this proper? . . .

The King knows the King of England is his good friend, for he has sent him handsome dashes [presents of gold]; he knows his officers are his good friends, for they come to see him. The King wishes the Governor to send to Elmina to see what is paid him there, and to write the King of England how much, as, the English say their nation passes the Dutch; he will see by the books given him by both forts. If the King of England does not like that, he may send him himself what he pleases, and then Sai can take it.

He thanks the King and Governor for sending four White men to see him. The old King wished to see some of them, but the Fantees stop it. He is but a young man and sees them, and so again he thanks God and his fetish.

Dictated in the presence of,

T. EDWARD BOWDICH.

WILLIAM HUTCHISON

HENRY TEDLIE

C. Treaty made and entered into by Thomas Edward Bowdich, Esquire, in the name of the Governor and Council at Cape Coast Castle, on the Gold Coast of Africa, and on behalf of the British Government, with Sai Tootoo Quamina, King of Ashantee and its Dependencies, and Boitinnee Quama, King of Dwabin and its Dependencies

[Italicized words are those that appear in Bowdich's version of the treaty but not in that of the Asantehene.]

1st. There shall be perpetual peace and harmony between the British subjects in this country and the subjects of the Kings of Ashantee *and Dwabin.*

2nd. The same shall exist between the subjects of the Kings of Ashantee *and Dwabin,* and all nations of Africa residing under the protection of the Company's Forts and Settlements on the Gold Coast, and, it is hereby agreed, that there are no palavers now existing, and that neither party has any claim upon the other.

3rd. The King of Ashantee guarantees *the security of* the people of Cape Coast from the hostilities threatened by the people of Elmina.

4th. In order to avert the horrors of war, it is agreed that in any case of aggression on the part of the natives under British protection, the Kings shall complain thereof to the Governor-in-Chief to obtain redress, and that they will in no instance resort to hostilities, *even against the other towns of the Fantee territory,* without endeavoring as much as possible to effect an amicable arrangement, *affording the Governor the opportunity of propitiating it, as far as he may with discretion.*

5th. The King of Ashantee agrees to permit a British officer to reside constantly at his capital, for the purpose of instituting and preserving a regular communication with the Governor-in-Chief at Cape Coast Castle.

6th. The Kings of Ashantee *and Dwabin* pledges himself/*themselves* to countenance, promote and encourage the trade of his/*their* subjects with Cape Coast Castle and its dependencies to the extent of his/*their* power.

7th. The Governors of the respective Forts shall at all times afford every protection in their power to the persons and property of the people of Ashantee *and Dwabin* who may resort to the water-side.

8th. The Governor-in-Chief reserves to himself the right of punishing any subject of Ashantee *or Dwabin* guilty of secondary offences, but in case of any crime of magnitude, he will send the offender to the Kings, to be dealt with according to the laws of his country.

9th. The King*s* agrees to commit *their* children to the care of the Governor-in-Chief, for education, at Cape Coast Castle, in full confidence of the good intentions of the British Government and of the benefits to be derived therefrom.

10th. The King*s* promises to direct diligent inquiries to be made respecting the officers attached to the Mission of Major John Peddie and Captain Thomas Campbell, and to influence and oblige the neighbouring kingdoms and their tributaries, to befriend them as the subjects of the British Government.

Signed and sealed at Coomassie, this seventh day of September, in the year of our Lord, one thousand eight hundred and seventeen.

The mark of Sai Tootoo Quamina X (L.S.)

The mark of Boitinnee Quama X (L.S.)

Thomas Edward Bowdich.

In the presence of William Hutchison.

Henry Tedlie

D. Dupuis's comment on Bowdich's version of the treaty

The Treaty, as published in Mr. Bowdich's work, compared with what was actually written, and deposited with the king, is a garbled statement. I cannot say less. In the original document, which is now in my keeping, the pompous name of Boitene Quama, king of Dwabin, is nowhere to be found. It would seem that this association of the two sovereigns was calculated to awaken a more lively interest, and thus only can I account for an attempt to deceive government and the public, by means, I believe, unprecedented in the annals of British diplomacy. The article, No. 9, showing the king's disposition to send his own children to Cape Coast for education is falsely inserted, and every other article is disfigured or misrepresented more or less.

E. Declaration of Messrs. Hutton, Salmon, Collins, and Graves, relative to the Message sent up to the King of Ashantee, by Mr. Smith

We, the undersigned officers and gentlemen, who accompanied the embassy, under charge of Consul Dupuis, being present at an audience . . . were witnesses to the truth of the following statement, resulting from a discussion which ensued between the king of Ashantee and the consul, on the subject of certain claims established by the former on the governor of Cape Coast Castle, and also on the town of Cape Coast, amounting, separately, to 1600 ounces of gold, and collectively to double the said sum.

The new treaty being read over and interpreted to the king, he expressed much dissatis-faction and declared it to be his determined resolution not to relinquish the demand he had made on the town of Cape Coast; alleging, at the same time, that he was actually negotiating with the governor of the Castle, who had become responsible to him for the payment of a cer-tain sum of money . . .

In reply to an observation, which was made by the consul at an early part of the debate, that the king of Ashantee had, in virtue of the treaty of 1817, consigned over to the protection of the British government the natives residing under the British forts, he, the king, produced the original treaties, preliminary and definitive, and caused them to be read over and ex-plained to him, which, when done, he declared he had been deceived by the author of those documents, who did not truly explain to him their contents, for he never could or would re-sign the command he possessed over a conquered people, who were his slaves, and conse-quently should be obedient to him their master. He moreover declared, that he had consigned these people over to the English, resident on the coast, giving and granting them authority to make use of their services as they pleased; but he never transferred to them the power to in-terfere with his government, in any shape; nor would he permit it, as they were, "*bona fide,*" his subjects only, as his dominions embraced the whole line of coast from Appollonia on the west to Danish Accra on the east, (both inclusive).

35 • The impact of the abolitionists on labor legislation (1828)

Missionaries at the Cape of Good Hope criticized the way that settler farmers, most of them of Dutch origin, treated their black employees, slaves and Khoisan alike. Joined in their criticism by allies among British merchants (whom local farmers accused of hoping to benefit from the growth of larger markets for their goods among a better-paid working class), the missionaries succeeded in pressuring the British government to rescind harsh labor regulations introduced earlier (especially the legislation of 1809 and 1812). Ordinance no. 20, July 17, 1828, established regulations "For Im-proving the Condition of Hottentots and other free Persons of Colour at the Cape of Good Hope, and for Consolidating and Amending the Laws affecting those Persons."[4]

WHEREAS certain Laws relating to and affecting the Hottentots and other free persons of colour, lawfully residing in this Colony, require to be consolidated, amended, or repealed, and certain obnoxious usages and customs, which are injurious to those persons, require to be declared illegal and discontinued: Be it therefore enacted, by His Honour the Lieutenant-Governor in Council, That from and after the passing of this Ordinance, the Proclamations of the 16th day of July 1787, 9th day of May 1803, 1st day of November 1809, 23rd day of April 1812, 9th day of July 1819, and 23rd day of May 1823, shall be, and the same are hereby repealed . . .

II. And whereas by usage and custom of this Colony, Hottentots and other free persons of colour have been subjected to certain restraints as to their residence, mode of life, and em-ployment, and to certain compulsory services to which others of His Majesty's Subjects are

4. G. W. Eybers, ed., *Select Constitutional Documents Illustrating South African History, 1795–1910* (New York: George Routledge and Sons, 1918), 26–28.

not liable: Be it therefore enacted, that from and after the passing of this Ordinance, no Hottentot or other free Person of colour, lawfully residing in this Colony, shall be subject to any compulsory service to which other of His Majesty's Subjects therein are not liable, nor to any hindrance, molestation, fine, imprisonment or punishment of any kind whatsoever, under the pretence that such Person has been guilty of vagrancy or any other offence, unless after trial in due course of Law; any custom or usage to the contrary in any wise notwithstanding.

III. And whereas doubts have arisen as to the competency of Hottentots and other free Persons of colour to purchase or possess Land in this Colony: Be it therefore enacted, [all transfers of land made to or by such Hottentot or other free person of colour are legal; and it is lawful for such persons born in the Colony or granted deeds of burghership to possess land].

IV. And whereas it is expedient to protect ignorant and unwary Hottentots and other free Persons of colour as aforesaid from the effects of improvident Contracts for Service: Be it therefore enacted, [that it shall not be legal for any person to hire by written agreement any Hottentot or free person of colour for a longer period than one calendar month at a time, except as hereinafter provided] . . .

36 • The settlers' revolt (1837)

Slave-owning farmers on the eastern frontier of the Cape of Good Hope reacted angrily to the legislation of 1828 because they considered it an unacceptable intrusion by the colonial government into employer-employee relations. They were particularly opposed to any official measures that prevented them from using physical means to punish their workers and to the enforcement of policies that resulted in the trial of farmers accused of ill-treating slaves and free black workers such as Khoisan. They were also unhappy with the refusal of the colonial administration to expand the eastern frontiers of the colony and thereby make more land available to farmers. From 1833 on, organized parties of Dutch farmers, almost all of them from the eastern districts of the cape, began moving into the interior of South Africa in an attempt to get beyond the reach of British authority and to find new areas of land to farm. During the rest of the decade approximately fifteen thousand men, women, and children (about half of whom were Khoisan "servants") joined this "great trek" into the interior. One of the leaders of this movement was Piet Retief, who, after an unsuccessful business career, little of which involved farming, had been declared bankrupt in June 1836, eight months before he joined the trek. Despite this checkered past, he became the main spokesman for Dutch settlers' aspirations at the cape. In a "manifesto" published in the Grahamstown Journal, *February 2, 1837, Piet Retief made a case for those farmers who objected to British rule.[5]*

Numerous reports having been circulated throughout the colony, evidently with the intention of exciting in the minds of our countrymen of prejudice against those who have resolved to emigrate from a colony where they have experienced, for so many years past, a series of the most vexatious and severe losses; and, as we desire to stand high in the estimation of our brethren, and are anxious that they and the world at large should believe us incapable of sev-

5. Eybers, *Select Constitutional Documents Illustrating South African History,* 143–45.

ering that sacred tie which binds a Christian to his native soil, without the most sufficient reasons, we are induced to record the following summary of our motives for taking so important a step, and also our intentions respecting our proceedings towards the native tribes which we may meet with beyond the boundary:

1. We despair of saving the colony from those evils which threaten it by the turbulent and dishonest conduct of vagrants, who are allowed to infest the country in every part; nor do we see any prospect of peace or happiness for our children in any country thus distracted by internal commotions.

2. We complain of the severe losses which we have been forced to sustain by the emancipation of our slaves, and the vexatious laws which have been enacted respecting them.

3. We complain of the continual system of plunder which we have ever endured from the Caffres [Africans] and other coloured classes, and particularly by the last invasion of the colony, which has desolated the frontier districts and ruined most of the inhabitants.

4. We complain of the unjustifiable odium which has been cast upon us by interested and dishonest persons, under the cloak of religion, whose testimony is believed in England, to the exclusion of all evidence in our favour; and we can foresee, as the result of this prejudice, nothing but the total ruin of the country.

5. We are resolved, wherever we go, that we will uphold the just principles of liberty; but, whilst we will take care that no one shall be held in a state of slavery, it is our determination to maintain such regulations as may suppress crime, and preserve proper relations between master and servant.

6. We solemnly declare that we quit this colony with a desire to lead a more quiet life than we have heretofore done. We will not molest any people, nor deprive them of the smallest property; but, if attacked, we shall consider ourselves fully justified in defending our persons and effects, to the utmost of our ability, against every enemy.

7. We make known, that when we shall have framed a code of laws for our future guidance, copies shall be forwarded to the colony for general information; but we take this opportunity of stating, that it is our firm resolve to make provision for the summary punishment of any traitors who may be found amongst us.

8. We propose, in the course of our journey, and on arriving at the country in which we shall permanently reside, to make known to the native tribes our intentions, and our desire to live in peace and friendly intercourse with them.

9. We quit this colony under the full assurance that the English Government has nothing more to require of us, and will allow us to govern ourselves without its interference in future.

10. We are now quitting the fruitful land of our birth, in which we have suffered enormous losses and continual vexation, and are entering a wild and dangerous territory; but we go with a firm reliance on an all-seeing, just, and merciful Being, whom it will be our endeavour to fear and humbly to obey.

> By authority of the farmers who have quitted the Colony,
> (Signed) P. RETIEF.

37 • A missionary talks with a king (1836)

Missionaries—British, French, and American—went into the interior of South Africa from the
1810s onward, aiming to introduce Christianity and "civilization" to Africans. George Champion
was the first missionary to travel to the Zulu kingdom, established by Shaka in the late 1810s and
1820s and ruled from 1828 onward by Dingane (or Dingaan; both spellings were current in the
nineteenth century), Shaka's half-brother and his assassin as well. Accounts of the Zulu written by
British traders who had visited Shaka in the 1820s stressed what they perceived as the brutality of
his regime and that of his successor. Champion found, however, a king very inquisitive about the
beliefs and practices of his European visitor, observations that he recorded in the entries below from
his daily journal.[6]

January 17, 1836, Sunday. The king sent for us early; of course our present must go with us as
an introduction. Providence had highly favoured us, in that we had been able to secure the
services of the only white man in the country who can speak Dingaan's language well, and
with whom the chief is well acquainted. Of course we were informed of all the minutiae of introduction and formality, on which often so much depends. Dingaan was sitting just outside
of his cattle-kraal, in a large old-fashioned arm-chair just brought him by Mr. N [Norden]. He
wore a cloak of red plush with two rows of buttons extending from head to foot in front. A
strip of the same was tied round his forehead. This is the place where he sits every morning for
the purpose of attending to business. Some fifty or eighty men were sitting in a semicircle on
either side of him on the ground. During some minutes after we had approached near him all
was silence. At length the chief sent his compliments to us, and wished to converse. He examined minutely the articles brought: the razor, the umbrella, the pictures, and the lock of a
tin trunk given him. A few beads also, a knife, a tea-canister, and some handkerchiefs were
among them. He appeared much pleased, and said he should like to see our wagon. This he
inspected narrowly. He found a piece of green baize which he fancied, and we gave it him. We
mentioned to him that it was the Sabbath, and that we rested from all secular business. He
seemed satisfied, and excused us till to-morrow. In the afternoon he sent a goat for slaughter,
and through his means probably the people were kept away from our wagon, so that our day
of rest has not been so much interrupted as we feared. A shower of rain also gave us a season
of quiet . . . We had brought with us a small turning-lathe, supposing that it would give the
chief a better idea of some things than any explanation of ours. Some rosewood upon the
wagon attracted his attention yesterday, and an enquiry brought the lathe on the carpet. He
must have it with us in his palace to-day, and see its operation in the turning of a snuff-box.
He sent for us early, to what may be called his hall of audience. This is an apartment somewhat in the shape of a triangle, with curved sides, surrounded by a fence of whittled sticks
woven very ingeniously together, and seven or eight feet high. It has three or four gates, each
one being surmounted by the sticks passing over the gateway, parallel to each other, in the
shape of a semicircle; and continued down its side to the ground. The king's house stands in
the centre, well constructed and very large, perhaps twenty feet high—but, after all, only a

6. Journal of George Champion, printed in John Bird, ed., *The Annals of Natal, 1495 to 1845* (Pietermar-
    itzburg, South Africa: P. Davis and Sons, 1888), 203–8.

Kafir hut. The king's great chair or throne stands in this room. Beside it there is nothing but a mound of clay, on which the king often stands to survey his town and land, no doubt with some of the pride of the Babylonian monarch. The king took us to different parts of his abode. It consists of apartments resembling the first, but usually containing three houses. He led us from one place to another till we were absolutely tired, and thought that if left to ourselves we should find it difficult to escape out of the labyrinth. In one apartment sixty or seventy of his girls were dancing and singing; and that not without some harmony and precision. And it must be added that we saw in his palace some three hundred girls, of whom a few, apparently, were in the position of servants, but the others evidently filled a different sphere. Completely beyond all description, their hips and necks loaded with beads of various sorts, and with no clothing on most, except a short coat around the loins, they present "in toto," as they drag their load over the ground, and in this warm weather, an appearance which excites in a stranger both ridicule and disgust.

We crept into one of the houses at the king's request. The dark earthen floor bore a fine polish, and was as smooth as marble. It is smeared every morning, I am informed, with fat. The fireplace in the centre was constructed with much neat taste, and the roof was so wattled on the inside as to appear like some well-braided basket.

Returning to the lathe, we found it surrounded by a whole host of the royal family, greatly admiring every part and parcel of the instrument. At length the box was finished, greatly to the satisfaction of the owner. But he must try his hand; and, to his credit it must be said, he succeeded very well for a beginner. He has an inquisitive mind, and often starts questions which show him to be superior to the generality of his people. Every part of the lathe underwent the strictest scrutiny, and nothing was left unexplained. But he is very proud and excessively fond of flattery. His subjects approach him in a bending posture or on the ground. No man comes into his palace without an express permit. His smith, however, was admitted to-day to view the curious machine. This man is of great service in fastening the rings and bangles upon his captains, and appears to be on very familiar terms with his chief. His language to the king is nothing but submissive adulation, as that of all his subjects, "Yes, father: O father! mighty chief," being appended to every sentence. He received a present of a file or two from Mr. Grout, whereat his eyes almost started out of his head for joy . . .

20th. This morning early, the king sent for us. He was sitting in the presence of his people. The doctor's skill was for some time the topic. He asked him if he could heal all diseases; if he went by any spirit in his art, and whether he could cure a man who was affected by paralysis in an arm or leg. When told that the man could be cured, he told us his own complaint, but said he would wait and see if the paralytic were cured. He wished to see some money; asked us what we thought of his dress yesterday; informed us now and then that the people were praising him; and as we were leaving him, asked if we could perform feats of leaping, such as some white men had once done. He asked us if we could get a bead-maker to live with him. When God's name happened to be mentioned, he asked us how we knew of Him, and then childishly turned to something else.

Took a walk round the town. It would occupy half an hour's constant walking. On the upper side we found the smith's shop. His work is wholly in brass. A very hot fire is made from the dried leaves of the sloe. Here the small brass wire is melted down into plates, which again are fluted by sharp hammers on rude anvils of stone, and bent so as to form the broad covering for the forearm, given by Dingaan to none but the greatest of his captains. The principal work now going forward here is the making of shields. These are made of large ox-hides, oval in shape, and are given, the black to the boys, the red to the men. In fact, Gungunhlovu seems to be little else than a camp of soldiers. The chief, is always talking of some warlike expedition, and inspiring them with a desire for plunder and blood. They live, as it were, at the king's table, and not on the fruits of their own labour . . .

21st. Again at the king's this morning. He improves in his skill at the lathe, and his fondness for it led him to ask it of us. This we had to refuse. The girls were at work. Some of them were receiving their calabashes of morning's milk, some engaged in fastening the brass about another's neck. The person to be operated upon was lying down with her neck across a block, while the rings were made to meet by pounding with a hammer. Ever after, the victim finds it difficult to bend her neck any way.

The king sat in a chair, very like an European one, but carved with an assegai [spear] out of a single block of wood. He wished us to write an order for some *brass dancing-rods*. The subject of our visit was mentioned, and he said that this afternoon he would see about it.

22nd. The king had appointed yesterday for our conference; but a true African shower prevented. The thunder was very loud, with lightning exceedingly vivid, and hailstones as large as bullets, and in such profusion as to whiten the ground, pelted our cloth habitation roundly.

Early this morning the king's messenger came for us. He was sitting in his usual morning seat, with his "amabutu," or young soldiers, in a half-moon in front of him, at thirty or forty yard's distance. He invited us near him, and also the three captains left in the place of two indunas in their absence. Our business came at once on the carpet, without form or ceremony. Some short account of God's word was given, and our object briefly stated. A Testament was shown as a part of God's word. He wished to know how many leaves it contained, and was surprised to hear us tell without counting them. He asked to hear some of it read. He then enquired about the Creation. A short account of the Saviour was given. They all seemed interested. One asked if God was not displeased with their treatment of His Son, and what He did to the people. We were asked if men knew anything about God before Christ came. One query was, if God was so powerful, why not pray to Him to take away all disease and misery?

Dingaan wished to know our relation to the Government of our country, and then said, "Here, now, are my three councillors, in place of the two great men; they must decide for you; I am favourable." The result was—for the councillors echoed but the voice of their chief— that they fear evils from the introduction of white men into their country, and wish the line of the whites to be beyond the Umtugela [river]; that they can hardly believe we can teach the people what we profess, to read and write; but that they wish the experiment to be tried in their country when we return with our wives. For this purpose we may begin in the district of Hlomenhline, containing several thousands. "And then," said the king, "if you succeed, I will bring the school right into the heart of my dominions, I will learn myself, and set an example to my people!"

We were mutually pleased. In present circumstances we can ask no more. Such is the gross darkness that reigns here, even in the mind of Dingaan, that the work must be gradual. In speaking of God to any of these people they have usually stared about the heavens in wonder, or listened to our words as an unmeaning story; and, perhaps, have interrupted us by asking for something that caught their eye. Soon we called upon the king for the last time. He was eating, and it was given us in very strict charge not to cough, or hem, or spit in his presence. He was in his hut. We were obliged absolutely to crawl in on our hands and knees. The chief was reclining on a mat, his head on a wooden bolster. Strung around the hut, behind his wives, were their bead dresses. The hut was not high within, but very wide, and supported by nine posts. In the centre the dogs were sleeping. We now saw the monarch reclining at his ease in our presence. Very little ceremony was required. He appeared to be our friend more than at any time previous. While in the house, we heard the loud song of his subjects previous to partaking of the king's meat. Several oxen are slaughtered daily by the chief. After a loud song, they all shout "God save the King," or its equivalent—and enter on the work of mastication.

Dingaan was as inquisitive as usual. He took much notice of a letter written for him to Mr. N. He asked us how we learned to read. He said it ran in his head that he should learn, and should ere long have one of us to teach him. Our interpreter received quite a rebuke for being a white man and not able to read and write. He then wished the names of all his girls, who were sitting around the sides of the house, and of the dogs which were sleeping in the centre, to be written, and to be read by one who had been absent during the writing. He asked when we should return, and gave us beads, as specimens of those which he wished us to bring. We must then make for him some candle-wicks, that he might supply his lantern and candlestick during our absence; and then he went out, leaving us the sport of his childish girls, till the heat and confinement of the house obliged us also to leave it. We found him outside, near some tallow, which probably his royal skill would soon manufacture into some sort of candles. Here he gave orders for five cattle, in addition to the two we had already received, to be brought to us for most on our journey, and charging the doctor not to forget his medicine, he wished us a good journey, saying that he regarded us as his friends, and wished soon to see us.

38 • Dingane kills the first settlers (1838)

Though initially welcoming to his first European visitors and always interested in discussing religion with missionaries, Dingane became concerned with the arrival of large numbers of Dutch settlers into his territory. He feared that they would undermine his authority, take his people's land, and perhaps even threaten his own life. In February 1838 he decided on a preemptive strike against the party of explorers led by Piet Retief. This eyewitness account of the killing of the explorers is by Francis Owen, an American missionary who lived at Dingane's capital and enjoyed the king's protection. Less than a year after Dingane's act, other explorers, working in alliance with the Zulu monarch's half-brother, Mpande, defeated the Zulu at the battle of Blood River. Dingane fled north as a refugee and within a few months was killed by Swazi enemies. Mpande succeeded him as king of the Zulu. The following eyewitness descriptions are from Owen's daily journal.[7]

February 6, 1838. A dreadful day in the annals of the mission. I shudder to give an account of it. This morning, as I was sitting in the shade of my wagon, reading the Testament, the usual messenger came, with hurry and anxiety depicted in his looks. I was sure that he was about to

7. Journal of Francis Owen, printed in Bird, *The Annals of Natal,* 346–48, 351–52.

pronounce something serious. And what was his commission? While it showed consideration and kindness in the Zulu monarch towards me, it disclosed a horrid instance of perfidy—too horrid to describe—towards the unhappy men who for a few days had been his guests, and are now no more. He sent to tell me not to be frightened, as he was going to kill the Boers. This news came like a thunderstroke to myself and to every successive member of my family as they heard it. The reason assigned for this treacherous act was that they were going to kill him; that they had come here, and that he had now learnt all their plans. The messenger was anxious for my answer; but what could I say? I was fearful on the one hand of seeming to justify the treachery, and on the other of exposing myself and my family to probable danger if I appeared to take their part. Moreover, I could not but feel that it was my duty to apprise the Boers of the intended massacre; while certain death would have ensued, I apprehended, if I had been detected in giving them this information. However, I was released from this dilemma by beholding an awful spectacle. My attention was directed to the blood-stained hill nearly opposite my hut, and on the other side of my wagon, which hides it from view, where all the executions at this fearful spot take place, and which was destined now to add sixty more bleeding carcasses to the number of those who have already cried to heaven for vengeance. "There!" said some one, "they are killing the Boers now!" About nine or ten Zulus to each Boer were dragging their helpless, unarmed victims to the fatal spot—where those eyes which awaked this morning to see the cheerful light of day for the last time, are now closed in death. I laid myself down on the ground. Mrs. and Miss Owen were not more thunderstruck than myself. We comforted one another. Presently, the deed of blood being accomplished, the whole multitude returned to the town to meet their sovereign; and, as they drew near to him, set up a shout which reached the [missionary] station, and continued for some time. Meanwhile, I myself had been kept from all fear for our personal safety; for I considered the message of Dingaan to me as an indication that he had no ill designs against the missionary . . .

February 7. I did not give an adequate description of the dreadful carnage yesterday. I omitted to state that many of the Boers had children with them, some under eleven years of age, as I am informed—and these were all butchered. They also had their Hottentot servants, and these were likewise slaughtered, besides their interpreter and his servant. The number slain must have been nearer a hundred than sixty . . . Dingaan afterwards sent for Mr. Venables and his interpreter . . . He said that he should never send us away, or drive us out; but if the teachers at any time wished to go and see their own people, and would come and say "Hlala guhle" (farewell, or rest quietly), he would not stop them . . .

February 9 . . . The king sent for my interpreter . . . and gave him a very plausible account of the late unhappy affairs. He said if he had not despatched the Boers, they would have fired at him and his people when they left; and that, when their guns were examined, they were all found to be loaded with ball.

39 • Advance by treaty in West Africa (1831–36)

Given the high financial and human costs of military action in West Africa, as evidenced by the fate of Governor Charles McCarthy, the British officially pulled back somewhat and tried to advance their antislavery and commercial interests in West Africa by forming alliances with African leaders and negotiating treaties with potential enemies. The British hoped to build up a network of alliances that would extend their reach into the interior. They developed alliances with the Fante people of the coast and, assisted by militias formed by Danish and African merchants, inflicted a heavy defeat on the Asante in 1827. The British government returned control of the coast to a group of merchants who appointed George Maclean as their governor. Maclean negotiated a new peace treaty with the Asante in 1831, in which the latter agreed to give up their claims to the coastal areas.

The British also sought to extend their commercial interests in the Niger Delta and thereby gain access to the enormous trading hinterland of the Niger River (especially the trade in palm oil). In the 1830s and 1840s representatives of the British government entered into a series of treaty agreements with the African merchant-kings who controlled the Niger Delta. They made annual payments (or "presents" or perhaps, in African eyes, "tributes") to convince local rulers to desist from participating in the export trade in slaves. Through treaties, they tried to establish the ways in which their merchants would be dealt with if disputes arose between European and African. In seeking to establish such extraterritorial jurisdiction, the British negotiated with one of the most important of the Niger Delta leaders, King Pepple of Bonny (a state that had grown throughout the eighteenth century as a center of the slave trade).[8]

A. British Peace treaty with Asante, April 27, 1831

We, the undersigned . . . Namely, the Governor of the Cape Coast Castle and British settlements, on the part of His Majesty the king of England; the princess "Aklanvah" and chief "Quagua," on the part of the king of Ashantee; "Aggery," king of Cape Coast; "Adookoo," king of Fantee; "Amonoo," king of Annamaboe; "Chibboo," king of Denkera; "Ossoo Okoo," king of Tufel; "Aminnie," king of Wassaw; "Chibboo," king of Assin; the chiefs of Adjumacon and Essacoomah, and the other chiefs in alliance with the king of Great Britain, whose names are hereunto appended—do consent to and hereby ratify the following treaty of peace and of free commerce between ourselves and such other chiefs as may hereafter adhere to it:

1. The king of Ashantee having deposited in Cape Coast Castle, in the presence of the above-mentioned parties, the sum of 600 ounces of gold, and having delivered into the hands of the Governor two young men of the royal family of Ashantee named "Ossor Ansah" and "Ossoo Inquantamissah," as security that he will keep peace with the said parties in all time coming, peace is hereby declared betwixt the said king of Ashantee and all and each of the parties aforesaid, to continue in all time coming. The above securities shall remain in Cape Coast Castle for the space of six years from this date.

2. In order to prevent all quarrels in future which might lead to the infraction of this treaty of peace, we the parties aforesaid, have agreed to the following rules and regulations for the better protection of the lawful commerce:

The paths shall be perfectly open and free to all persons engaged in lawful traffic, and persons molesting them in any way whatever, or forcing them to purchase at any particular

8. A, Metcalfe, *Great Britain and Ghana: Documents of Ghana History, 1807–1957,* 133–34; B, C. W. Newbury, ed., *British Policy towards Africa: Select Documents, 1786–1874* (Oxford: Clarendon, 1965), 375–76.

market, or influencing them by any unfair means whatever, shall be declared guilty of infringing this treaty, and be liable to the severest punishment.

Panyarring, denouncing and swearing on or by any person or thing whatever, are strictly
forbidden, and all persons infringing this rule shall be rigorously punished; and no master or
chief shall be answerable for the crimes of his servants, unless done by his orders or consent,
or when under his control.

As the king of Ashantee has renounced all right or title to any tribute or homage from the
kings of Dinkera, Assin, and others formerly his subjects, so, on the other hand, these parties
are strictly prohibited from insulting, by improper speaking or in any other way, their former
master, such conduct being calculated to produce quarrels and wars.

All "palavers" are to be decided in the manner mentioned in the terms and conditions of
peace already agreed to by the parties to this treaty.

Signed in the great hall of Cape Coast Castle, this 27th day of April, 1831, by the parties
to this treaty, and sealed with the great seal of the Colony, in their presence.

[Signed] George Maclean, Governor

B. British Treaty with King Pepple's House, Grand Bonny, January 25, 1836

ARTICLE I.

It is hereby agreed, between the undersigned H. B. Majesty's Subjects and the King of
Bonny, that no English Subject shall from this time be detained on shore or maltreated in any
way whatever by the King or natives of Bonny under any pretence; by so doing, they will bring
themselves under the displeasure of the King of England, and be declared enemies of Great
Britain, and that the Men of War, on any complaint will immediately come up the Bonny to
protect the English Vessels.

II.

In case of any misunderstanding between the Captains of the English Vessels and the
King or Gentlemen of Bonny, that all and every English Captain will go on shore, free of
molestation and will, with the King and Gentlemen of Bonny, peaceably settle all disputes
between the parties.

III.

English Captains having any complaint against any of the natives of Bonny, will come on
shore, and lay his or their complaint before the King, and they hereby promise to give the
complainant redress, by punishing the offender, and if any English seaman shall ill treat a
Bonny man he shall be punished by the Captain of the Vessel to which he may belong.

IV.

That for the future, all books made between the Traders and English Captains, shall bear
the signature of such responsible officer, belonging to the Ship with the date and name; by his
not doing so, the case shall be decided by the Captains of the Merchant Ships, lying in the
River, who will see, that the Trader's or Native's loss be made good.

V.

That after the Captain or Supercargo has paid the regular Custom, the trade shall be
opened, and upon no account, shall the trade of any Vessel be stopped; excepting the Cap-

tain or Supercargo act in opposition, to any of the annexed agreements, and refuses to pay the fine, imposed by the other Captains, for the infringing of these rules.

VI.

That every vessel's property shall be properly protected, and that no King, Gentleman, or Native of Bonny, shall roll away the casks of any Vessel from the Cask house on any pretence whatever.

VII.

That the King will be responsible for all monies, Oil, or goods, that may be owing to the English Captains, so that the Vessel may not be detained before sailing; and that the Captains of the English Ships, will see all just debts incurred by any vessel, are paid by her to Bonny men with Bars, or Oil, before leaving the River.

CHAPTER SIX

Technology Increases the Ease
of Conquest (1840–64)

40 • European mortality in West Africa before quinine (1840)

Since the time of the first Portuguese voyages in the mid-1400s, few Europeans escaped the effects of new diseases—especially malaria and yellow fever—whether on the West African coast or inland. The mortality rates were enormous, far higher than those elsewhere on the African continent or in the Americas or Asia. The average number of deaths among soldiers in the British settlements in Sierra Leone and on the Gambia in 1825 and 1826 ranged between 50 and 100 percent. In the Gambia the entire force died in eight months, and new supplies of men had to be brought in continually. These horrific death rates in and of themselves prevented Europeans from expanding their settlements on the West African coast and from moving into the interior. The following statistics, published in 1840 in an article titled "Western Africa and Its Effects on the Health of Troops," clarified for potential recruits to the military, as well as to other European settlers, the risks that they would face in going to West Africa.[1]

Troop mortality in Sierra Leone, 1819–36

1819–1836	Total Troops	Hospital Admissions	Deaths	Admitted/ 1000	Died/ 1000
Total	1843	5489	890	2978	483

[O]n the long average of 18 years, nearly half the force perished annually, and every soldier was about thrice in hospital in the course of the year.

Not only was the class of soldiers employed of the very worst description, but other circumstances, independent of climate, tended materially to swell the mortality. On the arrival of the principal part of the force in 1825, the barracks were found scarcely habitable, and the troops suffered every species of misery from the inclemency of the wet season before suitable accommodations could be provided for them. The rations, too, consisted principally of salt meat, which, in large quantities, is found to aggravate very materially the bowel complaints incident to that climate . . .

---

1. *United Service Journal and Naval and Military Magazine*, 1840, part 2, 510–11.

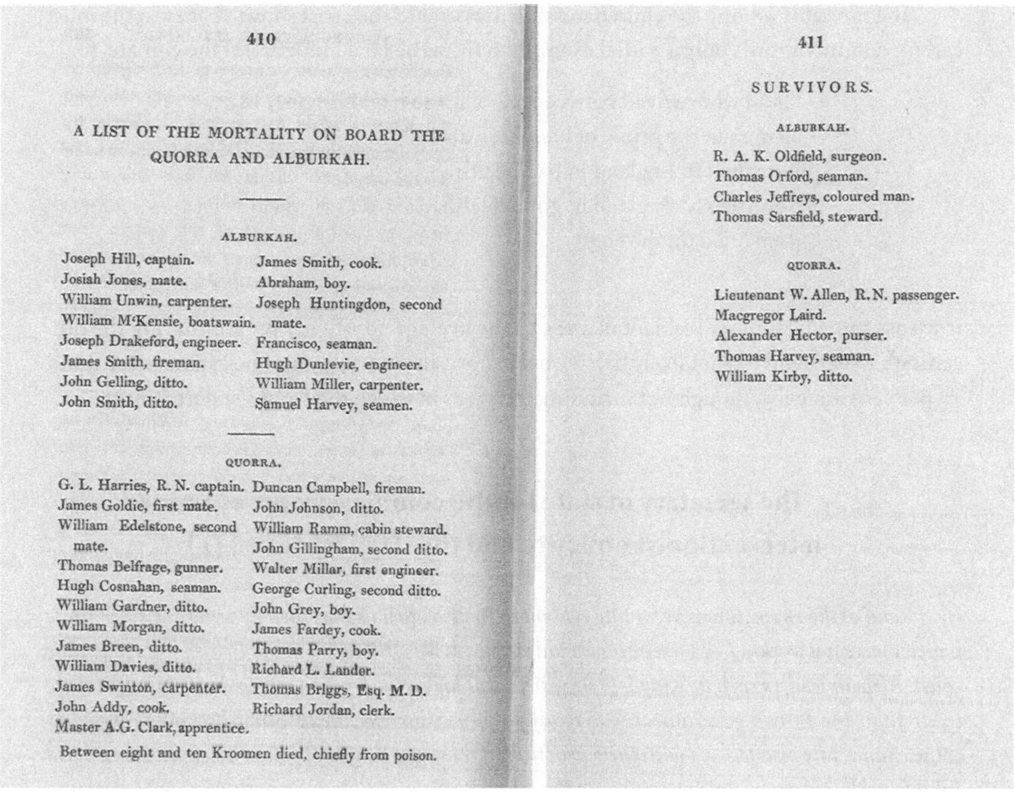

410

A LIST OF THE MORTALITY ON BOARD THE
QUORRA AND ALBURKAH.

ALBURKAH.

Joseph Hill, captain.   James Smith, cook.
Josiah Jones, mate.   Abraham, boy.
William Unwin, carpenter.   Joseph Huntingdon, second
William M'Kensie, boatswain.   mate.
Joseph Drakeford, engineer.   Francisco, seaman.
James Smith, fireman.   Hugh Dunlevie, engineer.
John Gelling, ditto.   William Miller, carpenter.
John Smith, ditto.   Samuel Harvey, seamen.

QUORRA.

G. L. Harries, R. N. captain.   Duncan Campbell, fireman.
James Goldie, first mate.   John Johnson, ditto.
William Edelstone, second   William Ramm, cabin steward.
   mate.   John Gillingham, second ditto.
Thomas Belfrage, gunner.   Walter Millar, first engineer.
Hugh Cosnahan, seaman.   George Curling, second ditto.
William Gardner, ditto.   John Grey, boy.
William Morgan, ditto.   James Fardey, cook.
James Breen, ditto.   Thomas Parry, boy.
William Davies, ditto.   Richard L. Lander.
James Swinton, carpenter.   Thomas Briggs, Esq. M. D.
John Addy, cook.   Richard Jordan, clerk.
Master A.G. Clark, apprentice.

Between eight and ten Kroomen died, chiefly from poison.

411

SURVIVORS.

ALBURKAH.

R. A. K. Oldfield, surgeon.
Thomas Orford, seaman.
Charles Jeffreys, coloured man.
Thomas Sarsfield, steward.

QUORRA.

Lieutenant W. Allen, R.N. passenger.
Macgregor Laird.
Alexander Hector, purser.
Thomas Harvey, seaman.
William Kirby, ditto.

FIGURE 9 West Africa in the early nineteenth century was known as "the white man's grave" for good reason. Fewer than a quarter of the men embarking on an inland exploration of West African rivers led by Macgregor Laird and R. A. K. Oldfield during the years 1832–34 survived the voyage, as this tally from their expedition shows. Macgregor Laird and R. A. K. Oldfield, *Narrative of an Expedition into the Interior of Africa, by the River Niger,* 1837.

This frightful loss of life was not confined to the period above referred to, however. During the nine years antecedent to 1819, which were not deemed particularly unhealthy, and when the barrack accommodation was less exceptionable, the loss of the troops was about one-fourth of their number annually; and the same was the case even in the earliest days of the settlement, as is shown by the following return of the soldiers and white colonists originally sent out by the Sierra Leone Company:—

	Company's civil servants	Overseers, clerks, etc.	families Settlers and	Soldiers	Total
Landed in 1792	26	59	18	16	119
Died 1792–1794	4	29	13	11	57

Being about half the aggregate number in the course of two years.

The mortality among the church missionaries sent to the coast shows that even the most careful conduct affords only a partial exemption from the fatal influence of the climate, for

Of 89 who arrived between March, 1804, and August, 1825, all men in the prime of life, there died	54
Returned to England in bad health	14
Returned to England in good health	7
Remained on the coast	<u>14</u>
	89

If we assume the number resident in 1825 as the average constantly present during the preceding 21 years, and it is not likely to have been more, the mortality may be estimated at about 17 per cent annually, though not including the years in which the troops suffered most.

41 • The secretary of state for the colonies proposes a more interventionist policy to end the slave trade (1841)

By the end of the 1830s, it was becoming evident to British officials that their existing antislave trade policies were not working. A surreptitious trade in slaves was still active in the British forts along the coast. African leaders such as King Pepple insisted on higher cash payments to desist from the slave trade than the British government was ready to pay. Moreover, Pepple and his peers refused to countenance any interference with their practices of domestic slavery. In these circumstances, Lord John Russell sent an official expedition up the Niger River in 1841 to meet with African leaders and to persuade them to cease the slave trade. The Niger commissioners traveled on three steamships, a new mode of transportation that for the first time allowed the British to sail against the outward flowing river currents and extend their sea power into the interior of Africa. In their travels, the commissioners followed the instructions given to them by Lord Russell in a letter dated January 30, 1841.[2]

10. On your arrival at each native settlement, you will ascertain the proper mode for opening a communication with the Chief; and in all your intercourse with him, you will take care that you are treated by him with proper respect; and you will not neglect, also, to treat him with the respect which is due to the rank which belongs to him.

11. You will tell the Chief that you are sent by the Queen of Great Britain and Ireland to express Her Majesty's wish to establish friendly relations with him; and to settle and agree with him for the extinction of the Foreign Traffic in Slaves in his dominions; and for the substitution instead thereof of a full and free intercourse and barter of all articles of innocent trade between the subjects of Her Majesty and those of such Chief, for his profit and advantage, and for the mutual use, comfort, and benefit of the subjects of both countries. You will ask him what articles he and his subjects are in want of, and you will express generally the readiness of this country to supply them; you will ask him what articles of trade he and his

2. C. W. Newbury, ed., *British Policy towards Africa: Select Documents, 1786–1874* (Oxford: Clarendon, 1965), 154–59.

subjects wish to dispose of; and you will express generally the readiness of this country to purchase them. You will inquire what further articles of native growth, or produce, or manufacture his country can supply as articles of useful export with Great Britain; and you will encourage him to the cultivation or production thereof, by expressing generally the readiness of this country to take off his hands, on fair and reasonable terms of barter, all such articles of useful trade for this country as he can supply, in return for all such articles of use, and comfort, and advantage to himself as he requires.

12. You will show to him the advantages of putting down the Foreign Slave Trade, and of building upon the abolition a lawful and innocent trade. You will say to him, that his subjects will thereby be induced to cultivate the soil, to value their habitations, to increase their produce, and to behave well, in order to keep the advantage which that produce will give to them; that they will thus become better subjects, and better men, and that his possessions will thus become more full of what is valuable. You will impress upon him, that he himself will no longer need to make, or to keep up, quarrels with his neighbours, or to undertake distant and dangerous wars, or to seek out causes of punishment to his own subjects, for the sake of producing from the odious Trade in Slaves an income for himself. You will explain to him, that the people of his country will, out of the produce of labour in cultivating, gathering, and preparing articles for trade, bring to him more revenues, and be consequently more valuable to him.

13. You will tell him, that Her Majesty, desirous to make that innocent commerce which is a benefit to all nations, a peculiar benefit to himself, proposes that, upon his abolishing the Slave Trade, not only he and his subjects shall have this free and advantageous commerce; but that he himself shall have, for his own share, and without any payment on his part, a sum not exceeding one-twentieth part value of every article of British merchandize brought by British ships and sold in his dominions; such proportion to be taken by himself without any reference to the amount of articles for which the remaining nineteen-twentieths shall be bartered with him or with his subjects; and you will make agreements with him on this subject conformable, as far as possible, with the draft agreement. You will, where possible, stipulate in return for a free right of barter for his subjects, and the abolition of any monopoly in his own favour, should such exist.

14. While explaining to the Chief the profit to be derived from the cultivation of the soil, you will not fail on all proper occasions, as far as you may deem it expedient and compatible with the main objects of your mission, to draw his attention to the superior advantages of free over slave labour: to impress upon him the impolicy as well as the injustice of slavery: and to acquaint him with the abhorrence in which it is held by Her Majesty and the people of England. You may remind him of the large tracts of waste land in his possession; state how unprofitable they are to him at present; and inform him that if he could procure such land to be cultivated by his subjects on a system of free labour, he would be justly entitled to receive a considerable share of the increased profits: far more than enough to counterbalance all the profits which could possibly arise from the continuance of the Slave Trade. You may further remind him that every man naturally works harder for himself than for another, and is more economical and more careful of his own property; consequently, that the produce of his country would be much greater by free labour than by any other system, and that he would derive a double advantage, first, from his share of the produce as a landlord, and afterwards from the

duties he would get as Chief on the sale of the remainder. You may further intimate to him, that a compliance with the wish of Her Majesty's Government and her people, in this respect, would certainly increase Her Majesty's interest in his welfare, and enable Her Majesty and her people to render much greater assistance and encouragement in improving the condition of himself and his people, than could be afforded them during the continuance of a system of slave labour. But you must always bear in mind that the main object of your commission is the extinction of the Foreign Slave Trade, and all other points must for the present be considered subordinate.

15. You will, at the proper time, exhibit the presents with which you are furnished from Her Majesty, as proofs of the desire of friendship which the Queen entertains towards the Chief, and as samples of the articles, with which, among others, this country will be glad to supply himself and his subjects in as great a quantity as they shall want and wish, on fair and reasonable terms of barter. You should not distribute these presents to any of the Chiefs, except in those cases where you are satisfied that the interests of the commission in which you are employed imperatively require it; and further, you will also bear in mind the necessity of giving no more than is absolutely requisite; and especially with a view to avoid all possibility of in future impeding ordinary traffic with British or other merchants. In case any of the Chiefs or Head-men of the country should be willing to make presents, you are authorized to exercise your discretion in receiving or rejecting the same; all presents received being for the use of Her Majesty.

16. You will finally propose to him an Agreement upon the basis of the draft with which you are herewith furnished.

17. If, after earnestly discussing this matter with the Chief, you shall find that your arguments have not so far prevailed with him, as to induce him to enter into this Agreement for the Extinction of the Foreign Slave Trade in his dominions; and if he shall resolutely resist your suggestions and the wishes of Her Majesty to that effect; you will entreat and urge him to reconsider this matter, you will ask him to assemble his elders or head-men, and consult with them, before he finally rejects the proposals made by you.

18. You will, if permitted to be present at such conference, declare that the Queen your Sovereign, however powerful, is anxious only to promote peace and prosperity among them; that she offers them, through you, every advantage that they can want and that she can give, towards increasing, in a harmless and sure way, the wealth and power of the country; that you come but to ask them to give up the custom of exporting human beings as slaves, and in return to offer them a more profitable substitute in innocent trade; that if they wish moreover any help towards the production of any article, or introduction of any commodity or art for the benefit of their country, your Sovereign is disposed to assist them, and her subjects will be willing to supply at a moderate rate what they desire; and that you will express to Her Majesty their wishes, and forward their views to that effect.

19. While you describe the power and wealth of your country, you will, in all your interviews with the African Chiefs, and with other African natives, on the subject of the suppression of the Slave Trade, abstain carefully from any threat or intimation, that hostilities upon their territory will be the result of their refusal to treat. You will state that the Queen and people of England profess the Christian Religion; that by this religion they are commanded to assist in promoting good will, peace, and brotherly love, among all nations and men; and

that in endeavouring to commence a further intercourse with the African nations Her Majesty's Government are actuated and guided by these principles. You will make allowance for the motives of fear, of distrust, of jealousy, of suspicion, by which native Africans, unaccustomed to treat with Europeans in this formal way, may, at first, naturally view the overtures made to them; you will make allowance also for misunderstanding, either of language, of manner, or of conduct, or of your object in seeking intercourse with them; you will also allow for any hardness of feeling you may witness in them on the subject of Slave Trade, a hardness naturally engendered by the exercise of that traffic, and, perhaps, in some cases, increased by intercourse with the lowest and basest of Europeans. You will endeavour to convince them by courtesy, by kindness, by patience and forbearance, of your most persevering desire to be on good terms with them; and you will be most careful to exhibit no signs of needless mistrust. You will on all occasions keep a strict watch, so that no mischief may, from open force or secret wile of the natives, ensue to the lives, liberties, and properties of yourselves, and of others committed to your care; and with this view you will be careful to be provided with adequate means of defence as far as possible; but you will on no account have recourse to arms, excepting for the purpose of defence; and you will bear in mind, that the language and conduct prescribed to you in this paragraph is that which you are to observe on all occasions in the course of your commission.

20. If, after all your attempts to attain the immediate object of your commission, you shall fail in it, you will conclude by telling the Chief and his head-men, that Her Majesty is bound to use all her naval means in conformity with the treaties already entered into with other Great Powers to endeavour entirely to put a stop to the exportation of Slaves from the dominions of every African Chief; and that the Chief and his subjects will, when perhaps too late, see cause to regret their conduct.

21. In those cases in which, all your arguments and representations failing, you will have been obliged to leave the Chief and his country, without accomplishing the immediate objects of your mission, you will be careful still even at parting to leave that Chief and his country in a friendly manner, in order to give room for future overtures, and for a reconsideration of the kindly meant efforts of Her Majesty; and you will, if time and circumstances allow it, take an opportunity of visiting again those Chiefs, who in your first visit declined your overtures; and strengthened by the weight which your success elsewhere may have given to your negotiations, you will again urge the Chiefs to conclude an agreement, on the before-mentioned basis of the abolition of the Slave Trade . . .

It is considered desirable by Her Majesty's Government to have power to erect one or more small forts on the Niger, from whence, and by means of which, to watch over the due execution of the Agreements, to assist in the abolition of the Slave Trade, and to protect and further the innocent trade of Her Majesty's subjects.

Bearing these views in mind, you will, in your course up that river, select some one or more appropriate spots for the erection of forts for the above-mentioned purposes; and you will make with the Chief of the country a conditional bargain for the land, stating the purpose for which it is intended; you will pay down a small portion of the price, as security for the purchase and permission; and you will send or bring home, for the consideration and ultimate decision of Her Majesty's Government, reports and drawings explanatory of the spot and its capabilities.

The spots should be chosen with reference both to defence and salubrity; to soil and to climate, not only of the spots themselves, but also of the immediate neighbourhood on both sides of the river; because the miasma from one side of a river will frequently, if carried by winds, produce diseases on the other side. They should be places where vessels may securely anchor and ride in safety. They should be in situations to which natives are likely to resort for trade; and if possible, in situations where natives have been accustomed to resort for the purpose. Means of a ready communication with the interior are also desirable for the positions; so that persons wishing to visit the interior from thence, for purposes of commerce or otherwise, may there find facilities for those objects. They should be in a neighbourhood where supplies for vessels may be got; and in a country where the inhabitants are well disposed towards friendly communication with British subjects; and they will be preferably situated if not far from some considerable mass of habitations. The establishment of a position near to the confluence of the rivers Niger and Tchadda, would, with its other advantages, have the additional and important one, that it would assist the British trade with both rivers . . .

33. If at any place, in an independent State within the range of your commission, it shall appear to you to be desirable, that a resident agent on the part of Her Majesty, shall be immediately appointed, and enter on his duties, you are empowered to leave at such a place provisionally, as British resident agent, any one of the gentlemen of your commission, or of the officers or others of the expedition, whom you may think competent and fitted to the duties of that situation. You may assure to such gentleman an allowance proportioned to the circumstances of his situation, for one year only.

42 • Treaties with "barbarians" are different from those with "civilised" people (1840–41)

Treaties that dealt ostensibly with antislavery policies had implications for African sovereignty. If an African leader agreed to bring an end to slavery and was unable to do so, did that mean that the British had the legal right (however they defined such a right) to intervene? The template drawn up by the British for treaties with African chiefs began with expressions of "peace and friendship," moved on to measures to reduce the trade in slaves, and ended with a requirement that the "person and property of the agent [of the British monarch be treated as though] sacred." In practice, as the treaty with the king of Kataba shows, antislavery treaties with African leaders resulted in the transfer of considerable powers from indigenous leaders to the British monarch. James Stephen, undersecretary of state for colonies, noted in a minute regarding the treaty that such fundamental changes could take place because diplomatic agreements made with Africans were not really "treaties" but rather "arrangements" that could be amended as the secretary of state for foreign affairs saw fit. That was how one dealt with "barbarous" as distinct from "civilised" people.[3]

3. Newbury, *British Policy towards Africa*, 150–53, 224–26.

A. Draft agreement with African chiefs, July 1840

Object:

There shall be peace and friendship between the people of England and the people of ———— and the slave trade shall be put down for ever in ————, and the people of England and the people of ———— shall trade together innocently, justly, kindly and usefully. And A and B do make the following agreement for these purposes:

Terms:

1. No white Christian persons shall be made slaves in the country in any case; and if any white Christians are now slaves in the ———— country, or shall be brought into it as slaves, they shall instantly be set free by the Chief of ————, and he shall assist them to return to their own country.

2. No persons of any colour, or wherever born, shall be taken out of the ———— country as slaves; and no person in the ———— country shall be in any way concerned in seizing, keeping, carrying, or sending away any persons for the purpose of their being taken out of the ———— country as slaves. And the Chief of ———— shall punish severely all those who break this law.

3. The officers of the Queen of England may seize every vessel or boat of ———— found anywhere carrying on the trade in slaves, and may also seize every vessel or boat of other nations found carrying on the trade in slaves in the waters belonging to the Chief of ————, and the vessels and boats so seized shall be taken into an England possession to be tried by English law; and, when condemned, shall be sold, and the produce of the sale shall be divided equally between the Queen of England and the Chief of ————, and the slaves who were found on board shall be made free.

4. English people may come freely into the ———— country, and may stay in it or pass through it; and they shall be treated as friends while in it, and shall receive every supply they need there; they may freely practice the Christian religion there, and shall not be harmed nor troubled on that account; and they may leave the country when they please.

5. English people may always trade freely with the people of ———— in every article which they may wish to buy or sell; and neither the English people nor the people of ———— shall ever be forced to buy or to sell any article, nor shall they be prevented from buying or selling any article; and the customs and dues taken by the Chief of ———— on English goods shall in no case be more altogether than 1/ th part of the price of the goods sold.

6. The paths shall be kept open through the ———— country to other countries, so that English traders may carry goods of all kinds through the ———— country to sell them elsewhere; and the traders of other countries may bring their goods through the ———— country to trade with the English people.

7. English people may buy and sell or hire lands and houses in the ———— country, and their houses shall not be entered without their consent, nor shall their goods be seized, nor their persons touched; and if English people are wronged or ill treated by the people of ————, and Chief of ———— shall punish those who wrong or ill treat the English people.

8. But the English people must not break the laws of the ———— country; and when they are accused of breaking the laws, the chiefs shall send a true account of the matter to the nearest place where there is an English force; and the commander of such English force shall send

for the English person, who shall be tried according to English law, and shall be punished if found guilty.

9. If the ———— people should take away the property of an English person, or should not pay their just debts to an English person, the Chief of ———— shall do all he can to make the ———— people restore the property and pay the debt; and if English persons should take away the property of the ———— people, or should not pay their just debts to the ———— people, the Chief of ———— shall make known the fact to the Commander of the English force, nearest to the ———— country, or to the resident agent, if there is one; and the English Commander, or the agent, whichever it may be, shall do all he can to make the English persons restore the property and pay the debt.

10. The Queen of England may appoint an agent to visit ———— or to reside there, in order to watch over the interests of the English people, and to see that this agreement is fulfilled; and such agent shall always receive honour and protection in the ———— country, and the ———— Chiefs shall pay attention to what the agent says; and the person and property of the agent shall be sacred.

11. The Chief of ———— shall, within 48 hours of the date of this agreement, make a law for carrying the whole of it into effect; and shall proclaim that law, and the Chief of ———— shall put that law in force from that time for ever . . .

Additional terms for special cases:

Article 1. Moreover, the Queen of England, for ———— years to come, will have ready every year, at ————, the following articles, viz: ———— and an English officer shall inquire in each year whether the Chief of ———— and his people have faithfully kept the foregoing agreement, and if, after enquiry, he shall be satisfied that they have kept the agreement, he shall then deliver the articles to the chief, or to the chief's agent for him; but when the English officer is not satisfied, he shall not deliver the articles.

Article 2. The practice of making human sacrifice, on account of religious or political ceremonies or customs, shall cease for ever in ————.

Article 3. The Chief of ———— sells and makes over to the English people of the Queen of England, the land from ———— to ———— and everything in it, entirely and for ever, for the sum of ————, of which ———— is now paid to him. And the English people shall have possession of the said land, and of whatever may be upon it, when they shall have paid to the Chief of ———— the remainder of the price above stated; and when the land shall be delivered over to the English people, they may do with it as they please.

Article 4. The Queen of England will assist in protecting the Chief and people of ———— against any attack which other chiefs and people may make on them on account of anything they may do for the purpose of giving up the slave trade according to the present agreement.

B. The treaty with Kataba (upper Guinea coast), April 23, 1841

. . . The Officer of England may seize every vessel or boat of Cartabar [Kataba] found anywhere carrying on the trade in Slaves, in the waters of Cartabar and the vessel and boats so seized shall be taken to an English possession to be tried by English law, and if condemned, shall with appurtenances and cargo be sold, the produce of the sale being equally divided between the Queen of England and the King of Cartabar.

Two Additional Articles:

1. The King of Cartabar seeing that he is unable of himself to prevent the incursion of neighbouring ill-disposed Chiefs delighting only in war and who have heretofore annually ravaged his Country, carrying off his people as Slaves; the cattle and produce; now and for ever places the Country of Cartabar under the sole protection of the Sovereign of England and he begs that Her Majesty Victoria the 1st. Queen of England may become in his own royal person and for Her Heirs and successors, the protecting Sovereign of the Cartabar Country; And the King of Cartabar freely cedes forever, to the Queen of England Her Heirs and successors one square mile of land in such part of his country as shall be pointed out by the Lieutenant Governor of the British Settlements of the Gambia or other officer authorized to do so.

2. The King of Cartabar agrees that he will not enter any alliances, negotiations or communication of any political nature whatever, with any power in the world without the knowledge and consent of the Queen of England; and the King of Cartabar declares the whole of the annexed Treaty, and these two additional articles to be binding equally to himself as to His Heirs and successors forever . . .

C. James Stephen's minute on the implications of the Kataba Treaty, September 6, 1841

. . . When the Niger Expedition was resolved on, it was also resolved to make war on the Slave Trade by Treaties with the Chiefs of the Interior. A model of such a Treaty was prepared, and was sent to each of the Governors. Capt. Huntley, the Governor of the Gambia, accordingly made a Treaty with a Chief called the King of Cartabar . . .

I have called this Agreement with the King of Cartabar a *Treaty*, but it should be observed that in devolving all these arrangements on this Office, Lord Palmerston [the prime minister] expressly stipulated against the use of any such Diplomatic language. He desired that the compacts to be made with the African Chiefs should be described as "Arrangements or Agreements," or by some other word which should exclude them from the class of Diplomatic Conventions. The distinction is not verbal or trivial. It means to reserve to the Secretary of State for Foreign Affairs his own exclusive power of negociating Treaties, and it is also meant to mark the distinction between Agreements with barbarous Chiefs and the international Compacts of Civilized States.

43 • A long-sought-for highway into the very heart of the continent (1854)

During the first half of the nineteenth century, British merchants, followed by government officials, sought a safe way into the interior of West Africa. In the words of one of the most persistent of these men, Macgregor Laird, the goal was to get access to "new and unrestricted markets" in the interior, particularly palm oil, without being subject to "the caprice and extortion of the petty chiefs at the mouths of the principal rivers of the African coast." Such access by river, especially the Niger, to an area in which "Nature had profusely bestowed her choicest treasures" and which already exported goods worth a million pounds annually (as Laird understood on the basis of information from English travelers and captured slaves), offered to the merchant "a boundless field of enterprise," to the manufacturer "an extensive market for his goods," and to youths, "the irresistible charms of novelty, danger, and adventure." Moreover, by introducing "legitimate commerce with all its attendant blessings into the centre of the country," a mortal blow could be struck at slavery, and millions could be rescued from "a religion characterized by violence and blood" and could learn "the truths of Christianity—that mild and beneficent faith, which proclaims 'peace on earth and good-will towards man.'" (See Laird and R. A. K. Oldfield, Narrative of an Expedition into the Interior of Africa, *1834.)*

However, Laird's voyage by steamer up the Niger in the years 1832–34 resulted in the death of more than 80 percent of the crew from "poison," the word used to describe any illness that could not otherwise be explained. The British government-financed expedition a few years later (1841–42) fared a little better, but not much. More than 35 percent of the Europeans on the expedition died, a mortality rate high enough to suggest that the interior was no more welcoming to the health of Europeans than was the coast.

In 1854, however, Macgregor Laird returned to his quest, this time financed by the British government and accompanied by the Reverend Samuel Crowther. On this expedition, led by Scottish explorer William Balfour Baikie, Laird demonstrated not only that the Niger could be navigated by steam far into the interior and that the trading potential of the interior was indeed as great as hoped for but also that, with the use of quinine, travel could be accomplished safely even if the nature of the "poison" still remained unknown. For the first time in the history of European exploration of the West African interior, an expedition returned without a single fatality. The account below was authored by Baikie.[4]

From the days of Herodotus to very recent times the theories which have been brought forward regarding the course and distribution of the Kwóra, or Niger, have been both numerous and varied. Geographers, both ancient and modern, have exerted their utmost ingenuity in endeavouring to solve the mystery; and, according as they believed in the westward or eastward course of the river, ranged themselves into two parties, the one pointing to the Senegal and the Gambia as the mouths of this mighty stream, while the other either conducted it through Lake Tsad to join the Nile, or else led it by a long and dreary route to be identified with the Congo. It certainly appears singular that, until a comparatively recent date, no one even hinted at its real termination. The numerous large bodies of fresh water falling into the bights of Benin and Biafra have for long been familiarly known, yet their source was never enquired after . . . it was not until 1808, that Reichard, judging from the vast amounts of alluvial deposits, first suggested the Rio Formoso as the outlet of the Kwóra, an idea since proved to be partially true. Major Laing and Captain Clapperton also believed in the discharge of its waters into the Bight of Benin, the former selecting the Rio Volta for the purpose, while the latter hypothesized an opening to the eastward of Lagos. But by no one was the enquiry pursued more seriously or more shrewdly than by Mr. Macqueen, who, having collected a vast amount

---

4. William Balfour Baikie, *Narrative of an Exploring Voyage up the Rivers Kwóra and Bínue (commonly Known as the Niger and Tsádda) in 1854. With a Map and Appendices. Pub. with the Sanction of Her Majesty's Government* (London: John Murray, 1856), 1–5, 29–30, 400–401, 403, 405, 406–7, 452–55.

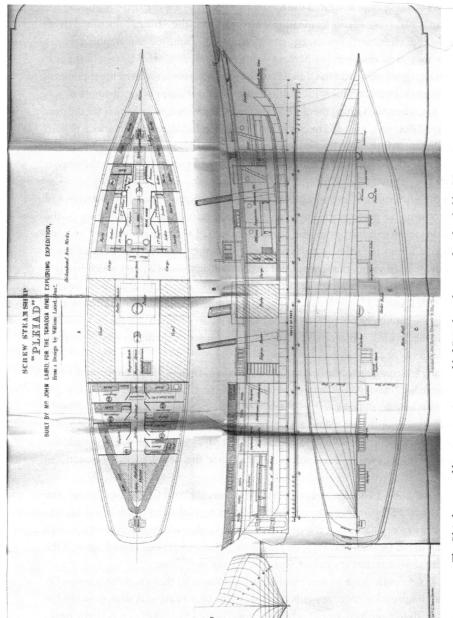

FIGURE 10 The *Pleiad*, powered by steam engines, enabled British explorers and traders led by Macgregor Laird and accompanied by the Reverend Samuel Crowther to sail against the river currents into the interior of Africa in 1854. Quinine, used for the first time on the *Pleiad*'s voyage, proved an effective prophylactic against malaria and prevented any deaths from that disease, up to that time the greatest cause of European mortality in Africa. William Balfour Baikie, *Narrative of an Exploring Voyage up the Rivers Kwóra and Bínue*, 1856.

of evidence on the subject, recommended in 1829, a careful examination of the rivers between the Rio Formoso and Old Kalabar. It must have been highly gratifying to this old ge-
ographer, whose knowledge of Central Africa is probably unsurpassed, to find only two years
afterwards his supposition verified by the splendid exploit of the Landers, who, at the expense
of so much risk and suffering, navigated the Kwóra from Yaúri to the sea, thereby proving the
existence of an available water communication with the heart of the African continent. His attempt, chiefly from climacteric causes, ended unfortunately: a spirited and graphic account
of its discoveries and its disasters [83 percent death rate] was published by two of the survivors, Mr. Macgregor Laird and Mr. Oldfield . . . The misfortunes met with by these pioneers
did not afford much encouragement for further trials, and no attempt of any magnitude was
made until 1841, when the Government fitted out three steamers, specially built for the purpose. This expedition was intended to carry out, besides extended research, various philan-
thropic but ill-matured schemes. Its ill success, with its fearful amount of sickness and loss of
life [35 percent death rate], still fresh in our memories, tended greatly to confirm the conviction of the deadly nature of the climate . . .

Such is the brief outline of the previous attempts to investigate and explore this river, and
though inducements to perseverance were far from wanting, still no one, reflecting on the
great probable sacrifice of European life, cared about taking the responsibility of advising
another attempt. But in 1852 the question was again started, in consequence of intelligence
received from Dr. Barth, who, the sole but still undaunted survivor of a party which had two
years before crossed the Great Desert, had boldly journeyed to the southward . . . On the 18th
of June, 1851, he crossed a large stream, named the Bínue, which, from the information he
received from the natives, he conjectured to be the upper part of the river hitherto known to
Europeans as the Tsádda. To ascertain this point, the present expedition was principally
destined . . .

[Admiralty Instructions to the British Consul, May 23, 1854 . . . The vessel prepared for
this expedition is the "Pleiad," an iron screw steamer of 260 tons burthen, rigged as a schooner.
She is 100 feet in length, 24 feet beam, engines of 60 horse power, and having 7 feet draught
of water, with three months provisions and stores on board, and twenty days' coal of twelve
hours each. She is officially reported on her trial of speed, at Liverpool, to have made ten
knots an hour in smooth water. There will be, in addition to this vessel, two 50 feet sectional
iron trade boats . . .

The Expedition has two main objects. One is to explore the river Chadda, or Benueh, the
eastern branch of the Káwara from Dágbo, the highest point reached by Oldfield and Allen in
1833, to the country of Adamauá, a distance of about 400 miles, where the river was crossed
at the junction of the Benueh and Faro, by Dr. Barth, in June 1851; and thence again, if the
season permits and the waters are still rising, to the limit of navigation.

The other is to endeavour to meet and afford assistance to that excellent traveler Dr.
Barth, who left England for Africa towards the close of the year 1849, and, who, from the lat-
est accounts received from him, would, after reaching Tumbuktu, make his way to the banks
of the Benueh . . . The same instructions hold good respecting Dr. Vogel, who left England in
1853, and who may have succeeded in penetrating to the banks of the Chadda.

In carrying out these two objects it is the desire of Her Majesty's Government, for the
benefit of commerce and civilization, to take every opportunity for opening trade with the

natives at each large town on the banks of the river . . . One hundred pounds' worth of suitable presents and samples of goods have been supplied by the Government for this purpose . . . These are to be freely given on all occasions; it is left to your judgment to limit the amount, but the practice is always to be observed in conformity with the custom of the country. It is further desirable to make careful enquiries as to the political power of the several chiefs, as to the state of civilization among them, as to the existence of foreign slave-trade, and if so, whether they would consent to put an end to it, if lawful trade could be ensured to them, and a market opened for ivory and other products of the country. Mr. Crowther will naturally enquire into the apparent disposition, willingness, or aptitude of the natives to receive religious or secular instruction . . .

The "Pleiad" being armed with a 12-pounder pivot-gun, four swivels, Minié rifles and double-barrelled guns for the officers, muskets for the crew, and with boarding nettings of wire, it is not probable that she will meet with any opposition in the lower parts of the river where there may be danger. But you will remember that the best security from attack consists in the natives seeing and knowing you are well prepared to meet it. At the same time you are strictly enjoined to use the greatest forbearance towards the people, and, while maintaining proper firmness in the event of any misunderstanding, to endeavour to conciliate as far as can possibly be admitted with safety to your party. You will, on all occasions, enforce the strictest justice, and never, on any account, permit one of your party to ill-treat, insult, or cheat the natives . . .

Macgregor Laird instructions to the sailing master, May 8, 1854 . . .

You will consider all trading operations subsidiary and auxiliary to the main design of the voyage, which is to ascend the river Chadda, the eastern branch of the Niger, as high as possible during the rise of the river . . .

In your intercourse with the natives you are not to assume any other character than that of a trader, which they will at once recognize and understand. You are not to mix yourself up with their local disputes; and, when they exist, change your location as quickly as possible, deal with them firmly and justly, and on no account allow the slightest insult or the smallest theft offered or committed on board your vessel to pass unnoticed or unpunished.

You will conform to the customs of the country in making the usual presents to the chiefs and leading men of the villages and towns you visit, using your judgment as to the amount, but never committing the practice, which corresponds to the Custom-House charges of civilized countries . . .

Your superiority is in your arms, and a few rounds of canister from your pivot-gun will be sufficient to show them that, after which you will have no more trouble. The cause of any collision is generally misunderstanding. As a rule the natives are well disposed, but in the lower parts of the river they cannot resist the temptation to plunder, if they think it can be done with impunity. Above Eboe there is no danger.

The Rev. Mr. Crowther, to whom I have offered a passage in the "Pleiad," will join at Fernando Po from Lagos. It is my desire that he has every opportunity given him of seeing the country and the people. His position on board is that of my guest, and you will see that he is treated with deference and respect.]

The peculiar features of this expedition were, first, the employment of as few white men as possible; secondly, entering and ascending the river with the rising waters, or during the rainy season; and lastly, it was anticipated that the use of quinine, as a prophylactic or preventive, would enable the Europeans to with stand the influence of the climate . . .

The Government party now consisted of myself and Mr. May, my assistant, and a black servant, and also Mr. Richards, whom I had engaged as interpreter . . . and Simon Jonas, an Igbo, who had been with the expedition in 1841; there were also Mr. [Samuel] Crowther and his servant, and the ship's complement comprised a sailing-master, three mates, a surgeon, three engineers, one supercargo, a steward, three black firemen, three interpreters, a cooper, a carpenter, four coloured seaman and two boys, and thirty-three Krúmen; in all, twelve Europeans, and fifty-four persons of colour . . .

Conclusion . . .

• We have discovered a navigable river, and available highway, conducting us into the very heart of a large continent . . .
• We have found these regions to be highly favoured by nature, teeming with animal life, and with fertile soils abounding in valuable vegetable products . . .
• We have met on friendly terms with numerous tribes, all endowed by nature with what I may term the "commercial faculty," ready and anxious to trade with us, and to supply us from their inexhaustible stores, with immense quantities of highly-prized articles . . .
• We can likewise indicate a most important outlet for home manufactures, as the unclad millions of Central Africa must absorb thousands of cargoes of soft goods, eagerly bartering their raw cotton, their vegetable oils, and their ivory, for our calicoes and cloths . . .

Appendix G. As I intend shortly to discuss at some length the question of African fever, I shall touch but very lightly on it here. It has been hitherto a great bugbear, and until very recently has been regarded and treated in an empirical and unscientific manner . . . It will be sufficient here to say that African fever has nothing specific about it; that it is certainly not *sui generis*, and that it is merely an aggravated form of the disease known in this country as ague. The various divisions into continued, remittent, and intermittent are only calculated to puzzle and to mislead; they refer to degrees and not to actual differences, and these forms gradually but surely merge into each other. In its mildest form the fever is intermittent, that is to say, between the paroxysms intervals of health occur: more aggravated, the complaint becomes remittent, meaning, that between the febrile accessions the symptoms only remit, but do not altogether disappear: in its greatest intensity the disease is quasi-continued, or to the unpractised eye seems to be devoid of paroxysmal changes, but to proceed with an undeviating deadly career. But in all these the poison, the original cause of the malady, is essentially the same and the results depend partly on constitutional causes, partly on the amount and virulence of the poison imbibed. The same amount of poison will, as is the case with alcohol, affect two persons inhaling it in very different degrees. The disease is what is termed by medical men *periodic*, and the remedies required are called *anti-periodics*, of which the best known and the most efficacious is quinine. This may be given as soon as the complaint shows itself, and the sooner the better, as it is the main-stay of the sufferer; of course, various occasional symptoms may occur during its progress, which will require to be treated according to circumstances. But the great modern improvement is the discovery that quinine not only cures, but that it actually prevents, and that by taking this invaluable drug while in unhealthy localities, persons may escape totally unscathed . . .

Much ingenuity has been displayed by those who believe in the specific nature of African fever in endeavouring to discover causes for its supposed malignity. At one time sulphuretted hydrogen was pronounced to be the *origo mali*, the theorists forgetting that if so, Harrowgate and Strathpeffer would be highly dangerous spots. Then putrid matters, moisture, vegetable decay, &c., each had their supporters, as well as many other hypotheses; but at present we only know that the poison, of the nature of which we are as yet ignorant, may arise from a dry soil. It is certainly more abundant where there is moisture, and generally more intense; but all that is really required for its production are a certain amount of heat and *previous* moisture. These conditions are widely spread, and therefore we find *malaria* also nearly ubiquitous, though more prevalent in warm climates. But in no *essential* does African endemic fever differ from the fever of Hindustan, of Borneo, of the Spanish Main, of the West Indies, or of fenny and marshy countries in Europe . . . Lastly, let it be always borne in mind that this disease is strictly and inherently non infectious.

44 • The persistence of "illegal" slaving (1848–61)

Despite the 1807 British and American legislation outlawing the export trade in slaves, and despite the activities of British antislavery vessels off the coast of West Africa, tens of thousands of Africans continued to be exported annually across the Atlantic. Though the export trade had been made illegal, Britain did not end the institution of slavery within its own colonial possessions until 1833, the United States not until 1865, and Brazil not until 1888. Moreover, travelers to Africa reported evidence of an increased use of slaves within indigenous communities, a result of utilizing the labor of some of those previously exported for the production of other goods for export from Africa to meet the changing demands of European merchants. The growth in slavery within Africa during the period when Europeans were traveling into the interior for the first time led to strong condemnations of slavery as a distinctly African phenomenon. Long-term European residents of Africa, however, such as Brodie Cruickshank, pointed out that slavery in Africa took a number of forms, including "pawning," and was not the same as the chattel slavery of the Americas.

A striking pattern that did arise from the antislave measures taken by the British and other European powers in the nineteenth century was a geographical shift in the slave export trade, with a decline along the west coast of Africa, a continued large-scale export from the Portuguese-dominated coast of West Central Africa, and a huge growth on the east coast. The expansion in the east (where exports had been negligible before about 1800) resulted from a combination of a rising demand for slaves on newly established French plantations in the Indian Ocean (this despite French emancipation in 1848); the development of spice plantations worked by slave labor on the Arab-ruled islands of Zanzibar, Pemba, and parts of the East African coast; increasing exports to the Persian Gulf and India; and the activities of Brazilian, Spanish, and American slavers seeking new sources of slaves for Brazil and Cuba to replace those under pressure on the west coast.

The following reports chart the move of the export trade from west to east and show the potential for African-European conflict arising from disputes about the terms of trade, the persistence and growth of slavery within Africa, and the issue of escapees. As on the west coast, European slave traders had to obtain supplies of slaves and negotiate prices with local merchants, often Arabs based in Zanzibar. Likewise, they often had to make tribute payments to local rulers as, for example, the Portuguese did on an annual basis to the Zulu. Each of the authors spent different amounts of time in Africa and had quite different experiences. Brodie Cruickshank lived on the Gold Coast between 1834 and 1854, was a member of the first legislative council of the Gold Coast when the colony gained independence from the administration of Sierra Leone in 1850, and briefly served as the colony's acting governor. Paul du Chaillu's account is based on four trips he made to Africa in the 1850s primarily to investigate the flora and fauna (he "shot, stuffed, and brought home over 2,000 birds . . . and . . . killed upwards of 1,000 quadrupeds"). Frederick Barnard was a British naval lieutenant who spent three years on an antislavery patrol on the coast of Mozambique.[5]

A. Brodie Cruickshank on indigenous slavery in West Africa, 1853

The condition of the slaves in the countries under our protection is by no means one of unmitigated hardship. In ordinary cases, the slave is considered as a member of his master's family, and often succeeds to his property, in default of a natural heir. He eats with him from the same dish, and has an equal share in all his simple enjoyments. He intermarries with his children, and is allowed to acquire property of his own, over which, unless under very extraordinary circumstances, his master exercises no control. He sometimes even acquires wealth and consideration far superior to his master, who may occasionally be seen swelling his importance, by following in his train. They address each other as "my father" and "my son," and differ in little in their mutual relations from the respect and obedience implied in these endearing epithets.

We see in the whole of their domestic economy a complete transcript of the patriarchal age; the same participation in the cares, and sorrows, and enjoyments of life; the same community of feeling and of interest; and the same external equality, conjoined with a devoted obedience, so marked and decided, as to assume the form of a natural instinct. This quality in the mind of dependents has a tendency to destroy the idea of personal accountability. The will of the master is in most instances more than a counterpoise for the volition of the slave, who yields obedience to his commands with an instinctive submission, without the intervention of any external compulsion, and often under circumstances where the natural inclination of the slave is opposed to the particular conduct required of him. Slavery of body and mind is thus thoroughly engrained in the constitution of the African. We have known cases of murder having been committed at the command of a master, and against the remonstrances of the slave, who however does not refuse compliance; and we have seen how completely the will of the master has been considered the test of the slave's conscience, by the perfect unconcern of the latter respecting the deed, and the absence of any idea of his accountability for it.

Scarcely would the slave of an Ashantee chief obey the mandate of his king, without the special concurrence of his immediate master; and the slave of a slave will refuse obedience to

5. A, Brodie Cruickshank, *Eighteen Years on the Gold Coast of Africa, Including an Account of the Native Tribes, and Their Intercourse with Europeans* (London: Hurst and Blackett, 1853), vol. 2, 236–50; B, Paul B. du Chaillu, *Explorations and Adventures in Equatorial Africa* (John Murray: London, 1861), 141–47; C, Frederick Lamport Barnard, R.N., *A Three Years' Cruize in the Mozambique Channel* (London: R. Bentley, 1848), 137–38, 153–54, 206–7, 217, 223–25, 258–59.

his master's master, unless the order be conveyed to him through his own master. This perfect identification of the mind of the slave with that of his master has no doubt given rise to the master's accountability for the acts of his slave, and to the laws which affect them. He has to pay his debts, and to make compensation and restitution for every injury committed by him, either wilfully or accidentally. This responsibility may be a cause of the kind and considerate treatment so often observable, the master's interest being so closely involved in the conduct of his slave, as to render him anxious to attach him to his person, and to engage his affectionate obedience. It will also account for the isolated cases of harshness and cruelty which occasionally come under our observation, the vindictive slave having it in his power to cause his master much annoyance and expense, for which the latter can only retaliate by corporal suffering. Where this discordant spirit exists, the master, after repeated ineffectual attempts to reclaim an incorrigible slave, gets rid of the annoyance by selling him.

There does not appear any limit to the extent of punishment which a master is permitted to inflict upon his slave. He is considered so entirely his property, that he may with impunity put him to death; although from applications for freedom, on the ground of severe personal injury, such as the loss of an eye or a tooth, there is reason to believe that, during some period of their history, the slave was protected by a more humane code of laws.

We have heard a slave argue for his emancipation on the score of the accidental loss of an eye, in his master's service, from the recoil of a branch of a tree, and appeal to a traditionary law which entitles him to this compensation.

Like the Hebrews, the Fantees make a distinction between the slaves, their countrymen, and those who have been taken in war, or purchased from another tribe. The latter, until they become amalgamated by a long period of servitude, and by intermarriage, do not receive the same considerate treatment. They are considered an inferior race, with the ordinary class of whom it is thought derogatory for the daughters of the land to intermarry. The burden of the labour of the country falls upon them. Immense numbers of these slaves are being annually imported into the country, through Ashantee, from the countries near the range of the Kong Mountains. Many of them, on their first arrival, manifest an extraordinary degree of stolidity and brutishness, and exhibit a very low type of intellect and breeding. They pass under the general name of "Donko," a word signifying a slave in the language of the interior, and which, from the great stupidity of these creatures, has come to be a word of reproach, tantamount to "fool." They are naturally a very obstinate, perverse, and self-willed race, upon whom it is difficult to make any impression by kindness. It is very difficult also to coerce them to labour; and yet, notwithstanding their many bad qualities, the Fantees eagerly purchase them from the Ashantees. They vary in price from £6 to £8, girls and boys being sold at a considerable reduction. They have scars on the face and person, distinctive of their native tribes; some with semi-circular lines covering the whole face, some with a few scarred lines on each cheek, some with a single raised mark upon the forehead, and others seamed and scarred over the whole of the upper part of their persons. Among this servant race, we find also a good many mongrel Moors, little superior to the others.

If they arrive in the country at an early age, they are by no means slow in acquiring knowledge, and become very useful to their masters, and sometimes obtain a consideration equal to the native of the country, intermarrying with the Fantees, and becoming members of their families. But if the Donko be grown up before his arrival upon the coast, he generally remains a dull, stolid beast of burden all the days of his life. It is only by comparing the native Fantee with these, that we are sensible of the very great advancement of the former, who appears a very civilized being in comparison with this foreign race. And yet these are not altogether devoid of some of the better qualities of our nature. They evince much sympathy and compassion for each other, and readily assist one another in their difficulties. A common fate appears to unite them by the ties of a patriotic attachment, and they delight to sing, in the place of their captivity, the songs of their native land. Their treatment by their masters depends much upon their own conduct, for interest, as well as natural inclination, make the Fantee a kind master. The great stubbornness of the Donko, however, often brings down upon him a severe chastisement, to which he submits with a sullen insensibility. Some thousands of these are added to the population of the country under our protection every year. Various considerations have induced the local government to tolerate this internal slave trade, which it would be difficult to suppress. The objects of it are either taken in war by the Ashantees, received as tribute from subjugated states, or purchased by them. If they were not bought by the Fantees, many of them would be sacrificed at the Ashantee customs, or kept in a worse bondage in that country. By being brought into the countries under our protection, their lives are spared; they receive a more humane treatment; they are shielded from oppression, and are placed within the influence of a higher degree of civilization. Their condition, in every respect, is improved by the change, and the second generation becomes an effective addition to a by no means superabundant population.

It will be seen, then, that while the diffusion of wealth and the progress of knowledge are creating a spirit of industry, and exciting a desire for greater freedom among the native Fantees, a fresh tide of slavery is pouring into the country from another direction. It may be questioned how far this state of matters is to be approved. But when we reflect, that the Ashantee wars are not undertaken expressly to supply this demand; that the transfer of the slaves from the Ashantee to the Fantee country is not adding to the ranks of slavery generally; that it greatly ameliorates the condition of the slaves in question, and brings them and their descendants within the scope of many civilizing influences, to which they would otherwise have remained strangers; that, moreover, an increase to the population is desirable to bring out the resources of a rich and fertile country, we are warranted in concluding that the cause of general civilization and of humanity is advanced by this movement. It is not unreasonable to hope that, after centuries of progress, the tide of emigration may again recede into the interior, carrying with it the seeds of civilization and Christian knowledge.

Besides the native-born Fantee slaves, and those purchased from the interior, there remains to be noticed another species of slavery existing, under the name of "pawns," to which we have already adverted. It has been seen that individuals form, in the present state of commerce, no small portion of the currency of the country. To obtain a loan or pay a debt, a master does not hesitate to place one or more of his family, or slaves, in temporary bondage to another. The terms of this contract are, that the pawn shall serve his new master until such time as the person pawning him shall make good the sum lent, with 50 per cent. interest; the services of the pawn, even if they should extend over a great number of years, counting for nothing in the liquidation of the debt. If a woman has been pawned, her new master has the right to make her his concubine, and her children continue to serve him also.

The cruel operation of this system will be best illustrated by an example. We will suppose A. to pawn his daughter B. to his friend C. for the sum of two ounces. He finds it impossible to redeem her, perhaps, under a period of many years, during which time we will suppose her to have borne seven children to her master. A. now is anxious to redeem his daughter, but he cannot do so without paying C. the original amount with interest, and four ackies and a half (22s. 6d.) for each child, which raises the original debt of two ounces (£8) to four ounces fifteen ackies and a half, or £9 17s. 6d. The money paid on account of the children is regarded as an equivalent for their maintenance.

If A. has had to borrow the money to effect this redemption, which frequently happens, it will be seen that the original sum of two ounces would go on accumulating at a rate which must eventually leave this family in a state of hopeless bondage. The death of the pawn does not cancel the debt. A. must substitute another pawn in her place, or pay the amount; but in this case B. generally, though not invariably, foregoes the interest. Neither is the master of a pawn, like the master of a slave, responsible for his pawn's debts. These recoil upon the head of the person pawning her.

A father cannot pawn his child without the concurrence of the mother's relations, unless she also be his slave. Neither can a mother pawn her child without the father's consent; but if he cannot advance the sum required, then she can do so. We have always regarded this system of pawning as much worse than actual slavery, and we have seen but too many of its victims irrecoverably reduced to perpetual bondage. The English authorities have greatly mitigated its hardships, by refusing to consider the loan in any other light than that of a common debt.

After the account which has been given, the reader will now be able to have a clear comprehension of the nature and condition of slavery upon the Gold Coast. It would appear that it is greatly influenced by the state of social progress, and that its exactions become more rigid in proportion to the advancement of a people. The closer the points of resemblance between the master and the slave, the easier will be the yoke; and where the improvement of both go on simultaneously, all distinctions gradually become effaced. We see the gradual operation of this process among the Fantee masters and their native-born slaves, while the diffusion of greater wealth among the former, and of increased knowledge, renders the condition of the "donkos," an inferior class, more truly that of a degrading servitude, and widens the distance between them and their masters . . .

Another difficulty which our Gold Coast government has to contend against, is the disposal of runaway slaves from Ashantee. It was stipulated in our treaties with the king, that his fugitive subjects should be redelivered to him in the same way that Fantees, flying into his dominions, were to be restored to the governor. This arrangement was necessary to prevent malefactors escaping punishment. But in many cases, the runaway Ashantee seeks a refuge from the fate which is likely to overtake him at the murderous customs which are often taking place at Coomassie, and a natural repugnance is, of course, felt about surrendering him.

Our position and power, however, do not enable us to follow the course most consistent with our feelings. If we were to refuse to deliver these runaways, the King of Ashantee would retaliate by seizing all the Fantees in his country, where a large number may at all times be found prosecuting their trade. He has also the means of cutting off all intercourse with his country, a measure which he invariably adopts upon occasions of misunderstanding with the governor. If redress were refused, war would be the consequence, a calamity in the present hopeful state of progress which would go far to undo the good which has been already effected, and which of all things is most anxiously to be avoided. Under these circumstances, the governor is obliged to mediate as he best can, and refuses to deliver up the runaway, except upon condition of sufficient security being given that his life will be spared.

Although this restriction must be galling to the king, yet he is induced to submit to it, rather than incur the risk of a doubtful war, into which he and his chiefs would not hesitate to plunge if such a vital question as the non-surrender of runaway slaves were involved in the issue. The security given for their safety is simply "the king's great oath," taken on his behalf by his messengers. There is no instance known of this oath given under such circumstances being violated. We remember a case, which will show the fearful regard which the king has for oaths.

Upon application being made for some runaways, the messengers were required to take the usual oath before they were surrendered. The refugees, however, were not satisfied with this oath alone, and positively refused to return to Ashantee, unless the king's messengers would give additional security for their safety, by "kissing the white man's book." They did not hesitate to agree to this, as they were perfectly satisfied that the king's oath would not be violated, and that, therefore, there could be no danger in kissing the book. But when they returned to Coomassie, and the king found that they had bound him, not only by his own, but also by the white man's oath, he became alarmed, lest any accidental injury might happen to the persons thus protected, which might bring him under the penalty of its violation; and to get rid of the liability, he sent the refugees back to the Fantee country, preferring to lose them to the risk of incurring an unknown danger.

It will be thus seen, that both to avoid insurrection among the Fantees, and the horrors of a war with Ashantee, the British authorities are compelled to adopt a policy with regard to this slave question, which appears never to have been openly avowed, and which is never brought under the notice of the Colonial Office without exciting a feeling of uneasiness, and calling forth a renewed declaration that slavery cannot be recognized within our settlements upon the Gold Coast, thus throwing back upon the governor the responsibility of its recognition.

B. Paul du Chaillu on the coast of West Central Africa, 1861

The next day I made a visit to the barracoons, or slave-pens, Cape Lopez [on the coast of West Central Africa, north of the outlet of the Congo river and in the same longitude as the island of Sao Tōmé where the Portuguese had first established slave plantations in the fifteenth century] a great slave-dépôt—once one of the largest on the whole coast—and I had, of course, much curiosity to see how the traffic is carried on.

My way led through several of the villages which are scattered about the extensive plain. Every head of a family makes a separate little settlement, and the huts of his wives and slaves which surround his own make quite a little village. Each of these groups is hidden from view by surrounding clumps of bushes, and near each are the fields cultivated by the slaves. The object of building separately in this way is to prevent the destruction which used frequently to fall upon their larger towns at the hands of British cruisers, who have done their best several times to break up this nest of slave-dealing. A town could be shelled and burned down; these scattered plantations afford no mark.

Cape Lopez boasts of two slave-factories. I now visited the one kept by the Portuguese. It was, from the outside, an immense enclosure, protected by a fence of palisades twelve feet high, and sharp-pointed at the top. Passing through the gate, which was standing open, I found myself in the midst of a large collection of shanties surrounded by shade-trees, under which were lying about, in various positions, people enough to form a considerable African town.

An old Portuguese, who seemed to be sick, met and welcomed me, and conducted me to the white men's house, a two-story frame building, which stood immediately fronting the gate. This was poorly finished, but contained beds, a table, chairs, &c.

Unfortunately I do not speak either Spanish or Portuguese, and my conductor understood neither French nor English. We had, therefore, to make use of a native interpreter, who made slow work of our talk. The Portuguese complained that it was now very hard to land a cargo in the Brazils, as the Government was against them, and that each year the trade grew duller. To put myself on a right footing with him, I told him I had not come to trade, but to collect objects in natural history, and to see the country and hunt.

I was now led around. The large house I have mentioned was surrounded by a separate strong fence, and in the spacious yard which was thus cut off were the male slaves, fastened six together by a little stout chain which passed through a collar secured about the neck of each. This mode of fastening experience has proved to be the most secure. It is rare that six men are unanimous in any move for their own good, and it is found that no attempt to liberate themselves, when thus fastened, succeed. They reposed under sheds or shelters built about the yard, and here there were buckets of water from which they could drink when they felt inclined.

Beyond this yard was another for the women and children, who were not manacled, but allowed to rove at pleasure through their yard, which was protected by a fence. The men were almost naked. The women wore invariably a cloth about their middle.

Behind the great houses was the hospital for sick slaves. It was not ill-arranged, the rooms being large and well-ventilated, and the beds—structures of bamboo covered with a mat—were ranged about the walls.

Outside of all the minor yards, under some trees, were the huge cauldrons in which the beans and rice, which serve as slave-food, were cooked. Each yard had several Portuguese overseers, who kept watch and order, and superintended the cleaning out of the yards, which is performed daily by the slaves themselves. From time to time, too, these overseers take the slaves down to the seashore and make them bathe.

I remarked that many of the slaves were quite merry, and seemed perfectly content with their fate. Others were sad, and seemed filled with dread of their future; for, to lend an added horror to the position of these poor creatures, they firmly believe that we whites buy them to *eat* them. They cannot conceive of any other use to be made of them; and wherever the slave-trade is known in the interior, it is believed that white men beyond sea are great cannibals, who have to import blacks for the market. Thus a chief in the interior country, having a great respect for me, of whom he had heard often, when I made him my first visit, immediately ordered a slave to be killed for my dinner, and it was only with great difficulty I was able to convince him that I did not, in my own country, live on human flesh.

The slaves here seemed of many different tribes, and but few even understood each other. The slave-trade has become so great a traffic here (here I speak of the country and foreign trade alike) that it extends from this coast quite to the centre of the continent; and I have met slaves on the coast who had been bought much farther in the interior than I ever succeeded in reaching. The Shekiani, Bakalai, and many other tribes far inland sell their fellows into slavery on various pretexts (chiefly witchcraft), and thus help to furnish the Sangatanga slave-barracoons. The large rivers which, joining, form the Nazareth, provide an easy access to the coast, and give Cape Lopez great advantages for obtaining a regular supply of slaves; and the creeks which abound hereabouts afford the vessels good chances to conceal themselves from the watchful cruisers ...

The next morning I paid a visit to the other slave-factory. It was a neater place, but arranged much like the first. While I was standing there, two young women and a lad of fourteen were brought in for sale, and bought by the Portuguese in my presence. The boy brought a twenty-gallon cask of rum, a few fathoms of cloth, and a quantity of beads. The women sold at a higher rate. Each was valued at the following articles, which were immediately paid over: one gun, one neptune (a flat disk of copper), two looking-glasses, two files, two plates, two bolts, a keg of powder, a few beads, and a small lot of tobacco. Rum bears a high price in this country.

At two o'clock this afternoon a flag was hoisted at the king's palace on the hill, which signifies that a slaver is in the offing. It proved to be a schooner of about 170 tons' burden. She ran in and hove to a few miles from shore. Immediately I saw issue from one of the factories gangs of slaves, who were rapidly driven down to a point on the shore nearest the vessel. I stood and watched the embarkation. The men were still chained in gangs of six, but had been washed, and had on clean cloths. The canoes were immense boats, managed by twenty-six paddles, and besides each about sixty slaves. Into these the poor creatures were now hurried, and a more piteous sight I never saw. They seemed terrified almost out of their sense; even those whom I had seen in the factory to be contented and happy were now gazing about with such mortal terror in their looks as one neither sees nor feels very often in life. They had been content to lie in the factory, where they were well treated and had enough to eat. But now they were being taken away they knew not whither, and the frightful stories of the white man's cannibalism seemed fresh in their minds.

But there was no time allowed for sorrow or lamentation. Gang after gang was driven into the canoes until they were full, and then they set out for the vessel, which was dancing about in the sea in the offing.

And now a new point of dread seized the poor wretches, as I could see, watching them from the shore. They had never been on rough water before, and the motion of the canoe, as it skimmed over the waves and rolled now one way now another, gave them fears of drowning, at which the paddlers broke into a laugh, and forced them to lie down in the bottom of the canoe.

I said the vessel was of 170 tons. Six hundred slaves were taken off to her, and stowed in her narrow hold. The whole embarkation did not last two hours, and then, hoisting her white sails away she sailed for the South American coast. She hoisted no colours while near the shore, but was evidently recognized by the people on shore. She seemed an American-built schooner. The vessels are, in fact, Brazilian, Portuguese, Spanish, sometimes Sardinian, but oftenest of all American. Even whalers, I have been told, have come to the coast, got their slave cargo, and departed unmolested, and setting it down in Cuba or Brazil, returned to their whaling business no one the wiser. The slave-dealers and their overseers on the coast are generally Spanish and Portuguese. One of the head-men at the factories here told me that he had been taken twice on board slave-vessels, of course losing his cargo each time. Once he had been taken into Brest by a French vessel, but by the French laws he was acquitted, as the French do not take Portuguese vessels. He told me that he thought he should make his fortune in a very short time now, and then he meant to return to Portugal.

The slave trade is really decreasing. The hardest blow has been struck at it by the Brazilians. They have for some years been alarmed at the great superiority in numbers of the Africans in Brazil to its white population, and the government and people have united to discourage the trade, and put obstacles in the way of its successful prosecution. If now the trade to Cuba could also be stopped, this would do more to put an end to the whole business than the blockading by all the navies of the world.

It is impossible for any limited number of vessels to effectually guard 4,000 miles of coast. Eight or ten years ago, when I was on the coast of Africa, the British kept some 26 vessels of light draught on the coast, several of which were steamers, while the rest were good sailors. The French also had 26 vessels there, and the Americans their complement. But, with all this force to hinder, the slave-trade was never more prosperous. The demand in Brazil and Cuba was good, and barracoons were established all along the coast. Many vessels were taken, but many more escaped. The profits are so great that the slave-dealers could afford to send really immense fleets, and count with almost mathematical certainty on making a great profit from those which escaped the cruisers. The barracoons were shifted from place to place to escape the vigilance of the men-of-war; and no sooner was one of these dépôts broken up than another was established in some neighbouring creek or bay. So great was the demand that fearful atrocities were sometimes practised on innocent negroes by shrewd captains, who begrudged even the small price they had to pay for slaves. Thus it is related of one that he invited a number of friendly natives on board of his vessel, then shut them under hatches, and sailed away with them to Cuba to sell them.

A pregnant sign of the decay of the business is that those engaged in it begin to cheat each other. I was told by Portuguese on the coast that within two or three years the conduct of Cuban houses had been very bad. They had received cargo after cargo, and when pressed for pay had denied and refused. Similar complaints are made of other houses; and it is said that now a captain holds on to his cargo till he sees the doubloons, and takes the gold in one hand while he sends the slaves over the side with the other. While the trade was brisk they had no occasion to quarrel. As the profits become more precarious, each will try to cut the other's throat.

Now there are not many barracoons north of the equator, and the chief trade centres about the mouth of the Congo. The lawful trade has taken the place of the slave traffic to the northward; and if the French will only abolish their system of "apprenticeship," lawful trade might soon make its way to the south.

C. Lieutenant Frederick Barnard describes the slave trade on the coast of Mozambique, 1848

In the evening I learnt that about a week before our arrival, a large barque had embarked from 700 to 800 slaves at Ouilinda, the river to the southward of Quillimane, and I have since found out, that this was the same *Julia* which Trou, the captain of the *Gentil,* had detained in May last, and that the slaves actually went from the town of Quillimane in launches. Three or four days after our last visit, 300 slaves had been burnt alive in a baracoon some distance to the northward, where they had been sent ready for embarkation, one of them slipping his iron collar during the night, and setting fire to the building.

Upwards of 2,000 slaves were ready in the neighbourhood of the town for embarkation, purchased with merchandize, brought out by American vessels, and slave-vessels were expected from Rio daily, so that my arrival at Quillimane put those who had so much at stake in a great ferment, and I witnessed long and angry discussions amongst them as they came in and out of Azvedo's house. A brig, said to be under Sardinian colours, had attempted to land her captain at Luabo, where they say there is a flag-staff, but he with three of his boat's crew was drowned in crossing the bar, one man only reaching the shore, and no more has been heard of her.

The black schooner belonging to Senhor Isidore, which had embarked 400 slaves at Macuze, put back after having lost one-half of her human cargo, and relanded the wretched remnant half dead . . .

I must now add another page to the dreadful horrors of slavery. The bark *Julia,* which I have twice mentioned before, after sailing with 700 slaves, was eight days afterwards wrecked on the Bassas da India Rocks, when every soul perished except the Captain and three of the crew, who escaped to the Macuze in a small gig. The current had drifted them close to the breakers before they knew their danger, and they had barely time to get out of her before she opened and went down.

Thus, in the short space of six months, I have detailed the untimely end of 1,200 Negroes, by fire, disease, and wreck; and the suffering they must have endured whilst driven from the interior must have thinned considerably the original number; for frequently have I seen them, soon after their arrival at Quillimane, mere skeletons, with death depicted in their countenances.

I saw the schooner on the beach: she was not coppered, and about ninety tons burden; and on board this were 400 human beings crammed for a passage across the Atlantic . . .

When Alexander first got on board in the cutter, he found that her crew had deserted her, leaving the steward and supercargo sick in the bunks on deck, with 420 slaves, the greater part under hatches, fastened down with spike nails, and left by the merciless wretches to be drowned or smothered. Never was there a more dreadful attempt at cool, deliberate, and wholesale murder; and yet there is no means of punishing the perpetrators; no judge nor magistrate residing at Mozambique, and the judge at Quillimane being a coloured man, formerly, a gentleman's servant, and one of the greatest slave-dealers in the place. Never was an officer placed in a more awkward position, the cutters being all but stoved, and there appearing every chance of the brig's being knocked to pieces as the tide went down. Alexander thought the best plan was to allow them to swim on shore, and the greater part of them

* As the reader may scarcely credit so large a profit, I subjoin an account of the fitting of a slave vessel from Havana in 1827, and the liquidation of her voyage in Cuba:—

1.—EXPENSES OUT.

Cost of LA FORTUNA, a 90 ton schooner,	$3,700 00
Fitting out, sails, carpenter and cooper's bills,	2,500 00
Provisions for crew and slaves,	1,115 00
Wages advanced to 18 men before the mast,	900 00
" " to captain, mates, boatswain, cook, and steward,	440 00
200,000 cigars and 500 doubloons, cargo,	10,900 00
Clearance and hush-money,	200 00
	$19,755 00
Commission at 5 per cent,,	987 00
Full cost of voyage out,	$20,742 00

2.—EXPENSES HOME.

Captain's head-money, at $8 a head,	1,746 00
Mate's " $4 "	873 00
Second mate and boatswain's head-money, at $2 each a head,	873 00
Captain's wages,	219 78
First mate's wages,	175 56
Second mate and boatswain's wages,	307 12
Cook and steward's wages,	264 00
Eighteen sailors' wages,	1,972 00
	$27,172 46

3.—EXPENSES IN HAVANA.

Government officers, at $8 per head,	1,736 00
My commission on 217 slaves, expenses off,	5,565 00
Consignees' commissions,	3,873 00
217 slave dresses, at $2 each,	634 00
Extra expenses of all kinds, say,	1,000 00
Total expenses,	$39,980 46

4.—RETURNS.

Value of vessel at auction,	$3,950 00
Proceeds of 217 slaves,	77,469 00
	$81,419 00

RESUMÉ.

Total Returns,	$81,419 00
" Expenses,	39,980 46
Nett profit,	$41,438 54

FIGURE 11 Though Britain and the United States had both declared the trade in slaves illegal in 1807, it remained a highly profitable industry. This balance sheet for a slave voyage made from Cuba to Africa and back in 1827 shows a net profit of more than 100 percent, even allowing for the payment of "clearance and hush-money." Brantz Mayer, *Captain Canot, or, Twenty years of an African slaver,* 1854.

reached it in safety. On the two following days, the boats were employed in completing the destruction of the brig by fire, and brought on board the two sick Portuguese and seven negroes who had remained on board. A few bodies were found on the beach and buried . . .

The slaves that are brought from the interior are poor half-starved looking creatures, attached to each other by ropes round the neck; and famine is spreading its ravages throughout this ill-fated country. The province is in such a state of decay, that it cannot continue long under its present government, and a more powerful one would scarcely risk the expense and loss of life attendant upon the many changes that must take place before it could be bettered . . .

As the principal object of all my visits to the town was to gain information respecting the movements of the slave-dealers and their agents, I was obliged to be constantly on the *qui vive,* and found myself both suspected and watched since the affair of the brig. However, I managed to get the following, bit by bit, from various quarters.

Paulo Roderigue, the captain of the *Defensivo,* and the shipper of 1,800 slaves at Inhamban and Delagoa Bay, was again expected at the former place, in two or three months, for 800 blacks, which were in readiness. He was to have two American brigs under their own colours, one of which was to be delivered over to the slave-dealers, whilst the other was to take both American crews on board, touch at Quillimane with money to pay the authorities, who have been in the habit of conniving at the slave trade, and return to Rio; so you may easily conceive what little chance there is of putting down this detestable traffic, whilst the star-spangled banner, that boasted flag of liberty, waves over and protects the miscreants, to put down whom England has expended so many hundreds of lives of her bravest, and so many millions of treasure. Look at the results.

There are now at Quillimane and its neighbourhood 2,700 poor wretches for embarkation. Their owners are at Rio, 800 belonging to Manuel Pinto de Fonseca; 200 to Tavares, or Tavash; 2,000 to Bernadino de Sa'. Only one slave agent remained at Quillimane, named Martinhas, and he intended to leave for Rio in the American [vessel].

Of the 420 slaves allowed to swim on shore from the brig off Mariangombe, 110 were retaken, and the rest were supposed to have escaped into the interior. She had on board five officers, four of whom had died of fever since her destruction. Eight of her crew were taken and sent to Mozambique in the Don Juan de Castro, and the captain and steward remained at Quillimane, most probably soon to be victims of the approaching sickly season . . .

I made diligent inquiries about the slave trade carried on at Angonha, and am led to believe that it has only of late become a place for the exportation of slaves for the Brazils, and that the *Lucy Penniman, Kentucky,* and two others which escaped, are the only vessels which have attempted to take in cargoes there. The Majojos have, however, for many years carried on a brisk trade in human flesh, by means of Arab dows, with Zanzibar, Johanna, and the Red Sea; but of late, the *Sappho, Mutine,* and *Helena,* have taken and destroyed several of these vessels, and put a temporary check on it. But there are so many rivers and inlets on this coast which a man-of-war cannot approach, that we might as well try to alter the currents in the Mozambique channel as stop the slave trade with sailing vessels.

45 • Christianity and cattle killing (1856)

Though the missionaries won fewer converts than they had hoped, their religious teaching, especially the apocalyptic aspects of Christianity, managed to have a profound impact on African societies under stress because of the expansion of European settlement. This was the case on the eastern frontier of settler expansion in South Africa, where, from the 1770s onward, Europeans and Africans competed for and fought over essential resources such as land and water. By the 1850s conditions for the Xhosa people had become particularly dire. They had lost considerable amounts of land to European settlers, who were backed by the military power of the British colonial state. The British administration seemed determined to end Xhosa political autonomy. Moreover, African cattle herds were being greatly reduced by an epidemic of lung sickness during the middle of the decade. In this context of suffering, missionary teachings about redemption and resurrection had particular appeal. Nonetheless, the Xhosa wanted to liberate themselves through a combination of Christianity and indigenous religious beliefs rather than accept missionary teachings as a form of submission to European intellectual authority.

In 1856 a Xhosa man, Mhlakaza, who had years earlier converted to Christianity and taken the name William Goliath, began spreading word of a vision seen by two young girls in which foreign visitors called on the Xhosa to kill their cattle and consume all their corn. Mhlakaza was the first Xhosa confirmed as an Anglican (in April 1850), and he worked for a number of years as the servant of an Anglican minister, joining his employer on missionary trips along the eastern frontier. However, the minister dismissed Mhlakaza because his work as a servant was not satisfactory. Back among the Xhosa, Mhlakaza spread the message of his niece, Nongqawuse, that if the cattle were killed and the corn eaten, then all of the whites would be driven into the sea and the suffering of the Xhosa would end. Many Xhosa followed Mhlakaza's precepts, with disastrous results. With most of their cattle slaughtered and their crops gone, tens of thousands of Xhosa starved to death (including Mhlakaza). Many of the survivors became refugees in the Cape Colony, where they sought manual work from white settlers in order to stay alive. Most of the Xhosas' land ended up in the possession of the British. Nongqawuse was captured, interrogated by the chief commissioner, before whom she gave the deposition printed below, and placed briefly in a pauper's lodge. Later released, she returned to the eastern cape, where she remained in obscurity until her death, in the second or third decade of the twentieth century.[6]

Examination, before the Chief Commissioner, of NONQUASE, a Kafir Prophetess, who was a niece of, and resided with, UMHLAKAZA. She is a girl apparently between 15 and 16 years, intelligent, and gave her evidence freely. She was given over to Major Gawler, by MONY, Chief of the Amabomvanas.

My name is Nonquase. Umhlakaza was my uncle, and a counsellor of Xito, a petty chief. My father's name was Umhlanhla, of Kreli's tribe. He died when I was very young. I lived with Umhlakaza. He lived at Xaha on the Kei, near the sea. Umhlakaza is dead. He died about six moons ago of starvation. Umhlakaza's son, and elder brother, and my brother lived at the same kraal. After Umhlakaza's death we went and lived with the Amabomvana, across the Bashee, near Mony's kraal. We originally intended crossing the Umtato, but remained at this kraal near Mony.

Umhlakaza had many cattle before the talk about the new people. This talking commenced about seven sowing seasons back (two and a half years). It commenced after my having reported to Umhlakaza that I had seen about ten strange Kafirs in the gardens, and I told him I was afraid to go there. The people I saw were Kafirs—young men. I was afraid of them,

6. "Deposition made by Nonquase, a Kafir Prophetess, in an Examination before the Chief Commissioner of British Kaffraria," *Cape of Good Hope Parliamentary Paper*, G38, 1858. For the examination of Nonkosi, the other prophetess, see G5, 1858.

because I did not know them. Umhlakaza told me not to be afraid of them, as they would do me no harm. He told me to speak to them, and ask them what they were doing there. I did so. They replied, "We are people who have come to order you to kill your cattle—to consume your corn—and not to cultivate any more." Umhlakaza asked them through me, "What are we to eat when we kill our cattle, &c?" They answered, "*We* will find you something to eat." The people then said that was enough for that day—they would return some other day. We asked them who sent them, they answered, "We have come of our own accord, as we wish every thing in the country to be made new." They said they had come from *a place of refuge* (engaba). I asked them where this place of refuge was. They said, "You would not know if we even told you." I always pressed them to tell me where the place of refuge was, but they gave me the same answer. The next day Umhlakaza killed one head of cattle. He then called a meeting of the people and told them that strangers had come to tell them to kill their cattle—to destroy their corn, and that great plenty would be provided for them hereafter. The people dispersed, and from that day they commenced killing their cattle, &c.; and Umhlakaza continued killing his cattle, one a day. The people killed more cattle than they could use. The dogs and wild beasts ate the carcasses. About four days after we saw the strange Kafirs, three men came. We first heard of their arrival by an old woman, who told Umhlakaza that the people from the place of refuge had arrived. Umhlakaza took me with him to speak to them. I asked them for the news. They answered, "We do not know what news you expect; our only news is to tell you to kill your cattle—to consume your corn—and plenty will be provided for you." They left us the same day. In five days after two men came. I recognised them as two of the men who had come before. They said, "Our great chief has sent us to tell you, Umhlakaza, that all the people must kill their cattle, &c., as he wished to change the country; and that you must communicate this to Kreli and all the Kafir chiefs." Umhlakaza told me to ask them who their great chief was. They said they would not name him, for if they did, we would not know him, having never seen him or heard of him. They soon after left us. Umhlakaza then went to Xoti (Kreli's uncle), who is chief of the Galekas in the lower country between the Bashee and the Kei, and told him the news. Xito instructed Umhlakaza to spread the news, which he did. After Umhlakaza returned from visiting Xito's and other kraals, the three men came again. I heard Umhlakaza tell these men what he had told Xito, and that he had spread the news over the country. They answered him that he had done right. These men then said, "You must all be quick in killing your cattle, as in seven days the people will rise." I asked him what people? They replied, "The same people as ourselves—and they will rise at different kraals; that they would have cattle, corn, guns, and assegais; and that they would drive the English out of the country, and make them run into the sea."

Within seven days Umhlakaza killed all his cattle, and the killing of cattle throughout the country became general. Kreli, Xito, Ungubo (Kreli's cousin), and Lindixowa, frequently visited Umhlakaza, and had private meetings with him. These meetings were quite confidential and secret. There was no one present. I was not there.

The following chiefs also visited Umhlakaza: Pama, Dondashe, Zono, Umgwebi, and Sigidi, Galekas. Also Dina (Pato's son), Qabimbola, Sandili, Macomo, Pato, Qasana, and Xoxo, Gaika and T'Slambie chiefs, and many others whose names I did not know. They came attended by counsellors, and many people. Kreli's counsellors supplied cattle to feed the chiefs and people at these meetings. The chiefs always slept several nights at Umhlakaza's kraal.

They used to have secret meetings with Umhlakaza, at which I was not allowed to be present, and so I do not know what passed between them and Umhlakaza.

Shortly after the expiration of seven days, I saw the men who stated they had come from the place of refuge. They came with Kreli. I told them that Umhlakaza had killed all his cattle, but they made no reply.

Some time after this a petty chief, Lindixowa, came direct from Kreli, and told Umhlakaza that, though he (Umhlakaza) had killed his cattle, he was to remain where he was. Umhlakaza remained ten days after this, and then moved down towards the sea, for the purpose of living on roots and shell fish.

When we were starving, I often heard Umhlakaza regret his having killed his cattle and destroyed his corn. That he never thought he would be so reduced or come to such misery. I have often heard him blame Kreli as the sole cause of the cattle-killing, which was done for the purpose of leading the Kafirs to war, and driving the English out of the country. I heard Xito and Pama say, that the killing of cattle was to force the Kafirs to war with the English.

NOTE: Upon being asked whether she had heard any others than Umhlakaza, Xito, and Pama speak of war, she replied as follows: "The three men stated they came from the place of refuge, and they intended fighting with the English and driving them out of the country. They spoke of the whole country where the English lived. They said that their great chief had informed them that his intention was to drive the English out of the country. I also recollect when Kreli paid his first visit to Umhlakaza, after the killing commenced, he, Kreli, told me, in Xito's presence, to tell the strange people that the English were in his way, and that these people must assist him to fight against the English and drive them out of the country. I delivered Kreli's message to these men; they answered 'Yes, we will assist Kreli to fight against the English and drive them out of the country.'"

I went to Kreli, who was sitting near at hand, and gave him their answer. Kreli replied, "I am glad;" and called out in a voice sufficiently loud to be heard by the three men, "I thank you my friends. I have been at a loss to know what to do with the English, as they have been stronger than the Kafirs; you have come to strengthen us."

Xito was present upon this occasion; also a great many counsellors. I heard Kreli on several other occasions express his thanks in the same manner whenever he asked these people to assist them; and he also told them to be sure and keep their promise.

Did you hear of the Umpongo Prophetess? Yes. Her name is Nonkosi. I heard Umhlakaza say she spoke the same as I did. I also heard Umhlakaza tell his sons that Umhala had sent to him for news.

I have never seen Nonkosi. When Major Gawler came to the Bashee, Mony ordered me to be sent to him.

JOHN MACLEAN, Chief Commissioner

Truly Interpreted,
W. B. Chalmers, Clerk & Interpreter

46 • Boer slaving (1858)

In addition to wanting land, European settlers also wanted labor. What is more, they wanted to obtain this labor as cheaply as possible since the farming in which they were engaged was often little beyond subsistence level. After the British ended slavery throughout their empire in 1833, Dutch-speaking settlers trekked into the interior of southern Africa and aimed to secure their labor needs from the African communities among which they lived. David Livingstone, whose journals chronicle the cruelties of Portuguese and Arab slaving, denounced the ways in which Dutch settlers, or Boers, engaged in a new form of slavery. He also remarked on the way in which these Boers deemed themselves a "chosen people" of God, entitled by biblical teachings, as well as by physical force, to rule over Africans.[7]

Another adverse influence with which the mission had to contend was the vicinity of the Boers of the Cashan Mountains, otherwise "Magaliesberg." These are not to be confounded with the Cape colonists, who sometimes pass by the name. The word Boer simply means "farmer," and is not synonymous with our word boor. Indeed, to the Boers generally the latter term would be quite inappropriate, for they are a sober, industrious, and most hospitable body of peasantry. Those, however, who have fled from English law on various pretexts, and have been joined by English deserters and every other variety of bad character in their distant localities, are unfortunately of a very different stamp. The great objection many of the Boers had, and still have, to English law, is that it makes no distinction between black men and white. They felt aggrieved by their supposed losses in the emancipation of their Hottentot slaves, and determined to erect themselves into a republic, in which they might pursue, without molestation, the "proper treatment of the blacks." It is almost needless to add that the "proper treatment" has always contained in it the essential element of slavery, namely, compulsory unpaid labor.

One section of this body, under the late Mr. Hendrick Potgeiter, penetrated the interior as far as the Cashan Mountains, whence a Zulu or Caffre chief, named Mosilikátze, had been expelled by the well-known Caffre Dingaan; and a glad welcome was given them by the Bechuana tribes, who had just escaped the hard sway of that cruel chieftain. They came with the prestige of white men and deliverers; but the Bechuanas soon found, as they expressed it, "that Mosilikátze was cruel to his enemies, and kind to those he conquered; but that the Boers destroyed their enemies, and made slaves of their friends." The tribes who still retain the semblance of independence are forced to perform all the labor of the fields, such as manuring the land, weeding, reaping, building, making dams and canals, and at the same time to support themselves. I have myself been an eyewitness of Boers coming to a village, and, according to their usual custom, demanding twenty or thirty women to weed their gardens, and have seen these women proceed to the scene of unrequited toil, carrying their own food on their heads, their children on their backs, and instruments of labor on their shoulders. Nor have the Boers any wish to conceal the meanness of thus employing unpaid labor; on the contrary, every one of them, from Mr. Potgeiter and Mr. Gert Krieger, the commandants, downward, lauded his

7. David Livingstone, *Missionary Travels and Researches in South Africa: Including a Sketch of Sixteen Years' Residence in the Interior of Africa* (New York: Harper and Brothers, 1858), 35–39.

FIGURE 12 David Livingstone captured the imagination of the West in the mid-nineteenth century as the most prominent missionary to Africa. Despite his fame, during his lengthy career in Africa he succeeded in converting only one African to Christianity, and that person remained Christian for only a few months. J. E. Chambliss, *The Life and Labors of David Livingstone*, 1876.

own humanity and justice in making such an equitable regulation. "We make the people work for us, in consideration of allowing them to live in our country."

I can appeal to the Commandant Krieger if the foregoing is not a fair and impartial statement of the views of himself and his people. I am sensible of no mental bias toward or against these Boers; and during the several journeys I made to the poor enslaved tribes, I never avoided the whites, but tried to cure and did administer remedies to their sick, without money and without price. It is clue to them to state that I was invariably treated with respect; but it is most unfortunate that they should have been left by their own Church for so many years to deteriorate and become as degraded as the blacks, whom the stupid prejudice against color leads them to detest.

This new species of slavery which they have adopted serves to supply the lack of field-labor only. The demand for domestic servants must be met by forays on tribes which have good supplies of cattle. The Portuguese can quote instances in which blacks become so degraded by the love of strong drink as actually to sell themselves; but never in any one case, within the memory of man, has a Bechuana chief sold any of his people, or a Bechuana man his child. Hence the necessity for a foray to seize children. And those individual Boers who would not engage in it for the sake of slaves can seldom resist the two-fold plea of a well-told story of an intended uprising of the devoted tribe, and the prospect of handsome pay in the division of the captured cattle besides.

It is difficult for a person in a civilized country to conceive that any body of men possessing the common attributes of humanity (and these Boers are by no means destitute of the better feelings of our nature) should with one accord set out, after loading their own wives and children with caresses, and proceed to shoot down in cold blood men and women, of a different color, it is true, but possessed of domestic feelings and affections equal to their own. I saw and conversed with children in the houses of Boers who had, by their own and their masters' account, been captured, and in several instances I traced the parents of these unfortunates, though the plan approved by the long-headed among the burghers is to take children so young that they soon forget their parents and their native language also. It was long before I could give credit to the tales of bloodshed told by native witnesses, and had I received no other testimony but theirs I should probably have continued skeptical to this day as to the truth of the accounts; but when I found the Boers themselves, some bewailing and denouncing, others glorying in the bloody scenes in which they had been themselves the actors, I was compelled to admit the validity of the testimony, and try to account for the cruel anomaly. They are all traditionally religious, tracing their descent from some of the best men (Huguenots and Dutch) the world ever saw. Hence they claim to themselves the title of "Christians," and all the colored race are "black property" or "creatures." They being the chosen people of God, the heathen are given to them for an inheritance, and they are the rod of divine vengeance on the heathen, as were the Jews of old. Living in the midst of a native population much larger than themselves, and at fountains removed many miles from each other, they feel somewhat in the same insecure position as do the Americans in the Southern States. The first question put by them to strangers is respecting peace; and when they receive reports from disaffected or envious natives against any tribe, the case assumes all the appearance and proportions of a regular insurrection. Severe measures then appear to the most mildly disposed among them as imperatively called for, and, however bloody the massacre that follows, no qualms of conscience ensue: it is a dire necessity for the sake of peace. Indeed, the late Mr. Hendrick Potgeiter most devoutly believed himself to be the great peacemaker of the country.

But how is it that the natives, being so vastly superior in numbers to the Boers, do not rise and annihilate them? The people among whom they live are Bechuanas, not Caffres [Livingstone is here referring to Xhosa], though no one would ever learn that distinction from a Boer; and history does not contain one single instance in which the Bechuanas, even those of them who possess fire-arms, have attacked either the Boers or the English. If there is such an instance, I am certain it is not generally known, either beyond or in the Cape Colony. They have defended themselves when attacked, as in the case of Sechele [Livingstone's sole convert], but have never engaged in offensive war with Europeans. We have a very different tale to tell of the Caffres, and the difference has always been so evident to these border Boers that, ever since those "magnificent savages" obtained possession of fire-arms, not one Boer has ever attempted to settle in Caffre-land, or even face them as an enemy in the field. The Boers have generally manifested a marked antipathy to any thing but "long-shot" warfare, and, sidling away in their emigrations toward the more effeminate Bechuanas, have left their quarrels with the Caffres to be settled by the English, and their wars to be paid for by English gold.

The Bakwains at Kolobeng had the spectacle of various tribes enslaved before their eyes —the Bakatla, the Batlókua, Bahúkeng, the Bamosétla, and two other tribes of Bakwains were all groaning under the oppression of unrequited labor. This would not have been felt as so great an evil but that the young men of those tribes, anxious to obtain cattle, the only means of rising to respectability and importance among their own people, were in the habit of sallying forth, like our Irish and Highland reapers, to procure work in the Cape Colony. After laboring there three or four years, in building stone dikes and dams for the Dutch farmers, they were well content if at the end of that time they could return with as many cows. On presenting one to their chief, they ranked as respectable men in the tribe ever afterward. These volunteers were highly esteemed among the Dutch, under the name of Mantátees. They were paid at the rate of one shilling a day and a large loaf of bread between six of them. Numbers of them, who had formerly seen me about twelve hundred miles inland from the Cape, recognized me with the loud laughter of joy when I was passing them at their work in the Roggefelt and Bokkefelt, within a few days of Cape Town. I conversed with them and with elders of the Dutch Church, for whom they were working, and found that the system was thoroughly satisfactory to both parties. I do not believe that there is one Boer, in the Cashan or Magaliesberg country, who would deny that a law was made, in consequence of this labor passing to the colony, to deprive these laborers of their hardly-earned cattle, for the very cogent reason that, "if they want to work, let them work for us their masters," though boasting that in their case it would not be paid for. I can never cease to be most unfeignedly thankful that I was not born in a land of slaves. No one can understand the effect of the unutterable meanness of the slave-system on the minds of those who, but for the strange obliquity which prevents them from feeling the degradation of not being gentlemen enough to pay for services rendered, would be equal in virtue to ourselves. Fraud becomes as natural to them as "paying one's way" is to the rest of mankind.

47 • Legislating race and religion (1858)

The Dutch settlers in the interior of southern Africa established two independent political communities, the Orange Free State (OFS) and the Transvaal Republic (also known as the South African Republic, or SAR). Though the British did not recognize the independence of these states, they did not interfere with the political autonomy of these communities from the mid-1850s to the end of the 1870s. The OFS and the SAR were constituted as independent republics, with the right to vote given to all white males but not to women or to Africans of any gender. Though influenced in part by the constitution of the United States, the framers of the South African constitutions made explicit the connection that they considered essential between church and state and limited official recognition to one church only, Dutch Reformed.[8]

General regulations of the South African Republic, February 1858

    1. This State shall bear the name of the South African Republic.

    2. The form of government of this State shall be that of a Republic.

    3. It desires to be acknowledged and respected by the civilised world as an independent and free people.

---

8. G. W. Eybers, *Select Constitutional Documents Illustrating South African History, 1795–1910* (New York: George Routledge and Sons, 1918), 363–67.

4. The people seek no extension of territory, and desire it only according to principles of justice, when the interests of the Republic render it advisable.

5. The people desire to possess and retain their territory unimpaired inclusive of their rights and claims to the territory towards the East and South-East of this Republic, so far as those rights and claims extend, and so in like manner towards the West and South-West. And the Government of the South African Republic shall be obliged as soon as possible to take steps for fixing and publishing by Proclamation the limits and boundaries.

6. Its territory is open to every stranger who submits to the laws of this Republic. All persons who happen to be within the territory of this Republic have equal claim to protection of person and property.

7. The lands or farms situated within this territory which have not yet been given out are declared to be the property of the State, but are none the less obtainable as heretofore by the Public. No farm inspected for that purpose shall be larger than 3000 morgen. And no one shall be entitled to apply for or to obtain lands until he has reached the age of sixteen.

8. The people demand as much social freedom as possible, and expect to obtain it by retaining their religious faith, by fulfilling their obligations, by submitting to law, order and justice, and by upholding these. The people permit the spread of the Gospel among the heathen subject to definite safeguards against fault and deception.

9. The people desire to permit no equality between coloured people and the white inhabitants, either in Church or State.

10. The people desire to put up with no trading in slaves nor with slavery in this Republic.

11. The people reserve to themselves alone the protection and defence of the independence and inviolability of Church and State, according to the laws.

12. The people delegate the function of legislation to a Volksraad, the highest authority in the country, consisting of representatives or plenipotentiaries of the people, elected by burghers possessing the franchise, but it is provided that a period of three months be given to the people to enable them to convey to the Volksraad their views on any proposed law, should they so desire, except in the case of laws which can brook no delay.

13. The people delegate the proposal and the administration of the laws to an Executive Council, which shall also recommend all public officials for appointment by the Volksraad . . .

20. The people desire to retain the fundamental teachings of their Dutch Reformed Religion as laid down in the years 1618 and 1619 by the Synod of Dordrecht, and the Dutch Reformed Church shall be the State Church.

21. They prefer to allow no Roman Catholic Churches amongst them, nor any other Protestant Churches than those in which the same tenets of Christian belief are taught, as contained in the Heidelberg Catechism.

22. They shall appoint no other representatives to the Volksraad than those who are members of the Dutch Reformed Congregations . . .

24. The people desire the development, prosperity and welfare of Church and State, and with this view to provide for the wants of the Dutch Reformed Ministers and Teachers . . .

32. The members of the Volksraad shall be chosen by a majority of the votes of the people. Every burgher, who has reached the age of 21 years or more, shall possess the franchise, provided he be a member of the Dutch Reformed Church. . . .

48 • Expanding trade by taking territory, Lagos (1861)

Though African traders on the Niger Delta and the British had negotiated a commercial treaty in 1836, with the king of Bonny receiving thereafter an annual payment to encourage him to reduce the trade in slaves, British officials became dissatisfied with the way the agreement worked in practice. They decided, as the following memorandum by Lord John Russell shows, that the formal acquisition of territory, preferably by treaty, would help attain two goals: encourage British trade up the Niger River by establishing a local administration that would assist British merchants in their dealings with Africans and enable a more interventionist policy with regard to the suppression of slavery. The focus of official British activities was the trading city of Lagos, named after the town in Portugal from which the first regular trade in African slaves had begun in the fifteenth century.[9]

A. Lord John Russell, letter to the Duke of Newcastle, recommending the annexation of Lagos, February 7, 1861

But there is another measure which would in my opinion be attended with the most beneficial results, both as regards the suppression of the Slave Trade, and the encouragement of lawful Commerce in the Bight of Benin, namely that the Town and Island of Lagos should be taken possession of by the British Government.

Since the establishment at Lagos of its present Chief, King Docemo, that Island has virtually been under British protection, the King's authority being only maintained by the continued presence in the Lagos Lagoon of one of Her Majesty's Gun Boats. If that protection were withdrawn, the place would, in all probability, shortly fall into the hands of its former Chief King Kosoko, under whose rule it would speedily become again the head quarters of Slave Dealers, as it was until Kosoko was expelled by a British force.

King Docemo is moreover unable to govern the people under him, and to keep order among the traders assembled at Lagos without the constant support and interference of Her Majesty's Consul, who is in reality the Chief Authority in the place. Her Majesty's Government are thus in fact burdened with the responsibility of governing and defending Lagos, whilst they do not enjoy any of the advantages of Sovereignty.

If instead of this anomalous quasi Protectorate, Lagos were placed under British authority, the state of uncertainty and periodical alarm that prevails there would be put an end to, and the feeling of security which could not fail to spring up, would have a most beneficial influence in extending the valuable trade already carried on from Lagos and its neighbourhood, the existence of which is due to the expulsion of the Slave Dealers from Lagos by a British force . . . and their exclusion ever since, by the measures taken to prevent the return of Kosoko.

To shew Your Grace the extent and value of this Trade, and how rapidly it has sprung up, I have the honor to enclose for your information the accompanying Extracts from Reports which have been received from Her Majesty's late Consuls at Lagos. It will be seen from these Papers that the value of the Palm Oil & Cotton exported from the Bight of Benin in the Year

9. Newbury, *British Policy towards Africa*, 426–28, 429–30.

1857 amounted to the sum of £1,062,700 and the value of these exports since that date would have been made more considerable if it had not been for the Slave hunting Expeditions of the King of Dahomey.

I do not doubt that Your Grace will concur with me that it would be impossible for Her Majesty's Government to allow Lagos again to fall into the hands of the Slave Dealers, nor could they view with indifference the establishment there by French Agents of a Depôt for Negroes to be exported as Labourers to the French Colonies, a measure which might still be carried into effect if the French should fail in procuring a supply of labor for their Colonies from other than African sources.

But the defence of Lagos would be far more easy if the place was actually under British Government, and there would then be no difficulty in preventing the interference of foreign nations with Lawful Trade by Schemes of black Emigration.

Moreover, the occupation of so important a point as Lagos, could not fail to produce a great moral effect upon the minds of the Inhabitants of the surrounding Country, and would go far to secure the tranquillity of the neighbouring District. From this District we have, within the last few years, derived a supply of Cotton which tho' hitherto small, is rapidly increasing, and which, according to the information received by Her Majesty's Government, is capable of an almost unlimited extension.

For these reasons I do not hesitate to recommend to Your Grace's favorable consideration, that Lagos should be taken possession of and occupied. It might afterwards be considered whether it should be constituted a British Colony.

It would, it is believed, not be difficult to obtain from the present Chief the cession of his Rights, in return for which it would probably be necessary to assign him an allowance out of the Revenues of the Port, and there is no cause to doubt that the inhabitants would gladly become British Subjects.

The expense of maintaining such a Colony would not be considerable, and would, in my opinion, be amply repaid by the advantages which I have pointed out.

If your Grace should agree in these views, I would propose to trust Her Majesty's Consul at Lagos to enter into a negotiation with King Docemo for the cession of his rights.

B. Lagos treaty of cession, August 6, 1861

Treaty between Norman B. Bedingfeld, Commander of Her Majesty's Ship *Prometheus*, and Senior Officer of the Bights Division, and William McCoskry, Esq., Her Britannic Majesty's Acting Consul, on the part of Her Majesty the Queen of Great Britain; and Docemo, King of Lagos, on the part of himself and Chiefs.

Article 1. In order that the Queen of England may be the better enabled to assist, defend, and protect the inhabitants of Lagos, and put to an end to the slave trade in this and the neighbouring countries, and to prevent the destructive wars so frequently undertaken by Dahomey and others for the capture of slaves, I, Docemo, do, with the consent and advice of my Council, give, transfer, and by these presents grants and confirm unto the Queen of Great Britain, her heirs and successors for ever, the port and Island of Lagos, with all rights, profits, territories, and appurtenances whatsoever thereunto belonging, and as well the profits and revenue as the direct, full, and absolute dominion and sovereignty of the said port, island, and premises, with all the royalties thereof, freely, fully, entirely, and absolutely. I do also covenant and grant that the quiet and peaceable possession thereof shall, with all possible speed, be freely and effectually delivered to the Queen of Great Britain, or such person as Her Majesty shall thereunto appoint, for her use in the performance of this grant; the inhabitants of the said island and territories, as the Queen's subjects, and under her sovereignty, Crown, jurisdiction, and Government, being still suffered to live there.

Article 2. Docemo will be allowed the use of the title of King in its usual African signification, and will be permitted to decide disputes between natives of Lagos with their consent, subject to appeal to British laws.

Article 3. In the transfer of lands, the stamp of Docemo affixed to the document will be proofs that there are no other native claims upon it, and for this purpose he will be permitted to use it as hitherto.

In consideration of the cession as before-mentioned of the port and island and territories of Lagos, the representatives of the Queen of Great Britain do promise, subject to the approval of Her Majesty, that Docemo shall receive an annual pension from the Queen of Great Britain, equal to the net revenue hitherto annually received by him; such pension to be paid at such periods and in such mode as may hereafter be determined.

Additional Article to the Lagos Treaty of Concession, 18 February 1862. King Docemo having understood the foregoing Treaty, perfectly agrees to all the conditions thereof; and with regard to the 3d Article consents to receive as a pension, to be continued during his lifetime, the sum of 1,200 (twelve hundred) bags of cowries per annum, as equal to his net revenue; and I, the undersigned representative of Her Majesty, agree on the part of Her Majesty to guarantee to the said King Docemo an annual pension of (1,200) twelve hundred bags of cowries for his lifetime, unless he, Docemo, should break any of the Articles of the above Treaty, in which case his pension will be forfeited. The pension shall commence from the 1st of July of the present year, 1862, from which day he, the King, resigns all claim upon all former farmers of the revenue.

49 • French ambitions in West Africa (1858–64)

During the first half of the nineteenth century, while the British were spreading their trading efforts along much of the West African coast and sought entry to the interior via two riverine systems— that of the Gambia river, north of Sierra Leone, and that of the Niger—the French largely concentrated their presence at the mouth of the Senegal river. (They also developed trading posts along the Ivory Coast and in Dahomey). From their coastal base the French had traded for slaves in the seventeenth and eighteenth centuries and, after the return of their territories at the conclusion of the Napoleonic wars (the British had seized France's colonial bases), for new products.

They focused at first on the indigenous gum trade (used for glazing textiles) and then, with the growing demand for lubricants in Europe, switched to groundnuts in the 1840s. The French acquired gum and groundnuts through trade with African merchants and producers. Increasingly, however, as the potential for huge profit in the oil trade became clear, the French hoped to renegotiate the terms of trade by getting direct access to the areas of production. This meant looking to the interior and especially to the hinterland of the Niger River with its great resources of palm oil, monopolized at midcentury by British traders moving into the interior up the Niger River. The great "architect" of French ambitions at midcentury was Louis Faidherbe, governor of Senegal from 1854 to1861 and 1863 to 1865. In developing his expansionist ambitions, Faidherbe had the support of the French military (the outline for a new colonial army had been drawn up by an official commission of French officers in 1850), and the clergy (in 1858 the Holy Ghost Fathers quoted below were applying for an official subsidy for their operations).[10]

A. Louis Faidherbe drafts a policy for the French in West Africa, May 1864

The situation of our establishments on the West Coast of Africa deserves the attention of the Government. For nearly five centuries our ships have been frequenting this coast, and it may be said that France was the first of all European nations to carry her flag and her civilising ideas into this part of the world. After enjoying an almost exclusive position and possessing numerous establishments over a long period, in consequence of disastrous set-backs on the seas she witnessed her possessions passing successively into the hands of the Dutch, the Portuguese, and the British, and the influence of those three naval powers gradually replacing that which she formerly exercised without dispute . . . However, our forces soon recovered their advantage, Saint-Louis was recaptured, and by a Treaty signed on 3 September 1783 we received exclusive possession of the Senegal river and its dependencies, Gorée, and the *comptoir* of Albreda, situated a short distance from the mouth of the Gambia. England was confirmed in possession of the latter river and retained the right to trade for gum between the River St. John and Portendick . . .

As for that portion of the coast between the left bank of the Gambia and the Sierra Leone river, it was not attributed exclusively to any nation; the French continued to share with the English and all other peoples the right to frequent these waters and to form new establishments at any point not occupied.

The Treaty of Paris (30 March 1814) confirmed these provisions, and restored to us *unreservedly* all the establishments which we possessed on the West Coast of Africa at 1 January 1792 . . . To these establishments have been added, in consequence of treaties with native chiefs, those of Grand Bassam (19 February 1842), Assinie, Dabou and Gabon (18 March 1842) . . . By a convention of 7 March 1857 we exchanged our *comptoir* of Albreda against the British right to trade for gum at Portendick . . .

However, our commerce, which these establishments were intended to protect and attract to themselves, has not unreservedly entered upon the paths thus opened to it. At the same time as it was profiting from the support of our posts and the prestige of our arms in order to extend its operations in Senegal, it successively abandoned our *comptoirs* down the coast to try to find in the free rivers suitable conditions for trading without supervision or protection. The Department of the Marine and Colonies was soon obliged to recognise that, at the same time as business was expanding in the territories dependent on Saint-Louis, in the Senegal river, on the coast at Dakar, and in the rivers Sine, Saloum and Casamance, the factories on the Gold Coast and at Gabon were almost completely abandoned, while a consid-

10. John Hargreaves, ed., *France and West Africa: An Anthology of Historical Documents* (London: Macmillan, 1969), 99–101, 102–4, 144–47. All translations are by Hargreaves.

erable growth was taking place in transactions at points on the coast not submitted to our authority and open to foreign competition, especially in the Gambia, where the trade is almost exclusively French.

The position may be summarised thus. French trade with the West Coast of Africa may be estimated at an annual value of 40 million francs, namely 24,000,000 francs of imports into France and 15,600,000 francs of exports. Of this sum Senegal (Saint-Louis and Gorée) accounts for a value of 19 millions (8 millions of imports into France, 11 millions of exports); Gabon accounts for 500,000 francs only. At Grand Bassam and Assinie trade is almost nil. Thus the trade which we carry out in competition with other European powers, either on parts of the coast which are open to all comers or in actual foreign establishments, accounts for *more than half* of the general movement of French shipping to the West Coast of Africa. The creation of our *comptoirs* has had almost no discernible influence on this state of things, and although our trade has found for the most part a régime concerned to give it exclusive protection, it has successively abandoned these points, where for twenty years, at an annual cost of 470,000 francs to the government, and of regrettable casualties caused by fever in the ranks of the administrative and naval personnel, we have maintained our occupation without serious results for our shipping or our influence. The moment seems come to draw clear conclusions from this situation. Two principal facts emerge from our experience. The first is the *stable* character of our interests in the Senegal district [*cercle*], the second the essentially *inconstant* nature of our relations on other parts of the coast. Our commerce, which seems to have found at Saint-Louis, under effective and progressive supervision, a centre from which to spread out, inland by the river and southwards through our coastal establishments, is leaving Gabon and our posts on the Gold Coast and resolutely facing in other districts—often with marked success—the hazards of a trade exposed to arbitrary acts of the natives and to the difficulties of competition.

It appears that we would be responding to these present tendencies of our traders, in the first place by consolidating the territorial base so well established around Saint-Louis, and then by guaranteeing them on the rest of the coast, instead of a limited and costly armed protection about which they seem to care very little, active general supervision in their relations with the natives, and favourable treatment from European nations. To achieve this double purpose it would be appropriate to enter into an arrangement with England, the only power which today competes seriously with us in these waters . . . In exchange for the Gambia, the English might be offered Gabon, Assinie . . . Grand Bassam and Dabou, together with the rights conferred on us by the Protectorate of Porto Novo, which is considerably impeding British designs upon Dahomey . . . [If this compensation were judged insufficient, one might go so far as to grant access for their flag to our colony of Saint-Louis.] We would further stipulate for equality of customs, shipping and port duties in all places thus exchanged.

After such a transaction, our Senegalese colony would form a compact and homogeneous territory, bounded by its natural frontiers; all the sources from which the trade of these coasts is drawn would be completely in our hands. Those who are resisting our plans for colonisation and development would receive no more supplies with which to do so, and caravans from the interior would henceforth follow the routes we saw fit to indicate. The great projects which might be conceived for extending our influence towards Timbuktu and the upper Niger would henceforth have a large and solid base . . .

This negotiation would in my view be the starting point for a system on which I believe the commercial future of the West Coast of Africa depends, and which might be the culmination of European policies in these waters; I mean the neutralisation of the coast, and the admission of all countries and nations to trade in its rich products, under the guarantee of an agreement concluded among the great powers, and under the protection of all the navies of Europe. [The final paragraph was deleted from the official version.]

B. Plans for a new type of colonial army, 1850

[I]t is highly desirable that the Senegalese infantry should be composed of European and native troops in equal parts. Black soldiers have always given excellent service in the colony. Among others, those who belong to the Bambara race are, it may be said, as good as white soldiers, and they have the advantage over them of being immune to all the hardships of the climate. One can thus well appreciate the value which the support of such a force might have for Senegal in a host of circumstances, especially for the garrisons up-river. This is indisputably one of the most urgent needs of the locality. The remaining companies, already much reduced in strength following successive liberations of their personnel, will soon be run down completely, when the remainder have received their discharge. The Commission attaches the greatest urgency to consideration of methods of reconstructing this force.

There are two ways in which this reconstruction might be effected. Firstly, one might consider subjecting the population of Senegal to the metropolitan law of recruitment. But we must recognise that populations unaccustomed to military service would accept such obligations only with extreme repugnance. Moreover they could hardly provide an intake of more than 25 or 30 men a year, which is clearly insufficient for present needs. The alternative method of recruitment, the most hopeful and indeed the only effective one, would be that formerly employed, which consists of going up-country to enrol captives, to whom the sum needed to purchase their freedom is given as enrolment bounty. The Commission is aware that the terms of the emancipation decree [1848] now seem to put legal obstacles in the way of such an operation. It is also aware of the moral and humanitarian reasons which led to the inclusion in this act of a prohibition of long-term contracts of service—and which indeed had already caused them to be forbidden by the previous regime. These contracts, handed over to private interests as they formerly were in the Colony, had indeed degenerated into a veritable slave trade, and could no longer be tolerated. But if they are strictly confined to the needs of military recruitment and entrusted exclusively to the hands of the administration, they cannot give rise to any abuse. What after all is their effect?—that the government restores to freedom a certain number of captives who would otherwise be doomed to almost certain death, on the sole condition that they serve the government for several years. One might add that when these men return to their homelands at the end of their military service they should become excellent agents for the diffusion into the interior of Africa of the first notions of civilisation and commerce. In view of the major political interest, supported by this humanitarian interest, in not merely maintaining but increasing the strength of the black companies in Senegal, the Commission feels quite justified in asking that all steps be taken to reconcile the requirements of existing legislation with the obvious needs of our position in Senegal.

It further recommends that these troops should be completely assimilated to troops sent from Europe in regard to pay and rations, though care should be taken that they are organised in separate units . . .

C. The Holy Ghost Fathers explain the role of missionary education for Africans, 1858

These are the objectives which the Missionaries of the Holy Ghost and the Sacred Heart of Mary have set themselves, and these are the needs of their establishment. Our general aim is the religious—and thus, the social—regeneration of the Negroes of Africa; the means to this will be our holy religion, and next to religious knowledge, work. Literary and scientific work for those who have the capacity to engage in it; manual work supplemented by a certain cultivation of the intelligence for those whose vocation is more humble. Our particular aim is to provide the French possessions with intelligent and loyal servants.

Consequently there is a dual objective. On the one hand, to produce well-educated and responsible young men, able to render real and valuable services in the colony and in the trading-posts as employees of the administration, the engineering department, the military and naval establishments; on the other to make honest and competent workmen, who would assist and if necessary even supervise those whom the colonial government already has at its disposal. Hence we have a primary and secondary school, and a trades school.

In the former we study the child, who usually comes to us young, at the age of five or six. If his intellectual qualities permit his education will be continuous; he will pass in succession from the primary school to the secondary school, where so far as our resources allow he will receive the same education as in a French collège. If a pupil's undeveloped intelligence does not allow him to undertake such a heavy curriculum, we content ourselves with giving him some knowledge of the elementary principles of the French language, arithmetic and writing, and we make a workman of him.

At present we are educating seventy children at Dakar, and among them we have printers, book-binders, blacksmiths, joiners, wood-turners, cooks, shoemakers, weavers and tailors.

There is no need to dwell further on the real advantages for the French government of such an establishment on the African coast. Our colonies and trading-posts need honest, intelligent and loyal workmen, and especially foremen who can supervise the Negroes; they will be found among the children brought up in our work-shops, formed by a rule of discipline and accustomed to obey.

The better-off families from Saint-Louis, Gorée and elsewhere give their children an education beyond what the Brothers can offer in the Colony. Our secondary school will accept them. Our boarding fees, more in line with their present resources than those in France, will allow a large number of families to send their children; the climate of Dakar, being that in which they were born, will not prove unhealthy for these children, as that of France so often does; finally these young men, knowing only Africa, will not wish to leave it, but to serve in their own fatherland the French government, which will have become their own father. It is quite otherwise with those educated in France, who return home only with regret, and live only for the moment of leaving again.

Moreover, now Dakar is French it is destined to become the centre of all the maritime and commercial operations of Africa, and this will allow all points on the coast to send representatives there. We already have children from Gabon, Principe Island, Grand Bassam, Rio Pongos, Rio Nunez, Casamance, Bathurst, Gambia, the kingdoms of Sine and Baol, Gorée, Saint-Louis and Galam.

The Sisters of Immaculate Conception have a similar establishment within ten minutes of our own and their programme for the education and instruction of children is the same as ours, in due proportion . . .

CHAPTER SEVEN

Africa for Africans? (1854–81)

50 ◆ Samuel Crowther on the role
of African missionaries (1854)

European missionaries had little success converting Africans to Christianity during the first half of the nineteenth century. David Livingstone, the most famous of the British proselytizers, convinced only one African chief to convert, and that individual soon repudiated his decision. However, Africans freed from slave ships interdicted by British frigates and released in Sierra Leone offered a potential source of indigenous missionaries. Many of the freed slaves worked for members of the Church Missionary Society (CMS) and converted to the Christian faith of their British employers and rulers. Unlike the European missionaries, they knew the local languages. They had also often been captured into slavery from parts of Africa beyond the coastal reach of the British and could therefore lead the antislavery advance into the interior.

Samuel Crowther was the most prominent of these African missionaries in the nineteenth century. Born among the Igbo people of present-day Nigeria and given the name Ajayi by his parents, he took the name Samuel Crowther when in 1825 in his late teens he was baptized as a Christian and a member of the CMS. He trained first as a schoolteacher for the CMS and then, after further education in England, was ordained a minister and in 1843 went to Abeokuta (southern Nigeria) as a missionary. During the 1840s and 1850s, Crowther accompanied several British expeditions organized by the African Inland Commercial Company to explore the course of the Niger. These expeditions aimed to investigate the commercial potential of the interior and to establish inland missions along the Niger. Whereas other accounts of these expeditions focus on technology and trade, Crowther's journal emphasizes the importance of opening Africa to the endeavors of indigenous Christian missionaries.[1]

On the need for African missionaries

I believe the time is fully come when Christianity must be introduced on the banks of the Niger: the people are willing to receive any who may be sent among them. The English are still looked upon as their friends, with whom they themselves desire to have connexion as with the first nation in the world. Could the work have been begun since 1841, how imperfect

---

1. Samuel Crowther, *Journal of an Expedition up the Niger and Tshadda Rivers, Undertaken by Macgregor Laird, Esq., in Connection with the British Government, in 1854* (London: Church Missionary House, 1854), xvi–xviii, 21–22, 80–81.

soever it might have been, yet it would have kept up the thread of connexion with England and the countries on the banks of the Niger. God has provided instruments to begin the work, in the liberated Africans in the Colony of Sierra Leone, who are the natives of the banks of this river.

If this time is allowed to pass away, the generation of the liberated teachers who are immediately connected with the present generation of the natives of the interior will pass away with it also; many intelligent men who took deep interest in the introduction of trade and Christianity by the Niger, who had been known to the people, have died since; so have many of the chiefs and people in the country, who were no less interested to be brought in connexion with England by seeing their liberated countrymen return. Had not Simon Jonas been with us, who was well known to Obi and his sons, we should have had some difficulty in gaining the confidence of the people at Aboh at our ascent.

It would be of very great advantage if the colony born young men were introduced by their parents or countrymen to their fatherland; it has many advantages which have not been sufficiently noticed. It cannot be expected that children born in the Colony should become acquainted with the countries and characters of the people so soon as their parents and countrymen. Though the parents are illiterate, yet if they are sincere followers of the Lord Jesus Christ, their service will be of much worth in introducing Christianity to their own people. They are brought back to their country as a renewed people, looked upon by their countrymen as superior to themselves, as long as they continue consistent in their Christian walk and conversation, and do not disgrace themselves by following heathenish practices. The language of the people of Abbeokuta will be that of the natives on the banks of the Niger: "Let those who come from the white man's country teach us and condemn our heathenish practices, we shall listen to them." It takes great effect when returning liberated Christians sit down with their heathen countrymen and speak with contempt of their own former superstitious practices, of whom, perhaps, many now alive would bear testimony as to their former devotedness in their superstitious worship; all which he now can tell them he has found to be foolishness, and the result of ignorance; when he with all earnestness, invites them, as Moses did Hobab, Come with us, for the Lord has promised good to Israel; and all this in his own language, with refined Christian feelings and sympathy, not to be expressed in words, but evidenced by an exemplary Christian life. The services of such persons will prove most useful in the introduction of the Gospel of Jesus Christ among the heathens. Let such persons be employed as readers or Christian visitors, and thus they will gradually introduce their children into the country, who in the course of time will be able to carry on the work more effectually; as pioneers, we must not look for instruments of the keenest edge, anything that will open the path for the future improvement will answer as well at the onset.

Talking about Christianity

July 23 [1854]: Sunday. Had service on board at half-past ten, and preached from St. John i. 29 [The next day John seeth Jesus coming unto him and saith, Behold the Lamb of God, which taketh away the sin of the world]. The boat was just ready for me after the service, to go on shore and speak a few words with the chief on religious subjects, and also to ask his permission to address the people of the town, when his canoe appeared from the creek, with numerous attendants, so I postponed my going till his return; but he remained so long on board, that there was no prospect of his soon going away. When Captain Taylor had done with him, I took the opportunity to speak with him at length on the subject of the Christian religion, Simon Jonas interpreting for me. The quickness with which he caught my explanation of the all-sufficient sacrifice of Jesus Christ, the Son of God, for the sin of the world, was gratifying. I endeavoured to illustrate it to him in this simple way. "What would you think of any persons, who, in broad daylight like this, should light their lamps to assist the brilliant rays of the sun to enable them to see better?" He said, "It would be useless; they would be fools to do so." I replied, "Just so;" that the sacrifice of Jesus Christ, the Son of God, was sufficient to take away our sins, just as one sun is sufficient to give light to the whole world; that the worship of country fashions, and numerous sacrifices, which shone like lamps, only on account of the darkness and ignorance of their superstition, though repeated again and again, yet cannot take away our sins; but that the sacrifice of Jesus Christ, once offered, alone can take away the sin of the world. He frequently repeated the names, "Oparra Tshuku! Oparra Tshuku!" Son of God! Son of God! As I did not wish to tire him out, I left my discourse fresh in his mind. The attention of his attendants, with the exception of a few, was too much engaged in begging and receiving presents, to listen to all I was talking about. I gave Tshukuma a Yoruba primer, in which I wrote his name; and left some with Simon Jonas, to teach the children, or any who should feel disposed to learn, the Alphabet and words of two letters. Tshukuma and his attendants were perfectly at home in the steamer, and it was not till a gentle hint was given them, that the gentlemen wanted to take their dinner, that he ordered his people to make ready for their departure.

Advice for European travelers

What is generally related of the natives of Africa as to their hostility to Europeans is not strictly correct. The truth is, they take alarm, and consequently get ready for the defence of their country, which is divided by wars, marauding and robbery into many independent states, and every district must watch against surprize by its neighbours. It is but natural for such a people, shut out from communication with the civilized world, when they see for the first time such a huge and self-moving body as a steamer, to take alarm, not knowing the object of those who inhabit it, for to their ideas it is a town of itself. There is one thing which enterprising European explorers overlook, I mean the continual fear and insecurity the Natives are in, from the constant treachery of their enemies. This causes them to go about always armed with their bows and arrows, and at the least alarm they are ready to discharge their deadly weapons. Though travellers fear nothing themselves, yet, they should endeavour to take due precautions to allay the fears of those whom they intend to visit, by previous communication, which will soon be circulated in the neighbourhood, and then all will be right. A prudent man will not consider an hour or two wasted to effect this purpose, rather than risk the painful result of misunderstandings which may never be remedied. As far as I know, there is no place in Africa uncontaminated with European slave dealers, which Europeans have visited with the intention of doing good, where such an event has not been hailed as the most auspicious in the annals of the country. Every chief considers himself highly honoured to have white men for his friends.

51 • Africanus B. Horton on an autonomous Africa (1868)

James Africanus Horton, a near contemporary of Samuel Crowther, was born in 1835, the son of an Igbo man who had been freed from a slave ship by a British naval squadron and who had settled in Sierra Leone. Identified by CMS missionaries as a talented scholar, Africanus Horton was recommended by his teachers to the British army as a likely candidate for medical training. He was educated in Scotland and in 1859 graduated with an MD degree (his dissertation was titled "The Medical Topography of West Africa"). Horton spent his career in the British army, where he served in medical stations along the West African coast and accompanied British expeditions against the Asante in 1864 and 1873–74. He retired in 1880 with the rank of surgeon-major and died prematurely in 1882.

Horton was a strong admirer of the British, especially with regard to their systems of education and rule, and he thought that Africa benefited from their presence. However, he also believed that Africans could change their societies themselves without the need for outside intervention and was an opponent of the expansion of formal empire. He criticized in particular the rise of pseudo-scientific racism in Europe and America and argued that Africans were in no way inferior to other peoples. He also stressed that Africans had themselves developed organized systems of governance, which in his view were full of shortcomings yet quite unlike the images of barbarity popularized in most of the accounts by European travelers. A strong critic of the Asante, he favored the creation of a federation of the Fante peoples of the Gold Coast, independent of the Asantehene, though under the influence of the British, whose culture he much admired. The following passages are from a book Horton published in 1868, a critical time for West Africa, in his view. A parliamentary committee in 1865 had recommended that Britain withdraw any official presence it had on the west coast other than in Sierra Leone, and the Asante had begun their campaign to reconquer the Fante. Horton wanted the British to stay, but only to allow Africans to develop new forms of self-government, not to conquer.[2]

On racism

It must appear astounding to those who have carefully and thoughtfully read the history of England in connexion with the subject of the African race, when its greatest statesman, so long ago as 1838, stated in Parliament the endeavours his Government had been making to induce the various continental and transatlantic ones to put down slavery, that the abolition of that institution in the Southern States of America should have produced so much bile amongst a small section in England; who, although they have had undeniable proofs of the fallacy of their arguments, and inconsistency of their statements with existing facts, have formed themselves into an association (*sic* Anthropological Society) to rake up old malice and encourage their agents abroad to search out the worst possible characteristics of the African, so to furnish material for venting their animus against him. "Its object," as has been

2. James Africanus B. Horton, *West African Countries and Peoples, British and Native, with the Requirements Necessary for Establishing That Self Government Recommended by the Committee of the House of Commons, 1865, and a Vindication of the African Race* (London: W. J. Johnson, 1868), v–vii, 31–34, 39, 113–16, 246–49.

stated, "is to prove him unimprovable, therefore unimproved since the beginning and, consequently, fitted only to remain a hewer of wood and drawer of water for the members of that select society." It would have been sufficient to treat this with the contempt it deserves, were it not that leading statesmen of the present day have shown themselves easily carried away by the malicious views of these negrophobists, to the great prejudice of that race.

It is without doubt an uphill work for those who have always combated that vile crusade of prejudice, especially when considering themselves at the point of putting a crowning stroke to the superstructure which had taken them years to erect, to find the foundation undermined by rats of a somewhat formidable size, and therefore requiring a renewed and a more unassailable structure. One of the anthropological myths is to prove that, up to the age of puberty, the negro can combat successfully, and even show a precocity superior to that of the more enlightened race of a temperate climate, but that after this period, which corresponds to the closing of the sutures, he is doomed—a limit is set upon his further progress. But to prove more convincingly that this malign statement is fallacious, let those who are interested in the subject refer to the Principals of the Church Missionary College, Islington; King's College, London; and Fourah Bay College, Sierra Leone; where full-blooded Africans, who have had the complete development of their sutures, have been under tuition, and they will then be able to form an opinion from unbiassed testimony. I do not for a moment attempt here to prove that, as a whole, a race whose past generations have been in utter darkness, the mental faculty of whose ancestors has never received any culture for nearly a thousand years, could attempt to compete successfully in their present state with one whose ancestors have successively been under mental training and moulding for centuries. To think so would be to expect an ordinary-bred horse to have equal chances in a grand race with a thorough-bred one. But I say that the African race, as exemplified by the results of enterprizes in Western Africa, if put in comparison with any race on the face of the globe, whether Caucasian, Mongolian, Teutonic, Celtic, or any other just emerging from a state of barbarism, as they are, will never be found a whit behind. But to draw deductions by comparing their present state with the civilization of the nineteenth century is not only absurd, but most unphilosophical.

Even Captain [Richard] Burton, the *noli me tangere* of the African race, the greatest authority in the present school of English anthropologists (their vice-president), who, from his writings, has led everyone to believe that he has a fiendish hatred against the negro, whilst animadverting in all his works on Western Africa, in the most unmistakably malicious language, on the impossibility of improving that race he so hates, forgot himself in one place, and exclaimed, as to their intellectual superiority, "There are about 100 Europeans in the land; amongst these there are many excellent fellows, *but it is an unpleasant confession to make,* the others appear to be inferior to the Africans, native as well as mulatto. The possibility of such a thing had never yet reached my brain. At last, in colloquy with an old friend upon the Coast, the idea started up, and, after due discussion, we adopted it. I speak of *morale.* In intellect *the black race is palpably superior, and it is fast advancing in the path of civilization.*" The first and last italics are ours . . .

Dr Knox regards everything to be subservient to race; and his arguments are brought forward to show that the negro race, in spite of all the exertions of Exeter Hall, or as his commentators most sneeringly call them, the "broad-brimmed philanthropy and dismal science school," will still continue as they were. To him, as he says, "Race is everything—literature, science, art—in a word, civilization depends on it . . . With me race or hereditary descent is everything, it stamps the man."

Of late years a society has been formed in England in imitation of the Anthropological Society of Paris, which might be made of great use to science had it not been for the profound prejudice exhibited against the negro race in their discussions and in their writings, They again revive the old and vexed question of race, which the able researches of Blumenbach, Prichard, Pallas, Hunter, Lacepède, Quatrefages, Geoffroy St Hilaire, and many others, had years ago (as it was thought) settled. They placed the structure of the anthropoid apes before them, and then commenced the discussion of a series of ideal structures of the negro which only exist in their imagination, and thus endeavour to link the negroes with the brute creation. Some of their statements are so barefacedly false, so utterly the subversion of scientific truth, that they serve to exhibit the writers as perfectly ignorant of the subjects of which they treat . . .

Carl Vogt, who, perhaps, has never seen a negro in his life, and who is perfectly ignorant as to the capabilities of the negro race, must needs deceive his pupils in Geneva on subjects that he knows nothing about. He tells them that as the young orangs and chimpanzees are goodnatured, so is the young negro; but that after puberty and the necessary transformation has taken place, as the former becomes an obstinate savage beast, incapable of any improvement, so the intellect of the negro becomes stationary, and he is incapable of any further progress; that, in fact, the supposed sudden metamorphoses (which rest only in his ideas) in puberty, said to have taken place in the negro at this period, is not only intimately connected with physical development, but is a repetition of the phenomena occurring in the anthropoid apes . . .

Now, is this not a base prostitution of scientific truth? I have seen more than a hundred thousand negroes, but have not been able to find these characteristic differences which Carl Vogt, who has never seen one, or Prunner Bey, who saw Egyptian negro slaves, essay to describe. Indeed, as amongst every other tribe, white or black, there are to be found some with short necks, and others whose necks are peculiarly long; but where are to be found negroes with pendulous bellies as the anthropoid apes? Not in Africa surely, for from Senegal to the Cameroons the negroes I have met with are peculiar for the perfect flatness of their bellies. But Carl Vogt descends from the absurd to the ridiculous; when, writing on the peculiarities of the human foot as characters differentiating man and ape, he went on to state that "the foot of the gorilla is more anthropoid than that of any other ape, and the foot of the negro more apelike than that of the white man. The bones of the tarsus in the gorilla exactly resemble those in the negro." We must only dismiss these absurdities by referring him to M. Aeby's measurements, which led him to the conclusion that individual races are not distinguishable from each other when the proportion of their limbs and these parts are examined; that the difference between the forearm of the European and the negro amounts to less than one per cent, and even he thinks that this slight difference which he has obtained may, by further and more extended measurement, be greatly reduced. Thus, therefore, there is no material difference in the proportion of the limbs between the European and negro.

On self-government

Our government will . . . exercise sole authority over the countries from the Sweet River, near Elmina, to the River Volta. This should be divided into two separate independent self-governments—viz., the *Kingdom of Fantee,* extending from the Sweet River, to the borders of Winnebah; and the *Republic of Accra,* extending from Winnebah to the River Volta; the former to comprise the kingdoms of Denkera, Abrah, or Abacrampah, Assin, Western Akim, and Goomoor; the latter Eastern Akim, Winnebah, Accra, Aquapim, Adangme, and Crobboe.

The next point to be considered is the political union of the various kings in the kingdom of Fantee under one political head. A man should be chosen, either by universal suffrage, or appointed by the [British] Governor, and sanctioned and received by all the kings and chiefs, and crowned as King of Fantee. He should be a man of great sagacity, good common sense, not easily influenced by party spirit, of a kind and generous disposition, a man of good education, and who has done good service to the Coast Government. He should be crowned before all the kings and caboceers within the kingdom of Fantee; the kings should regard him as their chief; his authority should be recognized and supported by the Governor of the Coast, who should refer to him matters of domestic importance relative to the other native kings, advise him as to the course he should pursue, and see that his decisions be immediately carried out.

He should be assisted by a number of councillors, who, for the time, should swear allegiance to the British Government, until such time as the country is considered fit for delivery over to self-government. They should consist not only of men of education and good, sound common sense, residing in the Coast towns, but also of responsible chiefs, as representatives of the various kings within the kingdom.

One most important consideration is the yearly vote of a round sum out of the revenue as stipend to the king elect whilst under this probationary course, such as would allow him to keep up a certain amount of State dignity, and would enable him to carry out his authority over the kings and chiefs. Each State should be made to contribute towards the support of the temporary Government; a native volunteer corps should be attached to the Government, officered by natives of intelligence, who should be thoroughly drilled by paid officers and sergeants, supplied from West Indian regiments stationed on the Coast. The English language should be made the diplomatic language with foreign nations; but Fantee should be made the medium of internal communication and therefore ought at once to be reduced to writing.

The territory of the kingdom of Ashantee is larger than that of the Protected Territory of the Gold Coast, but we find the reigning king possesses absolute power over the different tribes composing it. True enough, the edifice was constructed on the blood of several nationalities, which gives it greater strength; but the kingdom of Fantee must be erected on a peaceable footing, supported, for a time at least, by a civilized Government, with a prince at the head who is versed in native diplomacy . . . a prince who would be able, like the potentate of Ashantee, to concentrate a large force at a very short notice, at any given point, when menaced by their powerful neighbours . . .

The aim, therefore, should be to form a strong, compact native Government, which would command the obedience of all the native kings and chiefs, and which would immediately undertake the quelling of all disturbances in the interior, and command the native force if attacked . . .

Let them, therefore, have a ruler in whom they have confidence, and generals experienced in bush fighting; let them be united, offensive and defensive, to one another, under one head, whose authority is paramount; let good, large, open roads be made connecting the kingdoms with one another . . . let the strength of every kingdom be known by the head centre . . . and I guarantee that a compact, powerful, and independent Government will be formed, which would defy Ashantee and give confidence to the whole country . . .

Advice to the rising generation in West Africa

Let the younger portion of the population, who are so susceptible and ready to take offence and retort at the least occasion, remember that all Europeans who enter their country, by the higher degree of intellectual and moral cultivation which they, as a race, have received, are entitled to a certain degree of respect as the harbingers of civilization, imitating the good and virtuous, while shunning those whose actions are a disgrace to civilization . . . [L]et them be uniformly courteous, cultivate their minds, and strive zealously for substantial worth. Let them seek independence without bravado, manliness without subserviency; and let them put their shoulders to the work . . .

They should make it their ruling principle to concentrate their mental powers, their powers of observation, reasoning, and memory . . .

Let them consider that their own interest is intimately bound up in the interest of their country's rise; and that by developing the principle of public interest they will bring the Government to take an interest in themselves, and thus their interest and that of the Government will not clash, but become identical . . .

Let the rising generation, therefore, study to exert themselves to obtain the combined attractive influence of knowledge and wisdom, wealth and honesty, great place and charity, fame and happiness, book-learning and virtue, so that they may be made to bring their happy influences to bear on the regeneration of their country.

52 ◆ Cetshwayo describes Zulu society (1881)

During the 1870s and early 1880s, the British government engaged in a series of wars to cement imperial control over southern Africa. This was a considerable change from previous policies, which had kept colonial frontiers as restricted as possible. The change was occasioned by the huge economic growth set off by the discovery of diamonds and the resulting demand for cheap African labor. In 1879 the British went to war with the Zulu, whom the British denounced as barbarians who were ruled by tyrants and had no understanding of regularized forms of law and government. Though the Zulu defeated a British army, under the command of Lord Chelmsford, at Isandlwana (the worst defeat of the British in a colonial war), their forces were soon crushed by the superior firepower of their opponents. Their king, Cetshwayo, was deposed and sent into exile.

In the early 1880s, the British established an official commission to provide advice as to the most effective manner in which the newly conquered African peoples of southern Africa could be governed. One of the most important witnesses to appear before the commission was Cetshwayo, who, despite the evident biases of his questioners, argued that Zulu society was not a barbaric autocracy but a society that operated along certain recognized rules and practices and in which common people and women were treated not as slaves (as commonly argued by European missionaries) but as having certain personal and property rights. On July 7, 1881, the following exchange took place as Sir J. D. Barry, judge and president of the Native Laws and Customs Commission, questioned the king.[3]

137. Did Mpanda ever acknowledge that he owed any fealty to the Boers?—No; at one time when Dingaan was killed by his subjects, Mpanda came over to the Boers and was protected by them, because it was intended to kill him too. Shortly afterwards he was taken back to Zululand and lived there as king, and of course the Zulus thought that everything was settled between them and the Boers, but in a few days the Boers came and said they were going to fight Mpanda. There was a breach between the Zulus and the Boors [Boers], and then the English came to Natal.

138. Did Mpanda ever do anything to show that he acknowledged the Boer authority over him?—No.

139. Did Mpanda ever acknowledge the English authority over him?—No, the Zulus never acknowledged the authority of the English at any time, but they were like relations of the English. They always sent to the English, and told them anything that happened in Zululand, and wanted their help . . . The Zulus said they would not have anything more to do with the Boers, because the Boers could not look after them. At the time when the Boers intended to invade Zululand, the English came to Natal and attacked the Boers, and the Boers could do nothing against the Zulus after that; but in my reign they did, and in the latter days of Mpanda.

140. After Mpanda's death, before you succeeded, did you in any way acknowledge the authority of Shepstone over you?—The king says, when his father died, he sent a messenger with a large ox to Shepstone, to report it to him, and to say that he wished Shepstone to see about the country being settled under him, because the Zulu nation was a relation of the English.

141. Did not Shepstone influence your father in making his will in your favour?—No, Shepstone had no influence in any way. The Zulu nation and Mpanda himself told Shepstone that Cetywayo was the heir, and was to be king after his death.

142. Before you were crowned by Shepstone, did you do anything to show that Shepstone had any authority over you, or did you consider up to that time that he had any authority over you?—No; the king says he did nothing to acknowledge the authority of Shepstone, but he used to talk to Shepstone in a friendly way, and he acknowledged the Queen.

143. You did acknowledge the Queen before you were crowned by Shepstone as the Queen's servant?—The king says he acknowledged the authority of the Queen in this way,

---

3. *Report and Proceedings with Appendices of the Government Commission on Native Laws and Customs, Cape of Good Hope Parliamentary Paper, G4,* 1883, Part 1, 523–30.

that he would have nothing to do with the Boers or any other nation, and he acknowledged Shepstone as her officer.

144. As king of the Zulus, was all power invested in you, as king, over your subjects?—In conjunction with the chiefs of the land.

145. How did the chiefs derive their power from you as king?—The king calls together the chiefs of the land when he wants to elect a new chief, and asks their advice as to whether it is fit to make such a man a large chief, and if they say "yes" the chief is made.

146. If you had consulted the chiefs, and found they did not agree with you, could you appoint a chief by virtue of your kingship?—In some cases, if the chiefs don't approve of it, the king requires their reasons, and when they have stated them he often gives it up. In other cases he tries the man to see whether he can perform the duties required of him or not.

147. In fact, you have the power to act independently of the chiefs in making an appointment, although you always consult them?—No; the king has not the power of electing an officer as chief without the approval of the other chiefs. They are the most important men. But the smaller chiefs he can elect at his discretion . . .

150. Are there any hereditary claims to the appointment of induna [civil or military official]?—It is not hereditary with the small chiefs, but with the important men of the land. The son of the chief wife is heir to the property of this important man.

151. Has the heir to this property of a chief the right to claim to be a chief?—No; if a man was known to be fit to hold the post he would be appointed.

152. What are the duties of the indunas?—They look after the land, and decide different cases.

153. Cases of murder?—Every criminal case.

154. Do you allot a particular province to each induna?—The king allots different parts of the country to different chiefs.

155. And each induna in his own province tries all the cases which arise in that province?—He is called "induna" when he is at the military kraal [settlement], but when he goes to his residence he is called headman, and he has to look after the cases which arise in that part of the country.

156. How is he assisted at the trials?—He calls together all the chief men of that district, and they discuss the case.

157. After they have discussed it, does he retire and form his own opinion upon all the evidence and discussion, and come to a conclusion alone, or does he give his judgment sitting with the other men altogether?—No; the headman does not hear the evidence and then go home and consider it, but he sits there and listens to the assembly talking about the case. Then they ask his opinion, and he says, "I think so and so." If they don't agree with him, they give their reasons.

158. And he gives the final verdict?—Yes; the headman.

159. Does the headman award the punishment upon his own decision, or does he consult the others upon it first?—The headman and the assembly award the punishment.

160. But suppose they differ, who finally decides?—Then the case is taken to the king's kraal.

161. Has the king absolute power to decide?—The chief men of the land talk about the case first, and bring it up to him.

162. And he finally decides?—Sometimes they decide before they come to him, and they come and tell him which way they decide, and he approves or disapproves as the case may be, and as he thinks it right or wrong.

163. Suppose there is a difference among them, who finally decides?—The king has the power to decide in this way, that when he has decided the chief men of the country have nothing to say against it, because they will not say that the king has decided against their wish.

164. Is all law and right of property supposed to come from the king in consultation with his chiefs?—The right of property comes from the king, but he does not exercise that power. The country has remained like it is now since the king's father and grandfather reigned . . .

168. If you want to make a new law, to be applicable to all Zululand, how do you set about it?—The king has a discussion with the chiefs about it, and they give out the law, but he cannot make a law without their consent. He consults the chiefs and gives his reasons, and if they conclude to agree to it, it is the law, but he cannot make a law against the wishes of his chiefs . . .

171. In England our laws are written, and so there is no misunderstanding them, but suppose there is a dispute in Zululand, as to what the law really is, who is supposed to be the best authority upon the law as given out by the chiefs?—The king cannot say, because it never happened that there was any doubt about the law of the country . . .

173. Have the people, independently of these chiefs and you as king, any sort of voice in the making of any laws? Are they heard directly or indirectly?—No.

175. Is every man bound to serve in Zululand as a soldier?—The old men of the country are called the white part of the nation, that is to say they are not soldiers; the young men are the soldiers.

176. Have all these old men been soldiers before?—Yes. Some of these are retired and old, and unable to serve any more, but the younger ones who have the [head]rings on can go to the king and serve as they please, and return home as they like. The young men are not forced to be soldiers.

177. Is there any young man there who is not a soldier?—No, everyone wishes to be a soldier. If anyone stops at home, the others laugh at him, and say he is a "Ungogo" = Button quail . . .

180. What are the duties of the petty chiefs?—They principally superintend work for their superior chiefs, and for the king. The larger chiefs send them out to look after men who are doing work for the king . . .

183. The people are never consulted about either big or little matters? The only consultation is between you and your big chiefs in big matters, and between you and your small chiefs in smaller matters?—Yes, he has a voice in that; he can go to a chief and say it should be done in this or in that way . . .

196. Is there not one particular divine power, who is supposed to be above all spirits and to be the father of the whole human race?—Yes.

197. What is he called?–Nkulunkulu . . .

199. What does "Zulu" mean?—The name of the nations' ancestor; the first man of the Zulu nation.

200. Where is he supposed to be?—At the military kraal in Zululand. "Zulu" also means "heaven." Zulu was one of the king's ancestors, the king of Zululand.

201. Are the Zulus all supposed to come from heaven or to go there?—Yes, every man came from heaven because he was made by God, the white as well as the Zulus.

202. Why are the old chiefs called "white men"?—Because they generally live at the military kraal, and go home when they wish; and because they have a white shield instead of a black one.

203. You told us that you make these laws. Are you bound to govern in accordance with the laws which you and your ancestors have made . . . ?—Yes.

204. What is your law as to land? To whom does it belong, and how is it apportioned?—The whole country belongs to the king, and different portions of it are inhabited by headmen, and smaller portions by common people.

205. Who allots the land?—The king . . .

218. The Zulus generally have a great wife, a right-hand and a left-hand wife?—Yes.

219. But the great wife is not necessarily the first wife that he marries?–No . . .

223. When a man has a number of wives, does he keep them all in one kraal?—No; in different kraals . . .

230. Every woman, married or unmarried, belongs to some one, to her husband, her father, or her father's heir?—Yes.

231. Can any woman require property for herself?—No; only the king's wife.

232. If a married woman obtains anything it becomes the property of her husband?—Yes.

233. And if an unmarried woman obtains anything it is the property of her father or her father's heir?—If a father wishes his daughter to have anything she can have it, and if a son wants it he can ask his sister for it, but she can keep it if she likes.

234. Has any woman the right of property independent of the will of her father or her husband?—Yes; they can have property independent of the father or husband . . .

291. How many missionaries were there in your country?—The king is not quite sure, but he thinks about fourteen . . .

293. Did you like to have them there?—Yes, they did good, they were able to help the people by giving them medicine; they were kind people; they were not troublesome . . .

295. Altogether you think it was good to have them?—There was a German missionary whom the king did not like, but as a whole he liked the missionaries very much because they were no trouble.

296. What trouble did this man give?—He quarrelled with the people, and was too fast with thrashing. . . .

53 • A university for Africa (1881)

Edward Blyden was born in the Danish Caribbean in 1832, the descendant of African slaves. As a teenager he accompanied an American Presbyterian missionary to the United States in order to pursue higher education, but because of the racial discrimination he experienced he moved in 1851 to Liberia, where he remained for most of the rest of his life. In 1861 he became a professor at the newly established Liberia College and in 1881 was appointed its president. Later he became Liberia's ambassador to Great Britain, was nominated as a candidate for the presidency of Liberia, and then worked for the British colonial service in Lagos and Sierra Leone, where he dealt primarily with the education of Muslim Africans. He died in Freetown in 1912. West African leaders in the first half of the twentieth century viewed him as a pioneer of pan-Africanism, someone who saw a basic unity between peoples of African descent on both sides of the Atlantic. In his inaugural address to Liberia College, given January 5, 1881, he argued for a program of study for Africans that built on what he saw as the strengths of Western education but incorporated as well the study of Africa and of the Muslim world and avoided those European works produced during the era of the slave trade and imperialism.[4]

A college in West Africa, for the education of African youth by African instructors, under a Christian government conducted by Negroes, is something so unique in the history of Christian civilization, that wherever, in the civilized world, the existence of such an institution is heard of, there will be curiosity as to its character, its work, and its prospects. A college suited, in all respects, to the exigencies of this nation and to the needs of the race cannot come into existence all at once. It must be the result of years of experience, of trial, of experiment.

Every thinking man will allow that all we have been doing in this country so far, whether in church, in state, or in school—our forms of religion, our politics, our literature, such as it is, is only temporary and transitional. When we advance further into Africa, and become one with the great tribes on the continent, these things will take the form which the genius of the race shall prescribe.

The civilization of that vast population, untouched by foreign influence not yet affected by European habits, is not to be organized according to foreign patterns, but will organize itself according to the nature of the people and the country. Nothing that we are doing now can be absolute or permanent, because nothing is normal or regular. Everything is provisional or tentative.

The College is only a machine, an instrument to assist in carrying forward our regular work, devised not only for intellectual ends, but for social purposes, for religious duty, for patriotic aims, for racial development; and when as an instrument, as a means, it fails, for any reason whatever, to fulfil its legitimate functions, it is the duty of the country, as well as the interest of the country, to see that it is stimulated into healthful activity; or, if this is impossible, to see that it is set aside as a pernicious obstruction. We cannot afford to waste time in dealing with insoluble problems under impossible conditions . . .

We have in our curriculum, adopted some years ago, a course of study corresponding, to some extent, to that pursued in European and American colleges. To this we shall adhere as nearly as possible; but experience has already suggested, and will, no doubt, from time to time suggest, such modifications as were required by our peculiar circumstances.

The object of all education is to secure growth and efficiency, to make a man all that his natural gifts will allow him to become; to produce self-respect, a proper appreciation of our own powers and of the powers of other people; to beget a fitness for one's sphere of life and action, and ability to discharge the duties it imposes. Now, if we take these qualities as the true outcome of a correct education, then every one who is acquainted with the facts must admit that, as a rule, in the entire civilized world, the Negro, notwithstanding his two hundred years' residence with Christian and civilized races, has nowhere received anything like a correct

4. Edward W. Blyden, *Christianity, Islam, and the Negro Race* (London: W. B. Whittingham, 1887), 82–93.

education. We find him everywhere, in the United States, in the West Indies, in South America, largely unable to cope with the responsibilities which devolve upon him. Not only is he not sought after for any position of influence in the political movements of those countries, but he is even denied admission to ecclesiastical appointments of importance . . .

To a certain extent, perhaps to a very important extent, Negroes trained on the soil of Africa have the advantage of those trained in foreign countries; but in all, as a rule, the intellectual and moral results, thus far, have been far from satisfactory. There are many men of book-learning, but few, very few, of any capability, even few who have that amount, or that sort, of culture, which produces self-respect, confidence in one's self, and efficiency in work. Now, why is this? The evil, it is considered, lies in the system and methods of European training to which Negroes are, everywhere in Christian lands, subjected, and which everywhere affects them unfavourably. Of a different race, different susceptibility, different bent of character from that of the European, they have been trained under influences in many respects adapted only to the Caucasian race. Nearly all the books they read, the very instruments of their culture, have been such as to force them from the groove which is natural to them, where they would be strong and effective, without furnishing them with any avenue through which they may move naturally and free from obstruction. Christian and so-called civilized Negroes live, for the most part, in foreign countries, where they are only passive spectators of the deeds of a foreign race; and where, with other impressions which they receive from without, an element of doubt as to their own capacity and their own destiny is fastened upon them, and inheres in their intellectual and social constitution. They deprecate their own individuality, and would escape from it if they could. And in countries like this, where they are free from the hampering surroundings of an alien race, they still read and study the books of foreigners, and form their idea of everything that man may do, or ought to do, according to the standard held up in those teachings. Hence, without the physical or mental aptitude for the enterprises which they are taught to admire and revere, they attempt to copy and imitate them, and share the fate of all copyists and imitators. Bound to move on a lower level, they acquire and retain a practical inferiority, transcribing, very often, the faults rather than the virtues of their models . . .

In all English-speaking countries the mind of the intelligent Negro child revolts against the descriptions given in elementary books—geographies, travels, histories—of the Negro; but, though he experiences an instinctive revulsion from these caricatures and misrepresentations, he is obliged to continue, as he grows in years, to study such pernicious teachings, After leaving school he finds the same things in newspapers, in reviews, in novels, in *quasi* scientific works; and after a while . . . they begin to seem to him the proper things to say and to feel about his race, and he accepts what, at first, his fresh and unbiased feelings naturally and indignantly repelled. Such is the effect of repetition . . .

Those who have lived in civilized communities, where there are different races, know the disparaging views which are entertained of the blacks by their neighbours—and often, alas! by themselves. The standard of all physical and intellectual excellencies in the present civilization being the white complexion, whatever deviates from that favoured colour is proportionally depreciated, until the black, which is the opposite, becomes not only the most unpopular but the most unprofitable colour. Black men, and especially black women, in such communities, experience the greatest imaginable inconvenience. They never feel at home. In the depth of their being they always feel themselves strangers in the land of their exile, and the only escape from this feeling is to escape from themselves. And this feeling of self-depreciation is not diminished as I have intimated above, by the books they read. Women, especially, are fond of reading novels and light literature; and it is in these writings that flippant and eulogistic reference is constantly made to the superior physical and mental characteristics of the Caucasian race, which, by contrast, suggest the inferiority of other races, especially of that race which is furthest removed from it in appearance.

It is painful in America to see the efforts which are made by Negroes to secure outward conformity to the appearance of the dominant race.

This is by no means surprising; but what is surprising is that, under the circumstances, any Negro has retained a particle of self-respect. Now in Africa, where the colour of the majority is black, the fashion in personal matters is naturally suggested by the personal characteristics of the race, and we are free from the necessity of submitting to the use of "incongruous feathers awkwardly stuck on." Still, we are held in bondage by our indiscriminate and injudicious use of a foreign literature; and we strive to advance by the methods of a foreign race. In this effort we struggle with the odds against us. We fight at the disadvantage which David would have experienced in Saul's armour. The African must advance by methods of his own. He must possess a power distinct from that of the European. It has been proved that he knows how to take advantage of European culture, and that he can be benefited by it. This proof was perhaps necessary, but it is not sufficient. We must show that we are able to go alone, to carve out our own way. We must not be satisfied that, in this nation, European influence shapes our polity, makes our laws, rules in our tribunals, and impregnates our social atmosphere. We must not suppose that the Anglo-Saxon methods are final, that there is nothing for us to find for our own guidance, and that we have nothing to teach the world. There is inspiration for us also. We must study our brethren in the interior, who know better than we do the laws of growth for the race. We see among them the rudiments of that which, with fair play and opportunity, will develop into important and effective agencies for our work. We look too much to foreigners, and are dazzled almost to blindness by their exploits—so as to fancy that they have exhausted the possibilities of humanity . . .

I propose now to sketch the outlines of a programme for the education of the students in Liberia College, and, I may venture to add, of the Negro youth everywhere in Africa who hope to take a leading part in the work of the race and of the country. I will premise that, generally, in the teaching our youth, far more is made of the importance of imparting information than of training the mind. Their minds are too much taken possession of by mere information drawn from European sources . . .

We shall devote attention principally, both for mental discipline and information, to the earlier epochs of the world's history. It is decided that there are five or six leading epochs in the history of civilization. I am following Mr. Frederic Harrison's classification. First, there was the great permanent, stationary system of human society, held together by a religious belief, or by social custom growing out of that belief. This has been called the Theocratic state of society. The type of that phase of civilization was the old Eastern empires. The second great type was the Greek Age of intellectual activity and civic freedom. Next came the Roman type of civilization, an age of empire, of conquest, of consolidation of nations, of law and government. The fourth great system was the phase of civilization which prevailed from the fall of the

Roman Empire until comparatively modern times, and was called the Medieval Age, when the Church and Feudalism existed side by side. The fifth phase of history was that which began with the breaking-up of the power of the Church on the one side, and of feudalism on the other, the foundation of modern history, or the Modern Age. That system has continued down to the present; but, if sub-divided, it would form the sixth type, which is the Age since the French Revolution, the Age of social and popular development, of modern science and industry.

We shall permit in our curriculum the unrestricted study of the first four epochs, but especially the second, third and fourth, from which the present civilization of Western Europe is mainly derived. There has been no period of history more full of suggestive energy, both physical and intellectual, than those epochs. Modern Europe boasts of its period of intellectual activity, but none can equal, for life and freshness, the Greek and Roman prime. No modern writers will ever influence the destiny of the race to the same extent that the Greeks and Romans have done.

We can afford to exclude, then, as subjects of study, at least in the earlier college years, the events of the fifth and sixth epochs, and the works which, in large numbers, have been written during those epochs. I know that during these periods some of the greatest works of human genius have been composed. I know that Shakespeare and Milton, Gibbon and Macaulay, Hallam and Lecky, Froude, Stubbs and Green, belong to these periods. It is not in my power, even if I had the will, to disparage the works of these masters; but what I wish to say is, that these are not the works on which the mind of the youthful African should be trained. It was during the sixth period that the transatlantic slave trade arose, and those theories—theological, social, and political—were invented for the degradation and proscription of the Negro. This epoch continues to this day, and has an abundant literature and a prolific authorship. It has produced that whole tribe of declamatory Negrophobists, whose views, in spite of their emptiness and impertinence, are having their effect upon the ephemeral literature of the day, a literature which is shaping the life of the Negro in Christian lands. His whole theory of life, quite contrary to what his nature intends, is being influenced, consciously and unconsciously, by the general conceptions of his race entertained by the manufacturers of this literature, a great portion of which, made for to-day, will not survive the next generation . . .

The instruments of culture which we shall employ in the College will be chiefly the Classics and Mathematics. By Classics I mean the Greek and Latin languages and their literature. In those languages there is not, as far as I know, a sentence, a word, or a syllable disparaging to the Negro. He may get nourishment from them without taking in any race-poison. They will perform no sinister work upon his consciousness, and give no unholy bias to his inclinations . . .

Passing over, then, for a certain time, the current literature of Western Europe, which is, after all, derived and secondary, we will resort to the fountain head, and in the study of the great masters, in the languages in which they wrote, we shall get the required mental discipline without unfavourably affecting our sense of race individuality or our own self respect. There is nothing that we need to know for the work of building up this country, in its moral, political and religious character, which we may not learn from the ancients. There is nothing in the domain of literature, philosophy, or religion for which we need be dependent upon the moderns. Law and philosophy we may get from the Romans and the Greeks, religion from the Hebrews . . .

But we shall also study Mathematics. These, as instruments of culture, are everywhere applicable. A course of Algebra, Geometry, and Higher Mathematics must accompany, step by step, classical studies. Neither of these means of discipline can be omitted without loss. The qualities which make a man succeed in mastering the Classics and Mathematics are also those which qualify him for the practical work of life.

It will be our aim to introduce into our curriculum also the Arabic, and some of the principal native languages, by means of which we may have intelligent intercourse with the millions accessible to us in the interior, and learn more of our own country. We have young men who are experts in the geography and customs of foreign countries; who can tell all about the proceedings of foreign statesmen in countries thousands of miles away; can talk glibly of London, Berlin, Paris, and Washington; know all about Gladstone, Bismarck, Gambetta, and Hayes; but who knows anything about Musahdu, Medina, Kankan, or Sego, only a few hundred miles from us? Who can tell anything of the policy or doings of Fanfi-doreh, Ibrahima Sissi, or Fahqueh-queh, or Simoro of Boporu, only a few steps from us? These are hardly known. Now as Negroes, allied in blood and race to these people, this is disgraceful; and as a nation, if we intend to grow and prosper in this country, it is impolitic, it is short-sighted, it is unpatriotic; but it has required time for us to grow up to these ideas, to understand our position in this country. In order to accelerate our future progress, and to give to the advance we make the element of permanence, it will be our aim in the College to produce men of ability. Ability or capability is the power to use with effect the instruments in our hands, the bad workman complains of his tools; but, even when he is satisfied with the excellence of his tools, he cannot produce the results which an able workman will produce, even with indifferent tools.

I trust that arrangements will be made by which girls of our country may be admitted to share in the advantages of this College. I cannot see why our sisters should not receive exactly the same general culture as we do. I think that the progress of the country will be more rapid and permanent when the girls receive the same general training as the boys; and our women, besides being able to appreciate the intellectual labours of their husbands and brothers, will be able also to share in the pleasures of intellectual pursuits. We need not fear that they will be less graceful, less natural, or less womanly; but we may be sure that they will make wiser mothers, more appreciative wives, and more affectionate sisters . . .

In the religious work of the College, the Bible will be our textbook, the Bible without note or comment, especially as we propose to study the original language in which the New Testament was written; and we may find opportunity, in connection with the Arabic, to study the Old Testament. The teachings of Christianity are of universal application. "Other foundation can no man lay than that which is laid." The great truths of the Sermon on the Mount are as universally accepted as Euclid's axioms. The meaning of the Good Samaritan is as certain as that of the forty-seventh proposition, and a great deal plainer . . .

All our traditions and experiences are connected with a foreign race. We have no poetry or philosophy but that of our taskmasters. The songs that live in our ears and are often on our lips are the songs which we heard sung by those who shouted while we groaned and lamented. They sang of their history, which was the history of our degradation. They recited their triumphs, which contained the records of our humiliation. To our great misfortune, we learned their prejudices and their passions, and thought we had their aspirations and their power. Now, if we are to make an independent nation—a strong nation—we must listen to the songs of our unsophisticated brethren as they sing of their history, as they tell of their traditions, of the wonderful and mysterious events of their tribal or national life, of the achievements of what we call their superstitions; we must lend a ready ear to the ditties of the Kroomen who pull our boats, of the Pessah and Golah men, who till our farms; we must read the compositions, rude as we may think them, of the Mandingoes and the Veys. We shall in this way get back the strength of the race, like the giant of the ancients, who always gained strength, for his conflict with Hercules, whenever he touched his Mother Earth.

And this is why we want the College away from the seaboard—with its constant intercourse with foreign manners and low foreign ideas—that we may have free and uninterrupted intercourse with the intelligent among the tribes of the interior; that the students, even from the books to which they will be allowed access, may conveniently flee to the forests and fields of Manding and the Niger, and mingle with our brethren and gather fresh inspiration and fresh and living ideas . . .

The time is past when we can be content with putting forth elaborate arguments to prove our equality with foreign races. Those who doubt our capacity are more likely to be convinced of their error by the exhibition, on our part, of those qualities of energy and enterprise which will enable us to occupy the extensive field before us for our own advantage and the advantage of humanity—for the purposes of civilization, of science, of good government, and of progress generally—than by any mere abstract argument about the equality of races. The suspicions disparaging to us will be dissipated only by the exhibition of the indisputable realities of a lofty manhood as they may be illustrated in successful efforts to build up a nation, to wrest from Nature her secrets, to lead the van of progress in this country, and to regenerate a continent.

CHAPTER EIGHT

A New River of Gold Increases the
Motivations for Conquest (1874–1905)

54 • Diamonds (1874)

In 1869, the year after Africanus Horton published his major work on West Africa, reports of a huge diamond find in the interior of southern Africa reached Europe. Within a few years thousands of people, African and European, had traveled to the diamond fields. The new industry was hugely profitable for the few, such as Cecil Rhodes, who succeeded in monopolizing control of the diamond mines, and enormously demanding on the labor of Africans. Gwayi Tyamzashe, a Xhosa convert to Christianity and a minister in the United Free Church of Scotland, came to the new city of Kimberley to engage in missionary work. In a newspaper article published in August 1874, Tyamzashe describes the urban culture developed at the diamond fields, noting especially the huge range of people coming from every part of southern and central Africa to work in the mining industry. Tyamzashe's son, Henry Daniel, became one of the chief aides to Clements Kadalie in organizing the Industrial and Commercial Workers' Union in South Africa during the 1920s.[1]

We have often heard of the industrious city—the Metropolis of Great Britain; the crowding of its streets, and the noise of the machinery and workmen. But I question if the noise there has ever been anything approaching what I have heard at the New Rush [Kimberley]. The hurry and din of the wheels, pulleys, wires, and buckets, in conveying the diamondiferous ground out of the gigantic mine; the noise of waggons, carts, carriages, sieves, sorting tables, and all the like, combined with the barbarous yells of the native labourers, and accompanied with a hurrah for every trifling thing that seems to be out of place, these things are as familiar to us at Kimberley as the touch bells are to you at Lovedale.

On my first arrival at the New Rush I observed that nearly every evening was devoted to private and public amusements, insomuch that there seemed to be no room left for the great work for which we had come. The evenings resounded with the noise of the concert, the circus, and all sorts of dances from one end of the camp to the other. The life then of both coloured and whites was so rough that I thought this place was only good for those who were resolved to sell their souls for silver, gold, and precious stones, or for those who were determined to barter their lives for the pleasures of a time. Diamond stealing was also regularly

1. Gwayi Tyamzashe, "Life at the Diamond Fields," article published in the bilingual missionary journal *Kaffir Express/Isigidimi* (August 1874), reprinted in Francis Wilson and Dominique Perrot, eds., *Outlook on a Century: South Africa 1870–1970* (Lovedale, South Africa: Lovedale Press, 1972), 19–21.

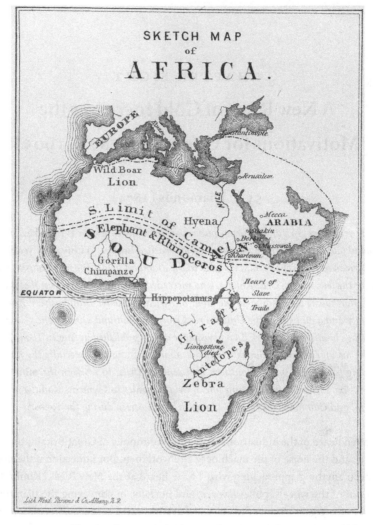

FIGURE 13 The West's image of Africa in the nineteenth century could be summed up by three words: animals, slaves, and Livingstone. This map comes from an account written by Alvan S. Southworth, secretary of the American Geographical Society, of a trip he made to Africa in 1874 to look for the sources of the Nile River and to describe the slave trade. In his preface Southworth expressed confidence that the day would soon come "when capital and Anglo-Saxon energy will release the degraded negro peoples from their ages of bondage" and argued that "Africa should be Americanized" (iv). Alvan S. Southworth, *Four Thousand Miles of African Travel*, 1875.

carried on on a large scale by persons of colour as well as whites. Even in the present days of order, peace, and good government, I fear that diamond stealing is still practised systematically and ingeniously. It is very effectively done by companies consisting of several natives and a European diamond buyer who is at the head of the Company. Like the old Spartans, these natives are taught to steal so that they cannot be found out, and are well compensated for it.

During the short period of about two years there has been a wonderful change with regard to the moral condition of the Diamond Fields. The invincible power of the Gospel has made itself felt in the hearts of many, so that now there are two opposite forces acting against each other, whereas before only one—namely, the evil influence—seemed to be the one ruling power in this camp.

Instead of the bustle and confusion of 1872, we have now that quietude and security of life and property which is characteristic of proper legislation and good government. About two years ago human life was, so to speak, reckoned as of less value than silver, gold, and precious stones. At that time you would hear nothing but cursing, swearing, screaming, and shouts of hurrah for new comers from the interior, for fighters, for a well dressed lady, for a diamond being found, and so forth. It is vain to expect order and smoothness here. The very purpose for which the people have rushed and crowded together in this camp—to get rich rapidly—speaks of itself that there can be neither order nor smoothness in such a rush as this. Add to this the severity of the climate and the unruly character of the diggers. All who have ever visited the fields will have complained of excessive heat, extreme cold, and choking dust occasioned by the every day storms of wind raising the gigantic heaps of sorted gravel, sometimes rendering the sun invisible, and breathing also difficult. You would be surprised to find at the Colesberg Kopje a person whom you knew to have been a respectable gentleman, dressed like a common labourer, with only a pair of trousers, a big flannel shirt purposely unbuttoned, and a big heavy belt round his waist. Every one who succeeds in making a fortune, whether he be white or coloured, will first have to be contented to live day after day like the Kaffir Bakwetas or white boys. When they are all at work you can hardly distinguish the whites from the coloured, for they all resemble the diamondiferous soil they are working.

A lady or a well dressed gentleman dare not come near the mine during the hours of labour, for the native labourers will make shouts of hurrah for them all round the Kopje. Day after day you hear shouts of hurrah for a diamond being found, for a rope or wire breaking, for a bucket falling and injuring some one, for a portion of a claim breaking down and burying some person or persons underneath it.

This is the reason why many persons wanting patience and perseverance have been thoroughly disappointed when they came here. To bear on for a year or so at this picnic life requires no ordinary degree of patience on the part of the digger. The summation of the above statements with regard to life at the Diamond Fields may be comprehended under the two English words, *rough and hard* . . .

In a mission point of view, it is not easy to deal with such a mixture of tribes as we have at the Diamond Fields. There are Bushmen, Korannas, Hottentots, Griquas, Batlaping, Damaras, Barolong, Barutse, Bakhatla, Bakwena, Bamangwatu, Bapeli, Magalaka, Batsuetla, Baganana, Basutu, Magwaba, Mazulu, Maswazi, Matswetswa, Matonga, Matebele, Mabaca, Mampondo, Mamfengu, Batembu, Maxosa, etc. Many of these can hardly understand each other, and in many cases they have to converse through the medium of either Dutch, Sisutu,

APPENDIX.

ANIMALS.

Believing that zoological gardens might wish in the future to make collections of animals in Central Africa, I made the following estimate, which was approved by those who had an extended acquaintance with the business:

No.	Animals.	Kinds.	.	Age.	Price.			
1..	Elephant	2		10 years ...	$200	×	8	=	$1,600
2..	Giraffe............................	1		3 years	100	×	4	=	400
3..	Hippopotami................	1		2 years . ..	100	×	4	=	400
4..	Ostrich	3		2 years . ..	25	×	12	=	300
5..	Lions	1		2 months ..	10	×	8	=	80
6..	Leopards...........	1		2 months ..	10	×	4	=	40
7..	Panther	1		2 months ..	10	×	4	=	40
8..	Wild Cat.......................	1		2 months ..	10	×	4	=	40
9..	Linx..........	1		2 months ..	10	×	4	=	40
0..	Monkeys........................	3		1 month ...	5	×	100	=	500
1..	Wild Ass.	1		2 months ..	100	×	4	=	400
12..	Wild Cat.......................	....		2 years ...	5	×	4	=	20
13..	Hyena...........................	2		2 months ..	10	×	8	=	80
14..	Fox.............................	3		....	5	×	12	=	60
15..	Abyssinian Cat.................	1		....	20	×	4	=	80
16..	Dromedary	2		5 years	100	×	8	=	800
17..	Antelopes	20		....	20	×	80	=	1,600
18..	Camel	....		....	20	×	4	=	80
19..	Rhinoceros.....................	1		....	100	×	4	=	400
20..	Zebra	1		....	100	×	4	=	400
21..	Crocodiles.....................	1		....	10	×	8	=	80
					Ani'ls, 290				$6,770

Cost of animals... ..	$6,770
Chains, 200 × $3..	600
Cages, 150 × $10...	1,500
Cases.......	1,000
To get the animals ready...........................	3,000
For care............................	1,000
Hunting expedition	500
Hunters, 10 × $100........ ....•....	1,000
Men, 30 × $50.........	1,500
Gunpowder, etc..................	2,000
Boats to Alexandria, 12 × $200.........	2,400
	$21,270
Cost of transportation to New York, including cases.......	10,000
Total	$31,270

FIGURE 14 Based on his experiences traveling four thousand miles through Africa in 1874, Alvan S. Southworth believed that "a few bold, rapid strokes of humanity and enterprise on the part of the Christian powers, would add 70,000,000 producers, now self-consumers [an allusion to the slave trade], to the modern arts and industries" (iv). As one example of how Africa could produce for the West, Southworth, inspired by the opening of the first American zoo (Philadelphia in 1874), published in 1875 this estimate of what it would cost an American city to acquire the animals needed to establish its own zoo. Alvan S. Southworth, *Four Thousand Miles of African Travel*, 1875.

or Kaffir. Those coming from far up in the interior, such as the Bakwena, Bamangwatu, Mapeli, Matebele, etc., come with the sole purpose of securing guns. Some of them therefore resolve to stay no longer here than is necessary to get some six or seven pounds for the gun. Hence you will see hundreds of them leaving the Fields, and as many arriving from the north almost every day.

55 • Cecil Rhodes's dreams of empire (1877)

*The most renowned of the diamond magnates was Cecil Rhodes. Born in 1853, the son of an En-
glish clergyman, Rhodes made a fortune in diamonds while still in his twenties, monopolized control
of the industry with his company, De Beers Consolidated Mines (which controls world diamonds
even today), became prime minister of the Cape Colony, and established his own private colony,
Rhodesia. Interested both in business and politics and an enthusiastic supporter of the British Empire, he attempted to perpetuate his beliefs by leaving practically his entire estate to fund scholarships for university study. These Rhodes scholarships would enable "young Colonists" (including
some Americans), males only (though with no restriction as to race), to study at Oxford University
(which Rhodes himself had attended, paying his own way from diamond profits) to acquire an understanding of "the advantage to the Colonies as well as to the United Kingdom of the retention of
the unity of the Empire." While a student at Oxford, Rhodes had sketched out his long-term aims
in a "confession of faith," reproduced below with Rhodes's original spelling and punctuation. The
scholarships, the qualifications for which Rhodes detailed in his will, were meant to create the society
of Empire boosters envisaged in the confession.[2]*

A. Cecil Rhodes's confession of faith, June 2, 1877

It often strikes a man to inquire what is the chief good in life; to one the thought comes
that it is a happy marriage, to another great wealth, and as each seizes on his idea, for that he
more or less works for the rest of his existence. To myself thinking over the same question the
wish came to render myself useful to my country. I then asked myself how could I and after
reviewing the various methods I have felt that at the present day we are actually limiting our
children and perhaps bringing into the world half the human beings we might owing to the
lack of country for them to inhabit that if we had retained America there would at this moment be millions more of English living. I contend that we are the finest race in the world and
that the more of the world we inhabit the better it is for the human race. Just fancy those parts
that are at present inhabited by the most despicable specimens of human beings what an alteration there would be if they were brought under Anglo-Saxon influence, look again at the
extra employment a new country added to our dominions gives. I contend that every acre
added to our territory means in the future birth to some more of the English race who otherwise would not be brought into existence. Added to this the absorption of the greater portion
of the world under our rule simply means the end of all wars, at this moment had we not lost
America I believe we could have stopped the Russian-Turkish war by merely refusing money
and supplies. Having these ideas what scheme could we think of to forward this object. I look
into history and I read the story of the Jesuits I see what they were able to do in a bad cause
and I might say under bad leaders.

In the present day I become a member in the Masonic order I see the wealth and power
they possess the influence they hold and I think over their ceremonies and I wonder that a

---

2. A, John Flint, *Cecil Rhodes* (London: Hutchinson, 1976), 248–52; B, Lewis Michell, *The Life of the Rt. Hon.
Cecil John Rhodes, 1853–1902* (London: Edward Arnold, 1910), vol. 2, 326–27.

large body of men can devote themselves to what at times appear the most ridiculous and ab-surd rites without an object and without an end.

The idea gleaming and dancing before ones eyes like a will-of-the-wisp at last frames itself into a plan. Why should we not form a secret society with but one object the furtherance of the British Empire and the bringing of the whole uncivilised world under British rule for the recovery of the United States for the making the Anglo-Saxon race but one Empire. What a dream, but yet it is probable, it is possible. I once heard it argued by a fellow in my own college, I am sorry to own it by an Englishman, that it was a good thing for us that we have lost the United States. There are some subjects on which there can be no arguments, and to an English-man this is one of them, but even from an American's point of view just picture what they have lost, look at their government, are not the frauds that yearly come before the public view a disgrace. to any country and especially their's which is the finest in the world. Would they have occurred had they remained under English rule great as they have become how infinitely greater they would have been with the softening and elevating influences of English rule, think of those countless 000's of Englishmen that during the last 100 years would have crossed the Atlantic and settled and populated the United States. Would they have not made without any prejudice a finer country of it than the low class Irish and German emigrants? All this we have lost and that country loses owing to whom? Owing to two or three ignorant pig-headed statesmen of the last century, at their door lies the blame. Do you perhaps ever feel mad? do you ever feel murderous? I think I do with those men. I bring facts to prove my assertion. Does an English father when his sons wish to emigrate ever think of suggesting emigration to a country under another flag, never—it would seem a disgrace to suggest such a thing I think that we all think that poverty is better under our own flag than wealth under a foreign one.

Put your mind into another train of thought. Fancy Australia discovered and colonised under the French flag, what would it mean merely several millions of English unborn that at present exist we learn from the past and to form our future. We learn from having lost to cling to what we possess. We know the size of the world we know the total extent. Africa is still lying ready for us it is our duty to take it. It is our duty to seize every opportunity of acquiring more territory and we should keep this one idea steadily before our eyes that more territory simply means more of the Anglo-Saxon race more of the best the most human, most honourable race the world possesses.

To forward such a scheme what a splendid help a secret society would be a society not openly acknowledged but who would work in secret for such an object.

I contend that there are at the present moment numbers of the ablest men in the world who would devote their whole lives to it. I often think what a loss to the English nation in some respects the abolition of the Rotten Borough System has been. What thought strikes a man entering the house of commons, the assembly that rules the whole world? I think it is the mediocrity of the men but what is the cause. It is simply an—assembly of wealth of men whose lives have been spent in the accumulation of money and whose time has been too much engaged to be able to spare any for the study of past history. And yet in the hands of such men rest our destinies. Do men like the great Pitt, and Burke and Sheridan not now exist. I contend they do. There are men now living with I know no other term the μέγα χόχέγις of Aristotle but there are not ways for enabling them to serve their Country. They live and die unused unemployed. What has been the main cause of the success of the Romish Church? The fact that every enthusiast, call it if you like every madman finds employment in it. Let us form the same kind of society a Church for the extension of the British Empire. A society which should have its members in every part of the British Empire working with one object and one idea we should have its members placed at our universities and our schools and should watch the English youth passing through their hands just one perhaps in every thousand would have the mind and feelings for such an object, he should be tried in every way, he should be tested whether he is endurant, possessed of eloquence, disregardful of the petty details of life, and if found to be such, then elected and bound by oath to serve for the rest of his life in his Country. He should then be supported if without means by the Society and sent to that part of the Empire where it was felt he was needed.

Take another case, let us fancy a man who finds himself his own master with ample means on attaining his majority whether he puts the question directly to himself or not, still like the old story of virtue and vice in the Memorabilia a fight goes on in him as to what he should do. Take if he plunges into dissipation there is nothing too reckless he does not attempt but after a time his life palls on him, he mentally says this is not good enough, he changes his life, he reforms, he travels, he thinks now I have found the chief good in life, the novelty wears off, and he tires, to change again, he goes into the far interior after the wild game he thinks at last I've found that in life of which I cannot tire, again he is disappointed. he returns he thinks is there nothing I can do in life? Here I am with means, with a good house, with everything that is to be envied and yet I am not happy I am tired of life he possesses within him a portion of the μέγα χοχέγις of Aristotle but he knows it not, to such a man the Society should go, should test, and should finally show him the greatness of the scheme and list him as a member.

Take one more case of the younger son with high thoughts, high aspirations, endowed by nature with all the faculties to make a great man, and with the sole wish in life to serve his Country but he lacks two things the means and the opportunity, ever troubled by a sort of inward deity urging him on to high and noble deeds, he is compelled to pass his time in some occupation which furnishes him with mere existence, he lives unhappily and dies miserably. Such men as these the Society should search out and use for the furtherance of their object.

(In every Colonial legislature the Society should attempt to have its members prepared at all times to vote or speak and advocate the closer union of England and the colonies, to crush all disloyalty and every movement for the severance of our Empire. The Society should inspire and even own portions of the press for the press rules the mind of the people. The Society should always be searching for members who might by their position in the world by their energies or character forward the object but the ballot and test for admittance should be severe.) [The section in parentheses did not appear in the first draft but was added later, when Rhodes was back in Kimberley, and then deleted when he wrote his will.]

Once make it common and it fails. Take a man of great wealth who is bereft of his children perhaps having his mind soured by some bitter disappointment who shuts himself up separate from his neighbours and makes up his mind to a miserable existence. To such men as these the society should go gradually disclose the greatness of their scheme and entreat him to throw in his life and property with them for this object. I think that there are thousands now existing who would eagerly grasp at the opportunity. Such are the heads of my scheme.

FIGURE 15 Cecil Rhodes was only forty-nine when he died in March 1902. One of the wealthiest men in the world, Rhodes's legacy, wrote his friend and biographer, Lewis Michell, in 1910, lay in his impact on South African mining, agriculture, and education and in "His Scholarship Foundation ... [which] in time may move the world," "his preservation of that immense territory called after his name [Rhodesia, now Zambia and Zimbabwe]—a territory which in alien hands would have barred our further expansion northward," and in having "preached" throughout his career "the salutary doctrine of equal rights" (311–12). Other contemporaries of Rhodes, such as Jan Smuts and Ndansi Kumalo (see DOCs 64A, 64D), would have assessed his legacy quite differently. This mask of Rhodes's face was cast from his corpse. Lewis Michell, *The Life of the Rt. Hon. Cecil John Rhodes*, 1910.

For fear that death might cut me off before the time for attempting its development I leave all my worldly goods in trust to S. G. Shippard and the Secretary for the Colonies at the time of my death to try to form such a Society with such an object.

B. Codicil to the last will and testament of Cecil Rhodes, October 11, 1901

23. My desire being that the students who shall be elected to the Scholarships shall not be merely bookworms I direct that in the election of a student to a Scholarship regard shall be had to (i) his literary and scholastic attainments (ii) his fondness of and success in manly outdoor sports such as cricket football and the like (iii) his qualities of manhood truth courage devotion to duty sympathy for the protection of the weak kindliness unselfishness and fellowship and (iv) his exhibition during school days of moral force of character and of instincts to lead and to take an interest in his schoolmates for those latter attributes will be likely in afterlife to guide him to esteem the performance of public duties as his highest aim. As mere suggestions for the guidance of those who will have the choice of students for the Scholarships I record that (i) my ideal qualified student would combine these four qualifications in the proportions of 3/10ths for the first 2/10ths for the second 3/10ths for the third and 2/10ths for the fourth qualification so that according to my ideas if the maximum number of marks for any Scholarship were 200 they would be apportioned as follows: 60 to each of the first and third qualifications and 40 to each of the second and fourth qualifications (ii) the marks for

the several qualifications would be awarded independently as follows (that is to say) the marks for the first qualification by examination for the second and third qualifications respectively by ballot by the fellow-students of the candidates and for the fourth qualification by the head master of the candidates school and (iii) the results of the awards (that is to say the marks obtained by each candidate for each qualification) would be sent as soon as possible for consideration to the Trustees or to some person or persons appointed to receive the same and the person or persons so appointed would ascertain by averaging the marks in blocks of 20 marks each of all candidates the best ideal qualified students.

24. No student shall be qualified or disqualified for election to a Scholarship on account of his race or religious opinions.

56 • The sack of Kumasi (1873–74)

In the mid-1860s, the British had considered abandoning their possessions in West Africa, with the exception of Sierra Leone, on the grounds that administrative costs were too high, the dangers of getting entangled in wars with African communities too great, and trading profits insufficient to make staying worthwhile. However, by the 1870s, perhaps anticipating economic returns like those newly developed in the southern African diamond fields, they had decided to stay. Staying meant dealing with the two issues that had bedeviled relations between the British and the Asante kingdom since the conclusion of the 1831 peace treaty: the authority of the Asantehene over African coastal peoples, and whether or not the British had to return to the Asantehene people (believed by the British to be mostly slaves) fleeing his authority. For the Asante, the ending of the slave trade had begun a long decline in their economic and political fortunes. In the late 1860s the new Asantehene, Kofi Karikari, went on the offensive. Arguing that the treaty terms of 1831 did not give the British authority beyond the reach of their guns at Cape Coast Castle, he engaged in a series of successful military campaigns against the coastal Fante people. He also argued that the Dutch, who had formerly been his allies and tributaries, had no right to transfer their territory, including the coastal fort of Elmina in particular, when the British bought out the Dutch in 1872.

Having to decide between withdrawal from the Gold Coast, continuous frontier wars, or further intervention, the British in 1873 decided to crush the Asante militarily. In the following correspondence, the Asantehene asserts his rights to the coast, the British colonial secretary instructs Sir Garnet Wolseley, the officer in charge of British forces (and the model for Gilbert and Sullivan's famous music hall figure, "the very model of the modern major-general"), as to his duties, and Henry Brackenbury, secretary to Sir Garnet, describes the destruction of Kumasi. Brackenbury's account, with its emphasis on Asante barbarity and bloodletting, became a very influential text in the development of an imperialistic literature at the end of the nineteenth century. By terms of the Treaty of Fomena (February 13, 1874), the defeated Kofi Karikari accepted the terms demanded by the British and gave up Asante claims to the coast (though retaining autonomy for the much-reduced territory of the Asante). In May 1874 the British consolidated their possessions on the Gold Coast into a single colony, thereby bringing an end to the Fante Confederation, which, supported by people like Africanus Horton, had attempted to bring about a self-governing state between 1867 and 1874. Later in 1874 the British banned the "selling, buying, or dealing in slaves" and emancipated all slaves in their Gold Coast territories, the first time that any colonial power had made slavery illegal in Africa since the emancipation of slaves in South Africa in 1833–34.[3]

A. Letter from King Kofi Karikari to Governor R. W. Harley with regard to Asante claims to the coastal communities of Elmina, Denkyera, Akim, and Assin, March 20, 1873

Sir . . . His Majesty states that, he being the grandson of Ossai Tutu, he owns the Elminas to be his relatives, and consequently the fort at Elmina and its dependencies being his, he could not understand the Administrator-in-Chief's sending Attah, *alias* Mr. H. Plange, to tell him of his having taken possession of them for Quake Fram, and notifying him also that in four months, he, the Administrator, would come to Ashantee to take power away from him.

He states that he has been made angry by this, and it was this which led to his sending great captains and forces to bring him Quake Fram, of Denkerah, who dares to take his Elmina fort, &c., and also the Assins and Akims, who are his slaves, and who have united with the Denkerahs to take power from him.

His Majesty further states that your Honour's restoring him these tribes . . . back to their former position as his subjects, and also restoring the Elmina fort and people back in the same manner as they were before, will be the only thing or way to appease him, for he has no quarrel with white men; but should your Honour come in to interfere as he hears you are, that you have not to blame him, because he will then start himself . . .

B. Instructions from the Earl of Kimberley to Sir Garnet Wolseley, September 10, 1873

Sir,

Her Majesty's Government wish to leave you a large discretion as to the terms which you may think it advisable to require from the king of Ashantee, but may I point out to you that the Treaty which was concluded with Ashantee in 1831 . . . seems to afford a reasonable basis for any fresh Convention.

It would certainly be desirable to include in such a Convention an explicit renewal by the king of Ashantee of the renunciation, contained in the Treaty of 1831, of all claim to tribute or homage from the native kings who are in alliance with Her Majesty; and further, a renunciation of all pretension on his part to supremacy over Elmina or over any of the tribes formerly connected with the Dutch, and to any tribute or homage from such tribes, as well as to any payment or acknowledgement in any shape by the British Government in respect of Elmina or any other of the British forts or possessions on the coast.

The king should also, for his own interest no less than with a view to the general benefit of the country, engage to keep the paths open through his dominions, to promote lawful com-

3. A and B, G. E. Metcalfe, ed., *Great Britain and Ghana: Documents of Ghana History, 1807–1957* (Legon: University of Ghana, 1964), 349, 351–52; C, Henry Brackenbury, *The Ashanti War: A Narrative Prepared from the Official Documents by Permission of Major-General Garnet Wolseley C.B. K.C.M.G.* (Edinburgh: William Blackwood and Sons, 1874), vol. 2, 223–44.

merce to and through the Ashantee country, and to protect all peaceful traders passing through his dominions to the coast; and it might be expedient that a stipulation should be made that a resident British Consul or Agent should be received at the Ashantee capital, if Her Majesty should think fit at any time to appoint one.

You will, of course, be careful to avoid as far as possible anything which may endanger the lives of the European missionaries and their families who have so long been held in captivity at Coomassie, without any fault of their own, so far as Her Majesty's Government are aware, and you will use every effort to secure their safe release. You will also endeavour to procure the surrender of all the prisoners taken by the Ashantees from the tribes in alliance with Her Majesty.

It is a usual practice with the native tribes to demand hostages for the faithful performance of Treaties of Peace. This was done in 1831, when two hostages of high rank were delivered over to the British Government by the king of Ashantee. If you should find it advisable to make a similar demand on the present occasion, you will bear in mind that the hostages should be men of high rank and position in Ashantee.

It would be reasonable to exact from the king the payment of such an indemnity as may be within his means, which are said to be considerable, for the expenses of the war and the injuries inflicted on Her Majesty's allies.

Lastly, the opportunity should not be lost for putting an end, if possible, to the human sacrifices and the slave hunting which, with other barbarities, prevail in the Ashantee kingdom.

C. Brackenbury describes the sack of Kumasi, February 1874

This entry into Coomassie is in its circumstances unrivalled in the annals of war. The town was full of armed men. The first wide open place reached immediately after crossing the swamp had houses on the right and left, in all of which armed men were seen, who ran away on the approach of our skirmishers, but returned again to watch the passage of the long column, disappearing into the bush if any attempt was made to disperse them. In the great main street hundreds of armed men were collected to observe the entry, yet not a single shot was fired. So strong, indeed, seemed their confidence in the white man, that they deliberately walked through the market-place, past the front of our troops, carrying their arms and ammunition away into the bush; and officers of rank were seen chasing and tripping men carrying kegs of powder on their heads, and rifles and ammunition-boxes in their hands. The main street commands both the town and the palace, and the Brigadier on arrival had placed the artillery so that it could sweep the streets ascending to the market-place, and thrown out picquets. A party was at once sent down to the king's palace . . . The palace was reached, but the king was nowhere to be found: he, the queen-mother, Prince Mensah, and all other personages of distinction, had disappeared.

Thus Coomassie was taken, and the goal of our enterprise was reached; the king had done his best, both by negotiations and the sterner policy of battle, to prevent our reaching his capital; but his efforts had failed. His policy of deceit and fraud had recoiled, broken to pieces upon the straightforward truthful dealing of our commander; and his troops had been scattered to the winds by the brave soldiers who had so well seconded the forethought, skill, and courage with which they had been directed by their general.

The king had in person been with his army; not in the fore-front of the battle; not seeking, like a brave man, to aid his troops by example, or staking his own life while others were staking theirs for him, but carried in his litter in rear, where no bullets came. But his presence showed the great effort that was made. "In Ashanti," said Prince Ansah, long before we went out, "the king never joins his army except on occasions when the full strength of the Ashanti power is to be put forth, and in pursuance of some solemn vow." And now, defeated, he takes refuge in flight, and, in his cowardly fear to come in, leaves his city and his people to be destroyed . . .

Of course the main question now occupying the Major-General's mind was to conclude a peace with the king, and if possible to obtain from him a treaty. His palace was left unmolested, only a guard being placed upon it . . . The following letter was addressed by Sir Garnet to the king:

> Coomassie, February 4, 1874
>
> KING, You have deceived me, but I have kept my promise to you.
> I am in Coomassie, and my only wish is to make a lasting peace with you. I have shown you the power of England, and now I will be merciful.
> As you do not wish to give up your mother and Prince Mensa, send me some other hostages of rank, and I will make peace with you tomorrow on the terms originally agreed upon.
> If either your majesty, or your royal mother, or Prince Mensa, will come to see me tomorrow early, I will treat you with all the honour due to your royal dignity, and allow you to return in safety. You can trust my word, I am, &c.,
>
> (Signed) G. J. WOLSELEY
> Major-General and Administrator, Gold Coast
> To His Majesty Koffee Kalkalli, King of Ashanti, Coomassie

The writer [Brackenbury] was commissioned to deliver this letter to the messengers, and at the same time to explain to them what were Sir Garnet's views; and it was impressed upon them that his Excellency had still only one wish—to make a lasting peace with the king; that he had no desire to break up his Majesty's kingdom, or to injure his position in the eyes of his people; that he had shown him how utterly impossible it was for him to resist the power of England, and had proved by coming to Coomassie that the white man always keeps his word. He now wished to make friends with the king, and urged upon him to come in person and treat with him. In order that he might do so, his palace was left untouched, and a guard was to be placed upon it in order to preserve unharmed everything that his Majesty had left. If the king himself would not come to see the Major-General, his Excellency would treat with his royal mother, or with Prince Mensa, the heir to the crown, but with no lesser personage. His Excellency promised that the king or either of these royal personages should be considered free, and treated with all respect due to their rank and dignity; and he would accept lesser chiefs as hostages for the payment of the indemnity which it was his duty to demand. If the king would thus come and treat, Coomassie should be left untouched, and the troops should leave it as they found it. At the same time, Owoosoo Koko [a representative of the Asantehene] was warned that every precaution had been taken against treachery; and that if in the night, or during our stay at Coomassie, one single shot was fired against our troops, Coomassie should be destroyed, and every living person in it unhesitatingly put to death . . .

[T]he Major-General and his staff lay down crowded together . . . to seek such rest as might be found. But there was little rest that night for any one in Coomassie. In the first place, the excitement of the day rendered us but little inclined for sleep; in the next place, we were sleeping or trying to sleep near the southern end of the town, and were sickened and nauseated by the loathsome smell of human bodies that pervaded this quarter, and which the fires in front of our place of shelter altogether failed to keep away. But even more sleep repelling was the fact, that at an early hour of the night, fires—evidently the work of incendiaries—sprang up all over the town, and through the night the troops were engaged in putting them out . . .

[The next day] the Major-General visited the palace . . . Descending the hill past the great fetish tree, which had blown down and shivered to pieces on the very day that Sir Garnet's summons to the king had left . . . past some other huge trees, whose gnarled roots spread across the road, passing on the left some large chiefs' houses, and on the right the house of the king's mother, we reached the high wooden paling which bounds the enclosure of the palace, and entered by a gate nearly opposite to a large enclosure on the opposite side of the road, where the bodies of dead kings and princes are buried for a year before being removed to the royal mausoleum at Bantama; and by the side of which enclosure is the mound on which human sacrifices are made on the occasions of great customs.

Entering by the gate in the paling, we found ourselves in the enclosure of the palace—a very large irregular pile of building, partly formed of thick walls of masonry, enclosing rooms two stories high, and partly of great open courts similar to those already described at Fommanah, only on a far larger scale, with the same raised rooms open to the court, and the same high pitched roofs. There are several entrances to the palace but we passed in, not by the porch on the south side, but by a large door on the west side of the palace, leading by a long passage, past some small courts to the right and left, which were apparently full of Ashantis, to the large court where the king holds receptions . . .

The great court would have held 200 men. The supporting pillars of the roofs of all the recesses were highly ornamented with scroll-work in glazed red clay, and the floor of the recess at the southern end, in which the king, sits to receive embassies . . . had the floor ornamented with various devices in white paint. At the foot of the steps leading up to this recess was a little wicker semi-circular fence, enclosing a tortoise, and some rubbish of different sorts, which we were told was great fetish. In another court was a splendid bird, apparently quite tame—a bird of many gorgeous colours, and most beautifully crested; this, too, was fetish. We also saw some of the king's cats, of which he has many, and with which the missionaries had told us he was very fond of playing. In one place we found a quantity of enormous umbrellas of various materials, amongst them the State umbrella sent home to her Majesty, and in the same court numerous litters covered with silks and velvets or the skins of animals, in which the king was wont to be carried. In rooms up-stairs were stored heaps of boxes, which appeared to contain articles of value, and silks, and many other treasures in profusion; all showed the signs of a hasty flight; and yet it was wonderful these things had not been carried away in the night.

Other things we saw of a different nature, which brought vividly before us the horrors of which this place had been a witness. There was the great death drum surrounded with human skulls and thigh-bones—the great drum on which three peculiar beats are given whenever a human victim is slaughtered as an offering to fetish. There were stools—the concave wooden stools common in the country—covered with clotted blood standing out from them in huge thick lumps, the blood of hundreds of human victims, in which they had been bathed as an offering to the memories of the king's ancestors, to whom they had belonged. Loathsome they were to see, as the flies rose in dense clouds from them at our approach.

We entered the king's bedchamber, closed by a heavy door, on which were many stamped placques of gold and silver; and we saw his Majesty's gorgeous four-post bed covered with silk, and on a stand beside it a large brass bowl filled with a compound of foul-smelling materials— the preparation of the fetish priests. But Sir Garnet Wolseley would not remain long enough in the palace where every association was horrible to the thought. Only, he had remained long enough to see that it would be well to protect it with a European guard, and that the guard must be a large one.

A hundred of the Rifle Brigade had already been ordered down, and the writer was left to see that the sentries were so posted as to prevent all ingress to, and egress from, the palace. Captain Carey accompanied the writer round the entire enclosure of the palace, and we endeavoured to post sentries, so that it should be impossible to enter it or leave it without being observed. The task was a most difficult one. On the north side there were but two entrances into the palace; on the west side but one; the eastern side also we easily protected by two sentries; but on the southern side, the palace itself in many places merged into one irregularly built cluster of houses, which we learnt belonged to the king's wives. Some idea of the size of the building and of its irregularity, may be gained from the fact that we posted 13 sentries in such positions that they were only just able to protect all the inlets to the building. After having apparently been all round the building once, we again marched round to see whether a sentry could not be economised; and though in one place we were enabled to remove one, we found that the whole of a long gallery, evidently the women's quarters, had been omitted, and we had to place another at the entrance of this. The guard of 100 men was placed in the great central court, and 1000 men might easily have been quartered in the main building.

In the mean time the Major-General had again received messages professing to come from the king, to the effect that his Majesty would come in in the course of the morning, and then that he would come later in the day. More messengers were sent, who professed that they would go to the king, urging him to come in, and saying that his palace was still at his disposal. But the king came not; the persons who professed to be his messengers, notably Owoosoo Koko and Boossumra Intakura, were found collecting, arms and ammunition and endeavouring to pass them out of the town, and were arrested. The policy of fraud and of deception which the king had hitherto displayed was again being attempted, and it was now scarcely to be hoped that the king would be wise enough to take the one last step in his power to save his capital by coming in, or sending his mother or his nephew to make peace . . .

A succession of tornadoes had seemingly set in; there seemed no apparent probability of their ceasing for some time; and the natives assured us that this was the prelude to the rainy season, evidently about to begin earlier than usual. The afternoon had passed, and the king had not fulfilled the promise said to have been made by him that he would come in; and there was now no probability of his doing so. His actual present position could not be ascertained; and even if we had found out where he was, it would have been impossible to capture him, as every village is surrounded with bush, and nothing, would be easier than to escape. To chase the king from one place to another was absolutely out of the question; it would but have been to add failure to what had hitherto been unbroken success; and whatever was to be done must now be accomplished without taking into consideration the possibility even of a meeting with his Majesty or his relations. In reply to all the invitations to act like a sensible man and make peace, the king, or those representing him, had only sent deceiving messages; and now the problem was, should the Major-General remain another day at Coomassie, and take advantage of it to march to Bantama, the royal mausoleum, or should he at once destroy Coomassie, and retire? . . .

It was out of the question to undertake any operation that might involve another battle; because any increment to our list of sick and wounded would have placed it beyond his [Wolseley's] power to remove them back to Agemmamu, as there would neither have been hammocks nor bearers sufficient for the purpose. A report was therefore circulated in the course of the afternoon, that the king having played the Governor false, and not having come in to make a treaty of peace, the army would advance in pursuit of him; and it was given out that all Ashantis found in the town after six o'clock the next morning would be shot . . .

As night set in, the rain again came down with merciless force, and peals of thunder shook the very earth. As soon as possible after dark, the prize agents proceeded to the palace to collect what they could of value; and the writer was allowed to accompany them. That night is one to be remembered with interest. The prize agents, and one or two other European officers, assisted by Andooa, chief of Elmina, and Vroom, Captain Buller's interpreter, worked with most ardent energy in despoiling King Koffee of his property. Candles were scarce at Coomassie; and only four were available for the search, of which economy forbade that more than two should be alight at a time. By the light of these two candles the search began. The first room visited was one which during the day had been seen to be full of boxes, some of which, at all events, contained articles of much value. Here were found those gold masks, whose object it is so difficult to divine, made of pure gold hammered into shape. One of these, weighing more than forty-one ounces, represented a ram's head, and the others the faces of savage men, about half the size of life. Box after box was opened and its contents hastily examined, the more valuable ones being kept, and the others left. Necklaces and bracelets of gold, Aggery beads, and coral ornaments of various descriptions, were heaped together in boxes and calabashes. Silver-plate was carried off, and doubtless much left behind. Swords, gorgeous ammunition-belts, caps mounted in solid gold, knives set in gold and silver, bags of gold-dust and nuggets; carved stools mounted in silver, calabashes worked in silver and in gold, silks embroidered and woven, were all passed in review. The sword presented by her Majesty to the king was found and carried off; and thousands of things were left behind that would be worth fabulous sums in cabinets at home . . .

Engineer labourers under Lieutenant Hare had set the town on fire. Commencing by applying their torches at the north edge of the town, they had worked down to the south. The town burnt furiously, all these three days of rain failing in any way to impede the progress of the devouring element. The thick thatched roofs of the houses, dry as tinder except just on the outside, blazed as though they had been ready prepared for the bonfire, and the flames ran down the framework which supported the mud walls. In the larger houses, more substantially built, only the roofs caught fire but the destruction was practically complete. Slowly huge dense columns of smoke curled up to the sky, and the lighted fragments of thatch drifting far and wide upon the wind showed to the King of Ashanti, and to all his subjects who had fled from the capital, that the white man never failed to keep his word.

At nine o'clock the firing party had reached the point where the rear-guard was stationed, and Major Home arrived with his Sappers from the palace, reporting that his work there was completed, that two of his eight mines had already exploded, and that the fuses of the remainder were lit. No sounds of explosion had been heard, the mines being so arranged that the thick masonry of the palace walls would be shaken throughout by their discharge, and would totter with the shock and fall.

Anxiety was exhibited by some of those remaining with the rear-guard at the great delay in the firing, of the mines at the palace, and the distance which in consequence existed between the main body and the 42d, which was to follow; but no such anxiety was shown by Colonel M'Leod. The same quiet demeanour was shown here as under the enemy's hottest fire; and he remained behind the rear company, till the party of Sappers and the last Engineer labourer had passed to the front.

At nine o'clock he rose and waved his hand; it was the signal for the rear company to march, and Coomassie was left a heap of smoking ruins.

57 • The Congo is as rich as North America (1885)

Henry Morton Stanley, born in Wales as John Rowland, reinvented himself under a new name after arriving in America as an eighteen-year-old in 1859. He first gained fame as the man who found Dr. Livingstone in 1871 and over the next three decades published a series of bestsellers extolling the economic potential of Africa for Western enterprise. Hired by King Leopold II of Belgium in 1878 to explore the resources of the Congo basin, Stanley was an ardent proponent of what he termed the "true civilizing influences . . . seen in the advancement of commerce and in the vitality of Christian missions." His cost accounting was exact. He argued that the investment of the equivalent of 1.75 English pennies per acre in the hinterlands of the Congo, Nile, Niger, and Shari (flowing into Lake Chad) rivers, most of the funds being spent on the building of railroad lines, would bring "an annual trade of over 3 shillings per acre almost guaranteed." With a population estimated at 43 million people, more than that of the other three river basins combined, and resources almost beyond imagination, Stanley considered the Congo one of the richest places on earth.[4]

Let us take North America for instance and the richest portion of it, viz., the Mississippi basin, to compare with the Congo basin, previous to its development by that mixture of races called modern Americans. When De Soto navigated the Father of waters, and the Indians were undisputed masters of the ample river basin, the spirit of enterprise would have found in the natural productions some furs and timber.

The Congo basin is, however, much more promising at the same stage of undevelopment. The forests on the banks of the Congo are filled with precious redwood, lignum vitae, mahogany, and fragrant gum-trees. At their base may be found inexhaustible quantities of fos-

4. Henry M. Stanley, *The Congo and the Founding of Its Free State: A Story of Work and Exploration* (New York: Harper and Brothers, 1885), vol. 1, x, xi, xv; vol. 2, 375–77.

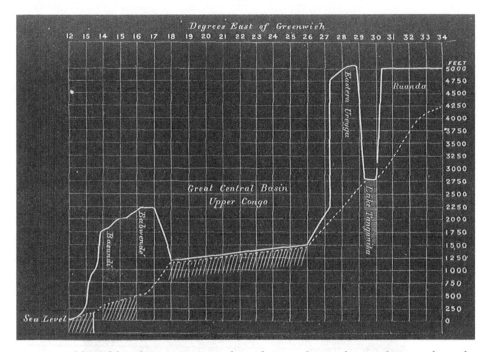

FIGURE 16 Most of the African continent is a huge plateau with steep drops to the ocean that make access to the interior physically very difficult. This graph of the elevation of Central Africa from the Atlantic Ocean in the west to Rwanda in the east, published by Henry Morton Stanley in a glowing account of the enormous resources to be found in the interior of Africa, shows a rise in elevation of five thousand feet, with two large physical barriers, one near the coast of the Congo, the other in the center of the continent. Henry M. Stanley, *The Congo and the Founding of Its Free State*, 1886.

sil gum, with which the carriages and furnitures of civilised countries are varnished; their boles exude myrrh and frankincense; their foliage is draped with orchilla-weed, useful for dye. The redwood when cut down, chipped and rasped, produces a deep crimson powder, giving a valuable colouring; the creepers which hang in festoons from tree to tree are generally those from which india-rubber is produced (the best of which is worth 2s. per lb.), the nuts of the oil palm give forth a butter, a staple article of commerce; while the fibres of others will make the best cordage. Among the wild shrubs are frequently found the coffee plant. In its plains, jungle, and swamp, luxuriate the elephants, whose teeth furnish ivory worth from 8s. to 11s. per lb.; its waters teem with numberless herds of hippopotamus, whose tusks are also valuable; furs of the lion, leopard, monkey, otter; hides of antelope, buffalo, goat, cattle, &c., may also be obtained. But what is of far more value, it possesses over 40,000,000 of moderately-industrious and workable people which the Red Indians never were. And if we speak of prospective advantages and benefits to be derived from this late gift of Nature, they are not much inferior in number or value to those of the well-developed Mississippi Valley. The copper of Lake Superior is rivalled by that of the Kwilu-Niadi Valley, and of Bembé. Rice, cotton, tobacco, maize, coffee, sugar, and wheat, would thrive equally well on the broad plains of the Congo. This is only known after the least superficial examination of a limited line which is not

FIGURE 17 The only way that Henry Morton Stanley was able to get a boat past the rapids of the lower Congo River was to haul it across land. It took him and several hundred African employees twelve months in 1880–81 to drag the forty-three-foot-long *En Avant* the 270 miles from the Atlantic Ocean to the Stanley Pool. Henry M. Stanley, *The Congo and the Founding of Its Free State*, 1886.

much over 50 miles wide. I have heard of gold and silver, but this statement requires further corroboration, and I am not disposed to touch upon what I do not personally know.

For climate, the Mississippi valley is superior, but a large portion of the Congo basin at present inaccessible to the immigrant is blessed with a temperature under which Europeans may thrive and multiply. There is no portion of it where the European trader may not fix his residence for years, and develop commerce to his own profit with as little risk as is incurred in India.

It is specially with a view to rouse the spirit of trade that I dilate upon the advantages possessed by the Congo basin, and not as a field for the pauper immigrant. There are over

40,000,000 native paupers within the area described, who are poor and degraded already, merely because they are encompassed round about by hostile forces of nature and man, denying them contact and intercourse with the elements which might have ameliorated the unhappiness of their condition. European pauperism planted amongst them would soon degenerate to the low level of aboriginal degradation. It is the cautious trader who advances, not without the means of retreat; the enterprising mercantile factor who with one hand receives the raw produce from the native, in exchange for the finished product of the manufacturer's loom—the European middleman who has his home in Europe but has his heart in Africa, is the man who is wanted. These are they who can direct and teach the black pauper what to gather of the multitude of things around him and in his neighbourhood. They are the missionaries of commerce adapted for nowhere so well as for the Congo basin, where are so many idle hands, and such abundant opportunities all within a natural "ring fence." Those entirely weak-minded, irresolute, and senile people who profess skepticism, and project it before them always as a shield to hide their own cowardice from general observation, it is not my purpose to attempt to interest in Africa. Of the 325,000,000 of people in civilised Europe there must be some surely to whom the gospel of enterprise preached in this book through the medium of eight languages will present a few items of fact worthy of retention in the memory, and capable of inspiring a certain amount of action.

I am encouraged in this belief by the rapid absorption of several ideas which I have industriously promulgated during the last few years respecting the Dark Continent. Pious missionaries have set forth devotedly to instil into the dull mindless tribes the sacred germ of religion; but their material difficulties are so great that the progress they have made bears no proportion to the courage and zeal they have exhibited. I now turn to the worldly wise traders for whose benefit and convenience a railway must be constructed.

58 • The scramble for Africa begins (1884–92)

At the same time that Africanus Horton was developing his ideas for an independent confederation of Fante peoples, Edward Blyden was elaborating his plans for a new university curriculum specifically designed to meet the needs of all peoples of African descent, Cetshwayo was testifying as to the regularized system of governance operating in Zulu society, and European speculators and adventurers were pursuing plans to obtain access to the reputed wealth of the interior of the continent. Expectations of interior wealth had grown enormously with the growth of the diamond industry and accelerated even more with the news of potentially vast gold finds, also in southern Africa, in 1886. From the 1870s onward, European merchants competed against each another to gain privileged access to African territory, primarily by negotiating treaties with indigenous rulers. In the Niger basin, for example, British representatives of the National African Company Limited (founded in 1882) and its successor, the Royal Niger Company (established by royal charter in 1886), concluded 343 separate treaties between 1884 and 1892. Representatives of the two companies used various templates in this treaty-making process; the following are the first template (used in 25 treaties) and the tenth (used in 22 cases).[5]

5. Edward Hertslet, *The Map of Africa by Treaty* (London: Her Majesty's Stationary Office, 1894), vol. 1, 457–58, 476–77.

FORM NO. 1

After the _____ year's experience, we, the undersigned _____ , fully recognize the benefit accorded to our country and people by our intercourse with the National African Company (Limited), and, in recognition of this, we now cede the whole of our territory to the National African Company (Limited), and their administrators, for ever. In consideration of this, the National African Company (Limited) will not interfere with any of the native laws and also not encroach on any private property unless the value is agreed upon by the owner and said Company.

The National African Company (Limited) will reserve to themselves the right of excluding foreign settlers.

Any palaver [negotiation] that may exist with any other tribe at any time, or in the event of any dispute arising between the _____ and territory, shall at once be referred to the National African Company (Limited) or their representative at the time.

We, the _____ and district, do hereby agree to afford assistance at any time for the protection of the said Company's property and people.

As per mutual consent of the _____ of the foregoing Agreement, the National African Company (Limited) agreed to pay _____

Pro the National African Company (Limited),

David McIntosh

FORM NO. 10

Treaty made on the _____ day of _____ , 18___ , between _____ on the one hand, and the Royal Niger Company (Chartered and Limited), for themselves and their assigns, for ever, hereinafter called "The Company," on the other hand.

1. We, the undersigned Kings and Chiefs of _____ , with the view of bettering the condition of our country and people, do this day cede to the Company, including as above their assigns, for ever, the whole of our territory, but the Company shall pay private landowners a reasonable amount for any portion of land that the Company may require from time to time.

2. We hereby give to the Company and their assigns, for ever, full jurisdiction of every kind, and we pledge ourselves not to enter into any war with other tribes without the sanction of the Company.

3. We give to the Company and their assigns, for ever, the sole right to mine in any portion of our territory.

4. We bind ourselves not to have any intercourse as representing our tribe or state, on tribal or state affairs, with any person or persons other than the Company, who are hereby recognized as the authorized Government of our territories: but this provision shall in no way authorize any monopoly of trade, direct or indirect, by the Company or others, nor any restriction of private or commercial intercourse with any person or persons of any nation whatsoever, subject, however, to administrative dispositions in the interest of commerce and order.

5. In consideration of the foregoing, the Company bind themselves not to interfere with any of the native laws or customs of the country, consistently with the maintenance of order and good government, and the progress of civilization.

6. The Company bind themselves to protect, as far as practicable, the said King and Chiefs from any attacks of any neighbouring aggressive tribes.

7. In consideration of the above, the Company have this day paid the King and Chiefs of _____ goods to the value of _____, receipt of which is hereby acknowledged.

This Treaty having been interpreted to us, the above-mentioned King and Chiefs of _____, we hereby approve and accept it for ourselves and for our people, and in testimony of this, having no knowledge of writing, do affix our marks below.

We, the undersigned witnesses, do hereby solemnly declare that the King and Chiefs whose names are placed opposite their respective marks have, in our presence, affixed their marks of their own free will and consent, and that _____ on behalf of the Company, has, in our presence, affixed his signature.

I, _____, for and on behalf of the Company, do hereby approve and accept the above Treaty, and hereby affix my hand.

Declaration by Interpreter. I, _____, native of _____, do hereby solemnly declare that I am well acquainted with the _____ language, and that on the _____ day of _____, 18__, I truly and faithfully explained the above Treaty to all the native signatories, and that they understood its meaning.

Witnesses to the above _____ mark or signature: Done in triplicate at _____, this _____ day of _____, 18__.

59 • The Berlin conference (1885)

Treaty making like that engaged in by the National African Company and competitors from Britain, France, Germany, Belgium, and Portugal set off a rush for territory. Between November 1884 and February 1885 an international conference, called together by Chancellor Otto von Bismarck of Germany, met in Berlin in an attempt to regulate this competitive rush. The main concern of the countries represented (every European state, as well as the United States) was not the partitioning of Africa but rather ensuring that their nationals not be excluded from any of the main trading areas of the continent, particularly the river basins of the Niger and the Congo. At the same time, they found it expedient in the interests of public opinion—strongly influenced by David Livingstone's antislavery writings and by the accounts of Henry Morton Stanley of traveling "Through Darkest Africa" in search of the lost missionary—to link commercial aims with a statement that greater intervention in Africa would lead to the suppression of the internal slave trade. The signatories to the treaty also agreed to ban the importation of firearms into Africa except when used by their own agents for self-protection or in order to suppress the slave trade. In practice, this meant that Europeans claimed (though were seldom able to achieve) a monopoly of guns.[6]

6. Hertslet, *Map of Africa by Treaty*, vol. 1, 20–45.

*General Act of the Conference of Berlin, relative to the Development of Trade
and Civilization in Africa; the free Navigation of the Rivers Congo, Niger etc;
the suppression of the Slave Trade by Sea and Land; the occupation of
Territory on the African coasts, etc. Signed at Berlin, February 26, 1885*

CHAPTER I. DECLARATION RELATIVE TO FREEDOM OF TRADE IN THE BASIN OF
THE CONGO, ITS MOUTHS AND CIRCUMJACENT REGIONS . . .

Art. I. The trade of all nations shall enjoy complete freedom . . .

Art. V. No power which exercises or shall exercise sovereign rights in the above-
mentioned regions shall be allowed to grant therein a monopoly or favour of any kind in matters of trade . . .

Art. VI. All the Powers exercising sovereign rights or influence in the aforesaid territories
bind themselves to watch over the preservation of the native tribes, and to care for the improvement of the conditions of their moral and material well-being, and to help in suppress-
ing slavery, and especially the slave trade.

They shall, without distinction of creed or nation, protect and favour all religions, scientific, or charitable institutions, and undertakings created and organized for the above ends, or
which aim at instructing the natives and bringing home to them the blessings of civilization.

Christian missionaries, scientists, and explorers, with their followers, property, and collections, shall likewise be the objects of especial protection.

Freedom of conscience and religious toleration are expressly guaranteed to the natives,
no less than to subjects and to foreigners . . .

CHAPTER II. DECLARATION RELATIVE TO THE SLAVE TRADE.

Art. IX. Seeing that trading in slaves is forbidden in conformity with the principles of
international law as recognized by the Signatory Powers, and seeing also that the operations,
which, by sea or land, furnish slaves to trade, ought likewise to be regarded as forbidden, the
Powers which do or shall exercise sovereign rights or influence in the territories forming the
Conventional basin of the Congo declare that these territories may not serve as a market or
means of transit for the trade in slaves, of whatever race they may be. Each of the Powers
binds itself to employ all the means at its disposal for putting an end to this trade and for punishing those who engage in it.

CHAPTER VI. DECLARATION RELATIVE TO THE ESSENTIAL CONDITIONS TO
BE OBSERVED IN ORDER THAT THE NEW OCCUPATIONS ON THE COASTS OF THE
AFRICAN CONTINENT MAY BE HELD TO BE EFFECTIVE.

Art. XXXIV. Any Power which henceforth takes possession of a tract of land on the
coasts of the African Continent outside of its present possessions, or which, being hitherto
without such possessions, shall acquire them, as well as the Power which assumes a Protectorate there, shall accompany the respective act with a notification thereof, addressed to the
other Signatory Powers of the present Act, in order to enable them, if need be, to make good
any claims of their own.

Art. XXXV. The signatory Powers of the present Act recognize the obligation to insure
the establishment of authority in regions occupied by them on the coasts of the African Continent sufficient to protect existing rights, and, as the case may be, freedom of trade and of
transit under the conditions agreed upon.

FIGURE 18 An American missionary, H. R. Phillips (middle row, second from right), sits with a group
of his converts in the city of San Salvador in the Congo. The woman to Phillips's right is blind; the
woman to her right was described by Phillips as the favorite wife of the old king, Dom Pedro V. At the
time the picture was taken, she had become a deaconess in the missionary church. Phillips arrived in San
Salvador with his wife in 1886, a year after the signing of the "General Act of the Conference of Berlin,
relative to the Development of Trade and Civilization in Africa." By 1900, the publication date of the
book in which this photograph appears and a year after Mrs. Phillips had died, two hundred Africans
"had been gathered into fellowship" at San Salvador, much of this achievement due to the work of Mrs.
Phillips among the African "girls and women of the town," and the efforts of four "native evangelists"
and their wives (vol. 2, 312). Images like this of missionaries and their converts appeared widely in popular media in the West in the nineteenth and early twentieth centuries and reassured readers of the benefits of "civilization" and Christianity for Africans. W. Holman Bentley, *Pioneering on the Congo*, 1900.

60 • Rhodes reaches north (1888)

*Though Cecil Rhodes succeeded in monopolizing control of the diamond industry under De Beers,
he was much less successful in the much larger and more profitable gold industry that developed in
the Transvaal beginning in the mid-1880s. Locked out of access to the best finds by other mining
magnates, Rhodes sought to compensate elsewhere by looking north to the old gold mines of Zimbabwe, worked by Africans from the twelfth to the fifteenth centuries but largely abandoned thereafter. Zimbabwe was ruled by Lobengula, king of the Ndebele people, who themselves had come to
the area only in the 1840s, refugees first from Shaka's Zulu empire and then fleeing from Dutch explorers and themselves conquering the Shona of old Zimbabwe. Lobengula had signed treaties with
Europeans since the 1860s, permitting them to prospect for minerals in exchange for paying him licensing fees. With demands for prospecting rights becoming incessant after the gold discoveries in
the Transvaal, in 1888 Lobengula agreed, in return for a substantial payment, to grant a monopoly*

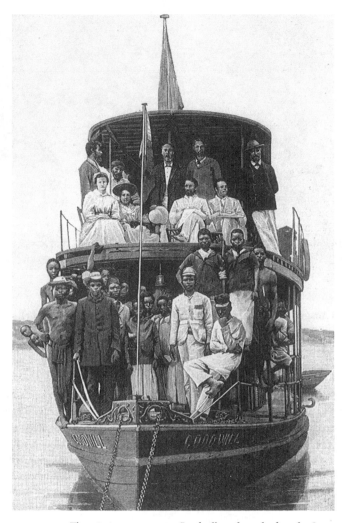

FIGURE 19 The missionary steamer *Goodwill* was launched on the Stanley Pool in December 1893 after being hauled overland from the Atlantic Ocean. Originally built in England, the *Goodwill* had been disassembled there under the watchful eye of Bungudi, the young son of an African chief from the Stanley Pool, who had been sent by the missionary George Grenfell to examine the process. Bungudi and fellow Africans reassembled the *Goodwill* at the Stanley Pool, ran the steamer, and did "all the work," as a result of which Bungudi became "a very efficient engineer" (vol. 2, 222). Despite the expertise and responsibilities of Bungudi and his African peers, the racial hierarchy of colonialism remained stark on the missionary vessel, with Europeans on the top, Africans on the bottom. W. Holman Bentley, *Pioneering on the Congo,* 1900.

over mining to representatives of Cecil Rhodes. Though the treaty was for prospecting and mining rights only, it did grant to the licensees "full power to do all things that they may deem necessary to win and procure the same [metals and minerals], and to hold, collect, and enjoy the profits and revenues," terms that, like others in the treaty, could be subjected to a wide variety of interpretations.[7]

Know all men by these presents, that whereas Charles Dunell Rudd, of Kimberley; Rochfort Maguire, of London; and Francis Robert Thompson, of Kimberley, hereinafter called the grantees, have covenanted and agreed, and do hereby covenant and agree, to pay to me, my heirs and successors, the sum of one hundred pounds sterling, British currency, on the first day of every lunar month; and, further, to deliver at my royal kraal one thousand Martini-Henry breech-loading rifles, together with one hundred thousand rounds of suitable ball cartridge, five hundred of the said rifles and fifty thousand of the said cartridges to be ordered from England forthwith and delivered with reasonable despatch, and the remainder of the said rifles and cartridges to be delivered as soon as the said grantees shall have commenced to work mining machinery within my territory; and further, to deliver on the Zambesi River a steamboat with guns suitable for defensive purposes upon the said river, or in lieu of the said steamboat, should I so elect, to pay to me the sum of five hundred pounds sterling, British currency. On the execution of these presents, I, Lo Bengula, King of Matabeleland, Mashonaland, and other adjoining territories, in exercise of my sovereign powers, and in the presence and with the consent of my council of indunas, do hereby grant and assign unto the said grantees, their heirs, representatives, and assigns, jointly and severally, the complete and exclusive charge over all metals and minerals situated and contained in my kingdoms, principalities, and dominions, together with full power to do all things that they may deem necessary to win and procure the same, and to hold, collect, and enjoy the profits and revenues, if any, derivable from the said metals and minerals, subject to the aforesaid payment; and whereas I have been much molested of late by divers persons seeking and desiring to obtain grants and concessions of land and mining rights in my territories, I do hereby authorise the said grantees, their heirs, representatives, and assigns, to take all necessary and lawful steps to exclude from my kingdom, principalities, and dominions all persons seeking land, metals, minerals, or mining rights therein, and I do hereby undertake to render them all such needful assistance as they may from time to time require for the exclusion of such persons, and to grant no concessions of land or mining rights from and after this date without their consent and concurrence; provided that, if at any time the said monthly payment of one hundred pounds shall be in arrear for a period of three months, then this grant shall cease and determine from the date of the last-made payment; and, further, provided, that nothing contained in these presents shall extend to or affect a grant made by me of certain mining rights in a portion of my territory south of the Ramaquaban River, which grant is commonly known as the Tati Concession.

7. Lewis Michell, *The Life of the Rt. Hon. Cecil John Rhodes, 1853–1902* (London: Edward Arnold, 1910), vol. 2, 244–45.

This, given under my hand this thirtieth day of October, in the year of our Lord 1888, at my royal kraal.

> LO BENGULA X his mark
>
> C. D. RUDD
>
> ROCHFORT MAGUIRE
>
> F. R. THOMPSON

Witnesses: Chas. D. HELM

　　　　　　 J. F. DREYER

61 ◆ The imperialism of chartered companies (1886–89)

The Berlin conference only intensified the competitive rush for territory and fortune in Africa. National governments now took a much greater role in supporting the interests of their merchants than had been the case before 1870. The British government, in particular, awarded a series of royal "charters" to companies in west, east, and southern Africa. These charters formally recognized the legality of the treaties made between merchant companies and African rulers and allocated to the companies the power (within British law) to operate in Africa as though they were themselves sovereign states. Royal charters were awarded in 1886 to Sir George Goldie's Royal Niger Company, in 1888 to Sir William Mackinnon's British East Africa Company, and in 1889 to Cecil Rhodes's British South Africa Company. Goldie came from an Isle of Man family that had made its money in smuggling and then legitimated itself through landholding. Mackinnon, a Scotsman, had made a fortune in shipping. Rhodes had added to his diamond fortune by investing in the Transvaal gold-mining industry and taking control of the gold areas of Zimbabwe. Each saw the enormous economic potential of monopolizing trade in their respective parts of Africa.[8]

Royal charter granted to the National African Company
(renamed the Royal Niger Company in 1887), July 10, 1886

1. The said National African Company Limited (in this our Charter referred to as the Company), is hereby authorized and empowered to hold and retain the full benefit of the several cessions aforesaid [the 343 treaties noted earlier], or any of them, and all rights, interests, authorities, and powers for the purposes of government, preservation of public order, protection of said territories, or otherwise of what nature or kind soever . . .

12. The Company is hereby further authorized and empowered, subject to the approval of our Secretary of State, to acquire and take by purchase, cession, or other lawful means, other rights, interests, authorities, or powers of any kind or nature whatever, in, over, or affecting the territories, lands, or properties comprised in the several treaties aforesaid, or any rights, interests, authorities, or powers of any kind or nature whatever in, over, or affecting other territories, lands, or property in the region aforesaid [the basin of the Niger river], and to hold, use, enjoy, and exercise the same for the purposes of the Company and on the terms of this our Charter . . .

8. Hertslet, *Map of Africa by Treaty*, vol. 1, 118–20, 177–80, 446–48.

Royal charter granted to the Imperial British
East Africa Company, September 3, 1888

(The petition of William Mackinnon and others for a charter with powers much like those of the Royal Niger Company was granted on the following grounds:)

That his Highness the Sayyid Barghash Bin-Said, Sultan of Zanzibar and its East African Dependencies . . . granted and conceded to the Petitioners . . . all his powers, and the rights and duties of administration . . .

That divers preliminary Agreements have been made on behalf of the Petitioners with Chiefs and tribes in regions which adjoin or are situate to the landward of the territories in the said Grants or Concessions . . . by which powers of government and administration such regions are granted or conceded to or for the benefit of the Petitioners.

That the Petitioners desire to carry into effect the said Grants, Concessions, and Agreements . . . within the sphere reserved for British influence, and elsewhere, as we may be pleased, with the view of promoting trade, commerce, and good government in the territories and regions . . . if the said Grants, Concessions, Agreements, or Treaties can be carried into effect, the condition of the natives . . . would be materially improved, and their civilization advanced, and an organization established which would tend to the suppression of the Slave Trade in such territories, and the said territories and regions would be opened to the lawful trade and commerce of our subjects and of other nations.

That the possession by a British Company of the coast-line . . . would be advantageous to the commercial and other interests of our subjects in the Indian Ocean, who may otherwise become compelled to reside and trade under the government or protection of alien powers . . .

Royal charter granted to the British South Africa Company, October 29, 1889

6. The Company shall always be and remain British in character and domicile, and shall have its principal office in Great Britain, and the Company's principal representatives in South Africa and the Directors shall always be natural born British subjects, or persons who have been naturalized as British subjects by or under an Act of Parliament of Our United Kingdom . . .

7. In case at any time any difference arises between any chief or tribe inhabiting any of the territories [the region of South Africa north of Bechuanaland and west of Portuguese East Africa] . . . that difference shall, if Our Secretary of State so require, be submitted by the Company to him for his decision, and the Company shall act in accordance with such decision.

20. Nothing in this Our Charter shall be deemed to authorize the Company to set up or grant any monopoly of trade; provided that the establishment of or the grant of concessions for banks, railways, tramways, docks, telegraphs, waterworks, or any other similar undertakings or the establishment of any system of patent or copyright approved by Our Secretary of State, shall not be deemed monopolies for this purpose.

22. The Company shall be subject to and shall perform and undertake all the obligations contained in or undertaken by Ourselves under any Treaty, Agreement, or Arrangement between Ourselves and any other State or Power whether already made or hereafter to be made . . . The Company shall appoint all necessary officers to perform such duties, and shall provide

such Courts and other requisites as may from time to time be necessary for the administration of justice.

62 • Voices of imperialism (1893–99)

The scramble for Africa accelerated in the 1890s, and treaty making was always accompanied by
the potential threat of armed force and often by its use as well, particularly in the form of the Maxim
gun, the first self-powered machine gun, capable of firing up to six hundred rounds a minute. Among
the British, the leaders of this scramble were for the most part men who had first come to Africa as
traders or as employees of the chartered companies. Such a background influenced their beliefs
about the benefits of international commerce and European rule for African societies. Frederick Lu-
gard, for example, went to East Africa as an employee of Mackinnon's British East Africa Company
and on its behalf concluded treaties with African rulers (including Mwanga, the king of Uganda)
by the terms of which the African leaders recognized the "sovereignty" of the company in exchange
for its "protection." In his published account of his East African exploits, Lugard stresses the eco-
nomic benefits of empire to Britain and Africa alike, and in his private diary he describes the exact
process by which he concluded a treaty with Mwanga on December 26, 1890. That trickery could
be used to considerable effect is illustrated by the account of R. S. S. Baden-Powell (who later
founded the Boy Scout movement) of how the British managed to get the king of Asante, Prempeh
I, to prostrate himself before their officers. Baden-Powell continues with a description of the second
British torching in twenty years of the Asante capital, Kumasi.

Whereas Mackinnon and his agent Lugard expanded British territorial control in East Africa
primarily by treaty, Sir George Goldie relied more on armed force. In a somewhat breathless ac-
count of his conquests in northern Nigeria in early 1897, he shows his determination to break any
form of resistance to British rule and to enforce complete submission.

That the exercise of armed force was not solely to be extended against African opponents but
also against anyone perceived to stand in the way of British Empire is made clear by the activities
of Joseph Chamberlain, secretary of state for colonies, and his agents in South Africa at the end of
the nineteenth century. Concerned that control of the South African gold industry, the largest in the
world, not remain in the hands of the Voortrekker descendants who ruled the Transvaal Republic,
Chamberlain corresponded with Sir Alfred Milner as to how British supremacy could be secured,
even at the cost of war.[9]

9. A, Frederick D. Lugard, *The Rise of Our East African Empire* (Edinburgh: William Blackwood and Sons,
    1893), vol. 1, viii–ix, 381–83, 395–97, 471, 473, 487–89; vol. 2, 585, 591–92, and Margery Perham, ed., *The*
    Diaries of Lord Lugard (Evanston: Northwestern University Press, 1959; first published by Faber and
    Faber, London, 1959), vol. 1, 40–42; B, R. S. S. Baden-Powell, *The Downfall of Prempeh: A Diary of Life with*
    the Native Levy in Ashanti, 1895–96 (London: Methuen, 1896), 19–22, 108–9, 123–31, 158–61; C, C. W.
    Newbury, ed., *British Policy towards West Africa, Select Documents, 1875–1914, with Statistical Appendices,*
    1800–1914 (Oxford: Clarendon, 1971), 148–50; D, Cecil Headlam, ed., *The Milner Papers: South Africa,*
    1897–1899 (London: Cassell, 1931), vol. 1, 525–28, 546–47.

A. Frederick Lugard envisions empire and makes treaties in East Africa

My aim . . . in these volumes, has been not so much to set forth a narrative of personal adventure, sport, and travel—a series of writing with which the public has been regaled by those who have far more to tell than I—but rather to place before thinking men subjects of more serious concern, both to ourselves in our dealings with Africa and to the subject races for whose welfare we have made ourselves responsible.

The rapid increase of population, the closing of the hitherto available outlets for emigration, as well as of the markets for our goods, and the sources of supply of our needs, indicate that the time is not far distant when the teeming populations of Europe will turn to the fertile highlands of Africa to seek new fields of expansion. It is possible, therefore, that British Central and British East Africa may be the embryo empires of an epoch already dawning—empires which, in the zenith of their growth and development, may rival those mighty dependencies which are now the pride of the Anglo-Saxon race. It behoves us, then, to take heed to the small beginnings of these great things, and in laying the foundations, to ensure that the greatness of the structure shall not suffer from lack of realisation on our part in the present.

There are many who have seemed to look on Africa as merely a field for romance and adventure—as a great blank continent on which explorers or adventurers were free to write their own names in capital letters. With the last decade of the century I trust that a new era has dawned for the African, and a new conception of our duties with regard to him has dawned upon ourselves . . .

FIGURE 20 Officials of the Imperial British East Africa Company negotiate a treaty with chiefs in East Africa. Frederick Lugard's private account of the process demonstrates that treaty making owed much more to his own dissembling than to the orderly negotiation conveyed in this image. Robert Brown, *The Story of Africa and Its Explorers,* 1895.

The "Scramble for Africa" by the nations of Europe—an incident without parallel in the history of the world—was due to the growing commercial rivalry, which brought home to civilised nations the vital necessity of securing the only remaining fields for industrial enterprise and expansion. It is well, then, to realise that it is for our *advantage*—and not alone at the dictates of duty—that we have undertaken responsibilities in East Africa. It is in order to foster the growth of the trade of this country, and to find an outlet for our manufactures and our surplus energy, that our far-seeing statesmen and our commercial men advocate colonial expansion.

Money spent in such extension is circulated for the ultimate advantage of the masses. It is, then, beside the mark to argue that while there is want and misery at home money should not be spent in Africa. It has yet to be proved that the most effective way of relieving poverty permanently, and in accordance with sound political economy, is by distributing half-pence in the street. If our advent in Africa introduces civilisation, peace, and good government, abolishes the slave-trade, and effects other advantages for Africa, it must not be therefore supposed that this was our sole and only aim in going there. However greatly such objects may weigh with a large and powerful section of the nation, I do not believe that in these days our national policy is based on motives of philanthropy only. Though these may be our *duties*, it is quite possible that here (as frequently if not generally is the case) advantage may run parallel with duty. There are some who say we have no *right* in Africa at all, "that it belongs to the natives." I hold that our right is the necessity that is upon us to provide for our ever-growing population—either by opening new fields for emigration, or by providing work and employment which the development of over-sea extension entails—and to stimulate trade by finding new markets, since we know what misery trade depression brings at home.

While thus serving our own interests as a nation, we may, by selecting men of the right stamp for the control of new territories, bring at the same time many advantages to Africa. Nor do we deprive the natives of their birthright of freedom, to place them under a foreign yoke. It has ever been the key-note of British colonial method to rule through and by the natives, and it is this method, in contrast to the arbitrary and uncompromising rule of Germany, France, Portugal, and Spain, which has been the secret of our success as a colonising nation, and has made us welcomed by tribes and peoples in Africa, who ever rose in revolt against the other nations named. In Africa, moreover, there is among the people a natural inclination to submit to higher authority. That intense detestation of control which animates our Teutonic races does not exist among the tribes of Africa . . . and if there is any authority that we replace, it is the authority of the Slavers and Arabs, or the intolerable tyranny of the "dominant tribe" . . . The experiment of an autonomous and civilised African state of freed negroes, such as was founded in "Liberia" in 1820 by the Washington Colonisation Society, and recognised an independent state by Europe in 1847, "can hardly be said to have been a success" . . .

[T]he question of the hostility of native tribes . . . is so important that it merits an additional word. The South African Company have the Matabeles [Ndebele] to deal with—an extremely powerful Zulu tribe of great organisation, who we are told are rapidly arming themselves with rifles. They have also had a collision with European neighbours in the Portuguese, and a similar collision with the Boers was narrowly avoided. The "British Central African Protectorate" is permeated by the slave-traders and their affiliated tribes, all armed with rifles and bitterly hostile, with whom the Administration is at chronic war, and who have hitherto proved themselves more than a match for its resources. There are also the fierce Angoni tribe, a tribe of Zulu origin. The Germans in like manner have tribes to deal with who are armed with thousands of rifles, and the whole country is full of arms . . . The French have in West Africa powerful negro states, well armed, on their frontiers, such as Dahomey and others, and still more powerful opposition in Algeria . . .

In the greater part at least of British East Africa there are no tribes to compare in power with any of these I have named . . . There are no settlements of armed slave-traders and no savage tribes armed with rifles, as in the case of every other territory in Africa, and the natives almost without exception are well disposed.

Another advantage which accrues to us in East Africa is the possession of at least three excellent harbours. Of these Mombasa is perhaps the finest natural port on the East African coast, and would form a most valuable coaling station for our fleet in these waters. But with its political importance we are not concerned here. With such a port at the base, and such an objective at the further point as . . . would be attained by communication with the lake and Nile waterways, surely the country offers indisputable natural advantages for commercial development?

Mr. Stanley has stated that we should be face to face with twelve millions of people as customers for our goods. Mr. Ravenstein's estimate of the population of British East Africa is 6½ millions, and probably if we extended our commerce to the shores of the lakes and the Nile, we should arrive at a total not far short of Mr. Stanley's estimate. Apart, however, from the wants of this native population are the requirements of alien immigrants. These form a very appreciable factor in the consumption of imports . . .

Whether European colonisation in the true sense of the term be feasible or not, it remains beyond a doubt that extensive areas suitable for European exploitation similar to that in India and Nyasaland, where large plantations of tea, coffee, cotton, &c., are raised, or for stock-rearing and sheep-farming, as in Australia and Canada, are available, and also that East Africa is eminently suitable for Asiatic colonisation . . .

The commercial value of East Africa is largely dependent on the labour available to develop its products. It has been said that the African is inherently lazy, and that he will do no more work than he is absolutely compelled to, and will relegate even that to his women . . .

So far . . . as my personal experience goes, I have formed the following estimate: (1) No kind of men I have ever met with—including British soldiers, Afghans, Burmese, and many tribes of India—are more amenable to discipline, more ready to fall into the prescribed groove willingly and quickly, more easy to handle, or require so little compulsion as the African. (2) To obtain satisfactory results a great deal of system, division of labour, supervision, &c., is required. (3) On the whole, the African is very quick at learning, and those who prove themselves good at the superior class of work take pride in the results, and are very amenable to a word of praise, blame, or sarcasm . . .

If . . . we accept the position that we go to Africa not merely for the good of the African, but for our own, it follows that, if the laziness of the natives should make it impossible for us to reap our advantage, we must find means to do it in spite of them. I have shown that in East Africa the population is restricted to certain areas, mainly through tribal wars and Masai raids. There are, therefore, large tracts of equally fertile country available for colonisation, without dispossessing or in any way incommoding the natives. Such colonies might consist of Africans—freed slaves, or the Sudanese from Equatoria, who would furnish labour. They might also consist of Asiatic immigrants . . .

From the overcrowded provinces of India especially, colonists might be drawn, and this would effect a relief to congested districts. From them we could draw labourers, both artisans and coolies, while they might also afford a recruiting ground for soldiers and police. The wants, moreover, of these more civilised settlers would . . . very greatly add to the imports, and the products of their industry to the exports of the country, thus giving a great impetus to trade. The African, too, is extremely imitative. The presence in his midst of a fully clothed people would be to him an example of decency which he would speedily imitate. His wants would become identical with theirs, and thus, while his status was improved, and a new encouragement given to trade, he would be compelled to exert himself and to labour in order to supply those wants. Moreover, the methods of agriculture, the simple implements of the Indian ryot, the use of the bullock, the sinking of wells, the system of irrigation and of manuring the soil, &c. . &c., would soon be imitated by the African, and the produce of his land would thus be vastly multiplied. As the population increased, both by the introduction of these aliens and by the cessation of war, famine, small-pox, and the slave-trade—a result which would follow on a settled government—the African would be compelled to work for his living, not, as heretofore, by the compulsion of slave labour, but in order to prove himself with the requirements of his increasing necessities and improved status, and by that law of competition which compels the indolent to labour . . .

[A]s long as our policy is one of free trade, we are compelled to seek new markets; for the old ones are being closed to us by hostile tariffs, and our great dependencies, which formerly were the consumers of our goods, are now becoming our commercial rivals. It is inherent in a great colonial and commercial empire like ours that we go forward or backward. To allow other nations to develop new fields, and to refuse to do so ourselves, is to go backward; and this is more deplorable, seeing that we have proved ourselves notably capable of dealing with native races, and of developing new countries at a less expense than other nations. We owe to the instincts of our ancestors, those vast and noble dependencies which are our pride and the outlets of our trade to-day; and we are accountable to posterity that opportunities which now present themselves of extending the sphere of our industrial enterprise are not neglected, for the opportunities now offered will never recur again . . .

We have a prescriptive right in East Africa and its lakes. They were all discovered by British explorers: Victoria by Speke and Grant, Nyasa by Livingstone, Tanganyika by Burton, Albert by Baker, and Albert Edward by Stanley. The steamers (three) placed on Nyasa have all been brought by the British; so has the one on Tanganyika; and those on the Albert and the Nile were brought down by Baker when in the Khedive's service. Our missionaries first penetrated to Uganda in the footsteps of our explorers. Thus, by right of discovery and of missionary effort, we had the prior claim to Uganda, and the time has now come for us to assert or forgo entirely that claim.

Those few who have given voice to the arguments against retention have, so far as I am aware, altogether avoided dealing with the strong array of facts which I have endeavoured to present to my readers. Briefly they are these:

1. Fulfilment of pledges to Europe, under (1) the Berlin Act, (2) the Brussels Act.
2. Pledges to the natives, and responsibility for anarchy, &c., on evacuation.

3. Political importance of retaining our hold on the Nile valley, and of the ports on the coast.
4. Commercial necessity of finding new markets, &c.
5. Obligation as regards missionaries, French and English.
6. Check to slave-trade—by establishing a protectorate in the heart of Africa.
7. Reflex action on other African possessions caused by loss of prestige.
8. Uniformity of policy inaugurated by cession of Heligoland, &c.
9. Preponderance of public opinion in favour of retention.
10. Prescriptive rights.

[In the following text extracted from his diary entry for December 26, 1890, Lugard, who was then in the employ of the British East Africa Company, describes the process by which he made a treaty with Mwanga, the king of Uganda]

I was ready at 8 A.M. but no message came. 9 past and 9.30 or more, and I made up my mind they had changed and it was war. Then I saw the Durbar break up, and crowds and crowds coming out. They came to us, and soon I got a message that they [the main advisors of Mwanga] would come and sign here, and go to the King afterwards. All the biggest knobs came in (not a single gun of any sort among them) and I sat them down on a big tarpaulin at the tent door, and had the table and everything ready. There was much long speechifying, and then they said they would sign provided they were allowed to write a Codicil, and I would sign that and give it to them. This they wrote themselves; it was mainly that the treaty was to be null, and another made, if the messengers from the coast came with other news than mine. Also that a compact which they would not show me made between themselves was still to be binding. Its main provision was religious toleration for both sides, I believe. This I signed, and then there was much discussion as to whether they should sign now first, or take it first to the King. At last they said I was to go alone to the King and he would sign and then all would sign. It eventually ended in all following on, so De W. came with me, and three or four Askari. Grant in camp with orders to send all Sudanese and 4 batches of men to our assistance in case he heard firing, and hold the camp with the other 2 troops and the Maxim, which he was to use freely if required. For the chiefs still spoke of some bad men of whom they seemed much afraid. It appears as far as I can understand that there really is a rabble of whom the king and all are afraid. They are, I believe, a drunken bang-smoking lot of blackguards, probably not Christians of either sect, and it was they who threatened to shoot if the Treaty was signed on 23rd. As a protection I wanted the Kimbugwe and Katikiro to accompany me—they said they would but the little Kauta was the only one who stuck close by us all the time, and ordered back the rabble when we entered. He is a right good little fellow, one of the very best, if not *the* best in the country, and I am most glad he is a R.C. because now if I favour him I can't be accused of partiality to the Protestants.

We found the King in undress reclining on a mat. I had brought no chair thinking it was to be a quick affair, but I stood till one was brought me. De W. brought his, all the rest (King included) on the ground. The King said I professed friendship but had given him no present. I said I knew it, but had come in haste and brought nothing but food, the Maxim and cartridges. By the way, they have keenly taken stock of our loads, and I heard on arrival here all about it. I had no cloth, and nearly all boxes which they supposed were *ammunition*. They are really all nearly bead boxes but it has helped to add to their fear of us, for supposing them all to be ammunition they were of course very afraid of us. I have not undeceived them! I added that Stokes was bringing me some loads and I wanted some canoes to fetch them from the South of the Lake, and in these were my presents for him. Then all the big chiefs came in one by one, till it was a full Durbar. Their Codicil was read to the King, and he at once asked if all the tributary states would still be compelled to pay tribute. I replied as before that I was a stranger and knew nothing of these States, that when I knew all about it we would see, that I had said nothing about it in the Treaty, one way or the other—this was merely a treaty of friendship with Uganda, and its tributary States, and did not touch the further question. I tried to turn the conversation by talking of the piece of Uganda lost which the Germans have taken, and told them that had they made a treaty with the British sooner they would not have lost it, but that even now I would write to Emin Pasha and see if I could get the tribute and if he refused would refer it to England. They would not be put off, however, and the King ordered them to add it to the Codicil. This was a poser, for it would considerably cripple my treaty to enter into such an obligation. So I got them to add, "and its tributary States" after the words "I Mwanga Sultan of Uganda," which of course meant nothing, or at least bound me to nothing.

Then the King told someone to sign for him. I would not have this, and insisted on his making a mark. He did it with a bad grace, just dashing the pen at the paper and making a blot, but I made him go at it again and make a cross, and on the 2nd copy he made a proper cross. Then one of the chiefs who could write wrote Mwanga's name opposite the mark, and "ilamu zake" as well and I was satisfied. Several of the head chiefs also signed, but it took about 10 minutes or ¼ hour per signature as they slowly formed each letter, and paused. At last the King left, and after one or two more signatures I left too, giving them their copy of the treaty and Codicil and taking mine. Need I say how delighted De W. and I were at our success! I had determined to arrive in Uganda by Xmas. I had not only done it but reached the capital, and spite of all trouble and opposition had got the Treaty made and signed within 12 hrs after Xmas. Not a bad 8 weeks' work from Dagoretti to Mengo and treaty made and signed!

B. R. S. S. Baden-Powell describes the
downfall of the Asantehene, Prempeh, 1896

[T]here exist more particular reasons for it [taking action against Asante] in the refusal of the king to carry out the provisions of the treaty of 1874.

The danger of allowing treaty contracts to be evaded is fairly well understood among European nations, but the results of slackness or leniency in their enforcement are none the less dangerous when the treaty has been made with an uncivilised potentate, since his neighbours are quick to note any sign of weakness or loss of prestige on the part of the white contracting party, and they in their turn gain courage to make a stand against the white ruler and his claims over them.

In Ashanti the abuse had been allowed to go on far too long. Natives near our border—ay, within it too—had seen year after year go by, and the Ashanti liberty taking the form of licence more and more pronounced, with little or no restraint beyond mild and useless remonstrance on our part. Naturally this raised the Ashantis once more in their estimation, while it lowered our prestige in a corresponding degree; and although the people were suffi-

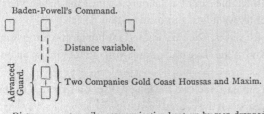

Baden-Powell's Command.

Distance variable.

Advanced Guard.

Two Companies Gold Coast Houssas and Maxim.

Distance, quarter mile, communication kept up by men dropped by the Gold Coast Houssas.

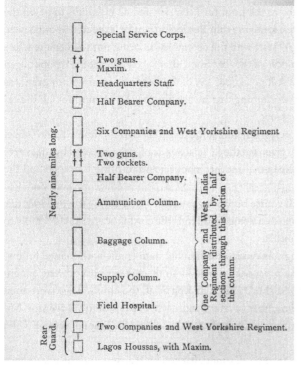

Special Service Corps.

Two guns.
Maxim.

Headquarters Staff.

Half Bearer Company.

Six Companies 2nd West Yorkshire Regiment.

Two guns.
Two rockets.

Half Bearer Company.

Ammunition Column.

Baggage Column.

Supply Column.

Field Hospital.

One Company 2nd West India Regiment distributed by half sections through this portion of the column.

Nearly nine miles long.

Rear Guard.

Two Companies 2nd West Yorkshire Regiment.

Lagos Houssas, with Maxim.

FIGURE 21 The British expeditionary force led by R. S. S. Baden-Powell to conquer the king of the Asante in 1895–96 stretched out in a line more than nine miles long, with Maxim guns at the front, middle, and rear. Baden-Powell later founded the Boy Scouts. R. S. S. Baden-Powell, *The Downfall of Prempeh; a Diary of Life with the Native Levy in Ashanti,* 1896.

ciently knowing to see that under our government they were their own masters and were able to carry out any ideas of commerce that they might entertain, still they also saw that, as far as local indications went, the Ashantis were equal in power to the white men, and, as a natural consequence, they were much inclined at least to waver in their allegiance to us.

"Britons never will be slaves," and Britons are so peculiarly imbued with a notion of fair-play that they will not see anybody else in a state of slavery either, if they can prevent it.

Slaves in some parts of the world form the currency of the country; in others they are the beasts of burden and the machinery; often their lot is mercilessly hard, though not always . . .

But in no part of the world does slavery appear to be more detestable than in Ashanti. Slaves, other than those obtained by raids into neighbours' territory, have here to be smuggled through the various "spheres," French, German, and English, which are beginning to hem the country in on every side . . .

They are not required for currency, since gold-dust is the medium here.

Nor are they required to any considerable extent as labourers, since the Ashanti lives merely on vegetables, which in this country want little or no cultivation.

And yet there is a strong demand for slaves. They are wanted for human sacrifice. Stop human sacrifice, and you deal a fatal blow to the slave trade, while you render raiding an un-profitable game . . .

The levy, being now 860 strong, is able to find two flanking parties on by-roads to the town [Kumasi], in addition to its main party on the central road.

THE DOWNFALL, 20TH JANUARY [1896]

. . . Six o'clock had been named as the hour for Prempeh and all his chiefs to be on the palaver-ground. This was done, well knowing that he might then be expected about seven, and it was desirable to make an early start with the ceremony, in order not to keep the white troops exposed to the sun in the middle of the day. Soon after seven o'clock the troops began to form on the parade-ground, but still no sign of any of the Ashantis coming; nor even was there any of the usual preliminary drumming that invariably goes on to summon all the re-tainers who usually form the procession.

Nearly two hours' grace had been given him; it looked as though Prempeh did not mean coming. The order was accordingly given for the Special Service Corps, assisted by the native levy, to surround the palace and the queen-mother's house, and to bring Prempeh and the queen to the Governor.

The native levy, in view of such course becoming necessary, had during the previous day cut away the bush adjoining the palace enclosure, and thus the cordon was enabled rapidly to take up its position to close every outlet.

In a very few minutes the king was carried forth in his state cradle with a small follow-ing, and, escorted by the troops, he proceeded hurriedly to the palaver-ground. The queen-mother, similarly escorted, followed shortly after, as well as all the chiefs. They were then marshalled in a line, with a limited number of attendants each, in front of the Governor, Mr. Maxwell, C.M.G., who was seated on a dais, together with Colonel Sir Francis Scott, K.C.B., and Colonel Kempster, D.S.O.

A square of British troops was formed all round, backed by Houssas and the native levy.

Then the doom of the nation was pronounced in a set-scene, and amid dramatic inci-dents such as could not fail to impress both natives and Europeans alike.

Through the medium of interpreters—Vroom, Secretary for Native Affairs, acting for the Governor; Albert Ansah, for the king—the conditions of the treaty to be imposed upon the Ashantis were demanded of them.

The first of these was that Prempeh should render submission to the Governor, in ac-cordance with the native form and custom signifying abject surrender. This is a ceremony which has only once before been carried out between the Ashantis and a British Governor, namely, Governor Rowe. On that occasion the king deputed officers of his court to perform the actual ceremony; but in this case it was insisted that the king must himself personally carry it out. Accordingly, with bad enough grace, he walked from his chair, accompanied by the queen-mother, and, bowing before Mr. Maxwell, he embraced his knees. It was a little thing, but it was a blow to the Ashanti pride and prestige such as they had never suffered before. Then came the demand for payment of the indemnity for the war. Due notice had been previously

FIGURE 22 The image of the king of the Asante, Prempeh (bottom left), and his Queen Mother, kneeling before three British officers in 1896, was a staple of late nineteenth-century Western images of European supremacy and African supplication. What the image did not show but which can be found in Baden-Powell's eyewitness account of the event was how the king and his mother had been forced by British troops to kneel before the officers, which they did in protest and "with bad enough grace." R. S. S. Baden-Powell, *The Downfall of Prempeh; a Diary of Life with the Native Levy in Ashanti,* 1896.

given, and the Ashantis had promised to pay it; but unless the amount, or a fair proportion of it, could now be produced, the king and his chiefs must be taken as guarantee for its payment.

The king could produce about a twentieth part of what had been promised. Accordingly, he was informed that he, together with his mother and chiefs, would now be held as prisoners, and deported to the Gold Coast.

The sentence moved the Ashantis very visibly. Usually it is etiquette with them to receive all news, of whatever description, in the gravest and most unmoved indifference; but here was Prempeh bowing himself to the earth for mercy, as doubtless many and many a victim to his lust for blood had bowed in vain to him, and around him were his ministers on their feet, clamouring for delay and reconsideration of the case. The only "man" among them was the queen.

In vain. Each chief found two stalwart British non-commissioned officers at his elbow, Prempeh being under charge of Inspector Donovan. Their arrest was complete.

But there was still an incident coming to complete the scene. The two Ansahs, although they held a large hand in causing the trouble between the British and Ashantis, appear in their own country to have little or no influence with the people, and, indeed, were looked on with jealousy and suspicion. These were surveying the scene—their handiwork—with a somewhat curious look, half amused, half nonplussed, when the Governor added to his remarks the suggestion that the present might be a suitable occasion for the arrest of these two gentlemen on a charge of forgery; and before they had fully realised between them that the charge was actually being preferred against them, they found that Mr. Donovan had adroitly handcuffed them wrist to wrist, and the scene was complete.

During the performance of this act another had been quietly preparing behind the scenes. Parties of the native levy had been withdrawn from the parade-ground, and were added to the cordon already drawn round the palace. All was silent there, and all the many doors were locked. But a path from the jungle leading to the back door, also locked, brought one within sound of the buzz of many men talking within, and of the soughing of bellows of smelting fires. At the close of the palaver on the parade-ground, two companies of the West Yorkshire Regiment, under Captain Walker, were detailed to take possession of the palace, clear it of all people inside, and to collect and make an inventory of all property found inside.

One company was accordingly sent to stiffen the cordon of native levies, and with the other company I proceeded to effect an entrance by a back way, which I had previously reconnoitred . . .

There could be no more interesting, no more tempting work than this. To poke about in a barbarian king's palace, whose wealth has been reported very great, was enough to make it so. Perhaps one of the most striking features about it was that the work of collecting the treasures was entrusted to a company of British soldiers, and that it was done most honestly and well, without a single case of looting. Here was a man with an armful of gold-hilted swords, there one with a box full of gold trinkets and rings, another with a spirit-case full of bottles of brandy, yet in no instance was there any attempt at looting.

It need not be supposed that all the property found in the palace was of great value. There were piles of the tawdriest and commonest stuff mixed indiscriminately with quaint, old, and valuable articles, a few good brass dishes, large metal ewers, Ashanti stools, old arms, etc. But a large amount of valuables known to belong to the king had disappeared, probably weeks previously—such as his celebrated dinner service of Dutch silver, his golden hat, his golden chair of state, and, above all, the royal stool, the emblem, *par excellence*, of the King of Ashanti.

These were all probably hidden, together with his wives, in various hamlets in the remote bush. The "loot" which we collected was sold by public auction, excepting golden valuables, which were all sent home to the Secretary of State.

The term "palace" has merely been used to denote the residence of the king. In reality there is very little that is palatial about it. It consists of a collection of the usual wattle-and-daub huts, with high walls and enormous high-pitched thatched roofs; endless courts, big and little, succeed each other, with narrow entries between, and with little or no attempt at architectural design or ornamentation.

The foundations of the old palace, built on more substantial principles, and destroyed in the last campaign, are still to be seen in the centre of the present place in a disused court.

Finding so little of real value in the palace, it was hoped that some treasure might be discovered in the sacred fetish-houses at Bantama, the burial-place of the kings of Ashanti, about a mile out of Bantama. This place had also been piqueted, but all its priests had disappeared previously, and when we broke in, only one harmless old man was found residing there. No valuables—in fact, little of any kind was found in the common huts that form the sacred place. In the big fetish building, with its enormous thatched roof, when burst open, we only found a few brass coffers—all empty! The door, which was newly sealed with mortar, showed no signs of having been quite freshly closed up, and it may therefore be inferred that the treasure had been removed some weeks previously.

Then, in accordance with orders, we set the whole of the fetish village in flames, and a splendid blaze it made. The great fetish-tree, in whose shade hundreds of victims have been sacrificed, was blown up with gun-cotton, as also were the great fetish-trees on the Kumassi parade-ground. Among the roots of these there lie the skulls and bones of hundreds, and possibly of thousands, of victims to the *regime* which to-day has so dramatically been brought to a close . . .

From the foregoing it will have been deduced that the success and bloodless victory of the expedition was due to the rapidity and the completeness of the movements of the force; and that this rapidity was in its turn the result of a thoroughly planned and well-equipped organisation. But then arises the question, *Cui bono?* What is the good of this victory when you have won it? What return is there for the half million that will have been spent upon it?

Inter alia, one may at once point out that it has, at any rate, put an end to the practice of human sacrifice, which, up till within three months ago, had gone on with all the unchecked force that it had ever enjoyed. Fetish superstition has an immense hold on the untutored children of the bush, and tradition and custom decreed that human sacrifice was the best form of propitiation of the fetish demons. Moreover, the men of the country have no kind of diversion or employment beyond very poor hunting and an occasional raid on a neighbouring tribe. Bloodlust, like many another vicious habit, rapidly takes root and grows on a man who is without other occupation. A bloody spectacle was naturally to the Ashantis a most attractive form of amusement, especially as at the same time it satisfied their superstition.

The popularity of human sacrifice was none the less great because it gave a direct impetus to the slave trade. As a rule, the victims of fetish sacrifice were slaves, and the supply had to be kept up to the demand. How great that demand was we may, perhaps, never know, but that it was little short of enormous may be guessed partly from the deposit of skulls and bones about the fetish groves, and partly from the fact that two streets in Kumassi consisted of the houses occupied by the official executioners. The suppression of this abuse has been one result of the expedition, and the disintegration of the Ashanti kingdom into its minor kingdoms will ensure its non-revival. This alliance of lawless chiefs into a common band, under the direction of the Kumassi king, has hitherto acted like a dam to a reservoir. Within five days' march of Kumassi, to the northward, the poisonous bush country comes to an end, and on beyond there lies the open country, rich and populous, which stretches thence to Timbuctoo. The natural outlet for this country's trade is by the Kumassi road to Cape Coast Castle and the sea. This is the reservoir which the Ashanti dam has kept closed up so long. In breaking down the Ashanti gang we have broken up the dam, and the stream which will now begin to flow should, in the near future, well repay the expenses of the machine with which it has been cut. An encouraging example lies to hand in the colony at Lagos, where, as a direct result of the Jebu campaign, the trade has in a single year leaped up to double what it was before.

The British prestige has, moreover, now extended its effect into the back country among tribes who were hitherto wavering with their future allegiance in the balance, and it may be inferred that they will not delay to come under our protectorate. This in its turn will mean the extension of our boundaries till they touch the Niger, and will thereby save the Gold Coast Colony from being shut out from up-country trade, as had been threatened, by the junction of the two French forces in Dahomey and in Timbuctoo. Indeed, the colonial party of our friends across the Channel are just beginning to suspect that, using Prempeh as a nail to hang our cloak upon, we have quietly beaten them in the race for the Gold Coast Hinterland—that instead of Dahomey joining hands with the French Soudan, the Gold Coast will ere long have marched its boundary on to that of the Royal Niger Protectorate. In gaining this enlarged territory, we may very probably also gain the assistance of a ready-made force with which to hold it, namely, the army, horse and foot, of Samory.

Thus, in the course of a few weeks, an enormous change has been wrought in the history of this part of Africa, and the vista of a great future has been suddenly opened to the Gold Coast Colony. And yet this great result has been gained by the use of a mere handful of men, and it is only when one realises the magnitude of the result that one sees with something akin to awe how much might have been lost by a little mismanagement or by a single false move.

C. Sir George Goldie reports to the British governor on his conquests in the Niger basin, February 18, 1897

In view of the interest felt by your Government in the Ilorin question, I venture to trouble you with the following brief report, and I shall be obliged if you will forward a copy to the Secretary of State for the Colonies. I am, of course, preparing a full report for the Secretary of State for Foreign Affairs, who will doubtless communicate it to the Colonial Office, but this fuller report cannot be completed at once, and I shall take it home with me, as I am returning at once to London, having fully succeeded, and to an extent beyond my expectations, in the three expeditions which I came out to direct.

Believing that Ilorin would accede peacefully to my suggestions after the fall of Bida, and having received the written submission of the Emir Suliman, I only brought from Jebba one half of the troops, and less than half of the guns, with which the battle of Bida had been won. I knew, however, that I could not find an opposing force more than one-fourth that of Bida; and, moreover, that our troops, flushed with success, were fit to combat much larger numbers.

On the 14th instant, at the River Araibi, ten miles from the City of Ilorin, I learnt from my spies that the four Baloguns, or War Chiefs, had compelled the Emir to agree to fight, and that the whole Ilorin forces were drawn up near the River Oyon, three or four miles from Ilorin, and were advancing to meet us.

The battle commenced about 8 A.M. on the 15th inst. and lasted till the afternoon of the 16th. We were compelled to inflict very heavy losses on the enemy. The Balogun Alanamu, the most warlike of the four War Chiefs, has just told me that we killed over 200 horsemen; and as the foot soldiers were in the proportion of about six to one, it may be assumed that their total loss exceeded a thousand. We then bombarded the town (which unfortunately caught fire) and took possession of it, the Emir, four Baloguns and all other Chiefs flying dispersed to distant villages.

While the troops were occupied in stopping the conflagration, I took active steps to enter in communication with the Emir, who has always been most faithful to his treaty with the [Royal Niger] Company. Today, at noon, the Emir and four Baloguns with other Chiefs surrendered to us and came here to negotiate a new treaty, which was signed in the presence of all the troops and many spectators in the great square. The Emir recognises the entire power of the Company over all the Ilorin territory, and that he will govern in accordance with the directions given him from time to time; that he must not make war without consent of the Company; that he must accept such frontier between Ilorin and Lagos as may be directed.

I told the Emir and Baloguns that, pending Her Majesty's decision, the frontier must be that fixed by Captain Bower some time ago on behalf of Sir Gilbert Carter. I carefully abstained from holding out any hopes that this frontier line would be rectified, but I think it right to inform you that I reserve to myself the liberty to reopen this question with Her Majesty's Government.

The Emir and Baloguns were greatly concerned with the difficulty they would have, after their crushing defeat, in organising any government in the Ilorin territory. I told them, however, that the Company felt that any government is better than anarchy, that they were at liberty to take the steps taken by all governments to enforce order in the regions left under their authority; but that they must wait for one month before taking such steps in the southern portion lying to the north of the Lagos frontier and Odo Otin, so as to give me time to inform you of what had taken place and to give you time to issue instructions to your officials and troops, so that the approach of Ilorin horsemen to the neighbourhood of the Lagos frontier should not be mistaken for a renewal of hostilities.

There is no fear of such renewal for a generation to come. The Ilorin power is completely broken. The four Baloguns, Alanamu, Salu, Ajikobi, and Suberu, were far more humble and broken than the peaceful Emir Suliman, whom they had forced into war, and who behaved today with great dignity, although with a keen sense of the entirely new position created by our conquest of Ilorin.

I have arranged that some of our troops shall move frequently along the Ilorin side of the temporary Lagos frontier, so as to ensure order and the roads being kept open. No garrison will be left permanently in Ilorin City, but troops will visit it occasionally.

We leave here to-morrow to receive the submission of another Sokoto province, Lafiagi . . .

I find to my regret, that the greater part of the City of Ilorin has been burnt.

D. Joseph Chamberlain, confidential letter to Alfred Milner, September 2, 1899

I am very glad to have your letters (Aug. 2nd and 16th received) when you can find time to write. The situation changes hourly. This afternoon I have suggested a Cabinet to Lord Salisbury to arrange for an ultimatum. Just now (1 A.M.) I have a telegram from Reuter to say that the Transvaal Govt. has sent a favourable reply! May it be so! but after recent experiences I am very sceptical. The incident however illustrates the difficulty of revising or of elaborating a policy which may be hopeless before the letter reaches you. Accordingly I propose to confine myself to generalities.

In the first place then I hope you are satisfied by now that although in the light of information which is incomplete and of telegrams which always are inadequate to explain fully the meaning of the sender, I may occasionally differ from you, yet that I am in the fullest sense of the word loyal to you as I believe you are to me. We have both a very difficult part to play and the atmosphere here is very different from that of Cape Town. Just consider how it strikes the ordinary patriotic Englishman . . . He sees that if there is a war it will be a very big affair—the biggest since the Crimea—with no honour to be gained, if we are successful, and with many most unpleasant contingent possibilities.

These things influence the outside politician, but in addition we, who are inside, have other difficulties. The War Office is not an ideal institution. The other day they were ready "to the last button"—now they talk of four months before they can put an army corps to the front. Of the Treasury I will say nothing since you were yourself an ornament of that great department . . . When I reflect on all these things I am really astonished at the progress we have made. It is a great thing to say that the majority of the people have, as I believe, recognized that there is a greater issue than the franchise or the grievances of the Uitlanders [English speakers resident in the Transvaal, most of them mineworkers] at stake, and that our supremacy in S. Africa and our existence as a great Power in the world are involved in the result of our present controversy. Three months ago we could not—that is to say we should not have been allowed to—go to war on this issue—now—although still most unwillingly and with a large minority against us—we shall be sufficiently supported. But please bear all this in mind if we move more slowly than you think wise, and than would be wise if we had only Cape opinion to think of—and the interests of the British Empire in South Africa.

What is going to happen next? If the reply from the Transvaal is unsatisfactory I hope you will get a report from your Commissioners in a very few days. I cannot see why there should be any careful examination of existing laws in the Transvaal. I should expect your men to report that the offer of 5 years' retrospective franchise and 8 additional seats would give substantial and immediate representation, if all the conditions of registration, residence, etc., etc., were the same as, say, in the Orange Free State and the Cape Colony. They might add that it would be necessary to allow the new members to use their own language in the Raad [parliament]—that it would be advisable that the amount of representation given to the Rand should be reconsidered in 5 years and increased in proportion to population and that these views should be embodied in a new Convention. Then shall we give Kruger one more chance by asking him to accept this Report and carry it out? At present I think we should. I can see clearly that the British in the Cape and in Natal are afraid that if he accepts at the last moment, he will do so with the intention of repudiating his obligations whenever we are otherwise engaged; and they would like us to increase our demands and send an ultimatum on other points such as Suzerainty, Disarmament, Federation, and I know not what which would certainly force a war. But can we do this yet? We must play this game out "selon les rè-gles," and it seems to me to-day that we ought to exhaust the franchise proposals and get a clear report before, on the principle of the Sybilline books, laid down by Lord Salisbury, we ask for more.

If and when we ask for more it means war, and therefore, before we do this, we must have a sufficient force in S. Africa to defend ourselves during the time that will be required to get the full fighting forces into the country. And besides this we must have Parliamentary sanction for the despatch of a large force, which means discussions, some division of opinion and delay. But suppose the time has come to put forward fresh demands and to obtain, at the price of war, a final settlement. What are these fresh demands to be? Perhaps they will have been settled by the Cabinet before this reaches you. If not let me have your views at the time by telegraph as well as by letter.

Here is a list of things for which we might ask—all to be embodied in a new Convention —1. Explicit recognition of Suzerainty. 2. Foreign affairs to be conducted through H.M.G. 3. Acceptance of Judicial Come. of P[rivy] Council, with Transvaal judge added, to deal with all future questions of interpretation. 4. Franchise, etc., as in Cape Colony. 5. Municipal rights for gold Mining Districts. 6. All legislation since 1884 restricting rights and privileges of Uit-landers to be repealed. 7. Disarmament. 8. Indemnity for expenses incurred since refusal of Franchise proposals. 9. Federation of S. African Colonies and States. I give these as a list of possible demands, but whether it would be good policy to put all of them forward before the war may well be a question . . .

Milner to Chamberlain, September 27, 1899, Confidential

I have to thank you for your long and most interesting letter of Sept. 2nd. For want of time I will not discuss all the useful information it gives me. Much that you tell me I had more or less surmised, both from the actual course of our diplomacy and the natural indications in the Press and in private letters. As far as home opinion is concerned the management of the controversy has been perfect. Seeing how hopelessly the British people were dead to the real issues 4 months ago, it is wonderful where they stand to-day. Unfortunately, inevitably, the long dragging controversy which has enlightened public opinion at home, has done harm here. It has discouraged many of our best supporters, but, what is worse than that, it has given time for the Afrikander propaganda to produce more and more effect throughout the Colony and has consolidated the Afrikander party. There is a good deal of actual plotting, but it is for the most part so cunningly concealed that one cannot lay hands upon it. In this respect the ne-cessity of keeping on terms with Ministers has been a great weakness to me. It was necessary —otherwise I should have had something like an insurrection in parts of the Colony before now—but it has been a fearful hindrance to finding out the secret workings of the enemy, as the officials and police, who are mostly in sympathy with us, have been in many more or less intangible ways hampered and discouraged in following up indications of sedition. And all the time the two Republics have been arming and colloguing. Until lately the O.F.S. [Orange Free State] was very wavering, but as weeks passed, our patience which was misinterpreted there, gradually turned against us and finally the bulk of opinion swung over to that side, to which Steyn and Fischer had all along been trying to incline it.

But after all, these are not our greatest difficulties. At a pinch I always felt pretty certain that we should have Afrikanderdom solid against us *in feeling*. But if we were able to strike a decisive blow quickly, that would not mean so much in actual physical force. The O.F.S. people would fight halfheartedly and the Colonial Afrikanders, with a few exceptions, would sit still, though secretly hostile. But here comes in the military, or perhaps as you hint really the financial obstacle. Owing to the fact that, as I suppose for financial reasons, provisional arrangements for the immediate transport of a large force have not been made during all these months, the large force cannot begin to arrive for at least two months, and during that time the military task it will have to perform may grow to much greater proportions. Moreover, we have an even more pressing problem and that is how to get over the next 3 weeks, if, as now seems most probable, the Republics decide to have a dash at us. However, it is no use dwelling on immediate contingencies, which will be decided one way or the other before this reaches you. We are doing our best in the dilemma, which especially in this Colony is great, viz. whether (*to*) scatter our small force along the border in order to keep the enemy in check and prevent risings—at the risk of being cut up or invested in detail, or to keep it concentrated down here at the risk of losing hold of the great part of the Colony and of the lines of communication. On the whole I think the former course is the better. The other is too suggestive of fear.

63 • Imperial slaughter at Omdurman (1898)

More than any other colonial battle, the British defeat of the forces of the Khalifa Abdullah Ibn-Mohammed at Omdurman on September 2, 1898, demonstrated in practice and symbolized for the Western public the triumph of Western military organization and technology over the forces of "fanaticism" and "barbarity." In the early 1870s Mohammed Ahmed, who termed himself the Mahdi, or guided one, led a religiously inspired revolt against the Egyptian occupiers of the Sudan and their Turkish overlords. In the early 1880s, when Britain had assumed control over Egypt as a way to protect its financial investments in the Suez canal, the Mahdi continued his struggle against the new imperialists and achieved his greatest victory in 1885 with the capture of Khartoum and the beheading of Charles Gordon, the evangelical Christian officer who was governor general of the Sudan and who commanded the British garrison at Khartoum. Later that year the Mahdi died of typhus, and he was succeeded by Abdullah Ibn-Mohammed, who had been born in Darfur in 1846.

After the fall of Khartoum, the British did not return to the Sudan for a decade and a half, but when they did, propelled by a growing concern that they were being outflanked by European competitors for control of the headwaters of the Nile, they came with a vengeance. Beginning in 1886, Lord Kitchener (known as the "Sirdar," Persian for commander, and appropriated by the British as the title for the commander of the Anglo-Egyptian army) organized in a thorough and meticulous fashion an invasion of the Sudan. He built a railroad line eight hundred miles across the sand from the Red Sea to Wady Halfa (on the Nile north of Omdurman) and brought armored boats down the Nile. He employed several batteries of machine gunners armed with the "light pattern Maxim gun," introduced in 1895, weighing only 25 pounds plus a 15-pound tripod and capable of being carried in an infantryman's backpack.

At dawn on September 2, 1898, Kitchener's army of approximately 22,000 men, almost half of them British soldiers, engaged the 50,000 men massed under the black flag of the Khalifa. During the next four hours the British annihilated their adversaries. The selections that follow are from two leading war correspondents of the time, both of whom were eyewitnesses to the slaughter, G. W. Steevens, and Winston Churchill.[10]

10. A and C, G. W. Steevens, *With Kitchener to Khartoum* (New York: Dodd, Mead, 1898), 1, 7–8, 22–23, 284, 286; B, Winston Churchill, *The River War: An Historical Account of the Reconquest of the Soudan* (London: Longmans, Green, 1902), 270, 271–73, 275–76, 280–81, 299, 300.

A. G. W. Steevens on the preparations for conquest

To walk around Wady Halfa is to read the whole romance of the Sudan. This is the look-out whence Egypt has strained her vision up-Nile to the vast, silent, torrid, murderous desert land, which has been in turn her neighbour, her victim, all but her undoing, and is now to be her triumph again. On us English, too, the Sudan has played its fatal witchery, and half the tale of Halfa is our own as well as Egypt's. On its buildings and up and down its sandy, windy streets we may trace all the stages of the first conquest, the loss, the bitter failures to recover, the slow recommencement, the presage of final victory . . .

And now we have come to the locomotive-sheds and the fitting-shops, the boiler-houses and the storerooms . . . the Halfa of to-day is the Egypt of to-day. Halfa has left off being a fortress and a garrison; to-day it is all workshop and railway terminus. To-day it makes war not with bayonets, but with rivets and spindleglands. Railways run along every dusty street, and trains and trucks clank up and down till Halfa looks for all the world like Chicago in a turban. In chains, too, for to Halfa come all the worst villains of Egypt . . . So the rails and sleepers are slung ashore to the jingle of ankle-chains; and after a day in Halfa it startles you in no way to hear that the black foreman of the engine-shop did his five murders, and that, nevertheless, he is a most intelligent, industrious, and harmless creature. On the contrary, you find it admirable that Egypt's ruffians are doing Egypt's work.

Halfa clangs from morning till night with rails lassoed and drawn up a sloping pair of their fellows by many convicts on to trucks; it thuds with sleepers and boxes of bully-beef dumped on to the shore . . . From the shops of Halfa the untamed Sudan is being tamed at last. It is the new system, the modern system—mind and mechanics beating muscle and shovel-head spear. It takes up and digests all the past; the bits of Ismail's railway came into the Dongola line; the engine of Wolseley's time has been rebuilt, and is running again; the military barracks are a store for all things pertaining to engines. They came together for the fourth act—the annihilating surprise of Ferkeh, the masterly passage of Hafir, the occupation of Dongola and Merawi, the swift march and sharp storm of Abu Hamed, the swoop on Berber. They were all coming together now for the victorious end, ready to enter for the fifth act and the final curtain on Khartum . . .

For in Halfa was being forged the deadliest weapon that Britain has ever used against Mahdism—the Sudan Military Railroad. In the existence of the railway lay all the difference between the extempore, amateur scrambles of Wolseley's campaign and the machine-like precision of Kitchener's. When civilization fights with barbarism it must fight with civilized weapons; for with his own arts on his own ground the barbarian is almost certain to be the better man . . . without the railway there could never have been any campaign at all. The battle of Atbara was won in the workshops of Wady Halfa . . .

B. Winston Churchill describes the day of battle

[Churchill] It was a quarter to 6 [September 2]. The light was dim but growing stronger every minute. There in the plain lay the enemy, their numbers unaltered, their confidence and intentions apparently unshaken. Their front was now nearly five miles long, and composed of great masses of men joined together by thinner lines . . .

The emblems of the more famous Emirs were easily distinguishable. On the extreme left the chiefs and soldiers of the bright green flag gathered under Ali-Wad-Helu; between this and the centre the large dark green flag of Osman Sheikh-ed-Din rose above a dense mass of spearmen, preceded by long lines of warriors armed presumably with rifles; over the centre, commanded by Yakub, the sacred Black banner of the Kahlifa floated high and remarkable; while on the right a great square of Dervishes was arrayed under an extraordinary number of white flags, amid which the red ensign of Sherif was almost hidden. All the pride and might of the Dervish Empire were massed on this last great day of its existence . . .

The advance continued. The Dervish left began to stretch out across the plain towards Kerreri—as I thought, to turn our right flank. Their centre, under the Black Flag, moved directly towards Surgham. The right pursued a line of advance south of that hill. This mass of men were the most striking of all. They could not have mustered fewer than 6,000. Their array was perfect. They displayed a great number of flags—perhaps 500—which looked at the distance white, though they were really covered with texts from the Koran, and which by their admirable alignment made this division of the Khalifa's army look like the old representations of the Crusaders in the Bayeux tapestry.

The attack developed. The left, nearly 20,000 strong, toiled across the plain and approached the Egyptian squadrons. The leading masses of the centre deployed . . . and marched forthwith to the direct assault . . . the division with the white flags . . . moved up into the general line and began to climb the southern slopes of Surgham Hill . . .

The Dervish centre had come within range . . . One after another four batteries opened up on the enemy at a range of about 3,000 yards . . . Above the heads of the moving masses shells began to burst, dotting the air with smoke-balls and the ground with bodies. But a nearer tragedy impended. The "White Flags" were nearly over the crest. In another minute they would become visible to the batteries. Did they realize what would come to meet them? They were in a dense mass, 2,800 yards from the 32nd Field Battery and the gunboats. The ranges were known. It was a matter of machinery. The more distant slaughter passed unnoticed, as the mind was fascinated by the approaching horror. In a few seconds swift destruction would rush on these brave men. They topped the crest and drew out into full view of the whole army. Their white banners made them conspicuous above all. As they saw the camp of their enemies, they discharged their rifles with a great roar of musketry and quickened their pace. For a moment, the white flags advanced in regular order, and the whole division crossed the crest and were exposed. Forthwith the gunboats, the 32nd Field Battery, and other guns . . . opened on them. About twenty shells struck them in the first minute. Some burst high in the air, others exploding in their faces. Others, again, plunged into the sand and, exploding, dashed clouds of red dust, splinters, and bullets amid their ranks. The white banners toppled over in all directions. Yet they rose again immediately, as other men pressed forward to die for the Mahdi's sacred cause and in the defence of the successor of the True Prophet. It was a terrible sight, for as yet they had not hurt us at all, and it seemed an unfair advantage to strike thus cruelly when they could not reply. Under the influence of the shells the mass of the "White Flags" dissolved into thin lines of spearmen and skirmishers, and came on in altered formation and diminished numbers, but with unabated enthusiasm. And now, the whole attack being thoroughly exposed, it became the duty of the cavalry to clear the front as quickly as possible, and leave the further conduct of the debate to the infantry and the Maxim guns . . .

FIGURE 23 The Maxim gun, the prototype of the modern machine gun, was invented by Hiram Maxim, an American-born British citizen, in 1884. The first use of the gun in actual combat was in Africa, by Henry Morton Stanley on an expedition from the Congo to the Sudan in 1887–90. It was later used by the British against the Ndebele in 1893–94 and against the Sudanese at Omdurman in 1898, on the latter occasion with especially devastating effect. Henry M. Stanley, *In Darkest Africa, Or, the Quest, Rescue and Retreat of Emin, Governor of Equatoria,* 1890.

while the shells from the gunboats screamed overhead and the whole length of the position began to burst into flame and smoke . . .

The Khalifa's plan of attack appears to have been complex and ingenious. It was, however, based on an extraordinary miscalculation of the power of modern weapons; with the exception of this cardinal error, it is not necessary to criticize it . . .

The attack languished . . . The ground, although it appeared flat and level to the eye, nevertheless contained depressions and swellings which afforded good cover . . . The artillery now began to clear out these depressions by their shells, and in this work they displayed a searching power very remarkable when their flat trajectory is remembered. As the shells burst accurately above the Dervish skirmishers and spearmen who were taking refuge in the folds of the plain, they rose by hundreds and by fifties to fly. Instantly the hungry and attentive Maxims and the watchful infantry opened on them, sweeping them all to the ground—some in death, others in terror . . .

[10.15 A.M.] The Dervishes were weak in cavalry, and had scarcely 2,000 horsemen on the field. About 400 of these, mostly the personal retainers of the various Emirs, were formed into an irregular regiment and attached to the flag of Ali-Wad-Helu. Now when these horsemen perceived that there was no more hope of victory, they arranged themselves in a solid mass and charged the left of MacDonald's brigade. The distance was about 500 yards, and, wild as was the firing of the Soudanese, it was evident that they could not possibly succeed. Nevertheless, many carrying no weapon in their hands, and all urging their horses to their utmost speed, they rode unflinchingly to certain death. All were killed and fell as they entered the zone of fire—three, twenty, fifty, two hundred, sixty, thirty, five, and one out beyond them all—a brown smear across a sandy plain. A few riderless horses alone broke through the ranks of the infantry . . .

Thus ended the battle of Omdurman—the most signal triumph ever gained by the arms of science over barbarians. Within the space of five hours the strongest and best-armed savage army yet arrayed against a modern European Power had been destroyed and dispersed, with hardly any difficulty, comparatively small risk, and insignificant loss to the victors . . .

C. Steevens on the balance sheet of conquest

[Steevens] Over 11,000 killed, 16,000 wounded, 4,000 prisoners—that was the astounding bill of dervish casualties officially presented after the battle of Omdurman. Some people had estimated the whole dervish army at 1,000 less than this total; few had put it above 50,000. The Anglo-Egyptian army on the day of battle numbered, perhaps, 22,000 men; if the Allies had done the same proportional execution at Waterloo, not one Frenchman would have escaped . . .

By the side of the immense slaughter of dervishes, the tale of our casualties is so small as to be almost ridiculous. The first official list was this. British troops: 2 officers . . . killed, 7 wounded; 23 non-commissioned officers and men killed, 99 wounded. Egyptian army: 5 British officers and 1 non-commissioned officer wounded; 1 native officer killed, 8 wounded; 20 non-commissioned officers and men killed, 221 wounded. Total casualties: 131 British, 256 native = 387.

64 • Voices of resistance (1893–1905)

The establishment of European rule was never a straightforward matter, particularly because of the determined resistance of Africans. Such resistance meant that the process of conquest sometimes stretched over several decades. It also meant that indigenous people developed new ways of combining, often across regional and ethnic boundaries, in their determination to overthrow foreign rule. In an oral account recorded in the 1930s, Ndansi Kumalo, an Ndebele chief born around 1860 and a subject of Lobengula, describes what happened when Rhodes and Lobengula disagreed about the terms of the treaty signed in 1888; Lobengula believing that he had only extended mineral rights to the diamond magnate, whereas Rhodes thought that the entire territory had become his personal fiefdom (as symbolized in the name he gave the country, Rhodesia). The events that Kumalo narrates took place in 1893 and ended with the British conquest of the Ndebele and the presumed suicide of Lobengula. Still, the British had to fight another even more violent war in 1896, ultimately dynamiting the caves in which African resistors fought to the last.

In an account from German Southwest Africa (present-day Namibia), Hendrik Witbooi calls on a German officer to respect the autonomy of the local inhabitants. Witbooi, a leader of the Nama people, had fought against German encroachment in the early 1890s and formed an alliance with his long-term enemies, the Herero, in order to strengthen the forces of resistance. Though Witbooi soon concluded (after the death of many Nama women and children) a peace treaty with the Germans, he continued to complain about the way in which he and his people were treated, subjected to heavy taxation and forced labor. The refusal of the Germans to treat the people of Namibia as anything but a conquered and servile people eventually caused Witbooi to rise again in rebellion. In 1904, when he was eighty years old, he led a revolt of Nama and Herero against colonial rule. The Germans responded by waging a war of extermination in which they drove their opponents into the desert, sealed the wells behind them so that they were without water, and placed the survivors in forced labor camps, where most died. Witbooi was killed leading an attack on a German supply column. He was not alone. A 1911 census recorded only half as many Nama living as had been the case in 1900 and only one-fifth as many Herero as a decade before.

Some Africans fought back with words, as did the Brass traders in the Niger delta, who in 1895 complained to the British government about the unfair way they maintained the Niger Company was treating them. Their letter directly challenges the arguments of exponents of commercial empire like Lugard, who contended that Europeans brought economic development to Africa and that the chartered companies sought to better the lot of backward people. The British government ignored the Brass merchants.

Jan Smuts, who fought with the Boers against the British, also had little doubt about what he believed motivated British imperialism—it was "the new forces of Capitalism" that he blamed. British greed for Boer gold resulted in the greatest casualty figures of any British colonial war: 20,000 British dead, 7,000 Boer men, and 30,000 Boer women and children (the women and children incarcerated in concentration camps, which, because of poor sanitation and the lack of medical treatment, quickly turned into death camps), and at least 15,000 African fatalities, likewise mostly among people incarcerated as the British pursued a scorched-earth policy.

In German East Africa (present-day Tanzania), the very ways in which imperialism took practical form forced the production of new crops for the export market, and harsh labor conditions on these new plantations (which meant little African land and labor devoted to growing food for their own needs) led rapidly to widespread opposition that, as in Namibia, transcended old ethnic boundaries. From July 1905 until August 1907, Africans from more than twelve different ethnic groups, assumed by German colonial officials of being incapable of working together, organized a large-scale resistance movement covering more than one hundred thousand square miles (or at least a third of the colony). Led by a prophetlike figure, Kinjikitile Ngwale, who claimed to be possessed by a powerful ancestral spirit and to have a war "medicine," maji [water] maji, that could render European arms ineffective, the movement persisted long after the Germans hanged its leader in August 1905. African casualties in the war exceeded 120,000. Still, leaders of movements that supported African independence in the 1940s and 1950s looked back to Maji Maji and its leader, Kinjikitile, as symbols of African defiance of European colonialism.[11]

11. A, Margery Perham, ed., *The Africans* (London: Faber and Faber, 1936), 69–75; B, Georg M. Gugelberger, ed., *Nama/Namibia: Diary and Letters of Nama Chief Hendrik Witbooi, 1884–1894* (Boston: Boston University African Studies Center, 1984), 117–18; C, C. W. Newbury, ed., *British Policy towards West Africa, Select Documents, 1875–1914, with Statistical Appendices, 1800–1914* (Oxford: Clarendon, 1971), 143–45; D, J. C. Smuts, *A Century of Wrong* (London: Review of Reviews, 1899), issued by F. W. Reitz, with preface by W. T. Stead, 89–98; E, G. C. K. Gwassa and John Iliffe, eds., *Records of the Maji Maji Rising* (Dar es Salaam: East African Publishing House, 1967), Part 1, pp. 5–6, 8–10, 11–12, 25–26.

A. Ndansi Kumalo describes the defeat of
Lobengula and the Ndebele, July–December 1893

. . . When I first saw a white man I could not make it out and ran away. When we got used to them we would go with goats and sheep and buy European clothing. Later people used to take cattle and barter for beads and blankets.

We were terribly upset and very angry at the coming of the white men, for Lobengula had sent to the Queen in England and he was under her protection and it was quite unjustified that white men should come with force into our country. Our regiments were very distressed that we were not in a fit condition to fight for the king because of the smallpox. Lobengula had no war in his heart: he had always protected the white men and been good to them. If he had meant war, would he have sent our regiments far away to the north at this moment? As far as I know the trouble began in this way. Gandani, a chief who was sent out, reported that some of the Mashona had taken the king's cattle; some regiments were detailed to follow and recover them. They followed the Mashona to Ziminto's people [Victoria district]. Gandani had strict instructions not to molest the white people established in certain parts and to confine himself to the people who had taken the cattle. The commander was given a letter which he had to produce to the Europeans and tell them what the object of the party was. But the members of the party were restless and went without reporting to the white people and killed a lot of Mashonas. The pioneers were very angry and said, "You have trespassed into our part." They went with the letter, but only after they had killed some people, and the white men said, "You have done wrong, you should have brought the letter first and then we should have given you permission to follow the cattle." The commander received orders from the white people to get out, and up to a certain point which he could not possibly reach in the time allowed. A force followed them up and they defended themselves. When the pioneers turned out there was a fight at Shangani and Bembezi.

I was in the Matoppos and had not recovered from smallpox. I did not see Lobengula at this time for we were isolated. We sent a message to the King asking for permission to join with his forces; he agreed and we reorganized our regiment. The King agreed that we might come out of quarantine and told us to go to Gwelo's to fetch some of his cattle, but we could not; we were too weak. Only fourteen of our regiment went to try and recover the King's cattle and on the way they heard that they were too late. The white men were there and had seized the cattle. These fourteen incorporated themselves in Imbizo's regiment and fought at Bembezi, and two were killed. The next news was that the white people had entered Bulawayo; the King's kraal had been burnt down and the King had fled. Of the cattle very few were recovered; most fell into the hands of the white people. Only a very small portion were found and brought to Shangani where the King was, and we went there to give him any assistance we could. I could not catch up with the King; he had gone on ahead. Three of our leaders mounted their horses and followed up the King and he wanted to know where his cattle were. They said they had fallen into the hands of the whites, only a few were left. He said, "Go back and bring them along." But they did not go back again; the white forces had occupied Bulawayo and they went into the Matoppos. Then the white people came to where we were living and sent word round that all chiefs and warriors should go into Bulawayo and discuss peace, for the King had gone and they wanted to make peace. The first order we got was, "When you come in, come in with cattle so that we can see that you are sincere about it." The white people said, "Now that your King has deserted you, we occupy your country. Do you submit to us?" What could we do? "If you are sincere, come back and bring in all your arms, guns and spears." We did so.

I cannot say what happened to Lobengula, but the older people said, "The light has gone out. We can do no more. There is nothing left for us but to go back to our homes." All that we could hear was that the King had disappeared alone; no one knew where he went. It could not be that his body, alive or dead, should pass into the hands of his enemies. Our King was powerful and a great king; he was invincible against other tribes. He ruled right up to the Zambezi. He was just; and if, unfortunately, many innocent men were killed it was through the jealousy and cunning of others who sent false reports which the King believed. At the beginning Lobengula was loved by everybody, but later bitterness arose in the families which had suffered loss and there was a good deal of dissension. I remember a tragedy when two of my relatives were killed. They were at the King's kraal and he was annoyed with them. He fired towards them with a shot-gun to frighten them and the warriors took it as a sign to despatch them and clubbed them to death. When news came to their kraal the children fled, but their wives said, "Let us die with them." The King sent them a message that it was mistake. It all arose from a dispute over cattle.

So we surrendered to the white people and were told to go back to our homes and live our usual lives and attend to our crops. But the white men sent native police who did abominable things; they were cruel and assaulted a lot of our people and helped themselves to our cattle and goats. These policemen were not our own people; anybody was made a policeman. We were treated like slaves. They came and were overbearing and we were ordered to carry their clothes and bundles. They interfered with our wives and our daughters and molested them. In fact, the treatment we received was intolerable. We thought it best to fight and die rather than bear it. How the rebellion started I do not know; there was no organization, it was like a fire that suddenly flames up. We had been flogged by native police and then they rubbed salt water in the wounds. There was much bitterness because so many of our cattle were branded and taken away from us; we had no property, nothing we could call our own. We said, "It is no good living under such conditions; death would be better—let us fight." Our King gone, we had submitted to the white people and they ill-treated us until we became desperate and tried to make an end of it all. We knew that we had very little chance because their weapons were so much superior to ours. But we meant to fight to the last, feeling that even if we could not beat them we might at least kill a few of them and so have some sort of revenge.

I fought in the rebellion. We used to look out for valleys where the white men were likely to approach. We took cover behind rocks and trees and tried to ambush them. We were forced by the nature of our weapons not to expose ourselves. I had a gun, a breech-loader. They—the white men—fought us with big guns and Maxims and rifles.

I remember a fight in the Matoppos when we charged the white men. There were some hundreds of us; the white men also were many. We charged them at close quarters; we thought we had a good chance to kill them but the Maxims were too much for us. We drove them off at the first charge, but they returned and formed up again. We made a second charge, but they were too strong for us. I cannot say how many white people were killed, but we think it was quite a lot. I do not know if I killed any of them, but I know I killed some of their horses. I remember how, when one of their scouts fell wounded, two of his companions raced out and took him away. Many of our people were killed in this fight. I saw four of my cousins shot.

FIGURE 24 Olive Schreiner, a founder of the modern feminist movement in Great Britain, used this photograph of employees of Cecil Rhodes's British South Africa Company lynching Shona men in 1896–97 as the frontispiece of her account of colonial atrocities in Rhodesia (now Zimbabwe). Olive Schreiner, *Trooper Peter Halket of Mashonaland,* 1897.

One was shot in the jaw and the whole of his face was blown away—like this—and he died. One was hit between the eyes; another here, in the shoulder; another had part of his ear shot off. We made many charges but each time we were beaten off, until at last the white men packed up and retreated. But for the Maxims, it would have been different. The place where we have been making the film is the very place where my cousins were killed.

We were still fighting when we heard that Mr. Rhodes was coming and wanted to make peace with us. It was best to come to terms he said, and not go shedding blood like this on both sides. The older people went to meet him. Mr. Rhodes came and they had a discussion and our leaders came back and discussed amongst themselves and the people. Then Mr. Rhodes came again and we agreed at last to terms of peace.

So peace was made. Many of our people had been killed, and now we began to die of starvation; and then came the rinderpest and the cattle that were still left to us perished. We could not help thinking that these dreadful things were brought by the white people.

B. Hendrik Witbooi, letter to Theodor Leutwein, August 17, 1894

Your Highness, dear Major Leutwein!

I received your long letter late last night. I take it from this letter of yours that you accuse me of various deeds. From this you seem to claim the right to condemn me to death as if I were a common criminal. You seem to try to reason with me by force of guns.

FIGURE 25 Hendrik Witbooi, born in what is now Namibia, was educated by German missionaries in the 1830s and died fighting against German soldiers in 1905. His extensive letters and diaries illuminate the ways in which Africans fought to defend and retain their independence. Bundesarchiv, Koblenz, Germany.

I. You accuse me of intending to attack Kirris. This is absolutely untrue.

II. You claim that I try to seduce people to do malicious things. This is blatantly untrue as well. You refer to Simon Kopper. You yourself have seen Simon Kopper and found out that he was quite against you long before I ever spoke to him. Why do you blame me for Kopper's present attitude? If Kopper's views have changed, what has that to do with me?

III. You say that I arrogantly claim to be ruler over certain territories and claim the sole right to sell such territories. I have this to give you for an answer: You white men, as well as the red men, know very well that this territory of which you speak has been my property since the death of my grandfather. The Red Nation attacked my grandfather without any cause. He conquered them. Later the same tribes attacked me as well. I conquered them a second time. This means that I have a double right to this territory. I have purchased these lands not with money, nor were they given to me as presents. Through bloodshed these lands came into my hands. This has been an old rule of war. You yourself indirectly acknowledge my right as proprietor to these lands by trying to take these lands away from me by force. Obviously you cannot see any other way of getting hold of these lands. If the said territory were not my own, why would you be attacking me? Again, I am not guilty of anything concerning this point.

IV. You claim that you are sorry that I do not accept German protection. You seem to think that I am guilty even of this. And therefore you seem to try to penalize me.

This is my answer: I have never in my life seen the German emperor and I am sure he has never seen me. Therefore it seems impossible that I could ever have hurt him.

God has made us rulers of some parts of the world. I don't think that one can call someone guilty if he wants to remain an independent ruler over his land and his people.

If you intend now to have me killed because of my love of independence, this is not shame or harm. If I have to die I shall die as an honest man defending my property and my rights.

What can be wrong with a man who refuses to be inferior to someone else? Why should I be condemned to death for things which are natural?

All the things you have said so far are constructs helpful for your own profit. You argue the way you do in order to appear to the rest of the world as a person who loves truth and rightful doings and to try to prove to this world that I have been wrong and guilty. But my dear friend! I must tell you that I have a clear conscience. I know that I have been innocent. I also know that you yourself are basically convinced of my innocence, but you seem to claim that strength and might precede truth and law. Since you have the guns, you force the right on your side. I fully agree with you in one thing: in comparison with you, we are nothing here. My dear friend! You arrive with such forces and guns and you tell me that you intend to attack me.

I guess this time I shall be forced to defend myself against you. I shall do so not so much in my own name but in the name of the Lord. Trusting in His aid and strength I shall defend myself. You also say that you are against bloodshed and that you are innocent in the event that people shall be killed in the near future. You claim that everything has been my fault.

This is blatantly impossible. I must say that I am astonished how you can think up such things.

I have told you that I am fully in favor of peace and that I shall never be the one breaking such a peace. But you say that you intend to attack me. The responsibility for the innocent blood of my men and yours therefore cannot be mine since I am not the instigator of another war. Since it is not I who plans another attack, how can I be guilty for what you plan to do?

V. Once more I must ask you, dear friend, to accept the truthful and honest peace I have offered you. You yourself have called this a true peace.

Please do leave us alone and withdraw!

Call your troops back and withdraw. Please do withdraw! Please do so!

This is my very serious plea! I am your friend and Captain,

Hendrik Witbooi

C. Letter from Warri, Karemma, Thomas O'Kea, and Nathaniel Hardstone, chiefs of the Brass District, to the British government, June 8, 1895, complaining about their treatment by the Royal Niger Company

The Company which is now known as the Niger Company has done us many injuries . . . for some time after the Charter was granted they drove us away from our markets in which we and our forefathers had traded for generations, and did not allow us to get in our trust, or trade debts, some of which remain unpaid to this day. Neither will they permit the Ejoh or market people to come down and pay us.

In 1889, Major Macdonald, now our big Consul, came to us, and we told him of all these things, and he promised that he would lay our complaints before the Queen's Government...

In 1891, he, Major MacDonald, came again and explained to us that it was the intention of the Queen's Government to send Consuls to these rivers and that we should then have a Consul of our own who would specially look after our interests. He pointed out to us that this could not be done without money, and explained how the money could be raised by means of duty, and asked whether we consented to pay these duties. At first we refused, because we could get no satisfactory answer about our markets; but eventually we signed, but begged the Major that he would do what he could to get some of our markets back for us...

Since then we have seen the Major many times, and he has always told us to be patient, but latterly things have gone from bad to worse, and the markets that we have are quite insufficient to maintain us.

We thoroughly understand that all markets are free, and open to everybody, black and white man alike; and we are quite willing to trade side by side with the white man at those markets. We do not now ask for any exclusive privileges whatever, but only that we may be allowed to trade without molestation at the places we and our fathers have traded in days gone by.

We are willing to pay fair duties: but we cannot understand, however, if all markets are free and open to black and white man alike, why there are many villages or markets in the Niger where neither are allowed to go and trade.

We submit that, if we have to go to Akassa, a distance of nearly 40 miles, to pay our duties, and are only allowed to trade at certain places selected by the Niger Company called "ports of entry," and have to take out trade and spirit licences, and pay a very heavy duty going into the territories and a heavy duty coming out, it is the same thing as if we were forbidden to trade at all.

The Niger Company say, "We (the Company) have to do these things, why not you?"

We can only say that, with our resources, to carry out these Regulations and pay these duties means ruin to us.

The Niger Company are cleverer than we are. We humbly submit that we have a right, confirmed by our Treaty, to go and trade freely in the places we have traded at for all these generations. We are ready to pay to do so, but let us pay a fair duty, and conform to fair Regulations.

The duties and Regulations of the Company mean to us ruin; of this there is no doubt.

We do not deny that we have smuggled, but under the circumstances can this be wondered at?

We have suffered many hardships from the Company's Regulations. Our people have been fired upon by the Company's launches, they have been fired upon from the Company's hulks, our canoes have been seized and goods taken, sometimes when engaged in what white men call smuggling, and sometimes when not.

The "chop" canoes coming from the Ejohs have also been stopped.

Within the last few weeks the Niger Company has sent messengers to the Ejohs and other tribes with whom we have always traded and said that any of them who traded with us at all, or who paid us their debts, would be severely punished, and their villages burnt.

We have evidence to prove all this, which we would like to lay before the big man who has been sent by the Queen.

All these unjust things that have been done to us, the many times we have been told to be patient and have been so, and the wrongs which we consider we have suffered are now worse than ever, all these drove us to take the law into our own hands and attack the Company's factories at Akassa.

We know now we have done wrong, and for this wrong we have been severely punished; but we submit that the many unjust oppressions we have borne have been very great, and it is only in self-defence, and with a view to have our wrongs inquired into, that we have done this thing. We have frequently asked the Consuls that have been put over us . . . to tell us in what way we have offended the Queen to cause her to send this trouble on us.

Traders we are, have been, and always will be. The soil of our country is too poor to cultivate sufficient food for all our people, and so if we do not trade and get food from other tribes we shall suffer great want and misery.

We fervently hope and pray that some arrangements may be arrived at which will enable us to pursue our trade in peace and quietness.

> Warri, his x mark
> Karemma, ditto
> Thomas Okea, ditto
> Nathaniel Hardstone, ditto

Witnesses: H. L. Gallwey, Deputy Commissioner and Vice-Consul, Benin District

D. Jan Smuts denounces British "capitalism" and "jingoism," 1899

In this awful turning point in the history of South Africa, on the eve of the conflict which threatens to exterminate our people, it behoves us to speak the truth in what may be, perchance, our last message to the world. Even if we are exterminated the truth will triumph through us over our conquerors, and will sterilise and paralyse all their efforts until they too disappear in the night of oblivion.

Up to the present our people have remained silent; we have been spat upon by the enemy, slandered, harried, and treated with every possible mark of disdain and contempt . . .

During this century there have been three periods which have been characterised by different attitudes of the British Government towards us. The first began in 1806, and lasted until the middle of the century. During this period the chief feature of British policy was one of utter contempt, and the general trend of British feeling in regard to our unfortunate people can be summarised by the phrase, "The stupid and dirty Dutch." But the hypocritical ingenuity of British policy was perfectly competent to express this contempt in accents which harmonised with the loftiest sentiments then prevailing. The wave of sentimental philanthropy then passing over the civilised world was utilised by the British Government in order to represent the Boers to the world as oppressors of poor peace-loving natives, who were also men and brethren eminently capable of receiving religion and civilisation . . .

The fundamental sentiment which governed the policy of the second period was a feeling of regret at having made this mistake [granting in 1852 and 1854 settlers in the Orange Free State and the Transvaal possession of the lands they then occupied as a result of the Great Trek], coupled with the firm determination to set aside its results. These wild and useless tracts, which had been guaranteed to the Boers, appeared to be very valuable after the Boers had rescued them from barbarism, and opened them up for civilisation. It was felt that they ought to gleam amongst the jewels of Her Majesty's Crown, notwithstanding the obstacle in the treaties that had been concluded with the Boers. As far as the means were concerned—they were, from the very exigency of inborn hypocrisy, partly revealed and partly concealed; the one differing from the other as light from darkness. The secret means consisted in arming the Kaffir tribes against us in the most incredible manner, and in inciting them to attack us in violation of solemn treaties and promises. If this policy succeeded the real objects and means could be suppressed, and England could then come forward and pose openly as the champion of peace and order, and as the guardian angel of civilisation in this part of the world . . . The British succeeded . . . annexing the Diamond Fields—a flagrantly illegal act . . .

The third period of our history is characterised by the amalgamation of the old and well-known policy of fraud and violence with the new forces of Capitalism, which had developed so powerfully owing to the mineral riches of the South African Republic. Our existence as a people and a State is now threatened by an unparalleled combination of forces. Arrayed against us we find numerical strength, the public opinion of the United Kingdom thirsting and shouting for blood and revenge, the world-wide and cosmopolitan power of Capitalism, and all the forces which underlie the lust of robbery and the spirit of plunder. Our lot has become more and more perilous . . . Every sea in the world is being furrowed by ships which are conveying British troops from every corner of the globe in order to smash this little handful of people. Even Xerxes, with his millions against little Greece, does not afford a stranger spectacle to the wonder and astonishment of mankind than this gentle and kindhearted Mother of Nations, as, wrapped in all the panoply of her might, riches, and exalted traditions, she approaches the little child grovelling in the dust with a sharpened knife in her hand. This is no War—it is an attempt at Infanticide . . .

Nor will a Chamberlain be more fortunate in effecting the triumph of Capitalism, with its lust for power, over us.

If it is ordained that we, insignificant as we are, should be the first among all peoples to begin the struggle against the new-world tyranny of Capitalism, then we are ready to do so, even if that tyranny is reinforced by the power of Jingoism . . .

[W]e now submit our cause with perfect confidence to the whole world. Whether the result be Victory or Death, Liberty will assuredly rise in South Africa like the sun from out the mists of the morning, just as Freedom dawned over the United States of America a little more than a century ago. Then from the Zambesi to Simon's Bay it will be

"AFRICA FOR THE AFRICANDER."

E. African oral testimonies about the Maji Maji uprising of 1905, recorded in the 1960s by G. C. K. Gwassa and John Iliffe

During the [cotton] cultivation there was much suffering. We, the labour conscripts, stayed in the front line cultivating. Then behind us was an overseer whose work it was to whip us. Behind the overseer was a jumbe, and every jumbe stood behind his fifty men. Behind the line of jumbes stood Bwana Kinoo [a German settler named Steinhagen] himself. Then, behold death there! And then as you till the land from beginning to end your footprints must not be seen save those of the jumbe. And that Selemani, the overseer, had a whip, and he was extremely cruel. His work was to whip the conscripts if they rose up or tried to rest, of if they left a trail of their footprints behind them. Ah, brothers, God is great—that we have lived like this is God's Providence! And on the other side Bwana Kinoo had a bamboo stick. If the men of a certain jumbe left their footprints behind them, that jumbe would be boxed on the ears and Kinoo would beat him with the bamboo stick using both hands, while at the same time Selemani lashed out at us labourers . . .

They [the people] waited for a long period because they were afraid. How could one clan face the Germans alone and not be wiped out? There had to be many.

It is true they were ruled for a very long time before they rose in arms against the Germans. The problem was how to beat him really well. Who would start? Thus they waited for a long time because there was no plan or knowledge. Truly his practices were bad. But while there were no superior weapons should the people not fear? Everywhere elders were busy thinking, "What should we do?"

He [Kinjikitile] was taken by an evil spirit one day in the morning at about nine o'clock. Everyone saw it, and his children and wives as well. They were basking outside when they saw him go on his belly, his hands stretched out before him. They tried to get hold of his legs and pull him but it was impossible, and he cried out that he did not want [to be pulled back] and that they were hurting him. Then he disappeared in the pool of water. He slept in there and his relatives slept by the pool overnight waiting for him. Those who knew how to swim dived down into the pool but they did not see anything. Then they said, "If he is dead we will see his body; if he has been taken by a beast or by a spirit of the waters we shall see him returned dead or alive." So they waited, and the following morning, at about nine o'clock again, he emerged unhurt with his clothes dry and as he had tucked them the previous day. After returning from there he began talking of prophetic matters. He said, "All dead ancestors will come back; they are at Bokero's in Rufiji Ruhingo. No lion or leopard will eat men. We are all the Sayyid Said's, the Sayyid's alone." The song ran: "We are the Sayyid's family alone. Be it an Mpogoro, Mkichi, or Mmatumbi, we are all the Sayyid Said's." The lion was sheep, and the European was red earth or fish of the water. Let us beat him. And he caught two lions which he tethered with a creeper, and people danced likinda before those two lions. They remained harmless. Then word of this new man spread afar . . .

Njwiywila meant secret communication such as at a secret meeting. At that time if you listened to Njwiywila you paid one pice. That was the meaning of Njwiywila. The message of Njwiywila was like this: "This year is a year of war, for there is a man at Ngarambe who has been possessed—he has Lilungu. Why? Because we are suffering like this and because . . . we are oppressed . . . We work without payment . . . This Njwiywila began at Kikobo amongst the Kichi, for they were very near Kinjikitile. It spread to Mwengei and Kipatimu and to Samanga. But the people of Samanga did not believe quickly. It spread quickly throughout Matumbi country and beyond. In the message of Njwiywila was also the information that those who went to Ngarambe would see their dead ancestors. The people began going to Ngarambe to see for themselves . . .

It was like a wedding procession, I tell you! People were singing, dancing, and ululating throughout. When they arrived at Ngarambe they slept there and danced likinda, everyone in his own group. The following morning they received medicine and returned to their homes . . .

The song of Mpokosi [a representative of Kinjikitile] during likinda was in the Ngindo language. He used to take his fly-switch and his calabash container for medicine, and he went around sprinkling them with medicine. It was like military drilling with muzzle-loaders, and under very strict discipline. Thus Mpokosi would say:

> "Attention!
> We are at attention.
> What are you carrying?
> We are carrying peas.
> Peas? Peas of what type?
> Creeping peas.
> Creeping?
> Creeping?"

And so on as they marched, until Mpokosi ordered:

> "Attention!
> Turn towards Donde country [inland].
> (The warriors turned).
> Turn towards the black water [the ocean].
> (They obeyed).
> Destroy the red earth.
> Destroy!
> Destroy?
> Destroy?"

And so on as they advanced as if to shoot.

During that time they were dressed in their military attire called Ngumbalyo. Further, each one was told where to go for this type of drilling. Thus, all gathered at Nandete for this type of likinda. The song was entirely in riddles. Thus the question "what are you carrying?" meant "what do you want to do?" The answer "we are carrying peas" meant "we are carrying bullets," and they used peas in their guns during drilling. "Creeping peas" are those that creep, and it meant that they were marching to the battlefield. "Creeping, creeping"—that was walking, that is military marching. "Destroy the red earth"—that meant tear the European apart or destroy him . . .

The District Officer let Fr. Johannes know that the sultans were to be hanged today. He could if necessary see for himself whether any of them wished to be baptised. (For Fr. Johannes had previously sought permission from the District Officer to baptise them if possible.) Fr. Johannes therefore went into the gaol, or rather into the passage between the gaols, in which the condemned men were lodged. They had just received sentence, and things in the gaol were therefore animated. Each still had commissions for his dependents to carry out. As soon as Fr. Johannes set foot in the place, some of those he knew came to him and asked him to undertake these commissions, which he said he was prepared to do. Then he asked some who had already received a certain amount of instruction at Peramiho, "Do you not wish to be baptised before you die?" They asked, "Can we do that?" When they were assured of this, many raised their hands and called out, "I want to be baptised, and I, and I!" A few who had not as yet received any instruction asked what this was all about. Fr. Johannes told them that if they would only be quiet he would explain it to them. Mputa [a paramount chief] himself then demanded silence, and Fr. Johannes instructed them briefly in the essential truths and on baptism and contrition. Then he asked who wanted to be baptised. Thirty-one men declared themselves ready for baptism, among them Sultan Mputa. Seventeen men, among whom were numbered a few Muslims, wished to know nothing of baptism. Despite exhortation, Mpambalyoto said briefly, I will die a pagan. Msimanimoto, a chief from the neighbourhood of Peramiho, also wanted to know nothing of baptism, for he protested that he would die blameless, he had done no wrong. Even those who had taken part in the attack on Kigonsera offered themselves for baptism, although they had not previously received instruction. Some —Fratera, for example—showed themselves especially pleased that they could still be baptised. One asked whether he would truly rise again. The District Officer had allowed half an hour, but not all had been baptised when this expired, so that he extended it slightly. When all were baptised, they were called out in threes and their hands bound. Then they were led out to the gallows, which were alongside the gaol, outside the boma. Some took leave of Fr. Johannes with the words, "Until we meet again." As he went out, Mputa, who showed genuine contrition, said in his bad Swahili, "But Kinjala led me astray."

The mood of the condemned men varied. Some cheered themselves with the fact that they could at least all die together. Kasembe declared: "Why should we fear to die? My father is dead, my mother is dead; now do I merely follow them." A few began to tremble somewhat as they were called out and bound. Others sat quietly by, and one could see from their behaviour that they were grieved and reluctant to die. On the whole, the business sat lightly on many, who chattered and laughed as at any other time. One asked Fr. Johannes for a pinch of snuff. Since he had none, he applied to Sergeant Leder, who stood watch, to get some from the guard. At this others also wanted snuff, but no more could be obtained. Some began to sing as they were led out. A few, however, cursed the District Officer especially. Mpambalyato declared that Chabruma would soon come to revenge them. Several asked Fr. Johannes to tell their families to bury them themselves, to buy cloth for the purpose and to wrap them in it. Bonjoli flatly demanded that Fr. Johannes should arrange it so that he was not hanged— from now on he would be true. Fratera prayed aloud the "Our Father" and "Hail Mary," and said, after he had been instructed, that at the end he would pray, "Jesus, Saviour, receive my spirit." For one the affair went on too long. He wanted to be led out before his turn. Fr. Johannes remained in the gaol until all had been led out, exhorting them to prayer and to a sense of contrition.

Thus many found at the end a merciful death, many who otherwise stood in grave peril of being lost eternally. God be thanked for it.

A vast crowd had naturally assembled outside to be witnesses of the "spectacle." At evening the hanged men were buried in a large common grave.

SELECTED BIBLIOGRAPHY

Bibliographic Guide

Norton, Mary Beth, and Pamela Gerardi, eds. *The American Historical Association's Guide to Historical Literature*, 3d ed. 2 vols. New York: Oxford University Press, 1995. The fullest bibliographic guide to world history, with comprehensive annotated entries.

Journals

African Affairs
Canadian Journal of African Studies
Imago Mundi: International Journal for the History of Cartography
International Journal of African Historical Studies
Journal of African History
Journal of Modern African Studies
Journal of Southern African Studies

Encyclopedias

Africana: The Encyclopedia of the African and African American Experience, ed. Kwame Anthony Appiah and Henry Louis Gates, 2d ed. 5 vols. New York: Oxford University Press, 2005.
New Encyclopedia of Africa, ed. John Middleton and Joseph Miller. 5 vols. Detroit: Thomson/Gale, 2008.

Maps

The most comprehensive published guides to historical maps of Africa are Oscar I. Norwich, *Norwich's Maps of Africa*, 2d ed. (Norwich, Vt.: Terra Nova, 1997); John MacIlwaine, *Maps and Mapping of Africa: A Resource Guide* (London: Hans Zell, 1997); and, especially, the definitive and beautifully illustrated volume by Richard L. Betz, *The Mapping of Africa: A Cartobibliography of Printed Maps of the African Continent to 1700* ('t Goy-Houten, the Netherlands: HES and De Graaf, 2007).

More dated but still the best sources of thematic maps of Africa are J. F. Ade. Ajayi and Michael Crowder, eds., *Historical Atlas of Africa* (New York: Cambridge University Press, 1985); J. D. Fage, *An Atlas of African History*, 2d ed. (London: Arnold, 1978); and Colin McEvedy, *The Penguin Atlas of African History*, rev ed. (New York: Penguin, 1996).

General Histories

The best one-volume histories of Africa are John Iliffe, *Africans: The History of a Continent*, 2d ed. (New York: Cambridge University Press, 2007), and Fred Cooper, *Africa since 1940: The Past of the Present*

(New York: Cambridge University Press, 2002). In addition, A. Adu Boahen, *African Perspectives on Colonialism* (Baltimore: Johns Hopkins University Press, 1989), is intellectually engaging.

Two older, multivolume series, the UNESCO and the Cambridge University Press histories of Africa, though not reflecting current scholarship, provide an enormous amount of information: UNESCO International Scientific Committee for the Drafting of a General History of Africa, *General History of Africa*, 8 vols. (Berkeley: University of California Press, 1981–93), and J. D. Fage and Roland Oliver, eds., *The Cambridge History of Africa*, 8 vols. (Cambridge: Cambridge University Press, 1982–86).

Books That We Use Regularly in Our Teaching

NOTE. This is not a comprehensive list but rather books that we find reflect high standards of scholarship, that are intellectually stimulating, and that students find useful and provocative in the classroom.

General

Appiah, Kwame Anthony. *In My Father's House: Africa in the Philosophy of Culture.* London: Methuen, 1992.

Birmingham, David, and Phyllis M. Martin, eds. *History of Central Africa.* 2 vols. New York: Longman, 1983.

Gilbert, Erik, and Jonathan T. Reynolds. *Africa in World History: From Prehistory to the Present,* 2d ed. Upper Saddle River, N.J.: Prentice Hall, 2007.

Hopkins, A. G. *An Economic History of West Africa.* London: Longman, 1973.

Meredith, Martin. *The Fate of Africa: From the Hopes of Freedom to the Heart of Despair: A History of Fifty Years of Independence.* New York: Public Affairs, 2005.

Africa in the Era of the Atlantic Slave Trade

Alpers, Edward. *Ivory and Slaves: Changing Patterns of International Trade in East Central Africa to the Later Nineteenth Century.* Berkeley: University of California Press, 1975.

Blackburn, Robin. *The Making of New World Slavery: From the Baroque to the Modern, 1492–1800.* New York: Verso, 1997.

Carney, Judith. *Black Rice: The African Origins of Rice Cultivation in the Americas.* Cambridge, Mass.: Harvard University Press, 2001.

Cooper, Frederick. *Plantation Slavery on the East Coast of Africa.* New Haven: Yale University Press, 1977.

Curtin, Philip. *The Atlantic Slave Trade: A Census.* Madison: University of Wisconsin Press, 1969.

Elphick, Richard. *Kraal and Castle: Khoikhoi and the Founding of White South Africa.* New Haven: Yale University Press, 1977.

Eltis, David. *The Rise of African Slavery in the Americas.* New York: Cambridge University Press, 2000.

Eltis, David, Stephen D. Behrendt, David Richardson, and Herbert S. Klein, eds. *The Trans-Atlantic Slave Trade: A Database on CD-ROM.* New York: Cambridge University Press, 2000.

Harms, Robert. *The Diligent: A Voyage through the Worlds of the Slave Trade.* New York: Basic Books, 2002.

Hawthorne, Walter. *Planting Rice and Harvesting Slaves: Transformations along the Guinea-Bissau Coast, 1400–1900.* Portsmouth, N.H.: Heinemann, 2003.

Hochschild, Adam. *Bury the Chains: Prophets and Rebels in the Fight to Free an Empire's Slaves.* Boston: Houghton Mifflin, 2005.

Isaacman, Allen F. *Mozambique: The Africanization of a European Institution: The Zambesi Prazos, 1750–1902.* Madison: University of Wisconsin Press, 1972.

Levtzion, Nehemia. *Ancient Ghana and Mali*. London: Methuen, 1973.

Lovejoy, Paul. *Transformations in Slavery: A History of Slavery in Africa*, 2d ed. New York: Cambridge University Press, 2000.

Miller, Joseph C. *Kings and Kinsmen: Early Mbundu States in Angola*. Oxford: Clarendon, 1976.

———. *Way of Death: Merchant Capitalism and the Angolan Slave Trade, 1730–1830*. Madison: University of Wisconsin Press, 1988.

Russell, Peter. *Prince Henry "the Navigator": A Life*. New Haven: Yale University Press, 2001.

Sheriff, Abdul. *Slaves, Spices and Ivory: Integration of an East African Commercial Empire into the World Economy, 1770–1873*. London: James Currey; Nairobi: Heinemann Kenya; Dar es Salaam: Tanzania Publishing House; Athens: Ohio University Press, 1987.

Thomas, Hugh. *The Slave Trade: The Story of the Atlantic Slave Trade, 1440–1870*. New York: Simon and Schuster, 1997.

Thornton, John K. *Africa and Africans in the Making of the Atlantic World, 1400–1800*, 2d ed. New York: Cambridge University Press, 1998.

Africa in the Era of Colonialism

Allman, Jean, Susan Geiger, and Nakanyise Musisi, eds. *Women in African Colonial Histories*. Bloomington: Indiana University Press, 2002.

Anderson, David. *Histories of the Hanged: The Dirty War in Kenya and the End of Empire*. New York: Norton, 2005.

Bender, Gerald J. *Angola under the Portuguese: The Myth and the Reality*. Berkeley: University of California Press, 1978.

Bonner, Philip, Peter Delius, and Deborah Posel, eds. *Apartheid's Genesis*. Johannesburg: Ravan, 1993.

Bundy, Colin. *The Rise and Fall of the South African Peasantry*. London: Heinemann, 1979.

Clark, Nancy L. *Manufacturing Apartheid: State Corporations in South Africa*. New Haven: Yale University Press, 1994.

Clark, Nancy L., and William H. Worger. *South Africa: The Rise and Fall of Apartheid*. New York: Pearson Longman, 2004.

Cooper, Frederick. *Decolonization and African Society: The Labor Question in French and British Africa*. New York: Cambridge University Press, 1996.

———. *From Slaves to Squatters: Plantation Labor and Agriculture in Zanzibar and Coastal Kenya, 1890–1925*. New Haven: Yale University Press, 1980.

Elphick, Richard, and Rodney Davenport, eds. *Christianity in South Africa: A Political, Social, and Cultural History*. Berkeley: University of California Press, 1997.

Human Rights Watch. *Leave None to Tell the Story: Genocide in Rwanda*. New York: Human Rights Watch, 1999.

Mamdani, Mahmood. *Citizen and Subject: Contemporary Africa and the Legacy of Late Colonialism*. Princeton: Princeton University Press, 1996.

Ranger, T. O. *Revolt in Southern Rhodesia, 1896–7: A Study in African Resistance*. London: Heinemann, 1967.

van Onselen, Charles. *Chibaro: African Mine Labour in Southern Rhodesia, 1900–1930*. London: Pluto, 1976.

Weiskel, Timothy C. *French Colonial Rule and the Baule Peoples: Resistance and Collaboration, 1889–1911*. New York: Oxford University Press, 1980.

White, Landeg. *Magomero: Portrait of an African Village*. New York: Cambridge University Press, 1987.

Worger, William H. *South Africa's City of Diamonds: Mine Workers and Monopoly Capitalism in Kimberley, 1867–1895*. New Haven: Yale University Press, 1987.

Wright, Donald R. *The World and a Very Small Place in Africa: A History of Globalization in Niumi, the Gambia,* 2d ed. Armonk, N.Y.: Sharpe, 2004.

Zwede, Bahru. *A History of Modern Ethiopia 1855–1991.* 2d ed. Oxford: James Currey, 2001.

Autobiographical Works

Emecheta, Buchi. *Head above Water.* Portsmouth, N.H.: Heinemann, 1994.

Mandela, Nelson. *Long Walk to Freedom: The Autobiography of Nelson Mandela.* Boston: Little, Brown, 1994.

Oliver, Roland. *In the Realms of Gold: Pioneering in African History.* Madison: University of Wisconsin Press, 1997.

Vansina, Jan. *Living with Africa.* Madison: University of Wisconsin Press, 1994.

Fiction

Achebe, Chinua. *Things Fall Apart.* London: Heinemann, 1962.

Dangaremgba, Tsitsi. *Nervous Conditions: A Novel.* Seattle: Seal, 1988.

Emecheta, Buchi. *The Joys of Motherhood: A Novel.* Portsmouth, N.H.: Heinemann, 1988.

Laye, Camara. *The Dark Child.* New York: Farrar, Straus, and Giroux, 1954.

Matshoba, Mtutuzeli. *Call Me Not a Man.* London: Longman, 1987.

Mda, Zakes. *The Heart of Redness.* New York: Farrar, Straus, and Giroux, 2002.

Sources for Illustrations

Ahmed, Akhter U., Ruth V. Hill, Lisa C. Smith, Doris M. Wiesmann, and Tim Frankenberger. *The World's Most Deprived: Characteristics and Causes of Extreme Poverty and Hunger.* Washington, D.C.: International Food Policy Research Institute, 2007. Http://www.ifpri.org/sites/default/files/publications/vp43.pdf.

Baden-Powell, R. S. S. *The Downfall of Prempeh; a Diary of Life with the Native Levy in Ashanti.* London: Methuen, 1896.

Baikie, William Balfour. *Narrative of an Exploring Voyage up the Rivers Kwóra and Bínue, (Commonly Known as the Niger and Tsádda) in 1854.* London: Murray, 1856.

Bentley, W. Holman. *Pioneering on the Congo.* 2 vols. London: Religious Tract Society, 1900.

Bovill, E. W. *The Golden Trade of the Moors,* 2d ed. New York: Oxford University Press, 1970.

Brown, Robert. *The Story of Africa and Its Explorers.* London: Cassell, 1895.

Chambliss, J. E. *The Life and Labors of David Livingstone, Covering His Entire Career in Southern and Central Africa.* Philadelphia: Hubbard Bros, 1876.

Dapper, Olfert. *Umbständliche und eigentliche Beschreibung von Africa.* Amsterdam: Jacob von Meurs, 1670–71.

Great Britain, Naval Intelligence Division. *French West Africa.* London: Her Majesty's Stationary Office, 1943–44.

Laird, Macgregor, and R. A. K. Oldfield, *Narrative of an Expedition into the Interior of Africa, by the River Niger: in the Steam-vessels Quorra and Alburkah in 1832, 1833 and 1834.* 2 vols. London: Bentley, 1837.

Livingstone, David, and Charles Livingstone. *Narrative of an Expedition to the Zambesi and Its Tributaries: and of the Discovery of the Lakes Shirwa and Nyassa, 1858–1864.* Harper and Brothers, 1866.

Major, Richard Henry. *The Life of Prince Henry of Portugal, Surnamed the Navigator.* London: Asher, 1868.

Mayer, Brantz. *Captain Canot, or, Twenty years of an African slaver, Being an Account of his Career and Adventures on the Coast of the Interior, on Shipboard, and in the West Indies.* New York: Appleton, 1854.

Michell, Lewis. *The Life of the Rt. Hon. Cecil John Rhodes, 1853–1902.* London: Edward Arnold, 1910.

Park, Mungo. *Travels in the Interior Districts of Africa, Performed under the Direction and Patronage of the African Association, in the Years 1795, 1796, and 1797.* London: John Murray, 1816.

Schreiner, Olive. *Trooper Peter Halket of Mashonaland.* Boston: Roberts Brothers, 1897.

Southworth, Alvan S. *Four Thousand Miles of African Travel: A Personal Record of a Journey up the Nile and through the Soudan to the Confines of Central Africa, Embracing a Discussion on the Sources of the Nile, and an Examination of the Slave Trade.* New York: Baker, Pratt and Co., 1875.

Stanley, Henry M. *The Congo and the Founding of Its Free State: A Story of Work and Exploration.* London: Sampson Low, Marston, Searle and Rivington, 1886.

———. *In Darkest Africa, Or, the Quest, Rescue, and Retreat of Emin, Governor of Equatoria.* 2 vols. New York: Chas. Scribner's Sons, 1890.

Twain, Mark. *King Leopold's Soliloquy: A Defense of His Congo Rule.* Boston: P. R. Warren Company, 1905.

Weule, Karl. *Native Life in East Africa: The Results of an Ethnological Research Expedition.* Translated by Alice Werner. New York: D. Appleton and Company, 1909.

WEB SITES

A. General Guides to Information Available on the Web

AfricaFocus
www.africafocus.org/
Up-to-the-minute, comprehensive, and informed reporting and links about contemporary events in Africa. Run by William Minter, a highly respected specialist on Africa and the author of several well-regarded books on southern and Lusophone Africa.

Stanford University Guide to Internet Sources on Africa South of the Sahara
www-sul.stanford.edu/africa/guide.html
A huge, continually updated, and fully annotated guide to Internet resources on Africa. The information on the Web site is organized by country, region, and topic.

University of Pennsylvania Electronic Guide for African Resources on the Internet
www.africa.upenn.edu/K-12/AFR_GIDE.html
The guide aims to assist not only teachers, librarians, and students, especially those in elementary and high schools, but also university faculty and students in locating online resources on Africa that can be used in the classroom.

H-Africa
www.h-net.org/~africa/ (Michigan State University)
H-Africa is an international scholarly discussion list on African culture and the African past. The focus is on university-level teaching and research, with up-to-date reviews of new books and online discussions about research questions and classroom resources.

B. Maps

Afriterra Foundation
www.afriterra.org/
Contains a searchable database of more than five thousand maps focused on Africa 1480–1900 in the Afriterra collection. More than one thousand of these maps are available as ultra-high-resolution digitized images.

Central Intelligence Agency (CIA) *World Factbook*
https://www.cia.gov/library/publications/the-world-factbook/index.html /
Site maintained by the Central Intelligence Agency. Contains up-to-date maps of every country in the world.

David Rumsey Historical Map Collection
www.davidrumsey.com/directory/where/Africa/
Contains approximately two hundred high-quality digitized historical maps of Africa, especially those from the 1700s and the 1800s.

Oscar I. Norwich Collection of Maps of Africa and Its Islands, 1486 to ca. 1865 (Stanford University)

www-sul.stanford.edu/depts/spc/maps/norwich_african_maps.html

One of the most comprehensive collections of historical maps of Africa, especially those of southern Africa, with 315 high-resolution maps available online.

C. Regional and/or Specialist Web Sites

African National Congress (ANC)

www.anc.org.za/show.php?doc=ancdocs/history/

The historical section of the ANC's official Web site contains documents that either were produced by the ANC, relate to the role of the ANC and its allies in the struggle for liberation, or are directly concerned with the ANC. The collection includes speeches, pamphlets, books, and photographs. New documents are continually being added to this section as they become available.

Aluka

www.aluka.org/

Aluka (derived from a Zulu word meaning "to weave") provides access to three collections. One focuses on cultural heritage sites and landscapes and includes photographs, 3-D models, GIS data sets, site plans, aerial and satellite photography, excavation reports, field notes, nineteenth-century European travelogues, and Arabic manuscripts from Timbuktu. Another collection focuses on African plant species and includes photographs, drawings, botanical art, field notes, and reference works drawn from published and unpublished material, especially from the Royal Botanical Gardens in Kew, London. The third collection includes material relating to the southern African peoples' struggle for freedom from colonial rule, including oral histories, speeches, nationalist publications, newspaper articles, fully digitized books and monographs, regional periodicals and magazines, posters, and pamphlets.

Centre Æquatoria Centre de Recherches Culturelles Africanistes

www.aequatoria.be/English/HomeEnglishFrameSet.html

This site contains full-text material on two major projects dealing with Belgian rule in the Congo. The first focuses on Belgian educational policy and practice from 1926 to 1972 and includes lists of students, inspection reports, exam results, statistics, school board regulations, several local disputes, curricula discussions, and circulars. The second project focuses on colonial schoolbooks and makes available online the full text of more than six hundred schoolbooks and religious textbooks dating from 1897. Originally published in more than thirty-five Congolese languages, an increasing number of these texts are being translated into French and English and made available online to researchers.

Digital Innovation South Africa (DISA)

www.disa.ukzn.ac.za/

DISA is a freely accessible online scholarly resource focusing on the sociopolitical history of South Africa, particularly the struggle for freedom during the period from 1950 to the first democratic elections in 1994. There are two primary collections of material: DISA 1, titled *South Africa's Struggle for Democracy: Anti-apartheid Periodicals, 1960–1994*, focuses on the Sharpeville massacre in March 1960, the rise of the black consciousness movement in the 1960s and 1970s, the independent trade unions, and the revival of the African National Congress after the Soweto uprising of June 1976 through the first democratic elections of 1994. The collection contains forty-five journals representing a wide spectrum of political views on a diversity of subjects such as trade unions, health, culture, and gender (e.g., *FOSATU Worker News, Sash, Isizwe, Clarion Call, Grassroots, African Communist*); DISA 2 is titled *Southern African Freedom Struggles, c. 1950–1994* and includes documents, interviews, articles, posters, commissions, trials, and legislation under the umbrella theme of freedom struggles, with carefully selected content in areas such as human rights, leadership, political parties, urban struggles, land issues, trade unions, and student unions.

Heritage Foundation
www.heritage.org/
Insight into conservative thinking about Africa and especially position papers that focus on the future energy concerns of the United States.

Human Rights Watch, Africa
www.hrw.org/doc/?t=africa
The first place to look for information about issues of contemporary significance such as child soldiers, Darfur, or conflict in the Congo.

National Intelligence Council (NIC) 2020 Project
www.dni.gov/nic/NIC_2020_project.html
The National Intelligence Council (NIC), a U.S. government body, is the intelligence community's center for midterm and long-term strategic thinking.

D. Trials

International Criminal Trial for Rwanda
http://69.94.11.53/
Up-to-the-minute, full transcripts of the daily proceedings of the trials of individuals charged with genocide and other crimes.

The Trial of Charles Taylor
www.charlestaylortrial.org/
Funded by the Soros Foundation, this Web site provides daily updates and full transcripts of the trial of the man viewed as being primarily responsible for the carnage in Sierra Leone and Liberia during the 1990s and the beginning of the twenty-first century.

Truth and Reconciliation Commission Maintained by the South African Department of Justice
www.doj.gov.za/trc/trccom.htm
This searchable, full-text site contains transcripts of the testimony of more than twenty-two thousand individuals who identified themselves as victims of the horrors of apartheid, as well as of the more than four thousand people who applied for amnesty for crimes committed during the apartheid era.

INDEX

ABOUT THE AUTHORS

WILLIAM H. WORGER is professor of history at the University of California, Los Angeles. A graduate of the University of Auckland, New Zealand, and Yale University, he previously taught at the University of Michigan and Stanford University. His research focuses on the history of South and southern Africa in the nineteenth and twentieth centuries.

NANCY L. CLARK is dean of the Honors College and professor of history at Louisiana State University. She studied African history at the University of California, Los Angeles, and at Yale University. She is completing a history of South Africa during World War II, which focuses on the war's impact on African and female workers.

EDWARD A. ALPERS is professor and chair of the Department of History at the University of California, Los Angeles. In 1994 he served as president of the African Studies Association. Alpers has published widely on the history of East Africa and the Indian Ocean. His current research focuses on Africans in the Indian Ocean.